LEIBNIZ

Selections

EDITED BY

PHILIP P. WIENER

CHARLES SCRIBNER'S SONS

NEW YORK

A–3.72[M]

Printed in the United States of America
SBN 684-12551-X (trade paper, SL)

ACKNOWLEDGMENTS

I am indebted to Professor Arthur O. Lovejoy for his incisive view of Leibniz's development of the principles of plenitude, continuity, and gradation presented in the fifth chapter of his authoritative study of the history of the idea of *The Great Chain of Being*, the William James Lectures delivered at Harvard University, 1933, and published by the Harvard University Press in 1936, with whose kind consent I have used that part of the text which translates Leibniz's utterances on the subject.

I wish to thank Professor Albert R. Chandler, Chairman of the Philosophy Department of Ohio State University, for his kind permission to use his revised translation of Dr. George Montgomery's version of Leibniz's *Discourse on Metaphysics*, first published by the Open Court Publishing Co. in 1902 and reprinted with Professor Chandler's revision in 1924.

Professor Donald Lach has kindly permitted me to use in my Introduction a quotation from his article on "Leibniz and China" which appeared in the *Journal of the History of Ideas* 6 (1945), pp. 436–455.

The *Philosophical Review* has co-operated also in permitting the use, in Part II of the Introduction below, of parts of my article, "Notes on Leibniz's Conception of Logic in its Historical Context," which appeared in that journal in November, 1939, pp. 567–586; however, these notes have been largely revised.

To Professor Paul Schrecker of the University of Pennsylvania, and the leading editor of many of Leibniz's unpublished writings, I owe some important suggestions in the choice of selections. Professor Leroy E. Loemker, Dean of the University of Georgia, has courteously and cooperatively shown me the table of contents of his two-volume edition and translation of Leibniz's works, in the course of publication by the University of Chicago Press, which the advanced student will surely wish to consult.

Dr. Huntington Cairns has in his writings indicated the historical significance of Leibniz as a legal philosopher, and kindly permitted me to draw on his expert knowledge of the subject.

Finally, the form in which I have chosen to acknowledge many suggestions from fellow-teachers of the history of philosophy has been to include as large a diversity of selections as they have proposed. Thus there should be enough source-material here to meet the needs of many kinds of students who do not have access to the original Latin, French, and German texts (see pp. 601–606). About half of these selections have never been translated into English, and the extant translations have had to be revised for accuracy.

Émile Ravier's *Bibliographie des Oeuvres de Leibniz* (Paris, F. Alcan, 1937) is the most exhaustive bibliography to date of all the known writings and editions of Leibniz's work. It has been used to supply the dates for the selections given here.

CONTENTS

vii

III. THEORY OF KNOWLEDGE AND METAPHYSICS

IV. ETHICS, LAW, AND CIVILIZATION

INTRODUCTION

I. BACKGROUND AND EARLY INTERESTS OF LEIBNIZ

Alfred North Whitehead, whose *Universal Algebra* and organic view of nature owe much to Leibniz, has placed him in "the century of genius." Gottfried Wilhelm Freiherr von Leibniz (1646–1716) belonged not only to that century but exemplified also the Renaissance ideal of the universal man in his many-sided activities, and ushered in the Age of the Enlightenment as well. He was a lawyer, scientist, inventor, diplomat, poet, philologist, logician, moralist, theologian, historian, and a philosopher who religiously defended the cultivation of reason as the radiant hope of human progress.

In order to place Leibniz's life in chronological relations to the great seventeenth-century philosophers, we may recall that Newton was born in the same year Galileo had died (1642), Robert Boyle was born in the same year Francis Bacon had died (1626), and that in the year of Leibniz's birth (1646), Descartes was fifty, Hobbes fifty-eight, Locke and Spinoza were only fourteen. In the natural sciences, then advancing rapidly, Leibniz corresponded with experimenters in physics, Huyghens, Von Guericke, Boyle, Newton, Papin, Perrault, Mariotte, and with biologists like Leeuwenhoek. In mathematics, Leibniz knew thoroughly the works of Pascal, Fermat, Descartes, Roberval, and corresponded with the Bernouillis, Sturm, Goldbach, Wallis, Wren, Varignon, Tschirnhaus (friend of Spinoza), and Newton. It was as a result of his correspondence with Newton that Leibniz was falsely charged with plagiarism in the discovery of the infinitesimal calculus. In the social sciences (as we now call them), among Leibniz's contemporaries were the founders of statistics, Graunt, Petty, and De Witt, the legal philosophers of "natural law," Grotius and Pufendorf; and finally, a group of Catholic and Protestant theologians, Arnauld, Malebranche, Clarke, De Volder, *et al.* discussed with Leibniz important questions of science, philosophy and religion which were not then studied as separate disciplines.

The wide range of Leibniz's intellectual interests was not unusual for the scientists and philosophers of his time, but few thinkers since Aristotle ever produced writings on so vast and varied a scale. They include thousands of letters and innumerable essays, finished and fragmentary, long and short, most of them posthumously published and many still unpublished. They deal with special and general topics in logic, mathematics, mechanics and mechanical inventions, biology and medicine, psychology and epistemology, metaphysics and theology, ethics and jurisprudence. There are also military and diplomatic plans and proposals, philological theories, documented researches in the medieval history of the Holy Roman Empire and the genealogy of the royal family of Hanover, projects for the reunion of the Protestant and Catholic Churches and for perpetual peace, and for the founding of academies of arts and sciences all over Europe on the model of the British Royal Society and the French Academy to which Leibniz had been elected. Only a few of the forty large volumes planned by the Prussian Academy as a definitive edition have appeared, and it is unlikely that the task will be completed in this century.

Leibniz's writings are both the delight and despair of students of his many-sided thought. They are a delight to a wide variety of scholars because they contain brilliant aperçus suggestive of many new ideas in the development of modern scientific and philosophic thought. However, the advanced character of his scientific thinking did not affect Leibniz's conservative respect for older, scholastic traditions and distrust of radical innovations, especially in ethics and theology. Still the mathematical student will admire his invention of determinants, non-metrical geometry (*analysis situs*), and the calculus (superior in its notation to Newton's), but will despair of Leibniz's unproved claims to deduce all the axioms of geometry and rules of algebra by means of a universal, logical language. The symbolic logician like C. I. Lewis, who has gone into the history of his science, will credit Leibniz with having taken the first steps toward a logical calculus, but will be disappointed by Leibniz's unrealized proposals. The experimentalist like Huyghens would have loved to see the possible experiments and inventions claimed by Leibniz, but was skeptical of his *a priori* rules for the art of discovery. The historian like Gibbon will admire Leibniz's labors in ransacking the medieval archives of feudal Germany, but will be cold to Leibniz's defense of his patron's feudal rights. The philosopher of science will admire Leibniz's acute analyses of the foundations of science or its first principles, but will wonder at the strange pre-established harmony of mind and body, of monads "without windows" reflecting each other's inner nature but opaque to external influences. He may with Bertrand Russell suspect that Leibniz sacrificed much of his logical rigor when he essayed to provide room in the foundations of science for extra-scientific value-judgments based on the traditional teleological conceptions of divine creation and planning. In any case it was natural for Leibniz to defend certain traditional ideas of God, freedom of the will, and immortality of the soul in the context of his own intellectual history, to which we now turn.

His father was a professor of moral philosophy at the University of Leipzig, and died when Leibniz was only six. The boy, precocious in learning things by himself, taught himself enough Latin (with the aid of Comenius' *Orbis Pictis*) to peruse the volumes of his father's library well stacked with classical and scholastic books on literature, history, and philosophy (Plato, Xenophon, Herodotus, Aristotle, Cicero, Quintilian, Polybius, Augustine and the other Church Fathers, Thomas Aquinas). But there were also the exciting modern books of Francis Bacon and René Descartes whose *Discourse on Method* might be compared with one of Leibniz's autobiographical accounts: "At school before I came to the grade in which Logic was taught, I had immersed myself in the historians and poets, having begun to read the historians almost as soon as I was able to read at all, and in verse I found great pleasure and ease; but as soon as I began to learn Logic, I found myself greatly fascinated by the division and order of thoughts which I was able to follow, and soon observed, as far as a boy of thirteen could, that there must be much more to the subject. I was most of all delighted with the Categories (Predicaments) which seemed to me to call the roll of all the things in the world, and I read Logic books of all sorts in order to find the best and most detailed account of the list of categories. I used to ask myself and my schoolmates to which category and subcategory anything that came up belonged." (Letter to Wagner, 1696).

This early fascination for such diverse subjects as history and logic is symptomatic of his intellectual versatility and, to a certain extent also, of his originality. His infinitesimal calculus was a masterly method for measuring rates of change, absent in the prevailing Cartesian theory that matter is extension or timeless spreadoutness. Leibniz, by insisting on the failure of Cartesian physics to include temporal, dynamic properties, provided physical nature with a historical dimension. And in his *Discourse on Metaphysics* there is a bold attempt to include the history of each individual substance within a "real definition" of its logically determined nature.

At the age of fifteen Leibniz was already preoccupied with the ancient problem of universal ideas: did they exist apart from changing particular things and processes (as Plato and the medieval realists like Anselm believed), or in the particular observations which are prior to the abstraction of general properties (as Aristotle and the nominalists maintained)? Leibniz took up the question in his baccalaureate thesis (*Disputatio metaphysica de Principio Individuo,* Leipzig, 1663), and argued in true scholastic style for a principle of individuation which would preserve the independence of universals with respect to ephemeral sensations, and yet embodied universal ideas in the eternal natures of individuals. In his youthful philosophizing, he thought, under the influence of Gassendi, that the essences of things were inseparable from the properties of material atoms and their motions. But this materialistic atomism was soon abandoned in favor of a scholastic principle of individuation, namely, that an individual is a determinate unity of form and matter, created by God. Leibniz was then ready to revert to the doctrine of substantial forms or embodied souls as the ultimate realities. The soul was understood in Aristotelian fashion as the "form" of the body, but "form" was not to be interpreted in a static, geometrical sense; this was the error of the Cartesians. Their two substances of thought and extension also left the relation of mind and body and the problem of personal immortality ungrounded; but the true interpretation of "substantial form" would do justice to the eternal purposive nature, final cause, or entelechy of each creature. Physics could then rid itself of the lifeless, purposeless motions of atoms in the void, and base its mechanical laws on the internal dynamic actions of groups of centers of energy. These substantial centers of living energy he called (following Augustine and Bruno) "monads." In them the spiritual and physical live in a pre-established harmony with one another.

On behalf of his substantial forms or monadic souls, Leibniz argues that he is only asking that they be considered to have the same sort of eternal existence which the atoms of Democritus already were presumed to have, and the same tendency or exigency to exist that the atoms had to move.

Not only does nature then do nothing in vain, but it operates in the most economical fashion according to the simplest laws, permitting no waste of space or identical empty spaces. For similar reasons, Leibniz opposed the Newtonian assumption of "action at a distance," for it violated the smooth continuity of causal action: "Nature makes no leaps" is Leibniz's favorite principle of continuity, and he applied it everywhere.

The economy and implied teleology of natural processes were illustrated in the laws of optical reflection and refraction where light always chooses the minimum path. Descartes' laws of motion preserved the quantity of motion (we should say momentum today), whereas Leibniz showed that there was also conserved a quantity of living force (we should say energy today). Finally, even Newton confessed that he was not satisfied with the action at a distance of gravitation, the universal force of attraction, and hoped that its underlying nature could some day be discovered.

So far as the purely scientific questions are concerned, the difference between the Cartesians and Leibniz is settled by crediting the former with the law of the conservation of momentum and the latter with the law of the conservation of energy. The difference between Newton's and Leibniz's views of space and time, discussed in the extensive correspondence with Samuel Clarke (a friend of Newton), is still of interest to students of the evolution and logic of modern physics. But there are also questions of broader philosophical import in these controversies. Leibniz challenged the adequacy of the mechanical conception of nature in both the Cartesian and Newtonian world-views. That conception seemed to Leibniz to fail to do justice to the organic, dynamic, and purposive features of life and thought. The idea of purposive activity provided Leibniz with a unifying principle for physical, biological, and psychological phenomena. It is historically relevant to note that he had come to the problems of the natural sciences only after deep absorption in humanistic studies, metaphysics, theology, and law.

Leibniz received his bachelor's and master's degrees at Leipzig in 1664–1666 for two theses on jurisprudence, and then moved to Altdorf nearby to receive a doctorate in law with a dissertation *On Perplexing Cases in Law* (*De casibus perplexis in jure,* 1666). This was followed a year later by an essay *On a New Method for the Study and Teaching of Jurisprudence* (*Nova methodus discendae docendaeque jurisprudentiae,* 1667) which secured him a position as legal adviser to the Elector of Mainz and Archbishop of Frankfurt. Now Huntington Cairns has observed in his authentic account of Leibniz as a legal philosopher that Leibniz's "early writings on jurisprudence, a field with which he began to occupy himself when he was eighteen years old, reveal clearly the mixture of scholasticism, novelty of insight, and scientific analysis that was to characterize his mature studies.

. . . The doctrine of law is to be treated rigorously beginning with definitions and proceeding syllogistically to the deductions and theories of law." *

Leibniz's success in applying his logical genius to the human questions of law opened a career for him in the diplomatic world; he refused an offer of a professorship in order to seek his fortune in the larger world of affairs.

When he arrived in Paris in 1672 on a diplomatic mission but fell in with the great mathematical scientists, he was caught between his wordly ambitions and his great admiration for the new developments in mathematical and physical sciences. An important clue to his philosophical development consists in observing how in nearly all of his writing he tried to accommodate traditional philosophy with its Platonic ideas, Aristotelian categories, scholastic substantial forms, to the new concepts and methods of the rapidly growing sciences.

While working on his doctorate, at the age of twenty, Leibniz had struck off an essay on the art of combining concepts (*De ars combinatoria,* 1666). It adapted the scholastic work of Lully, *Ars magna,* in the form of a universal ideographic language for symbolizing abstract concepts like Justice, Courage, etc. What Leibniz attempted was a universal method of analyzing concepts by means of numerical characters. Though he later confessed to the mathematical immaturity of this essay, he seems never to have abandoned the Pythagorean and semi-cabalistic notion of penetrating the mysteries of nature, man, and God by means of an esoteric universal language. Exaggerated as most of his claims for his "universal characteristic" seem to us today, the fact remains that in Leibniz's own opinion it led him to the discovery of the infinitesimal calculus as well as to "the

* H. Cairns, *Legal Philosophy from Plato to Hegel* (Baltimore, 1949), pp. 297, 299.

true method of metaphysics and theology." It is therefore central to an understanding of Leibniz's contribution to philosophy to examine his conception of the function of logic.

II. THE DUAL ROLE OF LOGIC

Leibniz himself more than once actually identified the basis of his new logic ("universal characteristic") with that of metaphysics and natural theology. "It is sufficient at present for me to notice that the foundation of my universal characteristic is the same as the demonstration of the existence of God." (Letter to Princess Elisabeth, 1678). But he also claimed repeatedly that his logic was the mother of all his discoveries in mathematics, physics, geology, philology, law and technology. Hence, for Leibniz, logic had to serve a double function; it had to offer proofs for the existence and structure of the divine source of all things, and also to further the arts and sciences.

These two functions of logic, bearing on theology and the sciences, vied with each other in Leibniz's thought with such equal force that it is often impossible to say which of them is more characteristic of his many logical writings, or how clearly he distinguished them in his own conception of logic. The rivalry in his orientation of logic between its theological uses, on the one hand, and its scientific function on the other, seems to be correlated with the changing intellectual traditions and social structure of his times. Although the foundations of the social order of seventeenth-century Europe rested on theological, legal and political traditions, the rise of the modern states, of experimental science, and of commerce displaced the feudal structure, and its scholasticism was confronted by far-reaching cultural changes. The development of more exact methods of measuring time, latitude and longitude, interest and insurance rates, and new techniques of agriculture, mining, shipbuilding, transportation, sanitation, medicine and accountancy required an intellectual reorientation and instruments which the traditional logic and science were unable to supply so long as they were subservient to theology.

The instrumental role which Leibniz assigned to his more general symbolic logic can be illustrated from his many concerns with the invention of adding machines for banks, of ready-reckoners for commerce, of submarines and magnetic compass for shipping, water-pumps for mines, telescopes and microscopes for war and medicine, etc.: "In natural philosophy, I have been the first, perhaps, to have completely demonstrated that the earth moves, and that the vacuum does not exist; this I have shown not through experiments, for they do nothing, but by geometrical demonstrations. . . . . In Mathematics and Mechanics I have by means of the Combinatory Art found several things which in practical life are of no small importance: first of all, an arithmetic machine which I call a Living Bank-clerk . . . of many uses in Business, military affairs, surveying, sine-tables and astronomy. Another instrument of mine which I call a Living Geometer, mechanically—for nothing exists in nature otherwise than mechanically—provides a way to resolve all conceivable lines and figures. . . . In Optics I have first of all men discovered (1) a certain kind of tube or lens which I call Pandochas because it makes the whole object uniform. . . . (2) Catadroptic tubes, for in one tube are juxtaposed a mirror and perspective . . . (3) a means, much sought until now, of measuring from a given position in perspective . . . which I found through the Art of Combinations. In nautical things . . .

on procuring sufficient data from a few experiments
. . . I will demonstrate how to find longitudes completely, and provide a way for a person on a ship to know
with certainty what his location is without the help of
the sun, moon and stars which cannot always be observed
(yet Huyghens' famous invention depends on them
alone). In Hydrostatics I have restored the lost invention of Drebel that enables one to go with a ship under
the surface of the water during a storm (for it is tran-
quil enough under water) or during an attack by sea-
robbers, and then to come up again; and this is what
Mersenne wanted so much to do. In Pneumatics . . . I
have compressed air into a box 1000 times normal pressure which can exert terrific force on water . . . like a
cannon shot." (Letter of Leibniz to Herzog Johann
Friedrich, Oct. 1671).

In hundreds of such letters written by Leibniz to all
the corners of scholarly Europe, our philosopher, inspired by his vision of the universal logical language,
claimed for his *art d'inventer* a power which taxes our
credulity. Almost all the mechanical, military, religious,
legal, and political phases of the life of his country and
age, were in Leibniz's mind to be benefited by his vision.
The universal characteristic deciphered the book of nature and revealed for him every link in the whole great
chain of being: the water that needed to be pumped out
of the Harz mines, the fossils in the mountains which
had to be described not as "sports of nature" but as
Nature's historical record of her illustrious works, the
physical phenomena of gravitation, elasticity, and magnetism which Leibniz thought he could deduce from the
purely geometrical laws of light. "I assumed that the
motion of the ether came from the daily motion of light
around the earth, without bothering to ask whether the
sun or earth turns. . . . All the phenomena of gravita-

tion, magnetism, electricity, and light are explicable by the resolution of a few problems of pure geometry: so much so that I believe I can be satisfied concerning the laws of motion by demonstrations entirely geometrical, without using any assumptions or principles from experience; and that whatever we will be able to say about these things, henceforth, will be only a matter of calculation and geometry (*res calculi et geometriae*)". (Letter to Ferrault, 1676).

The problems of medicine, of morals, of law, of theology and of metaphysics were all in Leibniz's mind to be duly resolved by the new symbolism. Thus logical rigor was important to him not merely for abstract theoretical reasons; it was necessary also, he thought, for the most practical interests of the seventeenth century, technological, medical, moral, legal, political, or religious. For example, Descartes is criticized by Leibniz not only for having failed to give a sufficiently rigorous proof of God's existence (a failure which weakens the defense of religion), but also because Descartes "of all men excelled in speculations, but has found nothing useful in life which falls under the senses and which may serve in the practice of the arts." (Letter to Philip, 1679).

It is in his correspondence concerning the experimentalists of the Royal Society of England (whom he had visited in 1673) that Leibniz reveals most clearly what he thought his logical instrument could do, and what the plain empiricists were not doing, namely, *to elicit all the knowledge deducible from a given number of presuppositions.* Lack of a proper art of demonstration had made it necessary, in Leibniz's opinion, for Baconian experimental philosophers like Boyle to resort to many observations in order to find out what Galileo and Descartes were able to know by reasoning. Some years after visiting the Royal Society in London, Leibniz reports:

"For they confessed to me in England that the great number of experiments they have amassed gives them no less difficulty than the lack of experiment gave the ancients." (Letter to Herzog Friedrich, 1679).

More than once does Leibniz take his experimental friends of the Royal Society to task for not having deduced more than they have from their many experiments. He and Huyghens admire the work of Robert Boyle, but find the Honorable Gentleman lacking in "application," or powers of generalization and inference. What Leibniz most admired in Boyle was his search for the simples or alphabetic elements of chemistry. Now Boyle thought his mechanical philosophy merely probable or no more true than his experimental observations, and reserved for theology a supernal place in "Things above Discourse," outside of science and logic. But Leibniz with his ambitious logical apparatus hoped to prove the teleological fitness of the grand laws of mechanics, so that the conservation of energy was a consequence of the continuity and universal harmony in all of nature.

In the physical sciences, what Hertz recognized in his *Principles of Mechanics* as the symbolic function of hypotheses, was first expressed by Leibniz as follows: "*Ars characteristica* is the art of so forming and arranging characters, in so far as they refer to thoughts, that they have among them those relations which the thoughts have among themselves: so that out of the ideas composing the idea expressing things, an expression of the things is composed out of characters of those things."

Leibniz constantly strove to reconcile the *a priori* elements of demonstrative reasoning with the more empirical side of scientific method. This stands out clearly if we compare the quotation just given with the empiricism in the following remark: "It is my habit to list a catalog of Experiments to do, when I examine some matter of Physics. And usually, I make such an enumeration of them that can assure me that by means of these experiments one will be able to find the cause or rule of what is in question through demonstration and not through Hypothesis. . . . In no wise content with the physical principles of Mons. des Cartes, I see that there is a way of establishing by means of experiments already done or easy to do, a Physics that is solid and without Hypothesis." (Letter to Berthey, 1677).

Thus a "solid Physics without Hypothesis" meant for Leibniz a more purely deductive logical system than either Descartes or Newton was prepared to offer. Leibniz had in mind apparently a postulational method for testing the compatibility or "compossibility" of the first principles or basic assumptions of any science. Compatibility of postulates in physics, for example, was demonstrable by experimental instances on the principle that what is actual is also possible, as in establishing the consistency of an axiom-set, we seek "interpretations." The superiority of the postulational treatment lay in the possibility of using the universal characteristic as a means or instrument for deriving new laws.

The criterion of "compossibility"—the compatibility of existing things—was also important in metaphysical theology, for Leibniz's main objections to Descartes' and Spinoza's proofs of God's existence rested on the logical point that their proofs had not established the compossibility of the attributes in the definition of God. Metaphysics or natural theology yields certainty because reference to empirical instances is not necessary in order to prove the consistency of the idea of God, the simplest of all ideas. Experimental physics can yield only probabilities because it is humanly impossible to refer all experimental laws to the logically simplest terms.

If adequate notice is taken of the postulation of

hypotheses or logically probable constructions, there will be more progress in Physics than if experiments alone are devised: "I agree with you, Sir, that it is necessary to follow the plans of Verulam in Physics, by adding to them, however, a certain art of conjecturing (*art de deviner*), for otherwise we shall hardly advance. I should be astonished if Mr. Boyle, who has so many fine experiments, would not come to some theory of chemistry after meditating so long on them. Yet in his books, and for all the consequences that he draws from his observations, he concludes only what we all know, namely, that everything happens mechanically. He is perhaps too reserved. Excellent men should leave us even their conjectures; they are wrong if they wish to give us only those truths that are certain." (Letter to Huyghens, Dec. 29, 1691).

Was Leibniz merely catering in his diplomatic way to the empiricism of his correspondents? Not if we consider the many times Leibniz reports his own empirical procedure; for example: "What made me believe that the variation of the compass-needle follows some rule (although still unknown) is the fact that I have seen some journals or log-books of long voyages in which it was often recorded as not changing by leaps but little by little." (Letter to Huyghens, Nov. 1690). Or again: "Is there nobody in philosophy at present who thinks about medicine? The late Mr. Crane was at home in it, but Messieurs les Cartésiens are too much preoccupied by their hypotheses. I prefer a Leeuwenhoek who tells me what he sees to a Cartesian who tells me what he thinks. It is however necessary to add reasoning to observations." (Letter to Huyghens, Feb. 1691).

Despite the traditonal text-book opposition of rationalists to empiricists, it is interesting to note that Hume in the next century claimed that he had the same interest as Leibniz in extending the logic of the sciences from formal demonstrations to empirical matters of probability. "The celebrated Monsieur Leibnitz has observed it to be a defect in the common systems of logic, that they are very copious when they explain the operations of the understanding in the forming of demonstrations, but are too concise when they treat of probabilities, and those other measures of evidence on which life and action entirely depend, and which are our guides even in most of our philosophical speculations." (Hume's *Abstract of a Treatise on Human Nature,* p. 7).

There was, then, a significant oscillation in Leibniz's writings between his *a priori* system of irreducible real definitions and the experimental aspect of his program for the use of logic as an instrument of discovery and invention. The task of reconciling the two aspects of Leibniz's logical theory was not successfully met by Leibniz nor by his successor, the dogmatic rationalist Wolff. A much more important attempt to resolve this old problem of rationalism and empiricism was made by Kant. Kant was greatly influenced by Leibniz's *Nouveaux Essais* (which was not published until 1765) with its point by point criticisms of Locke's *Essay Concerning the Human Understanding.*

There are two parts to Leibniz's universal characteristic: one is the system of primitive characters that stand for the irreducible simple concepts, the alphabet of the universal script; the other is the calculus of reasoning (*calculus ratiocinator*) which contains the rules of reducing all composite ideas to the simple ones and of combining the simple characters into composite ones. The former supplies the ultimate premises of all the sciences; the latter, the rules for combining concepts and propositions. Thus Leibniz's universal characteristic was both a metaphysical system and an instrument of demonstration and invention. It was not a novelty to conceive of logic as both a part of philosophy and an instrument. Boethius in the sixth century argued for this dual function of logic, comparing it to the eye which is both a part of the body and an aid to its orientation.

Nor was it a novelty to conceive of a universal language as the basis for the unification of the sciences. Since Lully's and Kircher's efforts, Jungius, the teacher of Leibniz, and various British philosophers known to Leibniz (Dalgarno, Wilkins, Hobbes, and Locke), had worked at the problem of simplifying language and logic on an international plane. In Bishop Wilkins' *Essay towards a Real Character and a Philosophical Language,* printed for the Royal Society in London, 1668, the following advantages of a universal language are cited in the Epistle Dedicatory: "More easy conversing with those of other nations . . . facilitating mutual commerce amongst the several nations of the world, and the improving of all natural knowledge; it would likewise very much conduce to the spreading of the knowledge of Religion . . . and contribute much to the clearing of some of our modern differences in Religion by unmasking many wild errors, that shelter themselves under the disguise of affected phrases; which being Philosophically unfolded, and rendered according to the genuine and natural importance of Words, will appear to be inconsistencies and contradictions. And several of these pretended, mysterious, profound notions, expressed in great swelling words, whereby some men set up for reputation, being this way examined, will appear to be, either nonsense, or very flat and jejune."

Leibniz approved of Locke's view, expressed in the last chapter of the *Essay Concerning Human Understanding,* that the study of Semiotics or the Doctrine of Signs "would afford us another sort of logic and critic than we have been hitherto acquainted with." But neither Locke nor his British compatriots had the mathematical training or skill to develop as Leibniz did the beginning of a symbolic logic through the generalization of algebraic and geometric reasoning.

Leibniz's aim was to find a common logical basis beyond the syllogism for algebraic, geometric, and theological reasonings. That he was not absolutely insistent that all science was completely reducible to an "alphabet of human thought" is intimated by such fragmentary notes of his as: "However, we must not imagine that we can always complete analysis to the first possibles, for that is not necessary for science." "Necessary" here can mean only "empirically possible," for it would take God's eternity to reveal the infinite number of absolute simples or compossibles.

It is not surprising therefore that the empiricist in Leibniz should have so frequently in his writings stressed the logical problem of estimating probabilities in matters of fact: "It is astonishing that the science of estimating probabilities is almost unknown, and that Logicians have not yet examined the degrees of probability or of likelihood that exist in conjectures or proofs . . . not in order to arrive at certainty, which is impossible, but in order to act as reasonably as possible on the facts and knowledge given us."

Thus, according to Leibniz, demonstrative certainty is impossible in matters of fact. He conceived the deductive procedure which yields certainty as consisting essentially in transforming one proposition into another by substituting in the former the definition of one or another of its terms. No deductive system was complete or rigorous until its premises (axioms or postulates) were reduced, as Pascal had insisted in *De l'Esprit Géométrique,* to the form of absolutely simple ideas by definitions. But Leibniz wished Pascal had offered a means of knowing when ideas were absolutely simple apart from conventional definition. Now, just as the prime numbers necessarily determine every composite number, so, Leibniz argued, the "real definitions" of terms would necessarily determine the axioms of any deductive system and yield theorems with a certainty *relative to the definitions*.

A "real definition" is the best kind of definition (*definitio optimi generis*) for it decomposes a term into its relatively "simple" constituent notions, e.g., "a parabola is the locus of points equidistant from a straight line and a point" is a real definition because the construction of the subject depends only on notions (point, line, equal distances) and operations known to be possible. A nominal definition, on the other hand, is merely a convenient abbreviation or convention about the use of terms, e.g., "ABC stands for a triangle." Only real definitions guarantee the possibility of things by means of a non-contradictory group of constituent concepts, e.g., "a square is an equilateral rectangle" has a real basis in the elements of equal sides and right angles which constitute the square.

The sciences for Leibniz are a group of real definitions together with all that can be deduced from them by means of the art of combinations. The two parts of the universal characteristic, viz., the inventory of real things and the rules for combining them, go to form a metaphysic and a logic. In practice, Leibniz realized, the number of simple constituent elements in any empirical object is so great that only God can identify them, that is, only God can reduce all empirical predications to simple identities.

Leibniz like Spinoza and Descartes adopted the traditional mode of theology and assumed there was an absolute set of simple ideas in God's mind through which all our knowledge is derived even though it is never complete: "A primitive concept is one which is not resolvable into others so long as the object which it signifies possesses no other character but is known through itself (*sed est index sui*). Now such a concept can get its existence only from that which is known through itself; namely from the highest substance, that is, from God. All derivative concepts, however, which we can have, we can possess only through the mediation of these primitive concepts, so that nothing can exist in things without the doing of God, even though we are not allowed to know altogether distinctly in which ways the nature of things depends on God or the ideas of things on the idea of God, wherein ultimate analysis or adequate knowledge of all things through their causes originates."

Now nothing in this theological tradition is more important for the mind of man than to strive toward the knowledge of God. Hence the attempt to demonstrate all axioms by reducing them to absolute primitives or simples is one of the ambitious but dubious metaphysical aspects of Leibniz's logic, at least of one function of logic as Leibniz conceived it.

There is only one language for all the sciences because there is only one God whose ideas are the ultimate simples and whose language is the language of nature. The seventeenth-century book of nature is not as simple as the ancient book. Nature is infinitely complex, for "in every particle of the universe there is contained a world of infinite creatures." Consequently the number of primitive ideas or real definitions must be infinite: "It is very important to conceive the number of primitive propositions as infinite, for they are either definitions or Axioms. The number of definitions as well as the number of terms is infinite. And so is the number of Axioms. I call an Axiom a proposition that is necessary and indemonstra-

ble. Necessary applies to propositions whose opposite
implies a contradiction. Now the only proposition whose
opposite implies a contradiction is a formal identity. The
latter is evident by itself, hence cannot be demonstrated;
to demonstrate means to make evident by reason and by
consequence. The senses show that 'A is A' is a proposition whose opposite 'A is not A' implies a contradiction.
Now what the senses show is indemonstrable. Therefore,
the true and indemonstrable Axioms are the identical
propositions. . . . If these primitive propositions are
infinite, the conclusions will also be so. . . . The primitive indefinables cannot be easily recognized by us, except
as prime numbers are. These we have so far been unable
to detect except by division by all the smaller numbers.
Likewise, irresoluble terms would only be recognized
negatively and provisionally. For I have a mark by
means of which the resolubility of a term can be recognized. It is as follows: When we meet a proposition
which appears to us necessary, and which is not demonstrated, it follows infallibly that there is in this proposition a definable term, provided that this proposition is
necessary. Next, we must try to give its demonstration;
and this cannot be done without finding the required
definition. By this method of not allowing any axiom to
pass without proof except the definitions and the identities, we shall come to the resolution of terms and to the
simplest ideas." *

The most interesting statement in the foregoing is
the one that appeals to the senses as part of the proof
of the irreducibility of the law of identity and of the
reducibility of all other statements to identities. This
made it possible to put propositions in the visible form
of equations, and to work with propositions as one did

* *L. Couturat, Opuscules et fragments inédits de Leibniz,*
pp. 186–7.

algebra, so that in any discussion the reasonings of men could be exhibited in the form of a calculus. An end would be put to clamorous controversy, claimed Leibniz, if the disputants would merely stop shouting, take out pencil and paper, and say to each other, "Let us calculate."

Although the operations of algebra (sum, product, factoring) were generalized in Leibniz's logic, the traditional algebraic science of quantity became merely a sample (*échantillon*) of the more general science and its enlarged field of applications, beyond the traditional limitations of mathematics to size or quantity: "Thus the best advantages of algebra are only samples of the art of characters whose use is not limited to number or size."

La vraie logique, la méthode d'universalité, was thus able to embrace a general geometry (analysis situs) and all the other branches of pure and applied mathematics, i.e., both necessary and probable reasoning. This theoretical consequence of a logic of contingent truths of fact (*vérités de fait*) had for Leibniz its practical social correlate: "We need a new logic to know degrees of probability in matters of fact, ... law, ... business." Frequently, prior to this, Leibniz had compared his new logic of estimating probabilities with the methods of bookkeepers. "The general science is to the particular sciences what the science of accounting is to the merchant or banker." In other words, a scientist or philosopher with a faulty logic will be as confused as a business man who does not know how to keep his accounts in order. And the divine order of things will reveal itself only to the philosopher who applies the most exact method of universal logic to his ideas if they are to account adequately for the supreme order of creation.

Leibniz's exacting logic did not meet with any imme-

diate success among either the scientific or metaphysical
thinkers of his time. It was not until the middle of the
nineteenth century that mathematical logic was applied
to the extension of the syllogism and to the calculus of
probability in any extensive way by Boole and De Mor-
gan. Boole devoted also a chapter of his *Investigation
of the Laws of Thought, on which are founded the
Mathematical Theories of Logic and Probability* (1854)
to refuting in Leibnizian fashion the metaphysics and
theology of Spinoza's *Ethics*. The axiomatic foundations
of arithmetic and algebra came even later in the works
of Weierstrass, Dedekind, Peirce, Frege, Peano, Whitehead, and Russell. Only in the last generation have applications of symbolic logic to relay-switch circuits, punch-
card systems, and calculating machines, and even to
biological theory, been made by scientists. They do not
seem aware that the immortal spirit of Leibniz is gaz-
ing with rewarding delight on their embodiment of his
visions. The smile undoubtedly changes to a deep frown
when that same spirit contemplates the dismissal of
metaphysics by specialists who lack cosmic perspective.

III. MONADISM

Bertrand Russell in his *Critical Exposition of the
Philosophy of Leibniz* maintains that "Leibniz's system
does follow correctly and necessarily from five premises"
which he enumerates as follows:

"I. Every proposition has a subject and predicate.

"II. A subject may have predicates which are qualities
existing at various times. (Such a subject is called a substance.)

"III. True propositions not asserting existence at particular times are necessary and analytic, but such as

assert existence at particular times are contingent and synthetic. The latter depend on final causes.

"IV. The Ego is a substance.

"V. Perception yields knowledge of an external world, i.e., of existents other than myself and my states."

Russell then finds that the first premise is inconsistent with the fourth and fifth premises, and this constitutes for a him a general objection to Leibniz's monadism.

If we followed Russell's method of logical atomism, we could make short shrift of any system of metaphysics in the history of philosophy. Such analysis, indeed, is not merely an exercise of logic, but is also an invaluable aid for the critical study of the history of philosophy. It ought to produce humility in would-be metaphysicians who believe themselves free of all inconsistencies. Nevertheless, if we depended on that method exclusively, we should be missing the historical vision of Leibniz, his dynamic view of the universe and of man's place in it. We should be forgetting that the human mind is, as it always has been, influenced by systems of thought which are never completely consistent, and we should thus fail to understand a good many of the pervasive and cumulative ideas that go into the evolution of our continually changing approach to scientific and moral problems. Though Leibniz is not a thoroughgoing experimentalist, his two uses of logic—to analyze the theoretical foundations of all the sciences and to integrate our scientific knowledge with its human or civilized values—stand out as the salient features of his rationalism.

Though Leibniz's system of microcosmic mirrors reflecting one another in various grades of energetic scintillation makes a pretty kaleidoscopic image, it is difficult to see how this optical analogy fits into Leibniz's other favorite analogy of the world as a pond teeming with living organisms. Such analogies, however, were illustrations of abstract principles which no thinker can ignore; for example, the interrelatedness and reciprocal causal action of bodies and of life processes as well as the evolutionary continuity of species of graded complexity and internal organization. Leibniz was so impressed with the details of internal structure, partly because of his logical sense of order and partly because of Leeuwenhoek's microscopic discoveries, that he tended to neglect the external factor of environmental interaction with organisms. His evolutionism and monadism are pre-formationist exactly because he regarded all processes and substances as governed by logical principles such as he found in mathematical series and the infinite terms generated by the law connecting them internally. The density of terms in such infinite series was generalized by Leibniz into a metaphysical principle of plenitude. Instead of atoms and empty spaces, swarms of monads fill the world in infinite abundance. One can also find mathematical analogies for Leibniz's hierarchy of monads. Now Professor Lovejoy has shown that the principles of continuity, plenitude, and gradation are the pervasive ideas that enter into the historic idea of "the great chain of being." Though this idea no longer enjoys the vogue it did for so many centuries of the history of thought, there are features of Leibniz's use of it which are still valuable to the modern philosopher, whenever he aims to frame a world-view within the bounds of what is scientifically intelligible and humanly valuable.

We may still appreciate Leibniz's suggestive discussions of the nature of individuals and of their spontaneous internal freedom, his analysis of processes, qualities and objective relations in the spatio-temporal order, his synoptic view of the great chain of being as a continuum of inter-related dynamic centers of energy, his worldly sense of the complexity and contingency of existence, his logical insight into the analytical character of the forms of thought, his epistemological distinctions of the degrees and kinds of knowledge, his psychological postulates of the integrative purposive action of the mind, its inseparability from bodily behavior, and the unconscious myriad of scarcely perceptible effects on the mind (*petites perceptions*), the possibility of organizing scientific research for peaceful purposes among thinkers in different fields and of different nationalities, and his toleration (without sparing logical criticism) of religious and ethical creeds as far apart as those of the Western and Oriental civilizations. In this summary recital of the high points of Leibniz's contributions to philosophy, we are ignoring for the time being the local and historical conditions in which Leibniz worked out his philosophical principles, though many of the defects in his philosophy may be explained by reference to his frequent concessions to the ruling political and ecclesiastical powers of his time, which we shall discuss later. To the extent that Leibniz formulated principles that are still philosophically important, we are justified in ignoring their immediate historical context.

Furthermore, we have seen that the roots of Leibniz's *Weltanschauung* are traceable to ideas which long antedate the seventeenth century. An important group of these ideas was developed in Leibniz's philosophy, as Arthur O. Lovejoy has so clearly demonstrated, to be the "most conspicuous, most determinative and most pervasive" conception of the Chain of Being among the great philosophic systems of the seventeenth century: "The essential characteristics of the universe are for him [Leibniz] plenitude, continuity, and linear gradation. The chain consists of the totality of monads, ranging in hierarchical sequence from God to the lowest grade of sentient life, no two alike, but each differing from those just below and just above it in the scale by the least possible difference. Since the metaphysics of Leibniz is a form of idealism, or more precisely, of panpsychism, the gradation is defined primarily in psychological rather than morphological terms; it is by the levels of consciousness which severally connect them, the degrees of adequacy and clarity with which they 'mirror' or 'represent' the rest of the universe, that the monads are differentiated. Nevertheless, the material world also, as a *phenomenon bene fundatum,* the mode in which these incorporeal entities necessarily manifest themselves to one another, has a derivative and somewhat equivocal, but essential, place in Leibniz's scheme of things; and he habitually employs without hesitation the ordinary language of physical realism, and discusses the problems of physical science as genuine, not as fictitious problems. And in the material world too the same three laws hold good; and they should be used by the investigator of nature as guiding principles in his empirical researches." *

This admirably succinct and authentic summary of Leibniz's metaphysics and theory of knowledge should be a valuable guide to the student as he reads through the selections of Parts II and III of this volume. It will be noticed that the principle of plenitude was used by Leibniz to refute the atomists' lifeless and mechanistic view of nature as a fortuitous concourse of particles in empty space. The plethora of real essences which crowd reality for Leibniz is marked by a dynamic propensity within each essence to come into existence in order to

* Arthur O. Lovejoy, *The Great Chain of Being: A Study of the History of an Idea,* The William James Lectures delivered at Harvard University, 1933. Cambridge, Mass.: Harvard University Press, 1936, p. 144.

cooperate in producing the richest or the greatest possible diversity within the economy of nature's laws. These laws, we have already noticed, are eternal decrees of God who never wills any existence incompatible with his reason. Monads come into existence as "fulgurations" or sparks of the divine, falling within the rational limits of a pre-established harmony. They are spiritual rather than physical points, but aggregations of them make up dynamic bodies in space.

It is remarkable how Leibniz in this principle of the dynamic inclination of essences to realize harmoniously the maximum of existence, unites physical, aesthetic, logical, metaphysical and theological considerations. In any case, what follows from this principle of plenitude is the principle of sufficient reason. The office of this principle is to explain or make rational the essentially contingent nature of existing things, why they should exist rather than remain mere possibilities in the mind of God. It posits that whatever exists has a reason or purpose for existing, derived from the order of creation. The ambiguous use Leibniz makes of this principle of sufficient reason appears in his two-fold way of explaining contingent truths, sometimes referring to God's willing the good in accordance with reason, and sometimes to man's empirical inability to reduce matters of fact to purely logical identities. If theologians did not take to Leibniz's principle of the exigency in essences to exist and the corollary principles of plenitude and of sufficient reason, it was because (as Professor Lovejoy has pointed out) such a principle seemed dangerously close to the materialistic theory of the inherent sufficiency of matter to move itself and to be intelligible without invoking divine decree or assistance.

Leibniz, however, did use his principle of sufficient reason to supplement the principle of contradiction, realizing that empirical science could not proceed by logical analysis alone and had to admit contingency in our knowledge of things, too complex and diverse for any understanding other than God's. This complexity and diversity was subsumed under his principle of the identity of indiscernibles which postulates that no two individuals, for example, two oak leaves, can be exactly alike in all their properties. This is an *a priori* principle and has ambiguous import also. Logically, it may be used as a definition of identity: two things (or, in logic, two terms) are identical if everything predicable of one is also predicable of the other; in that case, they differ only in their name; and the other meaning is that in observable nature no two things differ only numerically, for there are and must be inherent, individual, qualitative differences. The Cartesians who made extension or space the essence of substance would then be wrong in distinguishing two bodies merely by their geometrical properties or position, for space is homogeneous everywhere, whereas physical bodies being aggregates of living centers of energy have a more qualitative, dynamic basis for differentiation.

One might, as John Herman Randall, Jr. has suggested, derive the whole of Leibniz's metaphysics from his life-long polemic against the Cartesians. Their view of the conservation of motion was attacked by Leibniz because it failed to take into account the internal, dynamic interplay of natural forces. It is certainly true that Leibniz introduced his metaphysical principles of sufficient reason and continuity in defending his own version of the conservation of energy in the collisions of bodies or in their gravitational energy. That all physical bodies are elastic, resist motion, and acquire or expend energy according to the square of their velocity, could only be explained by reference to the internal dynamic essence of each individual substance. The latter is only partly fathomable by the human mind, since the striving effort (*conatus*) inherent in each ultimate substance is known completely only to God. Whatever manifestations of these essences we observe and measure in physics conform to the continuity we find in our own memories, in motion resolved by mathematical functions, and in the processes of natural growth. Rest is not absolute, but a limiting case of motion.

Furthermore, we cannot, according to Leibniz, explain why some substances act more freely and more powerfully than others unless we introduce the infinite gradations of internal activity characteristic of different grades of monads. As Professor Lovejoy has indicated, when it comes to differentiating the monads, Leibniz shifts from physics to psychology: each monad is graded according to its powers of mental activity, the higher monad perceiving changes within itself more clearly, distinctly, or adequately than the lower ones, and in so doing, "mirrors" more of the objective relations of the entire universe of monads from its point of view. The ensemble of these points of view forms an order of co-existence, and space is nothing but the simultaneous perception of co-existing qualities, as time is nothing but the order of successively perceived qualities. The spaces and times of each monad will be relative to the point of view of each. But there still remains the absolute space and time belonging to the ensemble of all points of view which only God can perceive intuitively, and which would constitute for him the objective relational order of the real universe. Leibniz thus had two orders of space and time, one for man's relative knowledge and one for God.

This ambiguous theory of space and time resembles Berkeley's phenomenal view which also made space an order of co-existing qualities, and time the order of their succession. Yet, though both admit the reality of secondary qualities, Leibniz criticized young Berkeley for denying the physical existence of bodies in space and time: "The man in Ireland who impugns the reality of bodies seems neither to give adequate reasons nor to explain sufficiently what is in his mind. I suspect he is one of those people who seek to become famous by their paradoxes." (Letter to Des Bosses, 1715).

The inherent effort of each essence to realize the maximum existence is the metaphysical basis for Leibniz's defense of a spontaneous freedom of will (made possible by divine grace) in the case of men's individual essences. The effective power of the will varies with the power of reason in each monad, though it is conditioned by an innumerable host of conflicting inclinations, unconscious perceptions, and unpredictable influences which act on the mind through the pre-established harmony in all things. This internal spontaneity does run afoul of Leibniz's cosmic determinism, but, at least, on the empirical side, it represents an attempt to do justice to the variety, complexity and contingency of human motivation.

The ultimate individuals (monads) of the universe are then active centers of energy containing all that they have been or will be within themselves. "Each monad is burdened by the past and pregnant with the future." The influence of the pre-formationist theory of biology is again very marked here, and again, is not consistent with Leibniz's notion of man's moral freedom. Also, so long as Leibniz explained his notion of an individual by comparing the latter to a place in a mathematical series or continuum, the substance or essential nature of each individual is determined rigorously by the formula of the series which fixes the internal relations of the individuals to one another. God, the king of monads, is not a monad, but the rule which generates the whole hierarchical series. Much of this is from Spinoza.

Leibniz's doctrine of internal relations compelled him logically to deny any external causal interactions among monads, thus paying a rather high premium for insuring their metaphysical individuality and moral privacy. Whatever changes they had to undergo were understood to be internal developments according to their pre-formed natures in the divinely pre-established harmony. The latter guarantees the perfect clock-like co-ordination of mind and body. That is what Leibniz meant when he wrote "the monads have no windows." They can only perceive with various degrees of discernment the changes which tick themselves off mentally in an order co-ordinated with their internal mechanism created by the perfect clock-maker, God.

There are *hypothetically* various possible alternatives in the varied detail of changes internal to the life of each monad, and an act of free will consists in choosing from among them. Each hypothetical possibility has strictly determined consequences, so that there is no absolute freedom to alter the metaphysically determined system of all compossibilities. Moral choice then rests on the hypothetical order of unrealized possibilities. This is true of man's voluntary actions and of God's choice of "the best of all possible worlds."

The problem of evil arises only because of the limitations of human understanding with respect to God's will whose providence is so often inscrutable. Like the scholastics Leibniz denies the metaphysical reality of evil as incompatible with the divine goodness of creation, and in his *Theodicy,* the only book published in his life-time, Leibniz prepared a long apologetic for the explanation of physical and moral evil. There are scarcely any new arguments here, and much use is made of the principle of sufficient reason even though man's knowledge is never sufficient to grasp the necessity for the existence of so much apparent evil. Leibniz also frequently indulges in the esthetic analogy of the apparent lack of harmony or beauty in the perception of an isolated piece of work of art, until the rest of it is brought into view. So we are reminded, with some empirical truth, that we often prematurely judge things evil until further consequences reveal a more just outcome to which the apparent evil was evidently a necessary prelude.

W. Somerset Maugham has expressed in a modern pragmatic way the Spinozistic-Leibnizian theory of free will. One of the characters in *Of Human Bondage,* Philip, says: "The illusion of free will is so strong in my mind that I can't get away from it, but I believe it is only an illusion. But it is an illusion which is one of the strongest motives of my actions. Before I do anything I feel that I have a choice, and that influences what I do; but afterwards, when the thing is done, I believe that it was inevitable from all eternity."—"What do you deduce from that?" asked Hayward.—"Why, merely the futility of regret. It's no good crying over spilt milk, because all the forces of the universe were bent on spilling it."*

IV. UNIVERSAL HARMONY AND WORLD PEACE

Leibniz repeatedly deplored the fact that men, including the most learned and scientific, so often bicker with one another, ridiculing others for holding opinions differing from their own, and refusing to make any

* W. Somerset Maugham, *Of Human Bondage* (New York: Doubleday and Co., 1917), ch. 67.

compromises in their own views. "The human race, considered in its relation to the sciences which serve our welfare, seems to me comparable to a troop which marches in confusion in the darkness, without any word or other signs for the regulation of their march and the recognition of one another. Instead of joining hands to guide ourselves and make sure of the road, we run hither and yon and interfere with one another." But the reason for this perpetual competition among men lies in the self-assertiveness essential to each individual as a center of active force, which Leibniz himself had insisted on as the ground of all individual existence. It is true that he optimistically and on religious grounds assumed also that all monads fell into a pre-established harmony. If men would follow the right method and use the universal characteristic as a means of expression, all wrangling would cease. Harmony rests on empirical conditions.

The temper of Leibniz's philosophy is not as naively optimistic as Voltaire with his literary wit and acidulous irony made it out to be in *Candide*. In Leibniz's frequent exhortations to advance the use of a more rational method of inquiry and discussion in scientific, social, philosophical and religious matters, he obviously presupposes that "the best of all possible worlds" does *not* imply preserving the present discordant appearance of things and the irrational habits of men. His many essays on method imply making fuller empirical use of the active power of reason in order to pursue goals to the best of our ability and knowledge. Whether such a melioristic program for promoting the progress of mankind is compatible with Leibniz's metaphysical theory of a pre-established harmony is, of course, an embarrassing question. Sometimes Leibniz writes optimistically—usually in order to obtain the support of a princely patron for some scientific or philosophical project—and sometimes

(perhaps, after being turned down or ignored) he writes
dourly that his age is not yet ripe for his ideas. In the
latter case, we must each be content with adding our
mite of creative intelligence, though at other times Leibniz thought it would not require many minds like his own
to bring about the millennium of Enlightenment under the
benevolent patronage of a heroic prince or princess.

This oscillation of mood in Leibniz between optimism
and pessimism concerning the possibility of a life of
reason for man reflects the radical dualism running
through Leibniz's life and philosophical writing. The
optimism runs high in his metaphysical and theodicic
theories of our knowledge of the dependence of all things
on a divine order and the ultimate reducibility of all
phenomena to logical identities expressing the nature
of immortal substances (monads) endowed with different
grades of active souls (according to their power to form
clear, distinct, adequate and intuitive ideas). The pessimism appears in our inability to divine the universal
harmony among the *apparent* physical, moral and metaphysical evils of existence, and in the fact that in three-
fourths of our knowledge, as Leibniz put it, we have to
be content with indistinct, symbolic, probable approxi-
mations to truth. Leibniz's optimism often rested on the
Platonic idea of a permanent rational order of justice,
truth and beauty lying behind the apparent evils, imperfect knowledge and discordance which marks the
finite earthly life of man. This span of man's life is only
a small transitory stage of the larger life of the immortal soul, as the life of the caterpillar is only a stage in
the life of a butterfly. Such metaphors, borrowed from
the biological discoveries in Leibniz's day by Swammerdam, Malpighi, Leeuwenhoek and others, were used by
Leibniz as analogical arguments for the immortality of
the soul and for the transience of life's ills.

For a philosopher who was so sure of the eternal nature of truth, goodness, justice, and many other Platonic ideas in the sciences of the mind, it is astonishing how many concessions Leibniz made to the temporal order of the semi-feudal princes and ecclesiastical officials of his day. He rarely criticized an established tradition or institution, and in fact warns against innovation in morals, politics or religion as socially disturbing. He thus subscribed to an almost literal interpretation of Christ's dictum: "Render unto Caesar what is Caesar's, and unto God what is God's." His whole philosophy teems with many dualities in addition to and yet in a sense paralleling this one of the temporal and the spiritual: the kingdoms of nature and of grace, the contingent truths of fact and the necessary truths of reason, the mechanical order of efficient causes and the teleological order of final causes, the empirical and the rational elements in knowledge.

But there is no doubt that Leibniz sought by means of his persistent vision of a universal harmony to reconcile logically incompatible elements in the classical, scholastic traditions and in the mathematical, experimental methods of the new or rapidly growing sciences of the seventeenth century to which he himself made such important contributions. The latter were largely a result of his sojourn in Paris among the brilliant mathematical scientists gathered there, though Leibniz, it should be recalled, came to Paris on a diplomatic mission. He had come as an envoy of the German princes to see Louis XIV and persuade him to divert his armies from war-devastated Germany to Egypt. Leibniz did not succeed in either meeting the Roi Soleil or changing the military ambitions of *Mars Christianissimus,* as Leibniz, smarting with disappointment, bitterly called the prince whom he had at first hailed as the Great Monarch of the age. "In fact to wish to subjugate by arms the civilized nations of Europe who are for the most part also the defenders and lovers of liberty, is not only impious but mad." But Louis XIV's armies proceeded to invade Holland, and Europe was at war until 1714. The German princes on the Rhineland, who were allowed by the Treaty of Westphalia (1648) to make separate treaties, were subsidized by Louis XIV, and thought they could play a double game of catering to France and intriguing for their own interests. Leibniz at first defended his friend and patron, Baron Boineburg, by agreeing with him that it was dangerous to have France for an enemy on the shores of the Rhine. But after Louis XIV's invasion of Holland, Leibniz attacked the French king for ignoring natural law, the law of all peoples (*jus gentium*), and the very idea of Christianity. He denounced Louis XIV for allying himself with the Turks against Christians and thus violating his vow as a Christian ruler to serve as the vicar of God.

Leibniz's interest in law and government was not confined to academic jurisprudence and its logic, though these were his early interests. He defined the universality of natural law not only in an abstract way but in political pamphlets, attacking the "inexcusable peace of Utrecht" of 1713, and defending the idea of the Holy Roman Empire for preserving on a temporal basis the universal order of peace and law against the aggressive, imperialistic policies of Louis XIV toward Austria, Spain, Holland and England. In Vienna, Leibniz even proposed a mass uprising against France, even as Richelieu had once had Louis XIII order a call to arms against Spain,—a forgotten fact which Leibniz had brought to light by exhuming the ordinances from the archives during his stay in Paris. But Leibniz was not advocating internal revolution: "As to that large question of the power of sovereigns and the obedience due them by people," he wrote to his friend Boineburg in 1695, "I am wont to say that it would be good for princes to be convinced that people have a right to resist them, and that, on the other hand, people be persuaded to passive obedience. However, I share enough of Grotius' opinions to believe that people ought as a rule to obey, the harm resulting from revolution being incomparably greater than what provokes it." This is a very utilitarian attitude quite separable logically from Leibniz's theodicic view that this is "the best of all possible worlds."

Leibniz aimed to form a single Christian body of European states so that as a result the whole of Europe might cease conspiring against itself. That is why he approved of l'Abbé de Saint-Pierre's project for perpetual peace in Europe on the basis of a sort of holy alliance among the rulers of Europe who would perpetuate peace by co-operative organization of the arts and sciences. Though he disagreed with that part of the plan which would abolish the Holy Roman Empire and give the Emperor only one vote, Leibniz said: "On the whole it is feasible, and its realization would be one of the most useful things in the world."

There is no explicit political philosophy in Leibniz though he was more politically active than any philosopher ever had been in Europe. The favor he enjoyed among the princes and princesses, church dignitaries and learned men of Europe made him a desirable ally in the religious and national competition of his age. He was offered a position as Chief Librarian of the Vatican, but preferred to keep on friendly terms with both Catholic and Protestant theologians and found it diplomatic not to take sides. This does not seem to be in Leibniz merely a matter of personal expediency, for he had a genuine love of peace and was imbued with the spirit of reconciliation, hoping to reunite the churches and join the cultures of West and East by interchange of ideas and goods with distant China. He was intensely interested, on behalf of Protestant missionary work in China, in the dispute in Rome concerning the modifications of the ritual for conversion proposed by some Catholic missionaries in China. Their purpose was to adapt the sacramental rites to Confucianism which was a state-religion and closely identified with civil service requirements.

There has been recently a growing interest in the intellectual history of China and its relations to Western civilization as the two cultures come into closer communication with each other, as Leibniz anticipated. Here the difficulties of language are very great for Western students, and the need of a universal medium of expression of ideas, such as Leibniz contemplated, is indeed of paramount practical importance. Meanwhile we must draw upon an expert sinologist like Professor Donald Lach who has made a study of "Leibniz and China" in a recent article:

"The influence of Leibniz upon his contemporaries and upon his successors was just as important in the field of Chinese studies as it was in general philosophy and mathematics. Of special significance was the stimulus which his thought gave to men of religion who were interested in opening China as a new field for Protestant missionaries. . . . Leibniz was the only major philosopher of the period to hold that the Chinese possessed a spiritualistic doctrine compatible in some of its aspects with Christianity .˙. . Leibniz studied Chinese life and institutions, not for themselves alone, but in an effort to corroborate with facts his theory of universal culture. Chinese political and social administration he believed to be far superior to the rule of favorites and the balance-of-power politics common to the monarchies of Europe.

. . . It was in this connection that Leibniz felt Europe might learn something of moral philosophy from China. According to Leibniz, China should profit from the revealed theology of Europe as exemplified in the Christian tradition. Chinese philosophy he considered not a foreign system of thought, but simply an alien counterpart of his own monadology and the Christian religion. In his analysis of I Ching's trigrams, he was not only looking for another mathematical device; he hoped also to reveal that the ancient Chinese were a logical and intelligent people. For a time, at least, he considered the Chinese language as a possibility in his search for a universal philosophic language. Moreover, in his consideration of historical subjects Leibniz recognized the necessity of studying Chinese history if the development of mankind is to be adequately co-ordinated and understood. In his great scheme of universal civilization, the philosopher pictured China and Europe, geographical opposites, as intellectual allies. Ideas and philosophies, as well as mechanical contrivances, were to serve as connecting links in the chain which Leibniz visualized and which men had hitherto—and have even yet—to forge." *

The whole last volume of Foucher de Careil's seven-volume edition of Leibniz's historical, religious and political works is devoted to Leibniz's projects and correspondence on the founding of scientific Academies in Berlin, Vienna, Amsterdam, and finally in Moscow. As his letter to Peter the Great shows, Leibniz in the last year of his remarkable scientific and worldly career, sought to extend the cultivation of science and learning to the vast reaches and primitive life of Russia, and then by way of this vast geographical link to connect the culture of Europe to that of China. Even in this last of his

* Donald Lach, "Leibniz and China," *Journal of the History of Ideas* (1945), pp. 453 f.

grand schemes, the old duality appears in the form of Leibniz's arguments for the advancement of the sciences including the systematic study of the languages of the peoples of Russia for the purpose of translating the Bible and doing missionary work among them.

Leibniz would have made an ideal Director for an international organization like Unesco whose program in many ways embodies his cosmopolitan ideas, far-sighted spirit of collaboration and co-operation for a more enlightened, peaceful, and morally progressive world civilization. Whether Leibniz was too optimistic about world harmony is no longer a question for academic dispute or literary wit, but one on which the very survival of civilization depends.

PHILIP P. WIENER

I. ON METHOD

1. FROM *ELEMENTS OF LAW AND EQUITY*
[1669–70]

The theory of law belongs to the sciences which are built not on experiments but on definitions, not on the senses but on demonstrations according to reason; it deals with questions, as we say, of law and not of fact (*juris non facti*). Since justice consists in a certain harmony and proportion, its meaning remains independent of whether anybody actually does justice to others, or conversely, is treated justly. The same holds for numerical relationships which remain true regardless of whether anybody does any counting or whether anything is counted. It is in the same sense that we may pass judgment on a house, a machine, or a society when we say that they would, if they existed, be beautiful, efficient, or happy respectively, even though they never will exist. Hence it is not surprising that the propositions of these sciences possess eternal truth. They are, namely, hypothetical propositions, and deal not with what exists but with what follows under the hypothesis of a defined existence. They also do not take their point of departure from the senses but from a clear and distinct intuition or, as Plato called it, idea, a word which itself signified discernment or definition.

. . . Thus the necessary connections of things and their implications are demonstrated without further ado, because they are derived from a clear and distinct idea which (when expressed in words) is derived from a definition by means of a concatenated series of definitions, in short, by means of a proof. Since the theory of law is a science, the basis of science proof, and the basis of

1

proof is definition, it follows that the definition of the
words "law," "more equitable," "justice" must first of
all be established. That is to say, we must make clearly
explicit the ideas with which we go about unwittingly
judging the truth of our assertions and the correctness
of the use of words.

The kind and method of this inquiry is one in which
we bring together the most significant and best examples
of the usage of words, and then think of what is common
to these and all other instances as well. For just as we
construct a hypothesis on the basis of an induction, that
is on the basis of a comparison of experiences, so we
similarly construct a definition as a result of comparing
many expressions in so far as in both situations the most
important cases previously investigated serve to give us
a summary expression that will cover the cases not yet
investigated. This method requires us, so long as it makes
no difference, to employ a word which is arbitrarily
chosen. For when we speak only to ourselves or our
intimates, or about something generally unknown, it is
within our power to attach to a defined idea a word which
need have only the particular function of helping our
memory; in that way it is unnecessary to repeat constantly a definition which may be composed of ten words.
However, when it comes to writing for publication about
a generally known subject not lacking in designations, it
is either the stupidity of one who will not be intelligible,
or the knavishness or arrogance of a person, which will
make him think up his own peculiar word or special applications of the same. . . .

2. ON THE METHOD OF UNIVERSALITY
[1674]

1. The method of universality instructs us how to find by means of a single operation analytical formulas and general geometric constructions for different subjects or cases each one of which would otherwise need a particular analysis or synthesis. As a result its use may be considered as extending to Algebra and Analysis and as spreading to all the parts of pure or applied mathematics. For it happens frequently that one and the same problem has several cases; their multitude is very bothersome and imposes useless modifications and wearisome repetitions from which this method will save us in the future.

2. Now as all the propositions of applied mathematical sciences may be stripped of their matter by means of a reduction to pure geometry, it will suffice to show its use in geometry. This boils down to two points; namely, first, the reduction of several different cases to a single formula, rule, equation, or construction, and secondly, the reduction of different figures to a certain harmony in order to demonstrate or resolve universally a number of problems or theorems about them. The first point diminishes difficulties, the other increases science and adds considerable light. For if in time the Geometry of infinites might be rendered a little more susceptible of Analysis so that the problems of quadratures, of centers, and of the Dimensions of curves could be solved by means of equations (as there is hope of doing although M. Descartes did not dare to aspire to do it), we should obtain a great advantage from the Harmony of the figures for the purpose of finding their quadrature as well as that of others.

3. It is true that Messieurs Desargues and Pascal believed they could reduce conic sections to a Harmony.

But beside the fact that their method is restricted and depends only on the particular properties of Conics, it is extremely awkward because we must still remain in the solid and confine the mind to a strong image of the cone. Indeed I well believe that there would be a great deal of trouble in solving difficult problems that way, unless they are already resolved by chance, *a priori,* or by means of a theorem demonstrated elsewhere. On the other hand, nothing can escape our method, which resembles the other parts of Analysis in that it spares the mind and the imagination; the latter, above all, must be used sparingly.

4. That is the aim of that great science which I am used to calling *Characteristic,* of which what we call Algebra, or Analysis, is only a very small branch, since it is this *Characteristic* which gives words to languages, letters to words, numbers to Arithmetic, notes to Music. It teaches us how to fix our reasoning, and to require it to leave, as it were, visible traces on the paper of a notebook for inspection at leisure. Finally, it enables us to reason with economy, by substituting characters in the place of things in order to relieve the imagination. . . .

[The remaining 51 paragraphs of this essay are mathematical, Leibniz showing how to remove the ambiguities of algebraic signs used in solving equations, e.g., the positive and negative roots of polynomial functions, the general equation of conic sections, the geometric interpretation of infinitesimal elements and asymptotic limits. This is followed by construction problems: "how to draw a perpendicular to a given conic section by means of a simple hyperbola," "how to find the intersection of a given conic section and a circle, following a rule common to all conic sections necessary for carrying out the calculations of the method of universality."]

2a. GENERAL GEOMETRY AND THE METHOD OF UNIVERSALITY
[1674]

Since theorems serve only to abbreviate or guide the solution of problems and since all theory should assist practise, all we need to do in order to judge the variety of kinds of geometry is to consider its problems. The problems of geometry are about straight lines or curves, and presuppose only the magnitude of some lines or figures, straight or curved. To the latter sort belong the problems of finding centers of gravity, and consequently, a good many problems of mechanics. Thus we may say that there are two kinds of geometry, an Apollonian and an Archimedean; the first was revived by Viète and Descartes, the second by Galileo and Cavalieri.

Problems of straight lines reduce to the solution of some equation whose roots must be extracted analytically by means of calculation, or geometrically by means of the intersection of loci, either exactly or approximately. Problems of curved figures in general are not yet subjected to a known method of analysis,* and if we wanted to reduce them to an equation, we should find it to be of infinite degree.

. . . I do not repeat here what I have recently said in a separate paper on the *Method of Universals,* which shortens calculation by including several cases under a single one, and which leads us to discover harmonies in the figures and gives us a means of ordering them in classes through general ideas.

---

* This was written a year before Leibniz discovered the infinitesimal calculus independently of Newton's prior but yet unpublished method of fluxions.

3. DIALOGUE ON THE CONNECTION BETWEEN THINGS AND WORDS
[1677]

A. If you were asked to bend a string so that it would enclose the largest possible area for its length, how would you bend it?

B. Into a circle; for, as geometry shows, of all figures with equal perimeters, the circle encloses the maximum area. Given two islands which can be circumnavigated in the same time, one having the shape of a circle and the other that of a square, the circular one would contain more land.

A. Do you believe this remains true even when you are not thinking about it?

B. Why, yes—even when geometers have not yet proven it, or people have not yet taken notice of it.

A. So in your opinion *truth* and *falsity* both reside in things, and not in thoughts?

B. Yes, of course.

A. But can we ever call any *thing* false?

B. No, I suppose only thoughts or statements about a thing are called false.

A. Then falsity is in thoughts, not things.

B. I must grant you that.

A. And, accordingly, truth as well?

B. So it seems; but I am still not thoroughly convinced about that, and still in some doubt about your conclusion.

A. When you are confronted with a problem and your opinion is not yet exactly settled as certain, are you not said to be in doubt whether you have the truth or falsity of the matter?

B. Certainly.

A. Then you recognize that it means the same to come to a decision about a question as to say we have a true or false answer to it?

B. I see now, and I concede that truth and falsity both pertain to thoughts and not to things.

A. But this contradicts your previous opinion that a proposition remains true even when you are not thinking about it.

B. Now you have me completely befuddled!

A. Well, then, we must look for a common ground in the two propositions. Would it be this: thoughts which might possibly be true are realized somewhere in fact, or to express myself more clearly, do you believe that every possible thought is actually thought?

B. No.

A. Then you see that truth really belongs to the class of thoughts which are possible, and that there is certainty only when somebody takes one or the other of the contradictory forms of his thought to be true or false.

B. It seems you have now found the correct answer to our difficulty.

A. However, since it is necessary to assume that a thought is to be called true or false, where, I ask, are we to find this true thought?

B. Well, I suppose by thinking about the nature of things.

A. How would it be, if it should come out of your own nature?

B. But surely not from it alone. For outside of my own nature there must be also the nature of the things I am thinking about, so that by pursuing the right method I may discover whether the proposition I finally arrive at is valid and true.

A. Quite right; yet there remain many difficulties.

B. Which do you have in mind?

A. Many scholars are of the opinion that truth originates in the human will and belongs to names or characters.

B. A very paradoxical position.

A. Nevertheless they prove it in the following way: The basis of every proof is definition.

B. Of course, we can prove many theorems simply by connecting definitions.

A. Does the truth of such theorems then depend on the definitions?

B. Certainly.

A. But definitions depend on our will?

B. How is that?

A. Is it not true that it is only the arbitrary will of the mathematician which makes him use the word "ellipse" to designate a defined figure? And again, is it not the arbitrary will of the Latin scholar which leads him to choose certain words to define "circulus"?

B. Well, what about it? Can thoughts not exist without words?

A. But not without some sign or other Ask yourself whether you can perform any arithmetical calculation without making use of any number-signs.

B. You have me quite confused, for I do hold characters or signs as indispensable in reckoning.

A. The truths of arithmetic are then expressed by some kind of signs or characters?

B. I cannot deny that.

A. Then they depend on man's will?

B. You are resolved to trick me with a curious sort of word juggling!

A. Not I but some very acute thinkers started this.

B. How can anyone be so irrational as to hold truth to be arbitrary and make it depend on names, when surely the same geometrical truth is expressible in Greek, Latin, and German?

A. That is correct, and for that reason we must meet the difficulty.

B. This one only makes me realize that in my thinking I never recognize, discover, or prove any truth without calling up to mind words or some other kind of signs.

A. Quite so; yes, if there were no signs, we should never think or conclude anything intelligibly.

B. However, when we look at geometrical diagrams, we frequently go ahead and bring to light many truths simply by studying the diagrams.

A. Quite so, but we must not forget that these diagrams are also to be regarded as characters. For the circle drawn on paper is not the true circle; but it is not necessary that it should be, for it suffices to substitute the drawn figure for the circle.

B. Yet it has a definite similarity to the circle, and that is not arbitrary.

A. By all means, and just for that reason diagrams are the most universal characters. But what similarity is there between the number of ten things and the mark "10"?

B. There exists among the marks, apart from whether they are properly chosen, a relation or order which corresponds to the order in things.

A. That may be, but what similarity do the first elements have to the objects they designate, for example, "O" to nothing, or the letter "a" to a line? You must admit that at least these elements need have no similarity to things. This holds, for example, for the word-stems "lux" and "fero," because their composite "lucifer" has certainly a definite relation to them, and, in fact, the relation is the one holding between the *objects* designated by *lucifer, lux, fero.*

B. In Greek, however, φώσφορος has the same relation to φῶς and φέρω.

A. Yes, yet the Greeks were also able to use another word here.

B. Quite right; I only mean that characters must show, when they are used in demonstrations, some kind of connection, grouping and order which are also found in the objects, and that this is required, if not in the single words—though it were better so—then at least in their union and connection. This order and correspondence at least must be present in all languages, though in different ways. And that leaves me with hope for a solution of the difficulty. For even though characters are as such arbitrary, there is still in their application and connection something valid which is not arbitrary; namely, a relationship which exists between them and things, and consequertly, definite relations among all the different characters ːsed to express the same things. And this relationship, this connection is the foundation of truth. For this explains why no matter which characters we use, the result remains the same, or at least, the results which we find are equivalent and correspond to one another in definite ways. Some kind of characters is surely always required in thinking.

A. Excellent! You have gotten yourself out of the difficulty marvelously. Your view is corroborated by analytical and arithmetical calculation; for, in the case of numbers, we arrive at the same results whether we use the decimal system or duodecimal system. If we apply the results of different kinds of systems of counting to grain or to any other countable materials, the result always remains the same. This is also true of algebraic analysis, although it is easier here to use a variety of characters than to modify things themselves in their relations to one another. Here also, the firm foundation of truth consists precisely in the connection and order of characters. If we designate the square of a by a^2 and set a equal to $b + c$, then we have a^2 equal to $b^2 + 2bc + c^2$; and if we set a equal to $d-e$, we have a^2 equal to $d^2 - 2de + e^2$. The first form states the relation of the whole (a) to its parts (b, c); the second states the relation of a part (a) to the whole (d) and to the difference between it and the whole (e). That both come to the same thing we find by substitution; if we substitute for d in the formula $d^2 + e^2 - 2de$ (which already equals a^2), its value $a + e$, we then obtain for d^2: $a^2 + e^2 + 2ae$, and for $-2de$: $-2ae - 2e^2$; then by addition:

$$d^2 = a^2 + e^2 + 2ae$$
$$e^2 = e^2$$
$$-2de = -2e^2 - 2ae$$

The sum $= a^2$

You see that no matter how arbitrarily we choose characters, the results always agree provided we follow a definite order and rule in using the characters. Although truths necessarily presuppose some characters and even sometimes have characters as objects—as when we demonstrate the rule for casting out nines—truth is not based on what is arbitrary in characters but on what is permanent in them: namely, the relationship which marks among themselves have to things. For it remains true, without our will having the slightest influence on the relations, that through the use of defined characters a definite form of calculation results which through the use of other marks in known relations to the defined ones, varies and yet preserves a constant relationship to them; the constant relationship results from the relation of the characters to the given ones, and emerges from the substitutions or comparisons made.

4. PREFACE TO THE GENERAL SCIENCE
[1677]

Since happiness consists in peace of mind, and since durable peace of mind depends on the confidence we have in the future, and since that confidence is based on the science we should have of the nature of God and the soul, it follows that science is necessary for true happiness.

But science depends on demonstration, and the discovery of demonstrations *by a certain Method* is not known to everybody. For while every man is able to judge a demonstration (it would not deserve this name if all those who consider it attentively were not convinced and persuaded by it), nevertheless not every man is able to discover demonstrations on his own initiative, nor to present them distinctly once they are discovered, if he lacks leisure or method.

The *true Method* taken in all of its scope is to my mind a thing hitherto quite unknown, and has not been practised except in mathematics. It is even very imperfect in regard to mathematics itself, as I have had the good fortune to reveal by means of surprising proofs to some of those considered to be among the best mathematicians of the century. And I expect to offer some samples of it, which perhaps will not be considered unworthy of posterity.

However, if the Method of Mathematicians has not sufficed to discover everything that might be expected from them, it has remained at least able to save them from mistakes, and if they have not said everything they were supposed to say, they have also not said anything they were not expected to say.

If those who have cultivated the other sciences had

imitated the mathematicians at least on this point, we should be quite content, and we should have long since had a secure Metaphysics, as well as an ethics depending on Metaphysics since the latter includes the sort of knowledge of God and the soul which should rule our life.

In addition, we should have the science of motion which is the key to physics, and consequently, to medicine. True, I believe we are ready now to aspire to it, and some of my first thoughts have been received with such applause by the most learned men of our time on account of the wonderful simplicity introduced, that I believe that all we have to do now is perform certain experiments on a deliberate plan and scale (rather than by the haphazard fumbling which is so common) in order to build thereupon the stronghold of a sure and demonstrative physics.

Now the reason why the art of demonstrating has been until now found only in mathematics has not been well fathomed by the average person, for if the cause of the trouble had been known, the remedy would have long since been found out. The reason is this: Mathematics carries its own test with it. For when I am presented with a false theorem, I do not need to examine or even to know the demonstration, since I shall discover its falsity *a posteriori* by means of an easy experiment, that is, by a calculation, costing no more than paper and ink, which will show the error no matter how small it is. If it were as easy in other matters to verify reasonings by experiments, there would not be such differing opinions. But the trouble is that experiments in physics are difficult and cost a great deal; and in metaphysics they are impossible, unless God out of love for us perform a miracle in order to acquaint us with remote immaterial things.

This difficulty is not insurmountable though at first

it may seem so. But those who will take the trouble to consider what I am going to say about it will soon change their mind. We must then notice that the tests or experiments made in mathematics to guard against mistakes in reasoning (as, for example, the test of casting out nines, the calculation of Ludolph of Cologne concerning the magnitude of circles, tables of sines, etc.), these tests are not made on a thing itself, but on the characters which we have substituted in place of the thing. Take for example a numerical calculation: if 1677 times 365 are 612,105, we should hardly ever have reached this result were it necessary to make 365 piles of 1677 pebbles each and then to count them all finally in order to know whether the aforementioned number is found. That is why we are satisfied to do it with characters on paper, by means of the test of nines, etc. Similarly, when we propose an approximately exact value of π in the quadrature of a circle, we do not need to make a big material circle and tie a string around it in order to see whether the ratio of the length of this string or the circumference to the diameter has the value proposed; that would be troublesome, for if the error is one-thousandth or less part of the diameter, we should need a large circle constructed with a great deal of accuracy. Yet we still refute the false value of π by the experiment and use of the calculus or numerical test. But this test is performed only on paper, and consequently, on the characters which represent the thing, and not on the thing itself.

This consideration is fundamental in this matter, and although many persons of great ability, especially in our century, may have claimed to offer us demonstrations in questions of physics, metaphysics, ethics, and even in politics, jurisprudence, and medicine, nevertheless they have either been mistaken (because every step is on slippery ground and it is difficult not to fall unless guided by some tangible directions), or even when they succeed, they have been unable to convince everyone with their reasoning (because there has not yet been a way to examine arguments by means of some easy tests available to everyone).

Whence it is manifest that if we could find characters or signs appropriate for expressing all our thoughts as definitely and as exactly as arithmetic expresses numbers or geometric analysis expresses lines, we could in all subjects *in so far as they are amenable to reasoning* accomplish what is done in Arithmetic and Geometry.

For all inquiries which depend on reasoning would be performed by the transposition of characters and by a kind of calculus, which would immediately facilitate the discovery of beautiful results. For we should not have to break our heads as much as is necessary today, and yet we should be sure of accomplishing everything the given facts allow.

Moreover, we should be able to convince the world what we should have found or concluded, since it would be easy to verify the calculation either by doing it over or by trying tests similar to that of casting out nines in arithmetic. And if someone would doubt my results, I should say to him: "Let us calculate, Sir," and thus by taking to pen and ink, we should soon settle the question.

I still add: *in so far as the reasoning allows on the given facts*. For although certain experiments are always necessary to serve as a basis for reasoning, nevertheless, once these experiments are given, we should derive from them everything which anyone at all could possibly derive; and we should even discover what experiments remain to be done for the clarification of all further doubts. That would be an admirable help, even in political science and medicine, to steady and perfect reasoning concerning given symptoms and circumstances. For even while there will not be enough given circumstances to form an infallible judgment, we shall always be able to determine what is most probable on the data given. And that is all that reason can do.

Now the characters which express all our thoughts will constitute a new language which can be written and spoken; this language will be very difficult to construct, but very easy to learn. It will be quickly accepted by everybody on account of its great utility and its surprising facility, and it will serve wonderfully in communication among various peoples, which will help get it accepted. Those who will write in this language will not make mistakes provided they avoid the errors of calculation, barbarisms, solecisms, and other errors of grammar and construction. In addition, this language will possess the wonderful property of silencing ignorant people. For people will be unable to speak or write about anything except what they understand, or if they try to do so, one of two things will happen: either the vanity of what they advance will be apparent to everybody, or they will learn by writing or speaking. As indeed those who calculate learn by writing and those who speak sometimes meet with a success they did not imagine, the tongue running ahead of the mind. This will happen especially with our language on account of its exactness. So much so, that there will be no equivocations or amphibolies, and everything which will be said intelligibly in that language will be said with propriety. This language will be the greatest instrument of reason.

I dare say that this is the highest effort of the human mind, and when the project will be accomplished it will simply be up to men to be happy since they will have an instrument which will exalt reason no less than what the Telescope does to perfect our vision.

It is one of my ambitions to accomplish this project

if God gives me enough time. I owe it to nobody but myself, and I had the first thought about it when I was 18 years old, as I have a little later evidenced in a published treatise (*De Arte Combinatoria,* 1666). And as I am confident that there is no discovery which approaches this one, I believe there is nothing so capable of immortalizing the name of the inventor. But I have much stronger reasons for thinking so, since the religion I follow closely assures me that the love of God consists in an ardent desire to procure the general welfare, and reason teaches me that there is nothing which contributes more to the general welfare of mankind than the perfection of reason.

5. TOWARDS A UNIVERSAL CHARACTERISTIC
[1677]

An ancient saying has it that God created everything according to weight, measure, and number. However, there are many things which cannot be weighed, namely, whatever is not affected by force or power; and anything which is not divisible into parts escapes measurement. On the other hand, there is nothing which is not subsumable under number. Number is therefore, so to speak, a fundamental metaphysical form, and arithmetic a sort of statics of the universe, in which the powers of things are revealed.

That the profoundest secrets are hidden in numbers has been a conviction of men ever since the time of Pythagoras himself who, according to a reliable source, transmitted this and many another intuition to Greece from the Orient. However, since the right key to the secret was not possessed, man's curiosity was led to nilities and superstitions of all sorts from which arose a kind of vulgar Cabal, far removed from the true one, and also—under the false name of magic—an abundance of phantasies with which books teem. Meanwhile there are still men who persist in the old belief that wonderful discoveries are imminent with the help of numbers, characters or signs of a new language, which the "adamite" Jacob Böhme calls a nature-language.

Nevertheless, no one perhaps has penetrated to the true principle, namely, that we can assign to every object its determined characteristic number. For the most learned men, whenever I divulged something of the sort to them, led me to believe that they understood nothing of what I meant by it. Indeed, for a long time excellent men have brought to light a kind of "universal language" or "characteristic" in which diverse concepts and things were to be brought together in an appropriate order; with its help, it was to become possible for people of different nations to communicate their thoughts to one another and to translate into their own language the written signs of a foreign language. However, nobody, so far, has gotten hold of a language which would embrace both the technique of discovering new propositions and their critical examination—a language whose signs or characters would play the same rôle as the signs of arithmetic for numbers and those of algebra for quantities in general. And yet it is as if God, when he bestowed these two sciences on mankind, wanted us to realize that our understanding conceals a far deeper secret, foreshadowed by these two sciences.

Now through some sort of destiny, I had as a boy already been led into these reflections, and they have since, as is often the case with first inclinations, remained most deeply impressed on my mind. This was wonderfully advantageous to me in two ways—though often both dubious and injurious to many—: first, I was thoroughly self-taught; as soon as I entered into the study of any science, I immediately sought out something new, frequently before I even completely understood its known, familiar contents. Thus I gained in two ways: I did not fill my head with empty assertions (resting on learned authority rather than on actual evidence) which are forgotten sooner or later; furthermore, I did not rest until I had penetrated to the root and fiber of each and every theory and reached the principles themselves from which I might with my own power find out everything I could that was relevant.

I had early in my youth shown a preference for historical books and rhetorical exercises, and shown such facility in prose and poetry that my teachers feared I might remain suspended in these delights. Consequently, I was led to logic and philosophy. Scarcely before I had understood anything at all of these subjects, I set down on paper an abundance of fanciful thoughts which had risen to the surface of my brain, and when I presented them to my teachers they were amazed. One of the things I explored was the problem of the categories. What I intended especially to show was that just as we have categories predicating classes of simple concepts, so there must be a new sort of category which embraces propositions themselves or complex terms in their natural order. I had no inkling at the time of methods of proof, and did not know that what I was advancing was already being done by geometers when they arrange their propositions in a consecutive order so that in a proof one proposition proceeds from others in an orderly way. Thus my reflection was absolutely superfluous, but since my teachers did not give up encouraging me, I took on the task all by myself to establish the aforementioned categories of complex terms or theorems. As a result of my assiduous concern with this problem I arrived by a kind of internal necessity at a reflection of astounding import: there must be invented, I reflected, a kind of alphabet of human thoughts, and through the connection of its letters and the analysis of words which are composed out of them, everything else can be discovered and judged. This inspiration gave me then a very rare joy which was, of course, quite premature, for I did not yet then grasp the true significance of the matter. Later, however, the conclusion forced itself on me, with every step in the growth of my knowledge, that an object of such significance had to be pursued further. Chance had it then that as a young man of twenty I had to compose an academic dissertation. So I wrote the dissertation on "ars combinatoria" (art of combination) which in 1666 was published in book form, and thus my astounding discovery was made public. Of course, people observe that this treatise is the work of a youngster who has just gotten out of school and has not yet become familiar with the sciences; for I lived in a place where mathematics was not cultivated, and had I like Pascal lived my early life in Paris, I should have succeeded earlier in advancing the sciences. Still I do not regret having written this dissertation, for two reasons: first, because it met with the approbation of many men of the highest intellect; secondly, because it already gave me an intimation of my discovery so that the suspicion that it was discovered only recently cannot be supported.

I have often wondered why nobody until now, so far as any written evidence indicates, had ever put his hands on such an important subject. For if one had only followed step by step a strict method of procedure from the start there should have immediately been forced on one's mind considerations of this sort—which I still as a boy missed in the study of Logic, without any acquaintance with mathematics, natural and moral sciences—

considerations which came home to me simply because I always sought first, original principles. The main reason, however, why people fail to go so far lies in the fact that abstract principles are usually dry and not very exciting, and after a momentary brush with them people let them alone. But there were three men, especially, who left me wondering why they had not entered into a problem of this significance: Aristotle, Joachim Jungius, and René Descartes. For Aristotle in the Organon and Metaphysics investigated with the greatest acuteness of mind the innermost nature of concepts. Joachim Jungius of Lübeck, however—who, of course, was himself scarcely known in Germany—is a man of such penetrating judgment and of so comprehensive a mind that one should have expected from him as from no other person—not excepting even Descartes—a fundamental renovation of the sciences, had he only been known and supported. He was already an old man when Descartes' work took effect, and it is regrettable that they both did not get to know each other. This is not the place to indicate what is to be extolled in Descartes whose mind stands far above any praise. He surely set foot on the true and right path in the country of ideas, the path which might have led to our goal—but for the fact that later, as it appears, in the course of his essay [*Discourse on Method*] he dropped the burden of the problem of method, and contented himself with metaphysical meditations and applications of his analytic geometry with which he attracted so much attention. In addition, he decided to investigate the nature of bodies for the purposes of medicine, which he was surely right in doing, had he only first solved the other problem, namely, the ordering of judgments and ideas. For from the latter there might have emerged a greater intellectual illumination than one was to believe possible, which would have shed light on experimental subjects also. That he did not direct his efforts to this end can be explained only by the fact that he did not grasp the deeper significance of the problem. Had he seen a method for establishing a rational philosophy with the same incomparable clarity as that of arithmetic, he would have chosen no other path than this one in order to establish a school which he so ambitiously strove to do. For a school which followed such a method in philosophy would naturally attract from among its tyros the same leadership in the kingdom of reason as geometry has, and would not totter or collapse if as a result of invasion, in a new barbaric era, the sciences themselves went under with mankind.

I, on the contrary, no matter how busy or diverted I might be, have steadfastly persisted in this line of reflection; I was alone in this matter, because I had intuited its whole significance and had perceived a marvelous and easy way to reach the goal. It took strenuous reflection on my part, but I finally discovered the way. In order to establish the Characteristic which I was after—at least in what pertains to the grammar of this wonderful universal language and to a dictionary which would be adequate for the most numerous and most recurrent cases—in order to establish, in other words, the characteristic numbers for all ideas, nothing less is required than the founding of a mathematical-philosophical course of study according to a new method, which I can offer, and which involves no greater difficulties than any other procedure not too far removed from familiar concepts and the usual method of writing. Also it would not require more work than is now already expended on lectures or encyclopedias. I believe that a few selected persons might be able to do the whole thing in five years, and that they will in any case after only two years arrive at a mastery of the doctrines most needed in practical life, namely, the propositions of morals and metaphysics, according to an infallible method of calculation.

Once the characteristic numbers are established for most concepts, mankind will then possess a new instrument which will enhance the capabilities of the mind to a far greater extent than optical instuments strengthen the eyes, and will supersede the microscope and telescope to the same extent that reason is superior to eyesight. Great as is the benefit which the magnetic needle has brought to sailors, far greater will be the benefits which this constellation will bring to all those who ply the seas of investigation and experiment. What further will come out of it, lies within the lap of destiny, but it can only be results of significance and excellence. For all other gifts may corrupt man, but genuine reason alone is unconditionally wholesome for him. Its authority, however, will not be open any longer to doubt when it becomes possible to reveal the reason in all things with the clarity and certainty which was hitherto possible only in arithmetic. It will put an end to that sort of tedious objecting with which people plague each other, and which takes away for many the pleasure of reasoning and arguing in general. For instead of testing an argument, an adversary usually makes the following objection: "How do you know that your reason is better than mine? What criterion of truth do you have?" If the first party then again refers to his reasons, his interlocutor lacks the patience to test them; since for the most part there must still be a great many other questions to settle, which would take a week's labor if he observed the traditionally valid procedures and rules of reasoning. Instead, after long pro and con discussions, most of the time it is emotion rather than reason that claims the victory, and the struggle ends there with the Gordian knot cut rather than untied. This is especially pertinent to the deliberations of practical life in which some decision must be finally made. Here it is only rarely the case that advantages and disadvantages which are so often distributed in many different ways on both sides, are weighed as on a balance. The stronger the representation or rather misrepresentation one party makes of this or that point according to his variable disposition, persuading others against his adversary by rhetorical effects of sharp relief and contrasting colors, the more dogmatically does he make up his own mind or indoctrinate others especially when he skillfully appeals to their prejudices. On the other hand, there is hardly anyone who is ever able to weigh and figure out the whole table of pros and cons on both sides, i.e., not only to count the advantages and disadvantages, but also to weigh them accurately against one another. Hence, I regard the two disputants as though they were two merchants who owe each other various moneys and have never drawn up a financial statement of their balance, but instead, always cross out the various postings of their outstanding debts and insist on inserting their own claims with respect to the legitimacy and magnitude of their debts. In this way, of course, conflicts could never end. We need not be surprised then that most disputes arise from the lack of clarity in things, that is, from the failure to reduce them to numbers.

Our Characteristic, however, will reduce all questions to numbers, and thus present a sort of statics by virtue of which rational evidence may be weighed. Besides, since probabilities lie at the basis of estimation and proof, we can consequently always estimate which event under given circumstances can be expected with the highest probability. Whoever is firmly convinced of the truth of religion and its implications and at the same time in his love of mankind longs for its conversion, will surely have to understand, as soon as he grasps our method, that (besides the miracles and acts of the saints or the conquests of a great ruler) there can be no more effective means conceived for the spread of the faith than the discovery under discusion here. For once missionaries are able to introduce this universal language, then also will the true religion, which stands in intimate harmony with reason, be established, and there will be as little reason to fear any apostasy in the future as to fear a renunciation of arithmetic and geometry once they have been learnt. I repeat, therefore, what I have frequently said, that nobody, whether a prophet or prince, can set himself a task of greater significance for human welfare as well as for the glory of God. We should nevertheless not remain content with words. Since, however, the wonderful interrelatedness of all things makes it extremely difficult to formulate explicitly the characteristic numbers of individual things, I have invented an elegant artifice by virtue of which certain relations may be represented and fixed numerically and which may thus then be further determined in numerical calculation. I make the arbitrary assumption, namely, that some special characteristic numbers are already given, and that some peculiar general property is observable in them. Thus, in the meantime, I take numbers which are correlated with the peculiar property, and then am able with their help immediately to demonstrate with astonishing facility all the rules of logic numerically, and can offer a criterion to ascertain whether a given argument is formally conclusive. Whether, however, a demonstration is materially conclusive may for the first time be judged without any trouble and without the danger of error, once we are put in possession of the true characteristic numbers of things themselves.

5a. PRINCIPLES OF A LOGICAL CALCULUS*
[c. 1679]

Axiom 1. A contains B and B contains C, therefore A contains C.

Demonstr. A = AB, B = BC, therefore A = AC, for substituting for B in the first premise its value BC taken from the second, we get A = ABC; and for AB here substitute its value A from the first premise and so obtain the result A = AC, or A contains C.

The primary Moods of the First Figure which follow immediately from the axiom:

Barbara: B is C,   A is B, therefore A is C
Celarent: B is not C,   A is B, therefore A is not C
Darii: B is C,   QA is B, therefore QA is C
Ferio: B is not C, QA is B, therefore QA is not C.

[QA stands for "Some A".]

Axiom 2. QB contains B or QB is B.

Demonstr. For QB = QBB, that is, QB contains B.

---

* Leibniz is here trying to reduce traditional forms of syllogistic and immediate inferences to something like an algebraic calculus. He has already shown that 'All A is B' (A is B) can be represented by an equation A = AB; similarly, 'No A is B' (A is not B) is represented by the equation A = Anon-B. The particular forms of proposition 'Some A is B' and 'Some A is not B' are represented as 'QA is B' and 'QA is not B,' and their expressions, which are inequations, are derived by negating the equations of their contradictories 'No A is B' and 'All A is B' respectively. Leibniz interprets classes intensionally as well as extensionally so that if man contains rationality, man is included in the class of rational beings; but the equation of men with men who are rational falls back on the extensional meaning. For Leibniz's place in the history of symbolic logic, cf. C. I. Lewis, *Survey of Symbolic Logic* (Berkeley, 1923), pp. 5–18 and Appendix which contains a translation of "Two Fragments from Leibniz" on a logical calculus.

Subalternation. B is C, QB is B (by Ax. 2). QB is C (Darii). B is not C, QB is B. QB is not C (*Ferio*).

The Secondary Moods of the First Figure

Barbari. B is C, A is B; QA is C.

Demonstr. For (from *Barbara*) B is C, A is B, therefore A is C. But since A is C, then QA is C by subalternation.

Celaro. B is not C, A is B; QA is not C.

Demonstrated in the same way from *Çelarent* by subalternation.

[Contraposition]: (If L is true, M is false; therefore, if M is not false but true, L will not be true but false. If L is false, M is true; therefore, if M is false, L is true.)

Axiom 3. Double negation of a term restores it: Not non-A is A. (Or this may be used as a definition of the sign for negation.)

Axiom 4. The non true is the false. (This likewise is a definition of the false.)

Corollary. The not false is the true. For the not false is the not non-true by Ax. 4. But the not non-true is the true by Ax. 3.

Axiom 5. If a conclusion is the consequence of premises and the conclusion is false, some one of the premises will be false.

Axiom 6. If B is C is true, then QB is not C is false.

(Demonstr. B = BC. Therefore QB = QBnon-C. For if QB = Bnon-C and BC is substituted for B, then QB would equal QBCnon-C, which is absurd.)

Corollary. If QB is not C is true, then B is C is false. For by Ax. 6, if B is C is *true,* then QB *is not C is* false. Therefore by Ax. 5, if it be false that QB is not C is false, the single premise in this case, B is C is true, must be

false. That is, by Ax. 4 and coroll., if it is true that
QB is not C, B is C is false.

Axiom 7. If B is C is false, QB is not C is true.

5b. A FRAGMENT ON LOGICAL SYNTAX*

All characteristic consists in the formation of an expression and in the transition from expression to expression. An expression is simple or well formed, and is
formed either through apposition, or through coalition.
A rule is made by apposition. A new character is made by
coalition. But in a calculus there is no need for coalition,
but a simple apposition or formula is sufficient, for the
sake of a short cut, by the adoption of arbitrary characters
whose expression is thus new. However, coalition is necessary for perfecting a development of the characteristics,
though the ingredients are indicated. In apposition there
again appears the order in which the calculation is to be
performed in such and such a manner, and it includes the
signs by means of which the apposition is modified.

The transition from expression to expression indicates
that in one given expression another can be placed.
Hence, a development or differentiation results from the
transition according to formulae for the transition
from proposition to proposition or to the consequence.
The simplest form of transition is substitution, and from
mutually substitutable formulas we obtain equipollence
or equivalence. A common transition is, that having
posited A and B one is permitted to say A B, except that
it is plain that since this is not general it does not belong
to the rules of calculus; it belongs to the general axioms.
Some such general propositions are convertible, and some

* Translated from an undated Latin fragment in Couturat,
Opuscules et fragments inédits de Leibniz (Paris, 1903), p. 326.

are not; moreover, the conversion of the relation that A^{be} O — B^{eb} is, therefore, B^{eb} O — A^{be}. Or if A is in some sense next to B, then B by having been limited in a certain manner is, by a relation converse to the previous one, next to A.

6. PRECEPTS FOR ADVANCING THE SCIENCES AND ARTS *
[1680]

. . . When I consider how many beautiful discoveries, how many solid and important meditations we have and how many excellent minds there are who lack no ardor for the investigation of truth, I believe we are ready to go far ahead and that in a short time wonderful changes could be accomplished in the affairs of mankind with respect to the sciences. But when I see on the other side the little concert in plans, the opposing routes people take, the animosity shown by some against others, destroying rather than promoting companionship, finally when I consider that practise does not profit from the light of theory, that we do not strive to lessen the number of disputes but to augment them, that we are content with specious argumentation instead of a serious and conclusive method, I fear we shall remain for a long time in our present confusion and indigence through our own fault. I even fear that after uselessly exhausting curiosity without obtaining from our investigations any considerable gain for our happiness, people may be disgusted with the sciences, and that a fatal despair may cause them to fall back into barbarism. To which result that horrible mass of books which keeps on growing might contribute very much. For in the end the disorder

* Title given by Erdmann to Leibniz's untitled manuscript.

will become nearly insurmountable; the indefinite multitude of authors will shortly expose them all to the danger of general oblivion; the hope of glory animating many people at work in studies will suddenly cease; it will be perhaps as disgraceful to be an author as it was formerly honorable. At best, one may amuse himself with little books of the hour which will run their course in a few years and will serve to divert a reader from boredom for a few moments, but which will have been written without any design to promote our knowledge or to deserve the appreciation of posterity. I shall be told that since so many people write it is impossible for all their works to be preserved. I admit that, and I do not entirely disapprove those little books in fashion which are like the flowers of a springtime or like the fruits of an autumn, scarcely surviving a year. If they are well made, they have the effect of a useful conversation, not simply pleasing and keeping the idle out of mischief but helping to shape the mind and language. Often their aim is to induce something good in men of our time, which is also the end I seek by publishing this little work. However, it seems to me better for the public to build a house, to plow a field or at least to plant some fruit or ordinary tree than to gather a few flowers or fruits. These diversions are to be praised rather than forbidden, but we must not neglect more important things. We are responsible for our talent to God and to the commonwealth; there are so many persons of ability from whom a good deal might be expected if they would combine the serious with the pleasant. It is not a question of composing great works; if each one contributed only one great discovery we should gain a good deal in a short time. A single observation or demonstration of consequence is enough to make one immortal and deserving of posterity; we have ancient geometers from whom we have no works, like Nicomedes and Dinostratus, whose reputation has been preserved because of a few propositions reported to be by them. The same can be said of a few nice machines like that of Ctesibus, and even still more of a solid demonstration in metaphysics and ethics; even the discoveries made in history are not to be neglected. And concerning experience, if each practising physician would leave us a few new very solid aphorisms, drawn from his observations as the fruits of his practise, if chemists and botanists, druggists and many others who handle natural bodies did the same either by themselves or through the care of those who knew how to question them, how many victories would we not score against nature? It is thus evident that if men do not make considerable progress it is most often for lack of will and good intelligence among them.

Now, though for many reasons I fear a return to barbarism, I do not give up expecting the contrary, for other very good reasons. Short of a sudden and general invasion of all Europe by barbarians, which is, thank God, not greatly apparent, the admirable facility of the printing-press to multiply books will serve to preserve the greater part of our knowledge. All we need to cause studies to fall into neglect would be to have all those in charge and·in authority fall into the hands of the military, a military quite different from that of our times. They would have to be barbarians, enemies of all science, resembling that Emperor of China who had taken on the task of destroying men of letters as disturbers of the public peace. But this change is hardly probable, and even our religion would have to be eclipsed in Europe before it can happen. Or else it would require something similar to that earthquake and flood which suddenly buried the great island Atlantis (about which Plato speaks on the word of the Egyptians), in order to interrupt the development of the sciences among mankind. That being the case, it appears that with books continuing to increase in number, we shall be wearied by their confusion and that some day a great, free and curious prince, a glorious amateur, or perhaps himself a learned man, understanding the importance of the matter, will cause to undertake under the best auspices what Alexander the Great commanded Aristotle to do with the natural sciences, what the Emperors of Constantinople, Justinian, Basil of Macedonia, Leon the Philosopher, and Constantine the Porphyrogenian, tried to have done (but badly, so far as we can judge from the works or from the fragmentary excerpts which remain, and from the curses of our contemporary critics hurled against the excerpters), and finally what Almansor or Mirandolin, the great Arabian prince, ordered done in his country; namely, that the quintessence of the best books be extracted and joined to the best observations, not yet written, of the most expert in each profession, in order to build systems of solid knowledge for promoting man's happiness. Based on experiments and demonstrations and adapted for use by repertories such a work would be a most durable and great monument of his glory and constitute an incomparable debt which all mankind would owe him. Perhaps, also, this great prince I am envisaging will offer prizes to those who make discoveries or disinter important knowledge hidden in the confusion of men or authors.

But why do I need any fiction? Why refer to some remote posterity what would be incomparably easier in our own day, since the confusion has not yet risen to the point it will reach then? Could any century be more suited than ours which will be recorded some day as the century of discoveries and wonders? And the greatest wonder that will be recorded is, perhaps, that great

prince * who is the glory of our time, and whom succeeding generations will envy in vain. I do not touch here
on those meritorious acts of his as a statesman or warrior
which do not fall within the province of this essay; what
he has done for the sciences would alone suffice to make
him immortal. We do not need to picture him further.
He is too unique and universally recognizable. Why then
grope in the uncertain idea of future things for what is
actually among us and even surpasses the conception of
the average mind? Perhaps, among so many persons of
ability in his flourishing realm and especially at his court
at which are assembled so many extraordinary persons,
someone has long since drawn up at his command a general plan for the advancement of the sciences, worthy
of the sciences and of the King, and far surpassing the
project that I can conceive. But even if I should be
fortunate to write it up first, I am quite sure I cannot
anticipate or attain the general views of that Monarch,
views which are admired everywheres and extend undoubtedly to the sciences. All that we ought to hope for
is that nothing troublesome may deter progress, that
heaven continue to favor him, and that without being
embarrassed from outside, he may make Europe enjoy
that felicitous peace with which he has crowned his
wonderful exploits. In that peace which is full of glory,
his generous magnificence will carry the sciences as far
as is possible through the energies of the men of today,
the sciences, I say, which are the principal ornament,
the greatest instrument of war, and the greatest treasure
of mankind.

But putting aside what relates to the combination of
our energies, for that depends on a higher authority, let
us say something about what depends on each one of us
and what should be done if we plan to advance knowl-

* Louis XIV.

edge and to cultivate the mind in order to train it to judge solidly the thoughts of others and to discover promptly the truth about one's self as much as is needed for one's happiness and for use in living. The first thing I would recommend would be the famous precept of Epicharmus:

"nervos atque artus esse sapientiae non temere credere," not to believe rashly what the common run of men or authors advance, but to always ask one's self for proof of what is maintained. That should be done without affectation of idiosyncrasy or novelty, which I hold dangerous not only in practise but also in theory, as I shall mention later, for I have found after long investigations that usually the oldest and most accepted opinions are the best, provided they are justly interpreted. We must not then concentrate on doubting but we must make inquiries in the spirit of instructing ourselves and establishing within ourselves immutable and sound thoughts; for when our judgment is based only on slight appearances, it constantly wavers and is often upset by the first difficulties which present themselves, or else if we obstinately stick to our opinions, we expose ourselves to making serious mistakes. However, I do not think it necessary to recommend to people universal doubt, for, though this expression may be favorably interpreted, it seems to me that people may take it in the wrong sense, as experience has only too well shown. Also this precept has alarmed many persons among whom there were a few whose enthusiasm did not lack prudence. Moreover, it is neither necessary nor even useful, for, since all we are concerned to do is to recommend to people to try to ground themselves always on reasons, doubt accomplishes nothing on this score; in fact, we are constantly seeking reasons for thoughts about which there is no doubt at all. This is evident not only in matters of faith, when we refer to what the Theologians call the *motive of credibility,* but also in everyday matters, as when we seek in our minds for proofs fit to persuade others what we ourselves believe, these proofs are not actually before us. I am certainly convinced that the Berose of Annius and the Etruscan Antiquities of Inghiramus are assumed to be plays, but to conceive distinctly all the evidence which crowds into my mind, I should need time and reflection.

Further, we even see that Proclus and other Geometers try to give demonstrations of a few axioms which nobody doubted but which Euclid believed he could take for granted, as, for example, that two distinct straight lines cannot have more than a point in common. It was also the opinion of the late Mr. Roberval that it was necessary to demonstrate axioms themselves as far as possible, and from what I have been told, he wanted to do this actually in the *Elements of Geometry* which he had planned. And to my mind this concern with demonstrating axioms is one of the most important points of the art of discovery, for which I shall give the reason some other time, contenting myself now to make mention of them in order that it may not be imagined a useless and ridiculous task and because it is indeed a corollary of the great precept I have just given. And it is astonishing to me to see that that famous philosopher of our times Descartes, who has recommended so much the art of doubting, has so little practised it in good faith on the occasions when it would have been most useful, contenting himself with alleging the self-evidence he claims for ideas which Euclid and the other Geometers have very wisely refused to begin with; this is also the way to cover up all sorts of illusory ideas and prejudices. However, I agree that we can and should often be content with a few assumptions, at least while waiting until they can also be made into theorems

some day; otherwise we should sometimes be holding
ourselves back too much. For it is always necessary to
advance our knowledge, and even if it were only to establish many things on a few hypotheses, that would still
be very useful. Then at least we should know that there
remain only these few hypotheses to be proved in order
to arrive at a full demonstration, and in the meantime we
should at least have the hypothetical ones which will lead
us out of the confusion of disputes. That is the method of
Geometers; for example, Archimedes assumes that the
straight line is the shortest distance between two points,
and that of two lines in a plane both bent in or hollow
on the same side, the line included in the other is the
shorter, and on that basis he rigorously completes his
demonstrations. But it is very important to make explicit
all the assumptions which are needed without taking the
liberty of accepting them tacitly for granted on the
excuse that the thing is self-evident just by an inspection
of the diagram or by the contemplation of the idea. In
this respect I find that Euclid with all his exactness has
sometimes been deficient, and though Clavius has often
supplied by his diligence what was lacking in Euclid,
there are places where he has not been attentive; one
of the most noticeable and least noticed of these is met
at the start in the demonstration of the first proposition
of the first book where he tacitly assumes that the two
circles used in the construction of an equilateral triangle
must intersect somewheres, although we know that some
circles can never intersect one another. But we are not
easily mistaken in geometry by these sorts of tacit assumptions. Geometers have too many means for discovering
the smallest errors that might escape them by inatten-
tion.

It is in philosophy chiefly that we should employ that
exact rigor of reasoning because the other means of

obtaining certainty are most often lacking in it. And yet it is in philosophy that people take the greatest liberties in reasoning. People scarcely remember that admirable admonition of St. Augustine: "Do not permit yourself to think you have known truth in philosophy, unless you can explain the leap in which we deduce that one, two, three, and four together make ten." It is true, that several men of ability in our times have tried to reason geometrically outside of geometry, but we scarcely acknowledge anything along that line successful enough to use as a support and to quote as we quote Euclid. To be clear about this we need only examine the alleged demonstrations by Descartes in one of his *Replies to Objections* against his Meditations and those of Spinoza in his essay on the *Principles of Descartes* and in his posthumous work on God, a work which is so full of lacunae that I am amazed. There has appeared a metaphysical Euclid by Thomas White, and Abdias Trew, a skilful mathematician of Altdorf, has reduced Aristotle's Physics to a demonstrative form as much as that author was able, and Father Fabry has claimed he has dressed up all philosophy as geometry. But often, looking more closely, there is no resemblance between them except in the outer garb, and we are far from that certitude which is sought, either because of equivocations or because of illogically drawn consequences, or finally because of those mischievous assumptions, explicit or tacit, which we grant without making any formal demands on them. However, that very fact shows that it should not be as difficult to write geometrically as people imagine, for it is easy to avoid errors against logical form, and equivocations disappear by means of nominal definitions which are intelligible. And as it is difficult to demonstrate everything, we may assume what appears to be most clear, provided that the assumptions are not too numerous nor as difficult as the conclusions. We should also know that we do not lack demonstrations in morals and in subjects which appear to be the most uncertain, even entirely accidental. This can be judged by the demonstration of *Games of Chance* by Pascal, Huygens and others, and by that of the Pensioner Witt concerning life-insurance. We can make and have seen such demonstrations in the matters of commerce, money, and a quantity of other subjects, which preserve mathematical certitude. We may even boldly advance an odd but true paradox, that there are no authors whose manner of writing resembles the style of Geometers more than the style of the Roman jurisconsults whose fragments are found in the Pandects. After granting them certain assumptions based on some custom, or else, to be sure, on some rule established among them, we admire these jurists for their consistency and applications of logic; they reason with such simple orderliness and subtle exactness that they put our philosophers to shame in even the most philosophical matters which they are often obliged to treat. There is no excuse, therefore, in philosophy to claim it is impossible to preserve the required exactitude of reasoning.

Even if it is only a question of probabilities we can always determine what is most probable on the given premises. True this part of useful logic is not yet established anywheres, but it is put to wonderful uses in practise when there are hypotheses, indications, and conjectures involved in ascertaining degrees of probability among a number of reasons appearing on one side or another of some important deliberation. Thus when we lack sufficient data to demonstrate a certitude, the matter yielding only probability, we can always give demonstrations at least concerning the probability itself. I do not speak here of that probability of the *Casuists,* based on the number and reputation of scholastic doctors, but of that probability drawn from the nature of things in proportion to what we know of them and which we may call likelihood. It results from bargaining over the assumptions, but in order to judge their value it is necessary that the assumptions themselves receive some estimated probability and be reduced to a comparative homogeneity. That would take too long to explain here.

If the precept I have just explained that we must always seek reasons and express them distinctly with all the exactness possible, were rigorously observed, it would be enough to apply it alone in order to discover all the rest without needing further advice. But as the human mind finds it hard to bother itself for a long time with a long sustained undertaking, we shall not easily find a man capable of completing in one effort a demonstrative survey of the sciences independent of the imagination, such as I have just described, although I do not despair of anything when I consider the work, penetration and use of leisure characterizing a Suarez or similar author. But as it is rare to find all these circumstances combined with those admirable and great insights into the true method, we must believe that only gradually by diverse attempts or by the work of several persons shall we come to those demonstrative elements of all human knowledge, and that will happen sooner or later depending on the disposition of those who have the authority and hence the power to advance good plans. It would therefore not be opportune to limit all their views and expectations to that alone, and as we write not only for the public but for the advantage in each case of a particular individual, and since it is obvious that few people are prepared to make for themselves an exact chain of demonstrations of all the truths they would like to learn, we must resort provisionally to a successive application of that great method. That is done by examining each science with the effort necessary to discover its principles of discovery, which once combined with some higher science or general science (namely, the art of discovery), may suffice to deduce all the rest or at least the most useful truths without needing to burden the mind with too many precepts. It is most obviously true that even if we should have completed the whole of a demonstrative Encyclopedia, we should have to take recourse to that artifice in order to aid memory. Of course, if this Encyclopedia were made in the way I wish, we could furnish the means of finding always the consequences of fundamental truths or of given facts through a manner of calculation as exact and as simple as that of Arithmetic and Algebra. I could give a demonstration of this in advance in order to encourage men to undertake this great work; but as the most exact demonstrations do not affect people sufficiently without examples, I should prefer not to reveal this great artifice except when I could authorize it through a few completed essays, in order not to prostitute it by offering it at the wrong time and ineffectively. However, though we cannot yet arrive easily at this general calculus which is the ultimate perfection of the art of discovery, in any case the art of discovery continues to- subsist and we can give some excellent precepts from it which are very little known and which I shall touch on somewhat in this essay where it will be verified by some examples of actual discoveries having appeared as consequences.

Concerning the principles of scientific discovery, it is important to consider that each science usually consists of some few propositions which are either observations of experiment or veins of thought which have offered the occasion and means for discovery. They would suffice to recover the discovery if it were lost and to learn it without a teacher if one wished to apply himself enough, by combining those few propositions in the usual way with the precepts of a higher science, assumed to be already known, namely, either the general science or art of discovery, or another science to which the science in question is subordinate. For example, there are several sciences subordinate to Geometry in which it is enough to be a geometer and to be informed of a few leading facts or principles of discovery to which geometry may be applied, so that it is not necessary in addition to discover for one's self the principal laws of these sciences. For example, in the theory of perspective we have only to consider that an object may be outlined exactly on a given surface by marking the points of intersection of visual rays, that is to say, of straight lines going from the eye through the objective points and prolonged to meet or intersect the surface. That is why the position of the eye, the shape and location of the surface (I say shape, because it may be a plane or convex or even concave surface), and finally, the geometric properties of the object (that is, its position and shape) being given, a geometer can always determine the point of projection on the surface corresponding to the objective point projected. And when we go further with such considerations we find very convenient short-cuts in practise to determine projections immediately, that is, the projected lines and shapes which represent the objective lines and shapes without being obliged to trace each point. The doctrine of shadows is simply that of perspective in reverse and results from it if we replace the eye by the luminous source, the object by the opaque body, and the projection by the shadow.

The theory of the sun-dial is only a corollary of a combination of Astronomy and perspective, that is, the projection of a few celestial points on a wall or other flat convex or concave surface, by means of rays going through these celestial points and the style point; we may assume without fearing any sensible errors that this point is at the center of the earth or even at the center of the universe, and by that means draw the projection of the sun's path, particularly of its daily motion as indicated by its shadow. There is, however, still a consideration in the art of drafting which should not be omitted, namely, that a projection by itself does not ascertain the quality of the objective surface with respect to its being flat, convex, or concave; that has to be supplied by other circumstances, e.g., by means of shadows and shades of color of varying intensities skilfully used. All of this can also be determined geometrically.

Music is subordinate to Arithmetic and when we know a few fundamental experiments with harmonies and dissonances, all the remaining general precepts depend on numbers; I recall once drawing a harmonic line divided in such a fashion that one could determine with the compass the different compositions and properties of all musical intervals. Besides, we can show a man who does not know anything about music, the way to compose without mistakes. But as it is not enough to know Grammar and Prosody to compose a beautiful epigram, and since a schoolboy who is to be taught to avoid mistakes in his writing does not for that purpose have to compose a speech having the power of Cicero's eloquence, so in music what a man needs in order to compose successfully are practice as well as a genius and vivid imagination in things of the ear. And as the making of beautiful verses requires a prior reading of good poets, noticing turns and expressions which gradually tinge one's own style, "as they who walk in the sun take on another tint," in the same way a Musician, after noticing in the compositions of talented men a thousand and one beautiful cadences and, so to speak, phrases of Music, will be able to give flight to his own imagination furnished with these fine materials. There are even those who are naturally musicians and who compose beautiful melodies just as there are natural poets who with a little aid and reading perform wonders, for there are things, especially those dependent on the senses, in which we do better by letting ourselves go automatically by imitation and practise than by sticking to dry precepts. And as playing the clavichord requires a habit which the fingers themselves have to acquire, so imagining a beautiful melody, making a good poem, promptly sketching architectural ornaments or the plan of a creative painting require that our imagination itself acquire a habit after which it can be given the freedom to go its own way without consulting reason, in the manner of an inspired Enthusiasm. The imagination will not fail to succeed in proportion to the genius and experience of the person, and we ourselves sometimes have the experience in dreams of shaping images which we should have great difficulty in creating while awake. But reason must afterwards examine and correct and polish the work of imagination; that is where the precepts of art are needed to produce something finished and excellent. But as we are here proposing only the kind of knowledge worthy of a respectable layman, who is not a professional, we have said all these things only in order to forestall incidentally the false notions of those who might abuse what we have just said about the easy means of learning the sciences by some few precepts or principles of discovery.

As the common man is eternally befogged by a badly understood distinction between practice and theory, it is still appropriate to explain in a few words what is solid in that distinction and how it should be understood. I have already explained that there are things which depend rather on the play of imagination and on spon-

taneous impressions than on reason and that in such
things we need to form a habit, as in bodily exercises
and even in some mental exercises. That is where we need
practice in order to succeed.

There are other matters in which we can succeed
through reason alone, aided by a few experiments or
observations. We can even learn these at some other person's expense. We see excellent geniuses succeeding in
their first attempt within the profession they apply themselves to, and by virtue of their natural judgment put old
practitioners to shame. But that is not a usual occurrence, and this is how we must regard it:

In all matters where it is possible for judgment aided
by a few precepts to avoid application and experiment,
we can always reduce all of a science with its subordinate
parts to a few fundamentals or principles of discovery
sufficient to determine all the questions which can arise
in the circumstances by combining with the principles the
exact method of the true Logic or art of discovery.

But to succeed actually with this precept in practice
we must distinguish among the things encountered; we
must know whether decisions must be made immediately
or if we have the leisure time to reflect with exactness.
In the first case, the precepts combined with the method
will not suffice, at least in the present state of the art
of discovery, for I believe that if it were perfected as
it should, and as it could be, that we might penetrate with
ease a vein of thought which now takes too much time
and explanation. Therefore, in order to obtain good decisions quickly in an embarrassing situation we have to
have an extraordinary power of genius or long enough
practice to make us think automatically and habitually
what otherwise would require investigation by reason.
But when we have the leisure time to reflect, I find that
theory can forestall practice in all matters capable of

precepts and reasons even if the latter are based on the foundation of experience provided that after the foundation is laid we can give a rational account of everything done. But this holds only if we know how to reflect methodically in order not to let anything escape of the circumstances to be accounted for.

And even theory without practice will incomparably be superior to blind practice without theory, when the practitioner is obliged to face some situation quite different from those he has practised, because not knowing the reasons for what he is doing, he will be stopped short, whereas he who possesses the reasons discovers the exceptions and the remedies. Thus we see frequently that persons with good judgment who employ some workmen, and after getting to understand the matter and the reasons for their practice, know how to offer suggestions in unusual circumstances which the men in the trade do not think of because they have their mind buried in the images of their routine ways. But people are very often mistaken in calling practice what is theory, and *vice versa*. For if a workman who may not know either Latin or Euclid is a man of ability and knows the reasons for what he does, he will possess a genuine theory of his art, and will be capable of discovering expediencies in any sort of situation. And, on the other hand, a half-baked scientist puffed up by an imaginary science will project machines and constructions which cannot succeed beause he does not possess all the theory required. He will understand perhaps the common rules about moving forces, the lever, the wedge, the jack-screw, but he will not understand that part of mechanics which I call the science of resistance or rigidity which has not yet been put sufficiently into rules, and he will not understand that the rigid pieces which are to support the moving parts should have a great deal of resistance,

else what will yield is these parts rather than the big
load supposed to be moved, and the nearer these rigid
parts are to the final action, the more they need rigidity.
When we understand these things, we are not exposed
so vulnerably, and we do not need any longer the enormous masses which workmen of little ability use to assure
themselves of rigidity. We can also say that all those
who have undertaken to give us a perpetual-motion machine have failed in theory. Now, generally, all our
errors which another person more skilful than we are,
might correct in us with good reasons, are contrary to
a genuine theory. However, I remain agreed that we cannot take enough precautions in important practical enter-
prises, and as the method of reasoning has not attained
the perfection of which it is capable, and since, moreover, our emotions and distractions prevent us from taking advantage of our own inner lights, I maintain that
we must distrust reason alone, and that it is important
to have some experience or to consult those who have it.
For experience is in relation to reason what tests (like
that of casting out nines) are in relation to arithmetical
operations. But when it is a question only of knowledge,
we may be content with a few precepts as principles of
discovery in each science provided we possess the general science or art of discovery.

7. DISCOURSE TOUCHING THE METHOD OF CERTITUDE, AND THE ART OF DISCOVERY IN ORDER TO END DISPUTES AND TO MAKE PROGRESS QUICKLY

Concerning unwritten knowledge scattered among men
of different callings, I am convinced that it surpasses
in quantity and in importance anything we find in books,

and that the greater part of our wealth is not yet recorded. There are even some sorts of information privately possessed by certain persons and lost with them. There is no mechanical art so slight and scorned which may not furnish some important observations and considerations; and all callings have certain ingenious skills which it is not easy to be informed about and which may nevertheless lead to consequences of the highest importance. We may add that the important matters of manufacturing and commerce can only be regulated by an exact description of what belongs to all sorts of arts, and that the questions of militia, finance, and navigation depend a great deal on Mathematics and on Physics particularly. And the chief defect in many scholars is that they occupy themselves only with vague and well-worn arguments while there is such a fine field for exercising their minds in solid and real objects to the advantage of the public. Hunters, fishermen, merchants, sea voyagers, and even games of skill as well as of chance, furnish material with which to augment useful sciences considerably. Even in the games of children there are things to interest the greatest Mathematician. Apparently, we owe the compass-needle to the amusement of children intent on looking to see how the needle turns. It is a fact that we owe to children the air-gun which they practically invented by stuffing the hollow tube of a feather at both ends with a slice of apple into which they had stuck each end of the tube successively, forcing the stuff together towards the middle of the tube, and then expelling it by the force of the compressed air caught in the middle; this was long before a skilful Norman workingman took it into his head to imitate them on a large scale. Finally, without neglecting any extraordinary things observed we need a genuine exhibit of human life, based on the practical activity of men, quite different from the sort of museums which a few scholarly men have left us which, despite their size, are scarcely nothing but a multitude of pretexts for harangues and sermons. In order to grasp the enormity of what we should have to choose for these real descriptions appropriate to practice, just imagine how much knowledge one would need if suddenly transported to a desert island one had to make for himself everything useful and convenient which the abundance of a big city furnishes us, since the city is filled with the best workmen and most talented men from all social ranks. Or else, imagine that an art is lost and that it must be rediscovered; all our libraries could not help supply the art, for though I do not disagree that there are a great many admirable things in books which men in the professions are still ignorant of and should take advantage of, it is nevertheless a fact that the most important observations and turns of skill in all sorts of trades and professions are as yet unwritten. This fact is proved by experience when passing from theory to practice we desire to accomplish something.

Of course, we can also write up this practice, since it is at bottom just another theory more complex and particular than the theory in general; but workingmen for the most part, outside the fact that they are not inclined to teach anybody but their apprentices, are not people to explain themselves intelligibly by writing. Our writers jump ahead of these particular details, which, though essential, are regarded by them as minutiae which they do not deign to be informed about, apart from the difficulty there is in describing them.

But my purpose here is not to explain in detail everything we should have to do to make a general inventory of all the knowledge already existing among men. However important this project may be for our welfare, it requires too many collaborators to expect its realization soon without some higher direction, apart from the fact that it goes chiefly into observations and historical truths or facts of sacred, civil or natural history; for facts are what are most in need of summaries, authorities, and inventories, and the best method is to make the greatest number of comparisons we can and the most exact, detailed, and diversified indices possible. This method of carefully registering facts is not what I have primarily set out to discuss here, but rather the method of directing our reason to take advantage of facts given either by the senses or by reports of others or by the inner light, in order to discover or establish important truths not yet known or certain, or at least not yet brought to light in the way needed to clarify the mind. For the truths which are still in need of being established are of two sorts: those known only confusedly and imperfectly, and others not known at all. For the first kind we must use the *Method of Certitude;* the others need the *Art of Discovery,* although these two arts do not differ as much as is believed, as I shall show in the sequel. Now it is plain that men make use in reasoning of several axioms which are not yet quite certain. We also see that they are always heatedly discussing sundry philosophical questions, affecting Religion, Morals, and natural science, without seeking a true method to settle the argument. But we see above all that the art of discovery is little known outside of Mathematics, for the Topics of rhetoric usually serve only as ledgers in which to arrange our thoughts passably and contain only a Catalogue of vague Terms and apparent maxims commonly accepted. I admit their utility is very great in Rhetoric and in questions treated popularly, but when it is a question of obtaining certitude and of discovering truths hidden in theory and consequently of new advantages for practice, we must use other artifices.

Long experience and reflections on all sorts of matters, accompanied by considerable success in inventions and discoveries, have led me to know that there are secrets in the art of thinking as in the other arts. And that is the object of the *General Science* which I undertake to treat.

8. THE ART OF DISCOVERY
[1685]

Men have known something of the road leading to certitude: The logic of Aristotle and the Stoics is proof of it, but above all is the example set by the mathematicians, and I may add that of the Roman jurisconsults, for certain of their arguments in the digests do not differ in any way from a demonstration.

However, this road has not been followed because it is a little inconvenient, and because it has to be treaded slowly with counted steps. But I believe its neglect is due to ignorance of its results. We have not considered how important it would be to be able to establish the principles of Metaphysics, Physics, and Ethics with the same certitude as the Elements of Mathematics.

Now I have found that by this means we should arrive not only at a solid knowledge of several important truths, but also that we should attain the admirable Art of Discovery, and a method of analysis which would accomplish in other matters something similar to what Algebra does with numbers.

I have even found an astonishing thing, which is, that we can represent all sorts of truths and consequences by Numbers. More than twenty years ago I gave a demonstration of this important discovery, and devised a method which leads us infallibly to the general analysis

of human knowledge, as can be judged by a little treatise
I had soon after published [*De Arte Combinatoria,*
1666] in which there are a few things smacking of the
youth and apprentice, but its basis was sound. I have
since built on it as much as other matters and distractions permitted me to be able to do.

I therefore discovered that there are certain primitive
Terms which can be posited if not absolutely, at least
relatively to us, and then all the results of reasoning can
be determined in numerical fashion, and even with respect to those forms of reasoning in which the given
circumstances or data do not suffice for an absolute
answer to the question, we could still determine mathematically the degree of probability.

I have noticed that the reason why we make mistakes
so easily outside of Mathematics (where Geometers are
so felicitous in their reasonings), is only because in
Geometry and the other parts of abstract Mathematics,
we can continually submit to trials or tests not only the
conclusion but also, at any moment, each step made from
the premises, by reducing the whole to numbers. But in
physics after many inferences are made experiment often
refutes the conclusion and yet does not rectify the reasoning and does not indicate the place where we went
wrong. In Metaphysics and Ethics, it is much worse;
often we cannot submit to experiments any of the conclusions except in a very vague manner, and when it
comes to the subject-matter of Metaphysics, experiment
is often impossible during our lifetime.

The only way to rectify our reasonings is to make
them as tangible as those of the Mathematicians, so that
we can find our error at a glance, and when there are
disputes among persons, we can simply say: Let us calculate, without further ado, in order to see who is right.

If words were constructed according to a device that

I see possible, but which those who have built universal languages have not discovered, we could arrive at the desired result by means of words themselves, a feat which would be of incredible utility for human life. But in the meantime there is another less elegant road already open to us, whereas the other would have to be built completely new. The road open to us consists of making use as mathematicians do, of characters, which are appropriate to fix our ideas, and of adding to them a numerical proof.

For by this means, after reducing reasoning in ethics, physics, medicine, or metaphysics to these terms or characters, we shall be able at any moment to introduce the numerical test in such a way that it will be impossible to make a mistake except willfully. This is perhaps one of the most important discoveries anybody has made in a long time.

It will be appropriate to say something about those who have tried to give demonstrations outside of mathematics. Aristotle was the first in Logic, and we may say he was successful, but he was far from being as fortunate in the other sciences he treated; if we had the books of Chrysippus, or of some of the other Stoics, we should find some attempt. We can say that the Roman jurisconsults have given us some fine specimens of demonstrative reasoning.

Among the Scholastics there was a certain Jean Suisset called the Calculator, whose works I have not yet been able to find and I have seen only those of a few disciples of his. This Suiseth began to use Mathematics in scholastic arguments, but few people imitated him because they would have to give up the method of disputation for that of book-keeping and reasoning, and a stroke of the pen would have spared much clamor. It is a remarkable thing to my mind that John the Scot wishing to illustrate how an angel could be in heaven and on earth, as the famous one in Virgil who "Walks along alone and conceals his head in the clouds," he made use of a proposition in Euclid about the equality of parallelograms.

Raymond Lully also did mathematics and in a fashion discovered the art of combinations. Lully's Art would be undoubtedly a wonderful thing if those fundamental terms of his, Goodness, Magnitude, Duration, Power, Wisdom, Will, Virtue, Glory, were not so vague, and consequently, serve only to express but not at all to discover the truth.

I do not remember now having noticed any demonstrative philosopher belonging to the past century, unless we consider Tartaglia who did something on motion, and Cardan who spoke of proportions, and Francisco Patrizzi, who was a man of admirable views but who lacked the learning necessary to pursue them. He wanted to correct the ways of demostrating things in Geometry, he had indeed seen that there was something in them, and he wanted to do something also for Metaphysics, but he lacked the strength. The preface of his New Geometry, dedicated to the Duke of Ferrara, is admirable, but the contents are pitiful.

But it is our own century which has gone in for demonstrations on a large scale. Galileo broke the ice in his new science of motion. I have seen the work of a member of the Academy of the Lincei, Stelliola by name, dealing with Dioptrics in which I notice something of the method of proceeding demonstratively in physics outside of pure Mathematics; the same is true in Kepler, in Gilbert and Cabeus, and in Snell whose work on Dioptrics has not yet appeared but whose discoveries apparently have opened Descartes' eyes.

Marin having published a book on light undertook to insert some demonstrations of God's existence in the style of the Geometers. At the same time, Descartes driven by the persuasive views of Mersenne undertook to order Metaphysics in a demonstrative form, but if he ever showed his weak points, he did it then. And nearly at the same time Thomas Hobbes undertook to write in a demonstrative manner in Ethics as well as in physics. There is in Hobbes a mixture of a mind which shows itself both wonderfully penetrating and strangely weak by turns, because he had not taken advantage of Mathematics to save himself from paralogisms.

At this same time Father Fabry began to write demonstratively. We may say that he was one of the most brilliant, scholarly, and universal minds of his order, but he lacked the true method of analysis. He proceeded often very cavalierly in his proofs and if he had refrained from making so many propositions and demonstrated more exactly those he has given he might have accomplished a great deal.

In England, an Anonymous author [Seth Ward] publishes a very ingenious *Metaphysical Attempt* [*Tentamen Metaphysicum*] to prove that the world cannot be eternal, but he assumes that one infinite cannot be greater than another or else that the infinite is not certain.

Sir Digby also undertook to give demonstrations of the soul's immortality, and his faithful Achates, Thomas White, as excellent in Geometry and Metaphysics as Mr. Digby was in knowledge of the World and in Chemistry, has offered a few admirable works written in a demonstrative manner. I have only seen his metaphysical Euclid; it surely contains some profound thoughts but it is too obscure and lacks a great deal before its demonstrations can be convincing or clarifying.

Finally, Spinoza undertook to give demonstrations; those he published on a part of the *Principles of Descartes' Philosophy* were well received. It must be admitted that this author has had beautiful and profound thoughts, but his other ideas are so confused and so far from having the mathematicians' clarity that one does not know what to say when he wishes to have them accepted as irrefutable demonstrations. The demonstrations he gives are sometimes extremely involved, and often the proposition he uses in order to demonstrate another proposition is much more difficult than the conclusion.

Among the Aristotelians we find also men of very great ability who have undertaken demonstrations. Two of these men are not to be despised, namely Abdias Trew, a mathematician in Altdorf, who has reduced to demonstrative form the 8 books of Aristotle's *De Physics Audito,* and the other is John Felden, known for his book of observations on Grotius' work *De Jure Belle et Pacis;* Felden offered some Elements of jurisprudence in which there surely are some solid thoughts. There is a professor of very great ability at Jena, whose name is Weigel. He has published a fine work called *Analysis Euclidea* in which there are many beautiful thoughts for improving logic and for giving demonstrations in philosophy. Among other things he has communicated to a few friends an Essay to demonstrate the Existence of God based on the thesis that all other beings must be continually created. He has also offered a very ingenious Moral Sphere, an allegorical manner of explaining all ethics by relationship to the Astronomers' doctrine of the Sphere. This moral sphere is appended to the Jena edition of Pufendorf's *Elements of Universal Jurisprudence.* Pufendorf has also inserted some definitions and Axioms in the geometrical fashion and they are quite ingenious.

Ramus has taken up Euclid anew in such a way that while following the rigor of the Demonstrations, he has abandoned the Method which seems most appropriate to guide the mind. But the good Ramus who had changed Euclid's method has not only lost rigor but also truth and accuracy. The excellent author Antoine Arnauld of the *New Essays of Geometry* has combined in a way clarity of order with certitude. Mercator, one of the ablest Geometers of our times, has also given us an *Elements of Geometry* in which he shows in the course of a few essays how we could combine clarity with certitude in Geometry. I admit, however, that if we cannot obtain both at the same time it is much better to be exact at the expense of order than to save order at the expense of truth. And we might say many things in favor of the order which Euclid had used.

I notice also a defect in those who try to write demonstratively, namely, they cut the subject up into so many little propositions that the mind wastes itself that way. That is why it is well to distinguish the most important propositions from the least important ones.

Also there is that fault which some authors have of undertaking to write propositions without knowing when it is time to finish, for propositions go to infinity. I find two limits which reason prescribes to us: 1) it is necessary to continue the synthesis until we can change it into an analysis; 2) it is useful to continue the synthesis until we see progressions to infinity; 3) when there are a few beautiful theorems which have a special practical use, it is good to mark them thus. But the first rule is sufficient for what is needed.

The most general defect, from which Euclid himself is not exempt, is to assume as axioms what can be demonstrated. It is true that this defect does no harm to certitude when these axioms are justified by an infinity of experiments, as Mathematicians have tried them already. But this defect does harm to the improvement of the mind and is the principal reason why the synthesis of Geometers has not yet been transformable into Analysis. It may seem astonishing for me to say this, but it must be known that the Algebra and Analysis of Viète and Descartes is rather Analysis of Numbers than of lines; although indirectly Geometry is reduced by them in so far as all magnitudes can be expressed by Numbers, but that requires long detours whereas Geometers can demonstrate in a few words what the method of calculation takes a long time to do. And when an equation has been found in some difficult problem, there is still a long way to go before we have the construction required by the problem. The method of Algebra in Geometry is certain but it is not the best. It is like going from one place to another by always wishing to follow the course of rivers; an Italian traveller I have known who always went by boat whenever he could, preferred to take the water-route from Wurtzburg to Wertheim, which is 12 German leagues along the river Mayn, though it takes only 5 hours by land. But when the land-routes are not yet open and cleared, as in America, one is too happy to be able to use the river, and that is how it is in Geometry when one goes beyond the Elements, for the imagination would be lost in the multitude of figures, if Algebra did not come to its assistance until we establish a characteristic proper to Geometry which indicates spatial relations as Arithmetic indicates magnitudes. This is feasible and would be very useful for discoveries as well as for aiding the imagination.

I have been sent a writing of the late Pascal called "the geometric mind" in which that illustrious person observes that Geometers have the habit of defining everything which is in the least obscure and of demonstrating everything which is in the least doubtful. I should like to have been given by him a few indications for detecting

what is doubtful or obscure. And I am convinced that
for the perfection of the sciences it is even necessary to
demonstrate a few propositions we call axioms; indeed
Apollonius took the trouble to demonstrate a few of those
Euclid assumed without demonstration. Euclid was right
but Apollonius was also justified. It is not necessary to
do so but it still remains important to do it, and necessary to certain views. The late Roberval planned a new
Elements of Geometry in which he was going to demonstrate rigorously several propositions which Euclid took
or assumed without proof. I do not know whether he
completed his work before he died, but I know that
many people ridiculed it; if they had known its importance, they would have judged otherwise. It is not
necessary for apprentices or even ordinary teachers, but
in order to advance the sciences and to pass beyond the
columns of Hercules, there is nothing more necessary.

9. ON TRUE METHOD IN PHILOSOPHY AND THEOLOGY
[c. 1686]

As I turned in my zeal for knowledge from the serious
study of Holy Scripture and of divine and human law
to the mathematical sciences, and was soon delighted by
the thoroughly luminous teachings of the latter, I came
near to remaining caught on siren cliffs. For some wonderful theorems were revealed to me to which others
were opposed; I saw the road open then to more and
greater things and many a structure which had arisen
quietly in my mind at play, appeared to me also to bear
promise of fruit. With what joy a beautiful theorem fills
one can be judged only by those who are able to comprehend such inner *harmony* with a purified mind. Mean-

while the memory of the diviner science afflicted my soul
and I deplored the fact that that science should forego a
comparable clarity and order. I saw how the most distinguished men, Saint Thomas and Saint Bonaventura
and William Durand and Gregory of Rimini and many
other authors of former times, have offered not a few
theorems of marvelous subtlety to First Philosophy
which might have been demonstrated with the utmost
rigor. I recognized how Natural Theology, which had
been most gloriously created by these men, had been sub-
merged in a barbaric darkness, and through a confused
use of words floundered between doubtful distinctions,
and so I often actually played the mathematician in
theology, incited by the novelty of the rôle; I set up
definitions and tried to deduce from them certain elements which were not inferior to those of Euclid in clarity but far exceeded them in the magnitude of their
consequences. For I reflected as follows: Geometry clari-
fies configurations and motions; as a result we have discovered the geography of lands and the course of the
stars, and machines have been made which overcome
great burdens, whence civilization and the difference
between civilized and barbaric peoples. But the science
which distinguishes the just man from the unjust, and
through which the secrets of the mind are explained and
the path to happiness is paved, is neglected. We have
demonstrations about the circle, but only conjectures
about the soul; the laws of motion are presented with
mathematical rigor, but nobody applies a comparable
diligence to research on the secrets of thinking. The
source of human misery lies in the fact that man devotes
more thought to everything but the highest good in life,
like the negligent merchant who sleeps at the beginning
and with the growth of his account-book eschews order
and clarity, and is then unable to put together all the

entries of receipts and disbursements from the beginning. Whence we have the clandestine atheism planted in men, the fear of death, doubts about the nature of the soul, the weakest or at least, vacillating pronouncements about God, and the fact that many men are honest by habit or necessity rather than by virtue of their judgment.

I saw that certain philosophers could not have kept their excessive promises because they have written with prepossessed minds or have preached mathematical rigor but have themselves practised otherwise and taken to light, popular ways of speaking, obtaining applause rather than assent. For—just to give one example—if the very distinguished René Descartes had only once of his own free will converted his meditations into propositions and his discourses into demonstrations, he would have himself seen the large number of flaws in them. This resulted, under pressure from his friends rather than from his own conviction, in his dressing up his proof of God's existence in a mathematical garb. For if I should assume that he himself had taken it for a proof, I should be doing his genius an injury.

Many think that mathematical rigor has no place outside of the sciences ordinarily called mathematical. But they overlook the fact that to write mathematically is the same as what the logicians call reasoning according to form, and that a single definition can take the place of the captious distinctions on which so much time is wasted. For the Scholastics labored under only one vice, that is, with all the order they sufficiently showed for the most part, and, so to speak, in mathematical ratiocination, they left the use of their words in uncertainy. Whence instead of one definition arose many, instead of one irrefragable proof arose many arguments pro and con; their dogmas of God and their often admirable reflections could easily be purged or clarified by a mathematically schooled mind.

I thought such a task all the more useful because I saw dangerous expressions slipping into men's souls; they are a sort of mathematical larva from which arises a false philosophy, and with that the whole of scholastic doctrine would be rejected.

For how many at most are there of those who, educated in the custom of the present century, really regard these trivialities, as the scholastic doctrines are called, worth reading? I congratulate myself for my youthful days when I had the opportunity to learn these studies also, before my mind was imbued with mathematical studies, and I thus acquired the habit of attending patiently to other studies. There are historical periods for these studies; there was a time when scholastic theology alone obtained the principal part, but today it is scarcely kept alive anywheres but in religious orders and convents. With the glowing light of the humanistic studies we find a contrary extreme emphasis, and there is as much of a tumult made over a syllable of Plautus and Apuleius as there used to be over universals and modal distinctions.

Now that we are cured of this malady, we face a greater danger. We have grown into manhood and with the maturing of judgment have discarded all our juvenile clothes in the same way as though the world grown out of barbarism had taken on wisdom with the years. We have known how long it took for mankind to acquire an interest in learning to know nature and to establish the laws of space and motion through which our powers are enhanced. But just as man in a free republic works mostly for others and little for himself, so we gather by successful investigations into the hereafter only the material from which, after many centuries, the edifice of truth will be erected. And I see that great men who in their youth pursued the study of mathematics and the humanities, and later on did experiments on nature or went into the business of the world, with the advent of age return to the advancement of the sciences and of the mind with which they associate their own happiness. It is a wise saying of that distinguished man Francis Bacon: a little philosophy "inclineth man's mind to atheism, but depth in philosophy bringeth men's minds about to religion." I say the same to our century; the value of a religious philosophy will be recognized by those who return to it, and mathematical studies will be used partly as an example of more rigorous judgment, partly for the knowledge of harmony and of the idea of beauty, experiments on nature will lead to admiration for the author of nature, who has expressed an image of the ideal world in the sensible one, so that all studies finally will lead to happiness.

For the most part we hail those minds who blandish the novelty of their philosophy by dressing it up in mathematical attire at the expense of divine truth. It is an indubitable fact, and one recognized also by Aristotle, that everything in nature is derived from size, figure, and motion. The theory of size and figure has been developed in a pre-eminent way; the innermost nature of motion is not yet patent due to the neglect of First Philosophy from which its laws are derived. For it is the task of Metaphysics to treat of continuous temporal modifications in the universe, since motion is only one kind of modification. In so far as the nature of motion is not understood, important philosophers having attributed the essence of matter only to extension, there has resulted a notion of bodies, previously unheard of, which fails to do justice to either the phenomena of nature or the mysteries of faith. For it can be demonstrated that extension without the addition of other qualities is not capable of either action or its passive reception; that everything becomes fluid in the most extreme way, that is, becomes vacuous; that then the cohesion of bodies and what is felt as solid in them cannot be explained, and that, therefore, the laws of motion are thereby constituted contrary to experience. All of which appears illustrated plainly in the principles of Descartes, since he makes motion purely relative and has thought up a kind of body which is in no way different from the void, and he has derived the cohesion and solidity of bodies from mere rest, because on his view bodies must come to rest immediately after they have come in contact with each other, since there can be no forces to separate them. Furthermore, he has laid down laws about motion and the impact of bodies which the most exact experiments have made obsolete. He has also artfully evaded the mysteries of faith by claiming to pursue philosophy rather than theology, as though philosophy were incompatible with religion, or as though a religion can be true which opposes truths demonstrated elsewhere. Once when he had to discuss the Holy Eucharist, he substituted for real species only apparent ones, and thus revived a doctrine rejected by a universal consensus of theologians. But this would mean little, if his philosophy could allow bodies to exist in several places at once. For if body and space are one and the same, how can we avoid the consequence that in different spaces or places there must be different bodies? Those who in forming a theory of corporeal nature add to extension a certain resistance or impenetrability (or, as they call it, antitype ἀντιτυπία) or bulk—as Gassendi and other scholars have done— have indeed philosophized correctly but they have not gotten rid of the difficulties. For what is needed to analyze the idea of body is some positive notion, which impenetrability does not have, since it is not yet proven that the penetration of bodies is not present in nature: condensation provides an argument (many think it results from penetration), although another explanation for it can be recognized. Finally, the absolute impenetrability of bodies contradicts both the teachings of our faith and the doctrine of πολυτοπία (being in several places at the same time), and it is just as difficult to see how a body can be in several places as several bodies in the same place.

What must we then add to extension in order to complete the concept of body? Nothing except what the senses themselves testify to. They inform us at once of three things: first, that we observe, and that we observe bodies, and that what we observe is a variety of things, composite or extended. Consequently, action has to be added to the notion of extension or variety. Therefore, *body is extended activity* (*agens extensum*), and a substance may be said to be extended if we hold that every substance is active and every active thing is called a substance. Now we can show from the inner truths of metaphysics that what is not active is nothing, for there is no such thing as a mere potentiality to act without any initial action. The force of a taut bow is in no wise a small one; only we say it is not yet in action. In any case, it is already present before the shooting of the bow, for the bow tugs with an effort, and every effort is an activity. Moreover, there are certainly *many* and *important* things to be said of the nature of effort (*conatus*) and of the principle of activity, or as the Scholastics called them, substantial forms, things which also illuminate Natural Theology and the mysteries of faith and dispel the darkness due to the obscurantist objections of philosophers.

The result is that not only souls but all substances

can be said to exist in a place only through the operations
of their active principle; that souls cannot be destroyed
by any power of body and that all forces act for the
highest mind whose will is the final reason for all things,
the cause being the universal harmony; that God as
creator can unite the body to the soul; that, in fact,
every finite soul is embodied, even the angels are not
excepted (in which true philosophy is in agreement with
the teachings of the Church Fathers); and finally, that
neither πολυτοπία (the same body in several places) nor
μετουσιασμόν (several bodies in the same place) contains
anything contradictory. For we can find something wonderful in the fact that the consubstantiation of bodies
becomes resolved in transubstantiation. On the other
hand, whoever says that the body is contained in the
bread, does not realize that he is asserting the destruction
of the substance of the bread and still leaving its properties intact—all such fallacies can be avoided once the
true and inevitable concept of substance is understood.
Of what great significance these theorems are for the
firm foundation of religious faith and for peace among
the Churches, the understanding will appreciate.

10. ON A GENERAL PRINCIPLE, USEFUL FOR THE EXPLANATION OF LAWS OF NATURE

[Letter to Bayle, *Nouvelles de la république des lettres,*

1687]

I have seen the Reverend Father Malebranche's reply
to the observation I had made about a few of the laws
of nature he had established in his book (*Recherche de
la vérité*). He himself seems quite disposed to give them
up, and this turn of mind is very laudable, but since his

reasons and strictures for doing so leave the subject as obscure as it was, despite my effort at clarification and a certain *General Principle of Order* which I had observed, I hope he will be good enough to permit me to use this occasion to explain that principle. It is of great use in reasoning, and I do not think it is employed often enough nor sufficiently known in its entire extent. It has its origin in the *infinite,* it is absolutely necessary in Geometry, but it is successful also in Physics, because the sovereign wisdom which is the source of all things, acts like a perfect Geometer, in accordance with a complete harmony. That is why this principle often serves as a proof or test, enabling one to see from the start and from the outside the flaw in an opinion badly put together, even before entering into an internal discussion of it. The principle may be stated as follows: when the difference between two cases may be diminished below any magnitude given in the data, then that difference must be diminishable below any magnitude given in the problem or in what results from it. Or to talk in more familiar language: when the cases (or data) approach each other continuously and finally get lost in one another, then must the events in the sequel (or in what is sought) do so also. All this depends again on a more general principle, to wit: *objects of inquiry are ordered as the order in the data.* But to understand this, we need examples.

We know that the case or supposition of an ellipse may approach that of a parabola as closely as one pleases, so that the difference between the ellipse and the parabola may become less than any given difference, provided that one of the foci of the ellipse is removed far enough away from the other. The rays coming from the distant focus will differ from parallel rays by as little as you please, so that consequently all the geometric theorems generally verified for the ellipse will hold for the parabola when the latter is considered as a kind of ellipse whose foci are infinitely far apart or (in order to avoid this expression), as a figure which differs from some ellipse by less than any given difference. The same principle occurs in physics; e.g., rest may be considered as an infinitely small velocity, or as an infinite retardation. That is why everything true about retardation or velocity in general may be verified for rest, taken so; whence the law for rest should be considered as a special case of the law for motion; otherwise, if that fails, you have a sure indication that the laws are badly put together. Likewise, equality may be considered as an infinitely small inequality, and we may make inequality approach equality by as much as we wish.

It is, among other faults, for lack of this consideration that Monsieur Des Cartes, able as he was, failed in more than one way in his alleged laws of nature. For (in order not to repeat here what I have said previously about the other source of his errors, when he took the quantity of motion for the force) his first and his second laws do not harmonize: the second requires that when two bodies B and C meet one another with equal speed, and if B is heavier by a very small amount, then C will be reflected or rebound with the first speed while B will continue its motion; whereas, according to the first law B and C being equal, they will both rebound with a speed equal to their initial speed. But this difference of results in the two cases is not reasonable; for the inequality of the two bodies may be as small as you please, and the difference supposed to result from the two cases, namely, between so small an inequality and perfect equality, may be less than any given amount; hence, in virtue of our principle, the difference between the resulting events should be as little as any given amount. However, if the second rule were as true as the first, the contrary would happen, for according to this second rule an increase as small as one pleases in the body B, formerly equal to C, makes a very great difference in the effect, so that it changes an absolute rebound into an absolute continuation of motion; this is a great leap from one extreme to the other, whereas in this case the body B should react a little less and the body C a little more than in the scarcely distinguishable case of their being both equal.

There are several other similar incongruities resulting from the Cartesian laws, which the attention of a reader applying our principle will easily notice, and the one I had found in the laws of the *Recherche de la Vérité* came from the same source. Father Malebranche admits in a way that there is an incongruity here, but he does not cease believing that the law of motion depending on the good pleasure of God, is ruled by his wisdom, and Geometers would be almost as much surprised to see these sorts of irregularities happen in nature as to see a parabola to which one could apply the properties of the ellipse with an infinitely distant focus. Moreover, I think we scarcely meet any example in nature of such incongruities: the more we know her, the more geometrical we find her. It is thus easy to judge that those incongruities do not come properly from what Father Malebranche alleges, namely, from the false hypothesis of the perfect hardness (elasticity) of bodies, which I agree is not to be found in nature. For when you assume such a hardness by conceiving it as an infinitely prompt spring, there results nothing as a consequence which cannot be perfectly adjusted to the true laws of nature respecting elastic bodies in general and you will never come to laws so poorly tied together as those I have mentioned. It is true that in composite things sometimes a small change may produce a large effect, as, for example, a spark falling into a mass of cannon-powder is capable of destroying a whole city. But that is not contrary to our principle, and we can give the reason for it by means of general principles; but with regard to simple principles or things, nothing like that can happen, else nature would not be the effect of an infinite wisdom.

In that way we see (a little better than in what is commonly said on the subject) how the true Physics may be tapped from the source of divine perfection. God is the final reason of things, and the knowledge of God is no less the principle of sciences than his essence and will are the principles of beings. The most reasonable philosophers remain agreed on this, but there are very few of them who are able to make use of it in order to discover truths of consequence. Perhaps these small samples will arouse some to go much farther. Philosophy is sanctified by having its streams flow from the fountain of God's attributes. Very far from excluding final causes and the consideration of a being acting with wisdom, we must from these deduce everything in Physics. That is what Socrates in Plato's *Phaedo* admirably well observed in arguing against Anaxagoras and other philosophers who were too materialistic. They, after recognizing an intelligent principle above matter, when they come to philosophize about the universe, instead of showing that this intelligence makes everything for the best (and that this is the reason of things: that it has found it good to produce things in accordance with its ends), try to explain everything by the sole concourse of particles, thus confusing conditions or instruments with the true cause. It is as if (Socrates says), in order to explain why I am sitting in prison awaiting the fatal cup and why I am not on my way to live among the Beotians or other people among whom everybody knows I might have been able to save myself, one were to say that the reason is that

I have bones, tendons, and muscles which can be flexed in the way necessary for me to be sitting. By my faith (he says), these bones and these muscles would not be here and you would not see me in this posture, if my mind had not judged that it is more worthy for Socrates to submit to what the laws of the country order. This passage in Plato deserves to be read in its entirety for it contains very beautiful and very solid reflections. However, I agree that the particular effects of nature can and ought to be explained mechanically, without forgetting still their admirable ends and uses, arranged by Providence, so that the general principles of Physics and of Mechanics itself depend on the conduct of a sovereign intelligence and cannot be explained without having it enter into our consideration. It is thus that we must reconcile piety with reason, and that will enable us to satisfy people of good standing who have some apprehension about the consequences of the mechanical or corpuscular philosophy as though it might alienate them from God and immaterial substances, whereas with the required corrections and everything well understood, that philosophy should lead us to them.

11. ON SOME PHILOSOPHICAL AXIOMS AND MATHEMATICAL FICTIONS

[Extract from a Letter to Canon Foucher, *Journal des Savans*, 1692]

I share your thought that it would be good to seek proofs for all the important truths that can be proved. But that should not prevent us from going ahead with particular problems while we are expecting to establish first principles. That is how geometers proceed with them. However, I should like very much to have your opinion in explanation of this, for fear that those who do not understand it sufficiently may not improperly imagine that Academicians are opposed to the progress of the sciences.

Mr. Descartes does not seem to me to have taken pains to establish his axioms firmly, despite the fact that he for one began with that reasonable doubt which you Academicians first professed to introduce.

Moreover we know that *Proclus* and even *Apollonius* had already envisaged a plan for working on the proof of axioms. But those who like to go into scientific detail scorn abstract and general inquiries, and those who work on fundamental principles rarely go into particulars. For my part, I have an equally high regard for both general and particular investigations.

My axiom that nature never acts by a leap has a great use in Physics. It destroys atoms, small lapses of motion, globules of the second element, and other similar chimeras. It rectifies the laws of motion. Sir, lay aside your fears about the tortoise that the Pyrrhonian sceptics have made to move as fast as Achilles. You are right in saying that *all magnitudes may be infinitely subdivided. There is none so small in which we cannot conceive an inexhaustible infinity of subdivisions.* But I see no harm in that or any necessity to exhaust them. A space infinitely divisible is traversed in a time also infinitely divisible. I conceive no physical indivisibles short of a miracle, and I believe nature can reduce bodies to the smallness Geometry can consider.

Mr. Ozanam will, I hope, not be put out by my not having given him my first insight into the quadrature of the circle about which he and I had spoken, and I would have sent him my demonstration of it if he had asked me for it. He will also acknowledge that I am the first to have shown him the employment of local (geometrical) equations for constructions; he was delighted with it, and has made very fine use of it, as I see in his Dictionary. It is true that this use of local equations is not an invention of mine. I had learned it from Mr. Slusius.

Some time ago I had an insight profitable to Mr. Ozanam; namely, a plan for drawing up certain analytical or specious (algebraic) tables based on combinations. If this were done, it would be a wonderful aid to Analysis and Geometry, and the rest of mathematics; it would push Analysis to a perfection beyond its present limits. It would serve advanced geometry as much as the old table of sines serves trigonometry. And as Mr. Ozanam is one of the most facile men in the world when it comes to the ordinary algebraic calculations, I had thought that through his means a thing as useful as that could be accomplished.

The reason why I left behind me in Florence an essay on a new science of Dynamics * is that there was a friend there who promised to straighten it out and put it into shape and even to have it published. It is my fault that it has not appeared for I only had to send him the end. But every time I thought of doing so, a host of new ideas came to me which I have not yet had a chance to digest.

Expressions like "Extremes meet" go a little too far, e.g., when we say that the infinite is a sphere whose center is everywhere and circumference nowhere. Such expressions must not be taken too strictly or literally. Nevertheless, they still have a particular use in discovery, something like that of imaginaries in Algebra. Thus we conceive the parabola as an ellipse with an infinitely distant focus; and in that way we maintain a certain universality in the propositions of conic sections. Calculation leads us sometimes to infinity without thinking

* See Selection II. 5 below (*Specimen Dynamicum*), pp. 119 f.

about it in advance. It would be possible thus to arrive at a conclusion, at least in the case of a velocity assumed to be infinite, that each point of a circle is in the same place, although, after all, an infinite velocity as well as an infinite circle are impossible. With all that, that infinite circle may still have its use in calculating: for if analysis made me see that the radius of the circle posited in the given plane is infinite, I should conclude that the entire plane of the posited circle is the locus sought. Thus if I did not find what I am looking for, namely, a circle that is posited, I should at least find what I was to seek, namely, that the required locus is the plane, and there is no such circle in this plane. So that *omnia sana sanis* (all is reasonable to the reasonable) still stands, and analysis obtains real uses from imaginary expressions. I have very important examples of this. It is true that from truths we can conclude only truths; but there are certain falsehoods which are useful for finding the truth.

12. THE HORIZON OF HUMAN DOCTRINE
[After 1690]

The entire body of the sciences may be regarded as an ocean, continuous everywheres and without a break or division, though men conceive parts in it and give them names according to their convenience. And as there are seas which are either unknown or sailed only by a few boats venturing on them by chance, so we may say there are sciences about which something is known only by chance and without a plan. One of them is the art of combinations which for me has as much significance as the science of forms or formulas or else of variations in general; in a word it is the Universal Specious or

Characteristic. Such is the science that treats of the same
and the diverse; of the similar and the dissimilar; of the
absolute and the relational; as the usual Mathematics
deals with the one and the many, the large and the small,
the whole and the part. We may even say that Logistics
or Algebra is subordinate to it in a certain sense, for
when we make use of several marks indifferently which
at the beginning of a calculation might be exchanged and
mutually substituted without harming the reasoning (in
this respect the letters of the Alphabet come in handy),
and when these letters or marks signify magnitudes or
general numbers the result is the Algebra or rather the
Specious of Viète. And that is exactly where the advantage of Viète's and Descartes' Algebra over that of
the ancients resides: by making use of letters instead of
known or unknown numbers we obtain formulas in which
there is some connection and order, which gives our
mind a means for noticing theorems and general rules.
Thus the best advantages of algebra are only samples
of the art of characters whose use is not limited to numbers or magnitudes. For if these letters designated points
(a common practise actually among Geometers), we
could form a certain *calculus* or sort of operation which
would be entirely different from Algebra and would continue to enjoy the same advantages as the latter has
(about this I shall have more to say another time). When
these letters designate terms or notions, as in Aristotle,
we obtain that part of logic which treats of the figures
and moods. I had figured that out when I first began my
studies, when I hazarded publishing a little treatise on
the Art of Combinations, which was well received and
reprinted [in 1690 at Frankfurt] against my wishes, for
having since had many other views of the subject, I could
have treated things quite differently. However, I may say
in passing that I had since then noticed this general

theorem of Logic: that the four figures of syllogisms have each a like number of useful moods; and that in each figure there are six moods. Finally when the letters or other characters designate the actual letters of the Alphabet or of language, then the art of combinations together with the observation of languages yields the Cryptography of deciphering.

I have also remarked that there is a calculus of combinations in which the composite is not a collective but a distributive whole, that is to say, one in which the combined things do not come together except alternatively, and this calculus also has six laws quite different from those of Algebra. Finally, the general Specious takes in a thousand ways of expression, and Algebra contains only one. Now without entering into the particular discussion of the laws which diversify the Specious, we can combine it with Arithmetic by calculating the *number of possible variations* which the general marks may receive. These variations may be taken in different ways; in the writings we form by using letters of the alphabet there is variety as much with respect to the letters as to their arrangement, and intervals or separations (for we do not write everything without stop, but we leave some separation among the words). Now since all human knowledge can be expressed by the letters of the Alphabet, and since we may say that whoever understands the use of the alphabet knows everything, it follows that we can calculate the number of truths which men are able to express, and that we can determine the size of a work which would contain all possible human knowledge, in which there would be everything which could ever be known, written, or discovered; and even more than that, for it would contain not only the true but also the false propositions which we can assert, and even expressions which signify nothing. This inquiry helps us understand

better how little man is in comparison with infinite substance, since the number of all the truths which all men
together can know is quite mediocre, even if there were an
infinity of men who for all eternity should exalt themselves
in the advancement of the sciences, assuming all the time
that human nature is no more perfect than it is now, for we
are not considering here life in the hereafter when the
human soul will be elevated to a more sublime state. This
paradox differs quite in magnitude from the one Archimedes proposed to the courtesans of King Hero by
showing them that the number of grains of sand which
would fill not only the whole globe of the earth but also
the space of a good part of the universe extending from
here to the stars, is quite a small number and easy to
write. For this number is almost nothing in comparison
with the number of truths, since there is no grain of
sand without its particular shape and which could not
furnish a great number of truths, not to mention truths
drawn from other things. It does not, however, follow
that, if the world and mankind should last long enough,
we should not be able to discover any but truths already
known, for mankind could be content with a certain small
number of truths during a whole eternity which would be
only a part of those it is capable of attaining and thus
would always leave something behind. But assuming man
always goes forward as long as he can, though perhaps
slowly and steadily making progress all the time, in the
end everything must be exhausted, and a Novel cannot
be written which has not already been written, nor a
new dream be possible. Thus it would remain necessarily
true that literally nothing will be said any longer which
has not already been said. For we shall say what has
been said or else, if we want to continue to say new
things, we shall exhaust what remains to be said, since
that is finite, as we shall demonstrate by and by. It is a

question then of giving a number greater than the number of everything which can be said or asserted; that is what we are going to do. . . .*

13. ON WISDOM
[c. 1693]

Wisdom is a perfect knowledge of the principles of all the sciences and of the art of applying them. By *principles* I mean all the fundamental truths which suffice to enable us to derive any conclusions we may need, by dint of some exertion and some little application; in sum, that which serves the mind to regulate manners, to make an honest living, and everywhere (even if one were surrounded by barbarians), to preserve one's health, to perfect one's self in any sort of things we may need, and finally, to provide for the conveniences of living. The art of applying these principles to situations includes in it the art of judging well or reasoning, the art of discovering unknown truths, and finally, the art of recalling what one knows on the instant and whenever needed.

The *art of reasoning well* consists of the following maxims:

1. We must never recognize as true anything but what is manifestly indubitable. That is why it will be well in

---

* The paper breaks off here, but in at least one other fragment, Leibniz calculates the number of all the statements which can be made by starting with an alphabet of 24 letters, and reaches a number of the order of 1 followed by 73 trillion zeros; cf. L. Couturat, *Opuscules et fragments inédits de Leibniz,* p. 96, and also footnote 3 in which Couturat refers to another fragment in which Leibniz maintains the contrary view that the number of terms and consequently of primary propositions is infinite. Archimedes' Sand-Reckoner showed how to express a number as high as 1 followed by 80,000 zeros.

beginning these inquiries to imagine ourselves interested in supporting the contrary in order to see if such incitement might not stimulate us to see whether we can find something solid to be said in its favor. For we must avoid prejudices and attribute to things only what they include. But we must also never be dogmatic.

2. When there does not seem to be any means of arriving at such an assurance, we must be content with probability while waiting for greater light. But we must distinguish degrees of probabilities, and we must remember that whatever we derive from a merely probable principle will retain the imperfection of its source, especially when we must assume several probabilities in order to arrive at that conclusion, for again, the latter becomes less sure than each probability serving as its ground.

3. To derive one truth from another we must keep uninterruptedly to a certain chain. For as we may be sure that a chain will hold when we are sure that each separate ring is of sound material, and that it clasps the two neighboring rings, namely, the one before and the one after it, so likewise, we may be sure of the accuracy of the reasoning when the matter is sound, that is to say, when it contains nothing doubtful, and when the form consists of a perpetual linking of truths with no gaps. For example, A is B and B is C and C is D, therefore A is D. Such a connecting chain will teach us never to put into the conclusion more than there was in the premises.

The *art of discovery* consists of the following maxims:

1. In order to become acquainted with a thing we must consider all of its prerequisites, that is, everything which suffices to distinguish it from any other thing. This is what is called definition, nature, essential property.

2. After we have found a means of distinguishing it

from every other thing, we must apply this same rule to the consideration of each condition or prerequisite entering into this means, and consider all the prerequisites of each prerequisite. And that is what I call *true analysis,* or distribution of the difficulty into several parts.

3. When we have pushed the analysis to the end, that is, when we have considered the prerequisites entering into the consideration of the proposed thing, and even the prerequisites of the prerequisites, and finally have come to considering a few natures understood only by themselves without prerequisites and needing nothing outside themselves to be conceived, then we have arrived at a *perfect knowledge* of the proposed thing.

4. When the thing merits it, we must try to have this perfect knowledge present in our mind all at once, and that is done by repeating the analysis several times until it seems to us that we see it as a complete whole in a single act of the mind. And to obtain that result we must observe some gradation in the repetition.

5. The mark of perfect knowledge is that nothing appears in the thing under consideration which cannot be accounted for, and that nothing is encountered whose occurrence cannot be predicted in advance. It is very difficult to complete an analysis of things, but it is not so difficult to complete the analysis we need to make of things. Because the analysis of a truth is completed when we have found the demonstration of the proposition. Most often the beginning of the analysis of the thing suffices for the analysis or perfect acquaintance of the truth of the thing with which we are acquainted.

6. We must always begin our inquiries with the easiest things, like the most general and simplest things, i.e., those on which it is easy to make experiments and to account for, like numbers, lines, motions.

7. We must ascend in order, both by going from easy to difficult things and by trying to discover some progression in the order of our thoughts for the sake of having nature itself as a guide and guarantee.

8. We must try to omit nothing in all of our distributions or enumerations. And that is why dichotomies with opposite members are very good.

9. The fruit of several analyses of different particular matters will be the catalogue of simple thoughts, or those which are not very far from being simple.

10. Having the catalogue of simple thoughts, we shall be ready to begin again *a priori* to explain the origin of things starting from their source in a perfect order and from a combination or synthesis which is absolutely complete. And that is all our soul can do in its present state.

The *art of recalling what one knows on the instant and whenever needed* consists of the following observations:

1. We must accustom ourselves to having presence of mind, that is, to be able to think in a disturbance, on the spur of the occasion and in danger, as well as in our study. That is why we must test ourselves on occasions and we must even seek such occasions with this precaution, however, that we do not expose ourselves to irreparable harm. In the meantime it is good to try ourselves out on occasions where the danger is imaginary or small, for example, in games, lectures, conversations, exercises, and humorous stories.

2. We must get used to making enumerations. That is why it is good to practise reporting all the possible cases of the problem under consideration, all the possible species of a kind, all the conveniences or inconveniences of a means, all the possible means for arriving at some end.

3. We must accustom ourselves to making distinctions, namely, given two or more very similar things, to find immediately all their differences.

4. We must accustom ourselves to analogies, namely, given two or more very different things, to find their similarities.

5. We must be able to relate immediately things which resemble strongly the given thing or differ very much from it. For example, when people deny me some general maxim, it is good if I can bring in some examples immediately. And when another person brings up some maxim against me, it is good if I can mention a counter instance; when a story is told me, it is good if I can immediately relate a similar story.

6. When there are truths or familiar facts in which the natural connection of the subject with its predicate is not known to us, as happens with matters of fact and truths of experience, we must use a few artifices in order to retain them, as, for example, concerning the specific properties of simple things in natural, civil, or ecclesiastical history, in geography, customs, laws, canons, languages. I see nothing so good for retaining such things as humorous verses and sometimes diagrams; item, hypotheses concocted to explain them in imitation of natural things (like a suitable true or false etymology for languages—*Regula Mundi* by imagining certain orders of providence for history).

7. Finally, it is good to make a written inventory of things known by acquaintance which are most useful, with an index or alphabetical table. And we should draw up, finally, a portable manual of what is most necessary and most usual.

14. ON THE LOGIC OF PROBABILITY
[From *New Essays,* bk. IV, ch. II, On Probability, 1704]

Opinion, based on the probable, also deserves perhaps the name knowledge; otherwise nearly all historical knowledge and many other kinds will fall. But without quarreling over names, I hold that *the investigation of degrees of probability* would be very important, that we are still lacking in it, and that this lack is a great defect of our Logic. For when we cannot decide a question absolutely, we might still determine the degree of likelihood from the data, and can consequently judge reasonably which side is the most likely. And when our moralists (I mean the wisest ones, such as the present-day General of the Jesuits) join "the safest" with "the most probable" and even prefer the safe to the probable, they are not in fact far removed from the most probable; for the question of *safety* is the same as that of the small probability of an evil to be feared. The fault of the moralists, lax on this point, has been in good part due to too limited and inadequate notion of *the probable* which they have confused with Aristotle's *endoxon* or *opinable;* for Aristotle in his *Topics* meant only to show how one accommodates himself to the opinions of others, as the orators and Sophists did. *Endoxon* for him means what has been accepted by the greatest number of people or the most authoritative; he was wrong in restricting his *Topics* to that, and this view caused him to adhere only to the accepted maxims, for the most part vague, as if he wished to reason only by means of quodlibets or proverbs. But the probable is more extensive; we must derive it from the nature of things; and the opinion of persons whose authority has weight is one of the things which may contribute to rendering an opinion likely, but it is not what completes the whole verisimilitude. And when Copernicus was nearly alone in his opinion, it was still incomparably more *probable* than that of all the rest of mankind. Now I do not know but that *the art of estimating verisimilitudes* would not be more useful than a good part of our demonstrative sciences, and I have often thought about it.

(From *New Essays,* bk. IV, ch. XV)

Rather than say [with Locke] that probability is based on agreement with our knowledge or on the testimony of persons we know, I should prefer to hold that it is always based on likelihood (*vraisemblance*) or agreement with the truth; and the testimony of others is also pertinent to the truth regarding facts within their reach. It then may be said that the similarity between the probable and the true is grounded either on internal or external considerations. The rhetoricians employ two kinds of arguments: *artificial* ones, based simply on reasoning about things, and *non-artificial* ones, based exclusively on the expressed testimony of men or perhaps also on the evidence of things themselves. But then there are also *mixed* arguments, since testimony may supply a fact which is used to form an artificial argument.

The sworn testimony of men is undoubtedly of greater weight than mere opinions, and the testimony adduced in rational argument is a result of greater deliberation. As you know, a judge at times makes witnesses take an oath of credulity (*de credulitate*); in the examination of witnesses they are often asked not only what they have seen but also what they think, asking them at the same time to give their reasons for their judgment and whether they have carefully considered them as they should. Judges also very often heed the views and judgments of experts in each profession; private persons are equally compelled to do so to the extent that they find it inconvenient to appear at the examination proper. Thus a child, or other human whose condition is but little better in this respect, is obliged, whenever he finds himself in a certain situation, to follow the religion of the country so long as he sees nothing wrong in it and is in no position to inquire whether there is a better one. A supervisor of pages, whatever his own sect, will compel each of them to go to the church of those who profess the same belief as this young man. We may consult the disputes between Mr. Nicole and others on *the argument from the majority* in matters of faith, in which sometimes too much deference is given to it and at other times too little consideration. There are other similar preconceived judgments by which men too easily evade discussion. They are what Tertullian, in a treatise, expressly called *prescriptions* [against heretics appealing to Scriptures in their own defense], using a term which the old jurisconsults (whose language was not unknown to him) intended for several sorts of exceptions or irrelevant and incompetent allegations, but which today means simply the temporal injunction against another's claim because it was not made in the time fixed by law. Thus there was reason for making public the *legitimate prejudgments* on the part of both the Roman Church and the Protestants. For example, both have found means of opposing novelty in each church respectively: when the Protestants for the most part abandoned the old form of ordination of clergymen, and when the Romanists changed the old canon of the Old Testament in Holy Scripture, as I have shown clearly enough in a dispute I had with the Bishop of Meaux [Bossuet], who has just died, according to the news which came a few days ago. Thus, while these censures are reciprocal, although novelty gives rise to some suspicion of error, it is not a certain proof of error.

(From *New Essays,* bk. IV, ch. XVI)

. . . Jurisconsults in treating the proofs, presumptions, conjectures and indices have said a number of good
things on this subject (of degrees of assent), and have
entered into some considerable detail. They begin with
notoriety, where there is no need of proof. After that
they come to *entire proofs,* or those which pass as such,
on which they pronounce judgment, at least in a civil
suit, but in which in some localities they are more reserved
in a criminal action; and they are not wrong in demanding in such a case *more than full proof,* especially what
is called *corpus delecti* according to the nature of the
act. There are therefore *proofs more than full* as well as
customary *full proofs.* Then there are *presumptions*
which pass for entire proofs provisionally, that is to say,
so long as the contrary is not proved. There are *proofs
more than half complete* (to speak strictly) in which
the party who bases his action on them is permitted to
swear he will supply the rest; this is *juramentum sup-
pletorium;* there are others *less than half complete* in
which quite contrariwise the party that denies the act
is permitted on oath to purge himself (*juramentum
purgationis*). Beyond this there are many degrees of
conjecture and *indices.* And particularly in a criminal
case there are indices to proceed to the torture (*ad
torturam*) which itself has many degrees indicated by
the rules of arrest; there are indices (*ad terrendum*)
sufficient to show the instruments of torture and to pre-
pare things as though they were going to be applied.
There are some (*ad capturam*) to make sure of a suspect;
and some to make inquiries secretly and quietly (*ad
inquirendum*). And these differences may be useful again
on other corresponding occasions; the entire *form of
juridical procedures* is in fact nothing but a species of

Logic applied to questions of law. Physicians also have a number of degrees and differences in their *signs* and *indications* which may be seen among them.

The Mathematicians of our day have begun to estimate chances in connection with gambling games. Chevalier de Méré, whose *Agrémens* and other works have been printed, a man of penetrating mind who was both a gambler and a philosopher, provided the mathematicians an opportunity by forming questions about bets, in order to know how much the game would be worth if it were interrupted at such or such a stage. In that way he persuaded his friend Pascal to look into these things a little. The question aroused much interest and provided Huygens the occasion to write his treatise on chance (*De Alea*). Other scientific men got into the subject. They established some principles which the Pensioner De Witt used in a little treatise printed in Holland on annuities. The foundation on which he built goes back to *prosthaphaeresis,* that is, to taking an arithmetical mean among several equally acceptable hypotheses, and our peasants have long used it in doing their natural mathematics. For example, when some inheritance or land is to be sold they form three groups of estimators; these groups are called *Schurzen* in Low Saxon, and each group makes an estimate of the property in question. Then suppose that the first estimates the value to be 1000 crowns, the second 1400, the third 1500; they take the sum of these three estimates which is 3900 and because there were three groups, they take a third or 1300 for the required mean value; or else, what amounts to the same thing, they take the sum of the third part of each estimate. That is the axiom of *aequalibus aequalia,* equal hypotheses must have equal weight. But when the hypotheses are unequal, we make comparisons among them. Let us suppose, for example, that with two dice one is to win if he rolls a 7 but his adversary is to win if he makes a 9; we ask what is the ratio of their probabilities of winning? I say that the latter's probability is only two thirds that of the first, for the first can make 7 in three ways (1 and 6, or 2 and 5, or 3 and 4) and the other can make 9 in only two ways (3 and 6, or 4 and 5). And all these ways are equally possible. Hence, the probabilities, which are to each other as the number of equal possibilities, will be in the ratio of 3 to 2, or as 1 to $\frac{2}{3}$. I have more than once said that we should have a *new kind of Logic* which would treat of degrees of probability, since Aristotle in his *Topics* has done nothing less than that, and was content with putting in order certain popular rules distributed according to common topics which may be useful on some occasion where it is a question of amplifying a speech and giving it some semblance of truth. But he did not take the trouble to give us a necessary balance to weigh probabilities and to form solid judgments accordingly. It would be well for future investigators of this matter to pursue the examination of *games of chance*; and in general I should wish some skilful mathematician might want to write an ample work, with full details and thought out well, on all sorts of games; this would be very useful for perfecting the art of discovery, the human mind revealing itself better in games than in the most serious matters.

(Letter to Bourguet, 1714)

Syllogistic Logic is truly demonstrative, just as Arithmetic or Geometry. I have in my youth demonstrated not only that there are really four figures, which is easy, but also that each figure has six useful moods, and cannot have either more or less, whereas ordinarily only four are given to the first and second, and five to the fourth. I have also proved that the second and third figures are derived immediately from the first without the intervention of the conversions which are themselves demonstrated by the second or third figure; but that the fourth is of lower degree and needs the intervention of the second or third, or (what is the same thing) conversions. The art of conjecture is based on what is more or less facile, or else more or less feasible, for the latin *facile* derived from *faciendo* means feasible. word for word; for example, with a pair of dice, it is as feasible to throw a twelve as to throw an eleven for each can only be made in one way; * but it is three times more feasible to throw a seven, for that can be made by throwing six and one, five and two, four and three, and one of these combinations is as feasible as the other. Chevalier de la Méré (author of *Livre des Agrémens*) was the first to have given occasion to those meditations which Pascal, Fermat, and Huyghens pursued. The Pensioner De Witt and Hudde have also worked on these questions since. Lately Bernouilli has cultivated the matter at my exhortation. Probabilities are estimated *a posteriori* by experience; and we should take recourse to it in the absence of *a priori* reasons; for example, it is equally probable that a child about to be born is a boy, as a girl, because the numbers of boys and girls are found to be nearly equal in this world. We may say that what happens more or less is also more or less feasible in the present state of things, putting all the considerations together which should concur in the production of a fact.

* Leibniz erred here in not considering *two* ways in which the dice may turn up 11: 6 and 5 *or* 5 and 6; hence, the probability of 11 turning up is twice that of 12 which can happen in only one way. D'Alembert made a similar error when he calculated the probability of two heads with a coin thrown twice was $\frac{1}{3}$ instead of $\frac{1}{4}$.

15. ON GEOMETRICAL METHOD AND METHOD OF METAPHYSICS
[Mémoires de Trévoux, July 1712]

. . . It is laudable to wish to apply the geometrical method to metaphysical matters, but we must admit that until now it has rarely been done with success. Monsieur Descartes himself with all his undeniably great skill never had less success than when he attempted it in one of his Replies to Objections.* For it is easier to be successful in Mathematics where numbers, diagrams, and calculations make up for the hidden defects of words; but in Metaphysics where we lack such aids (at least in usual matters of reasoning), what has to make up for that lack is a rigorous form of reasoning and exact definitions of terms; but we see neither there. . . .

**. . . As everything in geometry can be explained by calculation with numbers and also by an analysis of the spatial situation, but certain problems are more easily solved by the first of these two methods and others by the second, in the same way I find there are diverse ways of considering phenomena. Everything can be explained by efficient and by final causes; but whatever concerns reasonable substances (the minds of men) is more naturally explained by the consideration of ends, whereas other substances (bodies) are better explained by efficient causes.

* Cf. *Secundae responsiones* in Adam and Tannery edition of Descartes (Paris, 1904), VII, 155 ff., translated in part by T. V. Smith and Marjorie Grene, *From Descartes to Kant* (Chicago, 1940), 154 ff.

** The following paragraph is translated from Couturat, *Opuscules et fragments inédits de Leibniz* (Paris, 1903), p. 329.

II. FIRST PRINCIPLES: FOUNDATIONS OF THE SCIENCES

1. ON ARISTOTLE'S AND DESCARTES' THEORIES OF MATTER
[Fragment, c. 1671]

Aristotle's primary matter is the same as Descartes' ethereal matter. Each is infinitely subdivisible. Each inherently lacks form and motion, and each acquires forms as a result of motion. In each, mind is the source of motion. Whirls are produced without solidity in Aristotle's as well as in Descartes' vortices. The cause of solidity in each is a motion greater than any which can break it up, though this is not how Descartes explains it. Each whirl propagates any action it receives through motion to another whirl because of the continuity of matter. For Aristotle, as well as Descartes and Hobbes, makes all particular motions depend on the universal circular motion of whirls. Hence, the principal circular motions alone possess intelligence for Aristotle, because it is their action which produces all other action. Aristotle fell into error when he made the earth the center of the universe and all its rotations. But this was a pardonable error since natural philosophy had not yet been sufficiently guided by observation.

My emendation is that *primary matter is nothing if considered at rest.* Certain Scholastics have expressed this more obscurely when they said that form gives existence to primary matter. But a proof can be given of this. For whatever is unthinking is nothing, and whatever lacks variety is unthinking. Now if primary matter simply moves in one direction in parallel lines, *it is uniformly at rest,* and consequently is nothing. But *all things are full* in so far as primary matter is identical with space. Hence, *all motion is circular,* or composed of circular motions, or those returning into themselves. Many of the circular motions oppose each other, and many blend into each other. Many try to unite in one, tending to make bodies come to rest or annihilation of motion. *If bodies are devoid of mind, it is impossible for motion ever to be eternal. Particular bodies are produced by conflicting universal circular motions. Matter is actually divided into infinite parts. There are infinite creatures in any given body whatever. All bodies form a coherent whole. All are separable by force from the others, but not without resistance. There are no atoms,* or bodies whose parts are never separable by force. There are two principles through which motion is changed: the one governing the compositions of efforts (*conatum*), and the other the compositions . . . [The fragment breaks off here.]

2. THE EXIGENCY TO EXIST IN ESSENCES: PRINCIPLE OF PLENITUDE *

From the conflict of all the possibles demanding existence, this at once follows, that there exists that series of things by which as many of them as possible exist; in other words, the maximal series of possibilities . . . And as we see liquids spontaneously and by their

* The following paragraphs except the last are from passages quoted and translated by Arthur O. Lovejoy in his penetrating discussion of the principle of plenitude in Leibniz: *The Great Chain of Being, A Study of the History of an Idea* (Cambridge, Mass., Harvard University Press, 1936), pp. 177 f. The last paragraph is from *Leibnitiana, Elementa philosophiae arcanae,* ed. Jagodinsky (Kazan, 1913), pp. 28 f. See also *The Monadology,* § 54, below (III 13).

own nature gather into spherical drops, so in the nature of the universe the series which has the greatest capacity (*maxime capax*) exists.

. . . Every possible is characterized by a striving (*conatus*) towards existence, and may be said to be destined to exist, provided, that is, it is grounded in a necessary being actually existing.

. . . The sufficient reason for God's choice can be found only in the fitness (*convenance*) or in the degrees of perfection that the several worlds possess, since each possible thing has the right to aspire to existence in proportion to the amount of perfection it contains in germ.

. . . To say that some essences have an inclination to exist and others do not, is to say something without reason, since existence seems to be universally related to every essence in the same manner.

. . . If there were not some inclination inherent in the nature of essence to exist, nothing would exist.

. . . Perfection is to be placed in form [i.e., as the context shows, in *quantity* of forms], or variety; whence it follows that matter is not everywhere uniform, but is diversified by assuming different forms; otherwise, as much variety as possible would not be realized. . . . It follows likewise that that series prevails through which there can arise the greatest possibility of thinking of things as distinct (*distincta cogitabilitas*) . . . The actual universe is the collection of the possibles which forms the richest composite.

. . . We must say [writes Leibniz to Malebranche] that God makes the greatest number of things that he can and [by means of the simplest laws of nature] to find room for as many things as it is possible to place together. If God had made use of other laws, it would be as if one should construct a building of round stones

which leave more space unoccupied than that which they
fill.

. . . For a thing to be rightly estimated, I state as
a principle the Harmony of things, that is, the greatest
amount of essence exists that is possible. It follows that
there is more reason in the existence of a thing than in
its non-existence. And everything would exist if that
were possible. . . . The most Perfect Being is the one
that contains the most of essence. Quality is being, capable of having ideas and reflections, for this multiplies the
varieties of things as a mirror does.

2a. THE PRINCIPLE OF SUFFICIENT REASON

All other developments depend on the principle that
the whole is greater than the part, as everything Euclid
established in his *Elements* with the sole aid of addition
and subtraction; on the other hand, the determination of
the resultant *conatus* of two forces (equal but acting in
different directions) depends on a principle of higher
rank: *Nothing happens without a reason.* The consequences of this principle are that we must avoid unstable
changes as much as possible, that between contraries
the middle term should be selected, that we may add
what we please to a term provided no other term is
harmed by doing so; and there are still many other
consequences which are important in political science.
. . . This most noble principle of sufficient reason is the
apex of rationality in motion.* . . .

* From *Theoria motus abstracti* (sec. 23–4), 1671. Cf. Gerhardt, *Die philosophischen Schriften von G. W. Leibniz* (Berlin,
1875–90), IV, 232. The next six paragraphs are translated also
from Gerhardt's edition in the following order: VII, 309; VII,
199; IV, 438; II, 40; II, 181. The last undated and untitled fragment is translated from Bodemann's *Catalogue of the Leibniz
MSS. in the Royal Public Library at Hanover* (1895).

[c. 1686]

There are two first principles of all reasonings, the principle of contradiction . . . . and the principle that a reason must be given, *i.e.,* that every true proposition which is not known *per se,* has an *a priori* proof, or that a reason can be given for every truth, or, as is commonly said, that nothing happens without a cause. Arithmetic and Geometry do not need this principle, but Physics and Mechanics do, and Archimedes employed it. . . .

In demonstration I use two principles, of which one is that what implies a contradiction is false, the other is that a reason can be given for every truth (which is not identical or immediate), that is, that the notion of the predicate is always expressly or implicitly contained in the notion of its subject, and that this holds good no less in extrinsic than in intrinsic denominations, no less in contingent than in necessary truths. . . .

The demonstration of this predicate of Caesar (that he resolved to cross the Rubicon) is not as absolute as those of numbers or of Geometry, but presupposes the series of things which God has chosen freely, and which is founded on the first free decree of God, namely, to do always what is most perfect, and on the decree which God has made (in consequence of the first), in regard to human nature, that man will always do (though freely) what appears best. Now every truth which is founded on decrees of this kind is contingent, although it is certain. . . . All contingent propositions have reasons for being as they are rather than otherwise, or (what is the same thing) they have *a priori* proofs of their truth, which render them certain, and show that the connection of subject and predicate in these propositions has its foundation in the nature of the one and the other; but they do not have demonstrations of necessity, since these reasons are only founded on the principle of contingency, or of the existence of things, *i.e.,* on what is or appears the best among several equally possible things. . . .

As there are an infinity of possible worlds, there are also an infinity of laws, some proper to one, others to another, and each possible individual of any world contains in its own notion the laws of its world. . . .

I think you will concede that not everything possible exists. . . . But when this is admitted, it follows that it is not from absolute necessity, but from some other reason (as good, order, perfection) that some possibles obtain existence rather than others.

(From Letter to Des Bosses, 1711)

In my opinion, if there were no best possible series, God would have certainly created nothing, since he cannot act without a reason, or prefer the less perfect to the more perfect. . . .

(Undated)

Another principle, hardly less general in application than the principle of contradiction, applies to the nature of freedom—*viz.,* the principle that nothing ever happens without the possibility that an omniscient mind could give some reason why it should have happened rather than not. Furthermore, it seems to me that this principle is of exactly the same use to us in contingent things as the principle of contradiction is in necessary things. That is why the laws of motion depend on it; they are not geometrically necessary but originate in the will of God, governed by reason. Now since the principle of contradiction is the principle of necessity, and the principle that a sufficient reason must be given is the principle of contingency, it seems to me that freedom cannot be an exception to these principles. Archimedes takes it for granted that a balance will not tip more in óne direction than in the other when there is perfect equality on both sides; and similarly, in reasoning about morals and politics for the purpose of discovering the causes of human actions, we avail ourselves tacitly of the same assumption that there is always a reason or cause which inclines the will. . . . It seems that the soul is never in that state of complete indifference in which nothing can affect it internally or externally. There is always a reason or greater inclination behind what we in fact choose to do; our choice may depend not only on arguments, good or bad, but also on passions, habits, dispositions of the organs of thought, external impressions, greater or less attention, etc. This does not destroy freedom although it inclines it.

2b. IDENTITY IN INDIVIDUALS AND TRUE PROPOSITIONS
[1686]

In my opinion each individual substance always contains the marks of whatever has happened to it and the features of that which will ever happen to it. . . . Now every individual substance of this universe expresses in its concept the universe into which it has entered. . . .

I am quite convinced regarding what St. Thomas has taught about intelligences, and what I hold to be true in general, namely, that it is not possible for two individuals to exist completely identical, that is, to differ only numerically. . . .

Let a certain straight line A B C represent a certain time, and let a certain individual, say myself, endure or exist during this period. Then let us consider the me

which exists during the time A B and the me which exists
during the time B C. Now, since we suppose that it is
the same individual substance which persists in me
during the time A B while I am in Paris and during the
time B C while I am in Germany, there must be some
reason why we can truly say that I persist or to say that
it is the same I who was in Paris and is now in Germany;
if there were not a reason, then it would be quite right
to say it was not I but another person. To be sure,
introspection convinces me *a posteriori* of this identity,
but there must also be some *a priori* reason. It is not
possible to find any other reason than the fact that my
attributes of the preceding time and state as well as the
attributes of the succeeding time and state are all predicates of the same subject (*in sunt eidem subjecto*).
Now, what is it to say that the predicate is in the
subject if not that the concept of the predicate is in
some manner involved in the concept of the subject?
Since from the very time that I began to exist it could
be truly said of me that this or that would happen to me,
we must grant that these predicates were principles involved in the subject or in the complete concept of me
which constitutes the so-called ego and is the basis of
the interconnection of all my different states. These
have been known to God from all eternity. . . . When I
say that the individual concept of Adam entails all that
will ever happen to him, I mean no more than what
philosophers understand when they say that the predicate
is contained in the subject of true propositions. . . .

My idea of a true proposition is such that every predicate, necessary or contingent, past, present, or future, is
included in the idea of the subject. . . . This is a very
important proposition that deserves to be well established, for it follows that every soul is as a world
apart, independent of everything else but God; that it

is not only immortal and impenetrable but retains in its
substance traces of everything that happens to it. It also
determines what the relations of communication among
substances shall be, and in particular, the union of the
soul and body. The latter is not explained by the ordinary hypothesis of the physical influence of one on the
other, for each present state of a substance occurs in it
spontaneously, and is nothing but a consequence of its
preceding state. Nor does the hypothesis of occasional
causes explain how it happens, as Descartes and his followers imagine. . . . My hypothesis of concomitant
harmony appears to me to demonstrate how it happens.
That is to say, every substance expresses the whole
sequence of the universe in accordance with its own viewpoint or relationship to the rest, so that all are in perfect
correspondence with one another.*

2c. ON THE ACTUAL INFINITE
[From *Specimen calculi universalis,* c. 1679]

The difference between necessary and contingent
truths is indeed the same as that between commensurable
and incommensurable numbers. For the reduction of
commensurate numbers to a common measure is analogous to the demonstration of necessary truths, or their
reduction to such as are identical. But as, in the case
of surd ratios, the reduction involves an infinite process,
and yet approaches a common measure, so that a definite
but unending series is obtained, so also contingent truths

---

* From Leibniz's "Remarks on Arnaud's letter concerning my
proposition: that the individual notion of each person includes
once for all everything that will ever happen to him," in a letter
to Hessen-Rheinfels, May, 1686.

require an infinite analysis, which God alone can accomplish. . . .

(Reply to Foucher, *Journal des Savans,* Aug. 3, 1693)

. . . As to indivisibles, while they are understood as the simple extremities of time or of line, they cannot be conceived as containing new extremities of either actual or potential parts. Whence, points are neither big nor small, and no jump is necessary to pass through them. However, the continuous, though it everywhere has such indivisibles, is definitely not composed of them, as sceptics seem to assume in their objections (which to my mind are not at all insurmountable, once they are drawn up formally). Father Gregory of Saint Vincent has very well shown by the very calculation of infinite divisibility the place where Achilles should catch the tortoise ahead of him, according to the ratio of their speeds. Thus Geometry serves to dissipate these apparent difficulties.

I am so much for the actual infinite that instead of admitting that nature abhors it, as is commonly said, I hold that it affects nature everywhere in order to indicate the perfections of its Author. So I believe that every part of matter is, I do not say divisible, but actually divided, and consequently the smallest particle should be considered as a world full of an infinity of creatures. . . .

(Letter to Bernouilli, 1698)

In fact many years ago I proved that the number or sum of all numbers involves a contradiction (the whole would equal the part). The same is true of an absolutely greatest number and of an absolutely smallest number (or absolutely smallest fraction).

. . . Just as there is no smallest number or smallest element less than and a part of unity, so there is no smallest line or line-element; for a line like unity can be cut into parts or fractions. . . . For suppose all the subdivisions of a line, $\frac{1}{2}$, $\frac{1}{4}$, $\frac{1}{8}$, $\frac{1}{16}$, $\frac{1}{32}$, etc., actually existed. To infer from this series that an infinitieth term absolutely exists would be an error, for I think nothing more follows from it than that there exists an assignable finite fraction as small as you please. . . . Hence, I conceive points, not as elements of a line, but as limits or termini of a line, bounding further elements.*

3. WHETHER THE ESSENCE OF A BODY CONSISTS IN EXTENSION
[*Journal des Savans,* June 18, 1691]

If the essence of a body consisted in extension, this extension alone should suffice to account for all the properties of the body. But that is not the case. We observe in matter a quality which some have called *natural inertia,* through which the body resists motion in some manner, in such wise that some force must be applied to set it into motion (not even taking into account the weight), so that it is more difficult to budge a large body than a small one. For example, if the body A in

Fig. 1   ○   □
            A   B

motion meets the body B at rest, it is clear that if B were indifferent to motion or rest, it would let itself be pushed by A without resisting it and without diminishing the speed or changing the direction of A; and after the impact, A would continue its path and B would accompany it ahead. But it is not so in nature. The larger the body B, the more it will diminish the speed

* See the selection from the New Essays, Book II, Chapter XVII (III, 6 below) for a later discussion by Leibniz of infinity.

of A until A is forced to rebound from B if B is very much larger than A. Now, *if there were nothing more in bodies than extension* or position, that is to say, what Geometers know about it, combined with the sole notion of change, this extension would be entirely indifferent with respect to this change, and the results of the impact of the bodies would be explained solely by the Geometric composition of the motions. That is, *the body after the impact would continue with a motion composed of the impulsion it had before the impact and the one it would receive from the colliding body in failing to stop its motion;* that is to say, *in this case of collision,* it would travel with the difference of the two velocities and in the resultant direction. . . . The moving body would (on this hypothesis) carry along the body B which is at rest, without receiving any diminution of its velocity, and without any possible change arising from the equal or unequal magnitudes of the bodies; this is a consequence which is entirely *irreconcilable with experiments.* And if we should assume properly that magnitude ought to cause a change in the motion, we should not have any principle to determine the way to calculate it in detail in order to know the resultant direction and speed. In any case, one would incline to the opinion of the conservation of motion, whereas I believe I have demonstrated (in *Actis Erudit.,* 1686) that the force itself is conserved and that the quantity of force is different from the quantity of motion.

All of this shows that there is in matter something else than the purely Geometrical, that is, than just extension and bare change. And in considering the matter closely, we perceive that we must add to them some *higher or metaphysical notion, namely, that of substance, action, and force;* and these notions imply that anything which *is acted on* must act reciprocally, and *anything which acts must receive some reaction;* consequently, a body at rest should not be carried off by another body in motion without changing something of the direction and speed of the acting body.

I still agree that naturally every body is extended and that there is no extension without body. None the less we must not confound the notions of place, space, or of pure extension with the notion of substance which, besides extension, includes resistance, that is to say, action and passivity.

This consideration appears to me important not only in order to know the nature of extended substance but also in order not to prejudice piety by scorning higher and immaterial principles in Physics. For although I am convinced that everything in corporeal nature is done mechanically, I also continue to maintain that the very principles of Mechanics, that is, the first laws of motion, have a more sublime origin than those furnished by pure Mathematics. And I imagine that if that were better known or considered, many pious persons would not have so low an opinion of corpuscular Philosophy, and that modern Philosophers would combine better the knowledge of nature with that of its Author.

I do not expatiate on other reasons touching the nature of body; for that would take me too far.

3a. FURTHER DISCUSSION OF THE SAME SUBJECT
[*Journal des Savans,* 1693]

In order to prove that *the nature of bodies does not consist in extension,* I had made use of an argument (explained in the *Journal des Savans* of June 18, 1691) based on the fact that we cannot account for *the natural inertia of bodies* by extension alone; that is to say, extension cannot by itself explain the fact that matter resists motion, or else the fact that a body already in motion cannot carry along with it another body at rest without having its own motion retarded. For since extension in itself is indifferent to motion or rest, nothing should prevent the two bodies from accompanying each other with all the velocity of the first which it tries to impress upon the second. To that a reply is given, in the *Journal* of July 16, 1691 (as I have only recently learned), that *in effect the body should be indifferent to motion or rest, assuming that its essence consists solely in being extended,* but that nonetheless a body about to push another body should be retarded by it (not on account of extension but on account of force) because *the same force which was applied to one of the bodies is now applied to both.* Now the force which moves one of the bodies with a certain velocity should move the two together with less velocity. This amounts to saying in other terms that body if it consists in extension should be indifferent to motion; but that in effect not being indifferent, since it resists the body which is to give it motion, we must employ in addition to the notion of *extension* that of *force.* But this reply grants exactly what I ask. And in fact those who favor the system of occasional causes have already well realized that force and the laws of motion dependent on it cannot be extracted from extension alone. And as they have taken for granted that only extension is involved, they have been obliged to refuse force and action in it and to take recourse to the most general cause, the pure will and action of God. In doing this it may be said that they have reasoned very well from a hypothesis (*ex hypothesi*). But the hypothesis has not yet been demonstrated; and as the conclusion appears to be scarcely suitable for Physics, it is more pertinent to say that there is some defect in the hypothesis (which suffers from other difficulties) and that we should recognize in matter something more than what consists in an exclusive relationship to extension. The latter, just like space, is incapable of action and resistance which belong only to substances. Those who want to make extension itself a substance reverse the order of words as well as that of thoughts. In addition to extension there must be a subject that is extended, that is to say, a substance in which it is proper to have repetition and continuity. For *the extended signifies* but the repetition and continued multiplicity of what is spread out, a *plurality, continuity, and co-existence of parts,* and consequently, it does not suffice to explain the very nature of the substance spread out or repeated, whose notion is prior to that of its repetition.

(Letter to Father Bouvet in Paris, 1697)

I see that a number of able people believe that the *Scholastic Philosophy* must be abolished, and an entirely different one substituted for it, several wishing it to be the *Cartesian* philosophy. But after weighing the matter, I find the philosophy of the ancients solid and that we must use the philosophy of the moderns not to destroy but to enrich that of the ancients. I have had many disputes on that score with some able Cartesians, and have shown them by mathematics itself that they do not have the true laws of nature, and that to obtain them we must consider not only matter but also force in nature, and that the old forms or *Entelechies* are nothing but forces. In that way I believe in rehabilitating the ancient or scholastic philosophy which is so useful to theology without derogating from any of the modern discoveries or mechanical explanations, since mechanics itself pre-supposes the consideration of force. And it will be found that nothing is more suited to encourage the considera-tion of spiritual causes than force in corporeal phe-nomena, and thus to introduce spiritual things to men buried in materialistic notions, as the Chinese no doubt are. Hence, I believe I have rendered some service to religion in that respect as in the fact that I hope it will contribute a great deal to stop the course of a too materialistic philosophy beginning to take hold of minds, in so far as I show that the reasons for the laws of force come from a higher source.

The true practical philosophy (*the true and not simu-lated philosophy,* as our Roman jurisconsults say) con-sists in good rules for education, intercourse and so-ciability among men, rather than in general precepts on virtues and duties.

I come now to Physics, and I include under that name all experimental observations of corporeal things which we cannot yet explain by geometrical or mechanical principles. For they have not been obtained by *a priori* reason but by experiment and tradition.

Medicine is the most necessary of the natural sciences. For just as theology is the highest point of the knowl-edge of things regarding the mind, containing sound morals and sound politics, we can say that medicine is the highest point and like the principal fruit of the knowl-edge of bodies in relation to ours. But all physical science, including medicine itself, aims in the end at the glory of God and the highest happiness of men, for by pre-serving men it gives them the means to work for the glory of God.

4. NEW SYSTEM OF NATURE AND OF THE COMMUNICATION OF SUBSTANCES, AS WELL AS OF THE UNION OF SOUL AND BODY

[*Journal des Savans,* June 27, 1695]

1. Several years ago I conceived this system and communicated with some learned men about it, especially with one of the greatest theologians and philosophers of our time [Mons. Arnauld] who, having learnt some of my thoughts through a person of the highest quality, had found them quite paradoxical. But after receiving my elucidations, he changed his attitude in the most generous and edifying way in the world; and having approved a part of my propositions, he withdrew his censure regarding the rest of them with which he had still remained in disagreement. Since then I have on occasions continued my meditations in order to give the public only well examined opinions, and I have tried thus to satisfy objections made against my Essays on Dynamics (*Act. Erudit.,* April 1695) connected with this one. Now, at last, since important persons have desired to see my thoughts elucidated more, I have hazarded these meditations, though they are in no way popular nor appropriately served to any kind of mind. I have brought myself to do it mainly in order to profit by the judgments of those who are enlightened in these matters; for it would be too embarrassing to seek and summon in particular all those who would be disposed to give me instructions, which I shall always be very glad to receive, provided the love of truth appears in them rather than a passion for prejudiced opinions.

2. Although I am one of those who have worked hard on mathematics, I have not ceased meditating on philosophy since my youth, for it always seemed to me

there was a means to establish in philosophy something solid through clear demonstrations. I had penetrated far into the land of the scholastics when mathematics and the modern authors made me emerge from it while I was still young. I was charmed by their beautiful ways of explaining Nature mechanically, and I despised with reason the method of those who use only forms or faculties from which nothing is learnt. But since, having tried to lay the foundations of the very principles of mechanics in order to give a rational account of the laws of nature known to us by experiment, I realized that the sole consideration of an extended mass did not suffice, and that we must again employ the notion of force which is very intelligible despite its springing from metaphysics. It seemed to me also that the opinion of those who transform or degrade animals into pure machines, though a possible one apparently, is against appearances, and even against the order of things.

3. In the beginning when I had freed myself from the yoke of Aristotle, I had taken to the void and the atoms, for they best fill the imagination; but on recovering from that, after many reflections, I realized that it is impossible to find the principles of *a true unity* in matter alone or in that which is only passive, since everything in it is only a collection or mass of parts to infinity. Now multitude can only get its reality from *true unities* which come from elsewhere and are quite different from points (it is known that the continuum cannot be composed of points). Therefore to find these *real unities* I was compelled to have recourse to a formal atom, since a material being cannot be both material and perfectly indivisible or endowed with a true unity. It was necessary, hence, to recall and, so to speak, rehabilitate the *substantial forms* so decried today, but in a way which would make them intelligible and which would separate

the use we should make of them from the abuse that has
been made of them. I thence found that their nature consists in force, and that from that there ensues something
analogous to feeling and appetite; and that accordingly
they must be conceived in imitation of the idea we have
of Souls. But as the soul should never be used to explain
any detail of the economy of the animal's body, I judged
likewise that these forms must not be used to explain
the particular problems of nature though they are necessary to establish true general principles. Aristotle calls
them *first Entelechies*. I call them perhaps more intelligibly, *primitive Forces* which do not contain only the
act or the complement of possibility, but further an
original activity.

4. I saw that these forms and these souls should be
indivisible, as our mind is, remembering indeed that that
was the thought of Saint Thomas regarding the souls
of animals. But this truth renewed the great difficulties
of the origin and duration of souls and forms. For every
substance, being a true unity and not capable of beginning or ceasing to exist without a miracle, it follows that
they can only begin by creation and end only by annihilation. Thus, except the souls that God wishes still to
create expressly, I was obliged to recognize that it is
necessary that the forms constitutive of substances should
have been created with the world and that they should
subsist forever. Thus a few scholastics like Albert the
Great and John Bacon had glimpsed a part of the truth
about their origin. And that should not appear extraordinary, since we are only giving to forms the duration
which the Gassendists give to their atoms.

5. I judged, however, that we must not be indifferent
to the different grades of minds or reasonable souls, the
higher orders being incomparably more perfect than
those forms buried in matter, being like little Gods by

contrast with the latter, and are made in the image of God, having in them some ray of the light of Divinity. That is why God governs minds as a Prince governs his subjects, and even as a father cares for his children, whereas he disposes of other substances as an engineer manipulates his machines. Thus minds have particular laws which put them above the revolutions of matter; and we may say that everything else is made only for them, these very revolutions being accommodated for the happiness of the good and the punishment of the wicked.

6. Nevertheless, giving back to ordinary forms or *material* souls that duration which must be attributed to them in the place of what had been attributed to atoms, might arouse the suspicion that they go from one body to another, which would be *metempsychosis,* almost as some philosophers have believed in the propagation of motion and that of species. But this is a piece of imagination far removed from the nature of things. There is no such passage; and this is where the 'metamorphoses' of Messrs. Swammerdam, Malpighi, and Leeuwenhoeck, who are excellent observers in our day, have come to my aid, and have made me admit more confidently that the animal as every other organized substance has no beginning, though we think so, and that its apparent generation is only a development and a kind of augmentation. Thus I have noticed that the author of the *Recherche de la Vérité* [Malebranche], Mr. Regis, Mr. Hartsoeker, and other able men, have not been very far from having this thought.

7. But there still remained the biggest question, what becomes of these souls or forms after the death of the animal or the destruction of the individual with organized substance? And that is a most embarrassing problem; in so far as it scarcely seems reasonable for souls to remain

uselessly in a chaos of confused matter. That made me finally judge that there was only one single reasonable line to take, and that is the conservation not only of the soul but also of the animal itself and its organic machine even though the destruction of the gross parts may have reduced it to a smallness which is as much beyond our senses as it was before being born. Thus nobody can really observe the true time of death; the latter may pass a long time for a simple suspension of noticeable actions, and at bottom is never anything else in simple animals: witness the resuscitations of drowned flies buried under pulverized chalk, and several other similar examples which make us sufficiently aware that there would be many other resuscitations, and even more than that, if men were able to restore the machine. And there is some evidence apparently that something of that sort was discussed by the great Democritus, atomist that he was, though Pliny makes fun of him. It is, hence, natural that the animal having always been alive and organized (as some persons of great penetration are beginning to recognize), he remains so always. And since there is no first birth nor entirely new generation of the animal, it follows that there will not be any final extinction, nor any complete death taken in a strict metaphysical sense. Consequently, instead of the transmigration of souls, there is only a transformation of the same animal, according to the different ways the organs are unfolded and more or less developed.

8. However, reasonable souls follow much higher laws and are exempt from anything which might make them lose the quality of being citizens of the society of spirits. God has so well seen to it that no changes of matter can make them lose the moral qualities of their personality. And we may say that everything tends to the perfection, not solely of the universe in general, but also of those

creatures in particular who are destined to such a degree of happiness that the Universe finds itself interested by virtue of the divine goodness which is communicated to each one as much as the sovereign Wisdom may permit.

9. Concerning the ordinary course of animals and other corporeal susbtances whose complete extinction has been accepted until now, and whose changes depend on mechanical rather than on moral laws, I noticed with pleasure that the ancient author of the book *On Diet,* attributed to Hippocrates, had glimpsed something of the truth when he said explicitly that animals are not born and do not die, and that the things believed to begin and to perish only appear and disappear. That is the thought also of Parmenides and of Melissus, according to Aristotle. For these ancients were more solid than people believe.

10. I am the most readily disposed person in the world to do justice to the moderns; however, I find they have carried reform too far. Among other things, they confuse natural with artificial things for lack of insufficiently broad ideas about the majesty of nature. They conceive the difference existing between her machines and ours to be only one of size, Nature's being larger. This view has recently led a very able man (Fontenelle), the author of *Entretiens sur la pluralité des Mondes* (*Dialogues on the plurality of worlds*), to say that on looking closely at Nature, we find her less admirable than we had thought, and more like the shop of a working man. I believe that that view does not give us a worthy enough idea of her. Only in my system is one able to realize at last the true and immense distance between the smallest productions and mechanisms of divine wisdom and the greatest masterpieces of art of a limited mind, this difference being not simply one of degree but of very kind. We must then know that Nature's machines have a truly

infinite number of organs, and are so well supplied and resistant to all accidents that it is impossible to destroy them. A natural machine still remains a machine in its least parts, and furthermore, it remains forever the same machine that it has been, being only transformed by the different habits it takes on, at one time expansive, at another restrictive and concentrated, when believed to be lost.

11. Besides, by means of the soul or form, there is a true unity which answers to what is called the Ego in us. This cannot take place in the machines of art, nor in the simple mass of matter no matter how organized it is. Matter can only be considered like an army or herd, or like a pond full of fish, or like a watch made up of springs and wheels. However, if there were no true substantial unities, there would be nothing substantial or real in the collection. That was what forced Mr. Cordemoi to abandon Descartes and embrace the Democritean doctrine of atoms in order to find a true unity. But *material atoms* are contrary to reason, apart from the fact that they are still composed of parts, since the invincible attachment of one part to the other (if one could conceive or suppose it with reason) would not destroy their multitude. There are only *substantial atoms,* that is to say, real unities, absolutely destitute of parts, which are the sources of actions; they are the first absolute principles of the composition of things, and like the last elements of the analysis of substances. They might be called *metaphysical points*: they have *something vital* and a kind of perception; *mathematical points* are their *point of view* for expressing the Universe. But when corporeal substances are close together, all their organs together make only one *physical point* relatively to us. Thus physical points are indivisible only in appearance; mathematical points are exact, but they are only modali-

ties; only metaphysical or substantial points (constituted by forms or souls) are exact *and* real; without them there would be nothing real, since without true unities there would be no multitude.

12. After establishing these things, I thought I had arrived in port; but when I began to meditate on the union of the soul with the body, I was cast back, as it were, into the open sea. For I found no way of explaining how the body causes something to happen in the soul, or *vice versa;* nor how a substance can communicate with another created substance. Descartes had given up the game on that point, so far as we can know from his writings; but his disciples seeing that the common opinion is inconceivable judged that we feel the qualities of bodies because God causes thoughts to arise in the soul on the occasion of the movements of matter, and when our soul wishes in its turn to move the body they judged that it is God who moves it for the soul. And as the communication of the movements appeared to them inconceivable again, they believed that God gives movement to a body on the occasion of the movement of another body. That is what they call the *System of Occasional Causes,* which has been made very fashionable through the beautiful reflections of the author of the *Recherche de la Vérité.*

13. It must be admitted that by noting what cannot be the case concerning the soul and body, the Cartesians have at least penetrated to the difficulty, but it has not been alleviated by simply describing what in fact happens. In strict metaphysical language, there is very truly no real influence of one created substance on another, all things with all their realities being continually produced by the power of God; but in order to solve problems it is not enough to employ the general cause and to invoke what is called *Deus ex machinâ.* For when that

is done without any other explanation drawn from the order of secondary causes, recourse is being taken to miracle, properly speaking. In philosophy we must try to give reasons by showing in what way things are brought about by divine wisdom in conformity with the notion of the subject under investigation.

14. Therefore, though I was obliged to agree that it is impossible for the soul, or any other true substance, to receive any influence from the outside except through divine omnipotence, I was gradually led to a thought which surprised me but seems to me inevitable and indeed has very great advantages and a very considerable attraction. That is, we must say that God has from the first created the soul or any other real unity in such a way that everything arises in it from its own internal nature through a perfect *spontaneity* relatively to itself, and yet with a perfect *conformity* to external things. Thus our internal thoughts, that is, those in the soul itself and not in the brain nor in the subtle parts of the body (which are only phenomena following on external beings, or else, true appearances, like well ordered dreams), these perceptions internal to the soul itself, must happen to it through its own original constitution, that is to say, through its representative nature (capable of expressing beings outside itself by the mediation of its organs) given to it since its creation and constituting its individual character. And that is what makes each one of these substances represent, each exactly in its own way, the whole universe from a certain point of view. The perceptions or expressions of external things occur in the soul at a fixed moment by virtue of its own laws, as in a world apart and as if there existed nothing but God and itself (to use a manner of speaking employed by a certain person [Mons. Foucher] of great spiritual elevation and famous for his holiness). There will be

a perfect harmony among all these substances which produces the same effect that would be noticed if they communicated mutually through that propagation of species or of qualities imagined by the common run of philosophers. Moreover, the organized mass in which the point of view of the soul lies, is expressed more proximately and finds itself in turn ready to act itself by obeying the laws of the bodily machine at the moment the soul wishes to act, without disturbing the laws of nature, the spirits and blood then having exactly the motions they need to correspond to the soul's passions and perceptions. It is this mutual relationship regulated in advance in each substance of the universe which produces what we call their communication, and which alone causes *the union of soul and body*.

15. This hypothesis is indeed possible. For why could not God first give to substance a nature or internal force which could produce in it, in an orderly way, everything which will happen to it (as in a *spiritual or formal automaton* but *free* in that it has a share of reason), that is, all the appearances or expressions it will have, and that, without the aid of any creature? All the more so since the nature of substance requires necessarily and conceals a progression or change without which it would not have the force to act. And this nature of the soul being representative of the universe in a very exact though more or less distinct manner, the series of representations produced in the soul will correspond naturally to the series of changes in the Universe itself: as, conversely, the body has also been accommodated to the soul in those transactions in which the soul is conceived as acting on external things. This is all the more reasonable in so far as bodies are made only for minds capable of entering into society with God and to appreciate his glory. Thus, as soon as one sees the possibility of this

hypothesis of harmonies, it is seen as most reasonable both for giving a marvelous idea of the harmony of the Universe and of the perfection of God's works.

16. There is to be discovered in it also this great advantage that instead of saying that we are free only in appearance in a way sufficient for practical life, as several intelligent persons have believed, we should rather say that we are determined only in appearance but that in strict metaphysical language we are perfectly independent relatively to the influence of all other creatures. This again puts in a marvelous light the immortality of our soul and the constantly uniform conservation of our individuality, perfectly well regulated by its own nature, protected from all external accidents, notwithstanding any appearance to the contrary. Never has a system put our elevation in greater evidence. Every mind being like a world apart, sufficient unto itself, independent of any other creature, containing the infinite, expressing the universe, is as enduring, as subsistent, and as absolute as the very universe of creatures. Thus one should judge that he ought to behave in the most proper way to contribute to the perfection of the society of all the minds which make their moral union in the City of God. We also have in our system a new and surprisingly clear proof of God's existence. For this perfect harmony of so many substances which have no mutual communication can only come from the common cause.

17. Besides all these advantages recommending this hypothesis, we may say that it is something more than a hypothesis, since it scarcely seems possible to explain the thing in any other intelligible way, and since several big difficulties which have until now worried minds seem to disappear by themselves when we have understood the system. Ordinary ways of speaking are still preserved quite well. For we can say that the substance whose dis-

position gives a reason for change in an intelligible way
(so that we can judge that other substances have been
harmonized with it on that point from the beginning,
according to the order of God's decree), such a substance
may be conceived in that respect as *acting* consequently
on the others. Thus the action of one substance on another is not the emission or transplantation of an entity,
as is commonly conceived, and cannot be taken reasonably except in the way I have just mentioned. It is true
that in matter we conceive very well both emissions and
receptions of parts through which many are right in
explaining all the phenomena of Physics mechanically;
but as the material mass is not a substance itself, it cannot be other than what I have just indicated.

18. These considerations, however metaphysical they
may appear, still have a marvelous use in Physics for
establishing the laws of motion, as our *Dynamics* will
enable us to show. For we can say that in the collision
of bodies each one suffers only through its own elasticity,
because of the movement already in it. And as to absolute motion, nothing can determine it mathematically,
since everything terminates in relations: which makes
for the perfect equivalence of hypotheses, e.g., in Astronomy; so that whatever number of bodies we take, we may
arbitrarily assign rest or any degree of velocity we
choose without being refuted by the phenomena of rectilinear, circular, or composite motion. However, it is
reasonable to attribute to bodies true movements following the supposition which gives a reason for phenomena
in the most intelligible manner, this denomination of
movement being in conformity with the notion of action
which we have just established.

4a. SECOND EXPLANATION OF THE SYSTEM OF THE COMMUNICATION OF SUBSTANCES

(Histoire des Ouvrages des Savans, Feb. 1696)

You do not understand, you say, how I could prove what I have proposed concerning the *Communication* or *Harmony* of two *Substances* as different as the *soul* is from the *body*. It is true that I believe I have found the way, and here is how I intend to satisfy you.

Imagine two clocks or watches in perfect agreement. That can happen in three ways:

(1) The first consists in a mutual influence.

(2) The second is to have a skillful worker continually adjust them and keep them in agreement.

(3) The third is to manufacture these two time-pieces with so much art and accuracy that their agreement is guaranteed thereafter.

Now substitute the *soul* and *body* for these two time-pieces; their agreement can be obtained through one of these three ways. The *way of influence* is that of popular philosophy; but as we cannot conceive of material particles which can pass from one of these substances to another, we must abandon this idea. The way of the *continual* assistance of the Creator is that of the system of occasional causes; but I hold that this introduces *Deus ex Machinâ* in a natural and ordinary occurrence where, according to reason, it ought not intervene except as it operates in all other natural things. Thus there remains only my hypothesis, that is, the way of *Harmony*. From the beginning God has made each of these two Substances of such a nature that each by following its own laws, given to it with its being, still agrees with the other, just as though there were a mutual influence or as though God always took a hand in it beyond his general

supervision of things. There is nothing further I have
to prove, unless you wish to ask that I prove God is
skillful enough to use this prearranged scheme, examples
of which we see even among men. Now assuming that he
can, you do see that this way is most admirable and most
worthy of God. You suspected that my explanation would
be opposed by the very different idea we have of the
mind and body; but you see now that nobody has better
established their independence. For while people are
compelled to explain the communication of mind and body
by a sort of miracle, there is cause for many people to
fear that the distinction between soul and body might
not be as real as they believe, since they have to go so
far in order to maintain it. I shall not be vexed if learned
persons sound out the thoughts I have just explained
to you.

5. SPECIMEN DYNAMICUM
(Part I of an *Essay on Dynamics*, 1695)

Ever since we first talked of a new *Science of Dynamics* yet to be established, a good many distinguished men
in various places have expressed their desire for a fuller
exposition of this science. Hence, since we do not now
have enough leisure to write a book, we should like to
offer here a sketch which might shed some light on the
subject, and which some day perhaps will be returned
to me with compound interest yielded by the elicited opinions of men who give as much attention to the power of
the intellect as to refinements of style. In any case their
judgment will be frankly appreciated, and we hope useful for the advancement of the work.

We have elsewhere explained that there was contained
in material things something which has to be added to

mere extension, and is really prior to it, viz., a natural *force* implanted by the Creator in all things. It does not consist in that mere "potentiality" with which scholastic philosophy seems to be content, but is characterized by an effort (*conatu*) or nisus which, were it not limited by a contrary effort would also come to complete realization. This tendency is often apparent directly to the senses, and also, even if not apparent to sensation, is, in my judgment, known everywhere in matter by means of reason. As it is not our concern now to refer this force miraculously to God himself, we must assume that it has been placed by him in bodies themselves, verily to constitute their innermost nature. Since *activity* is the characteristic mark of substances, extension on the contrary affirms nothing other than the continual reiteration or propagation of an already presupposed effort and counter-effort, that is, resistant substance, and therefore, extension cannot possibly constitute substance itself.

In this connection it is of no relevance that every bodily activity originates in motion; for this motion itself is derived from another motion already present in the body or impressed on it by something external to it. Thus, strictly speaking, motion just like time, when reduced by analysis to its elements, has no existence as a whole so long as it possesses no co-existing parts. And thus there is nothing real in motion itself apart from the reality of the momentary transition which is determined by means of force and a nisus for change. In that force, therefore, consists whatever there is in material nature apart from its also being the object of geometry or extension. In this way, finally, we take into account the truth as well as the teachings of the ancients. And as we have in our day modern apologists for Democritus' atoms, Plato's ideas, and the Stoic tranquillity of mind which is believed to come from an insight into the best possible constitution of things, we also attain here an understanding of the traditional Aristotelian doctrine of the forms or entelechies—which was justifiably regarded as puzzling and appeared scarcely to be understood by the authors themselves. Accordingly, we believe that this philosophy, which has been accepted for centuries, is not to be discarded in general, but only stands in need of an elucidation which may make it consistent as far as possible. We shall illustrate it and develop it with new truths.

This method of inquiry is most suited for the prudence of the teacher and for the progress of students. We must only avoid having a merely destructive passion win over a constructive desire, and thus avoid vacillating with uncertainty, tossed hither and thither by winds of perpetual changes of doctrine daily proposed by audacious minds. Thus we arrive at the point where mankind at last suddenly curbs the violent passion of sects that are goaded by the desire of innovation, and by taking sure steps according to strictly determined propositions —in philosophy no less than in mathematics—advances toward ultimate principles. For the writings of distinguished men of ancient as of modern times, apart from their too sharp polemics against opposing thinkers, contain for the most part much that is true and good and what well deserves to be excerpted and deposited in the common treasury of knowledge. Would that people preferred to apply themselves to this task, rather than waste their time with carping criticisms; they would sacrifice only their vanity! At least I find, despite many of my own new discoveries—made indeed with such success that friends have often advised me to devote myself exclusively to such inquiries—that I appreciate the views of others and know how to evaluate each view according to its own worth, though also in different degrees, perhaps because I have learnt, as a result of my many-sided

activity, not to despise anything. But let us now return
to our theme.

Active force—it is called virtue or power in persons—
has two forms: it appears, first, as *primitive force* at
work within every corporeal substance—since in my view,
the nature of things permits no bodies to remain thoroughly quiescent—or secondly, as *derivative force.* The
latter is just a limitation of primitive forces, arising
from the multiplicity of conflicting interactions of bodies.
Primitive force—which is none other than the first entelechy—corresponds to the *soul* or *substantial form,* and
pertains only to general causes which do not suffice for
the explanation of phenomena. And so we agree with
those who reject Forms as explanations of the particular
and specific causes of sensory things which turn up in
experience. I emphasize this important point not because
I wish to cast suspicion again on the eternal right of the
Forms to disclose the sources of things, any more than I
wish to revive scholastic polemics. True *philosophy* cannot dispense with the knowledge of forms; nor ought
anybody believe he has completely grasped the nature
of bodies so long as he has not attentively perceived that
the common crass concept of material substance is imperfect, indeed false; this concept is borrowed exclusively from the testimony of sensory imagination, and
was re-introduced only a few years ago through an
inconsiderate abuse of the corpuscular philosophy (excellent and true in itself) which does not completely exclude
passivity or absolute rest from matter; further, it contains no reason in itself which might make it possible
for us to grasp the rules and natural laws governing
derivative forces.

Similarly, *passive force* exists in two forms, namely,
primitive or *derivative.* It is *the primitive force of the
persistent force of resistance* which constitutes what the

scholastic philosophy, properly understood, called "primary matter." It amounts to saying that one body is not penetrable by another, but opposes a resistance to it, and so to speak, does so with a certain indolence or repugnance to motion; its inertia is such that the force of the body acting on it is weakened by the impact. The *derivative force of persistence* reveals itself in many ways in *secondary matter.* Just now, however, we do not wish to consider universal and primitive conditions, for having once established that every body acts by virtue of its form, and is persistent or offers resistance by virtue of its matter, we wish to proceed to the further problem and to deal with the theory of derivative forces and resistances. We, therefore, go on to consider the case in which bodies through their diverse dynamic tendencies produce an impetus or complex modifications in one another. Specifically related to these derivative forces are dynamical laws which are cognizable through reason as well as verified by sensation itself in phenomena.

Derivative force, on which concrete actions and reactions of bodies depend, is here considered by us as always associated with motion—i.e., local motion—and its rôle is directed to the continuation of local motion. For we recognize that only through local motion can we explain all other material phenomena. As motion is continuous change of place, it consequently requires time. The movable object, as it acquires in time a definite *motion,* then possesses a definite velocity at each instant, which is all the greater as it traverses a greater distance in less time. The velocity, to which we assign a definite direction, is called by us "effort" (*conatus*), because we understand and define the "impetus" as the product of the mass of the body by its velocity; this is the same as what the Cartesians usually call "quantity of motion," under which term we should properly understand the magnitude of the *instantaneous* motion. More exactly stated, the true quantity of motion over a period of time is ascertained as the integral of the individual impetuses (which come to the moving body during a definite interval of time) multiplied by the time in a cumulative manner. We have on this score been engaged in a polemic with the Cartesians against their ways of expression. We can, however, in good and proper scientific language distinguish an increase of motion which has already occurred, or will occur later, from the increase which is *just at this instant* about to occur, and designate the latter as the increment or *element* of the increase. In that way we can make a distinction between the instantaneous *action* of the impact and the path which has already been followed. Similarly, we also distinguish the present instantaneous element of motion from that motion which extends over a definite time-interval and can be called the "motion." Then what is commonly called the amount of change should be more accurately designated as a measure of "motion." And even though we do not wish to raise verbal difficulties, but only to have a clear explanation given of them, yet we must, so long as such is the case, attend to them all the more conscientiously in order not to be misled by their ambiguity.

Furthermore, as the calculation of the motion which extends over a definite time-interval is achieved by the summation of infinitely many impetuses, the impetus itself—even though it is something momentary—originates in the successive series of infinite influences acting on the same movable body. It also results from the infinite repetition of a definite *element* . . . Therefore, an effort (*conatus*) has a twofold nature, and we can distinguish the elementary, infinitesimal tendency of the effort from the impetus itself resulting from the constant repetition and continuation of the elementary efforts. I do not mean, however, that these mathematical entities actually act on things in nature, but I regard them as useful abstractions for the purpose of accurate calculation.

Thus there appears a new twofold distinction of forces; viz., one—which I call inert or inactive force—refers primarily to the element of force while the motion itself does not yet exist in it but only the tendency to motion, as, for example, the stone in a sling which tries to fly off in the direction of the tangent, even if it is pulled back by the chain which holds it securely. On the other hand, the other force, which I call living or active force, is the usual one which appears in actual motion.*
An example of inert force is centrifugal force, or gravitational or centripetal force, or also the force which tries to restore a stretched elastic body to its original state. However, active or living force appears in impact—e.g., the force or impact of a heavy body that has been falling for a certain time, or that of a stretched bow which gradually resumes its earlier position—and such an active force arises from an infinite number of constantly continued influences of inactive forces. That is also what Galileo meant when he paradoxically called the impact of percussion an infinitely large force as compared to the simple tendency of gravitational force. In spite of the fact that the impetus or impulse of a body is *connected* with active force, nevertheless we shall show below that the two are not *identical*.

The active living force (*vis viva*) of a system of bodies may also be understood in two ways; namely, as *total* or as *partial* force; the latter is again divided into *relative* or *directive* force, depending on whether it acts among the parts or has to do with the system as a whole. Relative force, proper to the parts, makes it possible for the

* Inactive and active force correspond to what physicists much later called potential and kinetic energy, respectively.

bodies internal to a closed system to exert reciprocal effects on one another, whereas by virtue of directive force the system itself as a whole can produce external effects. I call it directive because the conservation of direction is completely dependent on this partial force. This alone would remain in operation, if we abstracted and halted the relative motion of the parts, leaving the system internally rigid. Whence from the resultant of the relative and directive forces we obtain *the absolute force of the system as a whole;* this will become clearer from the further rules given below.

The ancients, so far as is known, had conceived only a science of inactive forces, which is commonly referred to as Mechanics, dealing with the lever, the windlass, the inclined plane—pertinent to the wedge and screw—though there is discussion of the equilibrium of fluids and of similar problems; only the effort or resistance of bodies and not the impetus they have acquired through their action, is discussed. Now even though the laws of inactive force are transferred in a certain way to active forces, it is nevertheless necessary to be very circumspect in this matter. Hitherto, the error has been made of mistaking the product of the mass and velocity for the whole absolute force because it was seen that the inactive force is proportional to these two factors. However, as already noted above, this depends on a quite separate circumstance, to wit, on the fact, for example, that at the very commencement of the motion of a falling heavy body, the path or space covered, so long as it is of infinitesimal or elementary magnitude, is proportional to the velocity. However, once the weight has progressed a finite distance and given rise to an active force, the velocity acquired in falling is no longer proportional to the distance covered (which is a measure of the force, as we have shown above and as will be further shown below), but to the element of velocity. *Galileo* was the first to conceive the theory of active force—although he used another name or even another concept for it—and was the first to explain that the acceleration of falling bodies was the key to their motion. Descartes was right in distinguishing velocity from direction, and knew that in the total momentum of bodies the change of state was a minimum. However, he did not give the correct formulation of this minimum itself, since he let either the direction or the velocity vary, whereas the total change must be determined from the joint effect of both these factors. How that was possible indeed, he had no way of seeing, because in so far as he started his investigation with merely formal rather than physically real distinctions, he regarded two such heterogeneous things as completely incomparable and incapable of being united in a single formula, not to mention here other errors in his doctrine.

Honoratius *Fabri,* Marcus *Marci,* Joh. A. *Borelli,* Ignatius *Pardies,* Claudius *Dechales,* and other acute minds have given us works on the science of motion which are worthy of attention; but they have all failed to avoid fundamental errors. Huyghens, who has favored our age with such outstanding discoveries, has also on this point been the first, so far as I know, to arrive at a clear and exact truth, and has exhibited the defects and fallacies in this theory by means of his rules which had already been published some time ago. Wren, Wallis, and Mariotte—all distinguished in these studies—have also reached the same rules in this field, though they differ in their methods. However, concerning the fundaental causes of motion there is no agreement, because even the most prominent men of science have not always pursued the same methods of reasoning. As a result the true sources of this science of motion have never apparently been disclosed; even the proposition, which appears certain to me, is not yet generally recognized: namely, that the reaction of rebounding (or reflection of motion of impact) depends only on the elastic force, i.e., on the resistance of an internal motion. In fact, the concept of force itself has never been clearly explained to us: a situation disturbing to the Cartesians and many others because they could not understand that the sum of the motions or velocities—which they regarded as the quantity of the forces—after an impact might be different from what it was before the impact, for then it seemed that the quantity of the force would also vary.

Even as a youngster and at a time when I assumed with Democritus (and with Gassendi and Descartes who were his disciples on this point), that inert mass alone constituted the nature of bodies, I had thought of publishing a book under the title "Physical Hypothesis," in which the theory of abstract as well as of concrete motion were both presented together. The book has, I see, met with the approbation of many distinguished men, far beyond its slight merits. In it, under the hypothesis of the above concept of bodies, I presented the proposition that each of the colliding bodies must continue to exert its effort against the body it has run into, and must transmit it as such to the body immediately resisting it. For since at the moment of collision it seeks to continue its motion and push the resisting body along with it, and this effort—since I assumed at that time the indifference of bodies to motion or rest—must succeed completely because it is not checked by a counter-effort. In fact, even in this case, what must ensue is what is produced only as the resultant of the different efforts. Thus there is no obvious reason why the colliding body should not completely realize the effect of its effort, i.e., why it should not impart its full onmoving effort to the resisting body so that the latter's motion is a synthesis of its own earlier impulse and the new one it has received from without. Accordingly, if we think of bodies only under mathematical concepts like size, shape, place and their modification, and introduce the modification of velocity only at the instant of collision, without resorting to metaphysical concepts, i.e., therefore, without going into what form has to do with active force and matter with passive force—in other words, if we must determine the data of collision only through the geometrical configuration of the velocities, the result will follow, as I have shown, that the velocity of the smallest body will be imparted to a much bigger body which it meets. A body at rest, no matter how big it may be, would then be shoved along by any much smaller one which collides with it, and without the smaller body suffering any retardation, since in such a purely geometrical concept of matter there is no talk of any resistance. but only indifference with regard to motion. Accordingly, there would be no great difficulty in displacing a large as well as a small body; there would be an action without a reaction, and every numerical determination of force would become impossible, for everything could be affected by any thing. Now since these and other similar consequences are contrary to the order of things and conflict with the principles of true metaphysics, I believed at the time, justifiably indeed, that the Creator of things in his wisdom had, in the ordering of the system of things, taken care to avoid the consequences which must result from the purely geometric laws of motion.

However, since I sought the more exact reason for things, I knew in what the rigorously systematic explanation of things consisted, and I noticed that my early definition of the concept of bodies was inadequate. I discovered, apart from other arguments, a corroboration of this in the fact that in addition to size and impenetrability in bodies, there was at bottom still another principle from which the formulation of *force* may be inferred. Only if we unite metaphysical laws with the laws of extension, do we obtain the *systematic* rules of motion, as I might call them; every change takes place gradually, every action is accompanied by a reaction, and a new force can only arise from the diminution of the force in another place. A body which pushes another along must therefore always suffer a retardation such that neither more nor less force is contained in the effect than in the cause. Since this law cannot be derived from the merely geometrical concept of mass, there must then be another basic principle immanent in bodies, viz., the force itself which is always preserved in the same quantity, although it is divided among different bodies. From this, then, I drew the conclusion that we must, in addition to purely mathematical principles which belong to sensory imagination, recognize metaphysical ones which are apprehended only in thought, and that to the concept of material mass we must add an equally formal and superior principle. For not all truths pertaining to the physical world can be obtained from merely arithmetical and geometrical axioms (including the axioms of greater and less, whole and part, shape and structure), but we must introduce other axioms about cause and effect, activity and passivity, and take account of the order of things. Now it does not matter whether we label this principle "Form," "entelechy," or "force," so long as we remember that it meets with an intelligible explanation only in the concept of force.

But if today a few exceptional men, aware of the defect of the prevailing concept of matter, revive the notion of a *"Deus ex machinâ"* in a kind of Mosaic philosophy (as Fludd used to call it), and deny any internal force and activity in things, I cannot agree with them. For although they have excellently adduced that in strict metaphysics one created body cannot make inroads on the nature of another, and although, as I even gladly admit, everything arises perpetually through the continual creativity of God, yet the reason, as I believe, for any natural truth whatsoever is never to be sought immediately in the activity or will of God, but rather in the fact that God has enclosed *in things themselves* properties and determinations from which all their predicates can be explained. Of course, he has created not only bodies but also souls, which correspond to the original entelechies, but all this will be shown elsewhere through their own deeper reasons.

Although I admit an active principle which is superior to merely material concepts and may be called a living principle present in all bodies, yet I am, despite this, not of the opinion of Henry More and other men, distinguished by their piety and genius, who use for the explanation of phenomena themselves something like an original life-force or hylozoistic principle (*Archeus*). As though it were not true that all natural processes lend themselves to mechanical explanation, and as if they who seek such an explanation wished to deny all immaterial realities in general and were hence suspect for harboring irreligious thoughts! Or as if it were necessary to plump for Aristotle's intelligences in the celestial spheres, things as artificially convenient as they are unfruitful, e.g., making the four elements strive upwards or downwards by virtue of their own forms! With all these things, I say, I do not agree, and this philosophy suits me as little as the doctrine of the ancient theologians who were so firmly convinced of the fact that thunder and snow depended on Jupiter himself that they accused as atheists all who inquired into proximate causes. In my opinion, the best disposition of the ques-

tion is one which equally satisfies religion and science,
so that we recognize the possibility of inferring all physical phenomena from mechanically efficient causes, but
understand at the same time that mechanical laws themselves in their generality originate in higher reasons, and
that, accordingly, we need a higher active cause which,
however, only serves for the establishment of general
and, accordingly, remote reasons. But once this is settled,
then when it comes to dealing with proximate and individual causes, we have no further concern with souls or
entelechies, of as little use to us as the idle faculties or
unintelligible sympathies of the scholastic metaphysics.
For the primary and most general active causes ought
not be intermingled with the treatment of particular
problems, except for the sake of reflection on the purposes to which the divine wisdom has adhered in his
ordering of things; that is, we should miss no opportunity to praise and glorify God.

In actuality (as I have shown in an example from
optics which the famous Molyneux fully applauded in
his *Dioptrics*), final causes themselves are very usefully
employed in particular physical problems, not only for
the sake of awakening in us admiration for the beauty
of divine works, but also meanwhile to provide a result
which we could not obtain or could only obtain with
problematic certainty by way of efficient causes. Philosophers until now have perhaps not yet paid sufficient
attention to this use of final causes. On that score it is
generally established that all events can be explained
in a twofold fashion: through the *kingdom of power* or
efficient causes and through the *kingdom of wisdom* or
final causes: that God as an architect created bodies as
mere machines according to *mathematical laws of quantity,* and yet has determined them for use by souls. However, he rules over souls that are capable of reason in the

fashion of a prince, or rather, indeed, of a father, who rules in a sort of community, according to the *moral laws of goodness* and guides everything to his greater glory. These two kingdoms everywhere interpenetrate without confusing or disturbing each other's laws, so that there always comes to pass the greatest in the kingdom of power and at the same time the best in the kingdom of wisdom. It was our design in this essay, however, to establish the universal rules of active forces in order to be able then to employ them for the explanation of particular efficient causes.

Next I came to work out accurately and exactly the same calculation of forces by quite different methods: one truly *a priori,* by the simplest consideration of space, time, and action (which I explain elsewhere); the other *a posteriori,* namely, by calculating the force through the effect produced in using itself up. For I here refer not to any effect, but to one produced by a force which completely expends itself and may therefore be called violent; such is not the case with a heavy body moving on a perfectly horizontal plane and constantly preserving the same force; this is a harmless sort of effect, so to speak, which we can also calculate by our method but it is not the one we wish to consider now. Furthermore, I am choosing to consider that particular kind of violent effect which is homogeneous or capable of being divided into similar and equal parts such as we have in the ascent of a heavy body: for the ascent of such a body two or three feet is exactly double or triple the ascent of the same body one foot; and the ascent of a body twice as heavy to a height of one foot is twice the ascent of the single body to a height of two feet, and hence, the ascent of a double heavy body to a height of three feet is exactly six times the ascent of the single body to a height of one foot. Here we assume for the sake of exposition that at the different heights the weights are equally affected by gravity, although in fact there is a slight though negligible difference. In an elastic body it is not so easy to establish homogeneity. Therefore, when I wished to compare bodies differing in weight or velocity, I found it easy to see that if the body A is single and the body B double in weight but equal to A in velocity, the force of the former is single and that of the latter double, for in B there is only twice the matter of A and nothing else. But if the bodies A and C are equal but the velocity of C double that of A, I saw that what is in the body of A is not doubled in C even though the velocity is doubled. And it was evident to me that an error was made by those who believed that the force is doubled simply by doubling the mode of being; for I had already once observed and suggested that the true and hitherto unknown art of calculating (despite the fact that so many *Elements of Universal Mathematics* have been written) consists in finally arriving at something homogeneous, that is, an accurate multiplying not only of modes of all kinds but also of things. No better or more remarkable specimen of this method could be given than the one shown by the argument here.

Therefore, in order to obtain these results, I asked myself whether these same two bodies A and C, equal in magnitude but different in velocity, could homogeneously produce some effects equal to their causes. For in that way the things which could not easily be compared by themselves might be accurately compared by their effects. Moreover, I assumed that the effect must be equal to its cause if produced by the expenditure or use of the complete force, so that it would not matter how much time it takes to produce the effect. Let us suppose, then, that the equally heavy bodies A and C expend all of their force in ascending to heights proportional to their velocities (C's being double that of A's velocity). This will happen if they are at the extremities of pendulums suspended from points P and E [see diagram] and of equal lengths PA and EC, and have risen to points A_2 and C_2 where they would have expended their initial velocities, that of C double that of A. It is clear from the demonstrations of Galileo and others that if the body A with

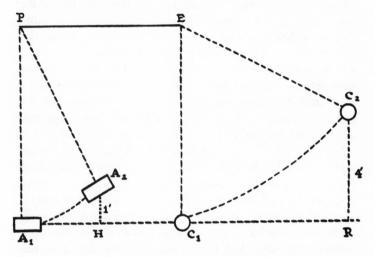

velocity 1 would ascend to a vertical height of one foot above the horizontal, then the body C with velocity 2 would ascend to a vertical height of four feet above the horizontal. Hence, it follows that a heavy body having a velocity of 2 has four times the force of energy than a body of the same weight but half the velocity, since in expending all its force it can do four times as much. For raising a pound, that is, itself, four feet raises four times one pound one foot. And in this manner we can by reason infer generally that the forces of equally heavy bodies are as the *squares* of the velocities.

I have reduced the contrary opinion, generally held

and especially by the Cartesians, that forces vary with bodies and velocities, to an absurdity, namely, to perpetual motion. The method I used was to define *a posteriori* two states unequal in force and to distinguish the greater from the less by a certain character. Then, by substituting one for the other, I show that perpetual mechanical motion or an effect more powerful than the cause does not arise, and therefore, that the two states are not at all equivalent, but that which was substituted for the other was more powerful because it has caused something greater to be done. But I take as certain that nature never substitutes things unequal to the forces themselves, and that the complete effect is always equal to the whole cause, and again, we can substitute what is calculated accurately to be equal to the forces and proceed safely as though that substitution corresponded to what took place in the action with no fear of perpetual motion. But if it were true, as is generally supposed, that a heavy body A assumed to have a weight of 2 and acquiring a velocity of 1 is equivalent to a heavy body C assumed to have a weight of 1 and acquiring a velocity of 2, we ought to be able to substitute one for the other without difficulty. But this is not true. For let us assume that A has acquired a velocity of 1 in its descent $A_2 A_1$ from the vertical height A_2H less than a foot from the horizontal. Now let us substitute at A_1 on the horizontal the supposed equivalent, viz., the weight C with its weight of 1 and acquiring a velocity of 2 by ascending to C_2 at a vertical height of 4 feet. This would mean that by the descent of the two pound weight A from the height A_1H of one foot, the substitution of the supposed equivalent has accomplished an ascent of one pound to a height of four feet. But this is twice the effect of the first body. Therefore we have gained an equal quantity of force, or we have produced perpetual mechanical motion, which is certainly absurd. And it does not matter whether we can actually make these substitutions by the laws of motion, for equivalents can always be substituted for one another, although, indeed, we have thought out various ways by which the entire force of the body A will be transferred to the body C, initially at rest but which is put into motion by A itself being brought to rest. Whence it will happen that in place of a two pound weight and velocity of 1 would be substituted a one pound weight of a velocity of 2, if they were equivalent; but we have shown that an absurdity would result.

These things are not worthless to consider, nor are they quibblings over words, for they are of the greatest importance in comparing machines and motions. For example, if power is obtained from water or animals or from some other cause, by which a weight of 100 pounds is kept in constant motion so that within a fourth of a minute it can be made to complete a circle of 30 feet diameter, but someone else maintains that a weight of 200 pounds can in the same time complete half the circle with less expenditure of power, his calculation seems to yield a gain; but you ought to know that you are being deceived and getting only half the power.

6. ON NATURE IN ITSELF; OR ON THE FORCE RESIDING IN CREATED THINGS, AND THEIR ACTIONS
[1698]

1. I have recently received from the very illustrious John Christopher Sturm, a man especially meritorious for his work in mathematics and physics, the Apology which he published at Altdorf in defense of his Dissertation, *De Idolo Naturae,* which Gunther Christopher

Schelhammer, the eminent and beloved physician of Kiel, attacked in his book on nature. As I have formerly examined the same question, and as I have had by letters some discussions on this subject with the eminent author of the Dissertation, mention of which he made in a way very gratifying to me in recalling publicly some details of our correspondence in the first volume of his *Select Physics* (Vol. I, Sec. 1, Chap. 3, epilog. § v, pp. 119, 120), I have been thereby but the more disposed to give serious attention to such an important subject, judging it necessary that my view and the whole question should be a little more distinctly set forth from those principles which I have already often indicated. This apologetic dissertation seemed to me to offer an opportunity favorable to my design, because it was easy to see that the author had there treated in a few words the essential points of the question. For the rest I do not take sides between these illustrious men.

2. Two points especially, it seems to me, are in question: first, in what consists the nature which we are accustomed to attribute to things, the commonly received attributes of which, according to the judgment of the celebrated Sturm, savor a little of paganism; next, whether there is in creatures any ἐνέργεια, a thing which he appears to deny. As for the first point, concerning nature in itself, if we examine what it is and what it is not, I admit indeed that there is no soul of the universe; I even admit that these marvels, which happen every day and of which we are wont to say with reason that the work of nature is the work of an intelligence, are not to be attributed to certain created intelligences endowed with a wisdom and virtue proportioned to so great a matter; but that universal *nature* is, so to speak, the *handiwork of God,* and one so great that every natural machine (this is the true but little observed difference

between *nature* and *art*) is composed of really infinite
organs, and consequently requires in the author and
director infinite wisdom and power. This is why I hold
the omniscient heat of Hippocrates and the soul-giving
Cholco-goddess of Avicenna and the very wise plastic
virtue of Scaliger and others and the hylarchic principle
of Henry More, as being either impossible or superfluous; and it is enough for me that the mechanism of
things is constructed with so much wisdom that all these
marvels come to pass through its very development, organized beings being evolved, I think, according to a
preconceived plan. I am therefore of the opinion of the
illustrious author when he rejects the figment of a certain created nature, whose wisdom forms and governs
the mechanisms of bodies; but it does not hence follow,
I believe, and reason does not admit, that all created,
indwelling, active force must be rejected.

3. We have just spoken of what it is not; let us now
examine more closely what this nature is which Aristotle
was not wrong in calling the *principle of motion and of
rest*, although this philosopher seems to me to take the
word in too broad a meaning, and understand by it not
only local motion or rest in a place, but in general *change*
and τάσσις or persistence. Whence, also, as I may say in
passing, the definition which he gives of motion is truly
obscure; it is, however, not so absurd as it seems to those
who suppose that he meant to define only local motion.
But let us return to the matter in hand. Robert Boyle,
a man eminent and skilled in the accurate observation of
nature, has written on nature in itself a little book, the
thought of which, if I remember correctly, is summed
up in this, that we ought to regard nature as being the
very *mechanism* of bodies; which indeed may be proved
ὡς ἐν πλάτει; but if he had examined the thing with
more ἀκριβεία he would have distinguished in the mech-

anism itself the principles from their derivatives. So it does not suffice, in order to explain a clock, to say that it is moved in a mechanical manner, without distinguishing whether it receives this impulse from a weight or from a spring. I have already declared more than once (what I think should be valuable in preventing the abuse of mechanical explanations of material things, to the prejudice of piety, as if matter could exist by itself and as if the mechanism had no need of any intelligence or of any spiritual substance) that the origin of the mechanism itself does not come merely from a material principle alone nor from mathematical reasons but from a certain higher principle, and, so to speak, metaphysical source.

4. One remarkable proof, among others, of this truth is that the *foundation of the laws of nature* must be made to consist not in this, that the same quantity of motion is preserved, as was commonly believed, but rather in this, that the *same quantity of active power,* still more (and I have discovered that this happens for an admirable reason), the *same quantity of moving force* [*actio*] *must be preserved,* the estimation of which must be very different from that which the Cartesians conceive under quantity of motion.

I have conferred on this subject, partly by letters, in part publicly, with two mathematicians of superior talent, and one of them embraced my opinion altogether; the other, after long and thorough examination, ended by renouncing all his objections and avowing frankly that he had not yet been able to find an answer to my demonstration. And I am all the more astonished to see that the illustrious man, in the edited portion of his *Select Physics,* in explaining the laws of motion, has admitted the common doctrine as if it did not permit of doubt (he has, however, recognized that it rests upon no demonstra-

tion but on a certain probability, and he has repeated it
in this last dissertation, Chap. 3, § 2); but perhaps he
wrote before my writings appeared and had not the
time or the thought for revising his own, especially as
he was persuaded that the laws of motion are arbitrary,
which appears to me not at all according to reason. For
I think that it is because of reasons determined by wisdom and order that God has been led to make the laws
which we observe in nature; and hence it is evident,
according to the remark which I formerly made on the
occasion of an optical law and which the celebrated
Molyneux later highly approved in his *Dioptrics,* that
final cause is not only useful to virtue and to piety in
ethics and in natural theology, but that even in physics
it serves to find and to discover hidden truths. So when
the renowned Sturm, where he treats of final cause in
his *Select Physics,* presented my doctrine among the
hypotheses, I could have wished that he had sufficiently
examined it in his criticism; for he would have found
opportunity for saying in favor of the importance and
fruitfulness of the argument many excellent things and
such as are useful for piety.

5. But we must now examine what he says of the
notion of nature in his apologetic dissertation, and what
seems to us insufficient in it. He grants, Chap. IV, § § 2,
3, and often elsewhere, that the movements which take
place now are the result of the *eternal law* once decreed
by God, which law he calls soon after volition and *command;* and that there is no need of a new command from
God, of a new volition, and still less of a new effort
or of a sort of laborious operation (§ 3); and he repels
as an unjust imputation on the part of his opponent the
thought that God moves things as a wood-cutter does his
two-edged ax, or as a miller governs his mill by retaining
the waters or by turning them loose on the wheel. But

in truth, as indeed it seems to me, this explanation does not suffice. For I ask if this volition or this command, or, if you prefer, this divine law, decreed originally, attributed to things only an *extrinsic denomination;* or if, in forming them, it created in them some permanent impression, or as Schelhammer, remarkable as well for his judgment as for his experience, well calls it, an *indwelling law* (although it is most often unknown to the creatures in whom it resides), whence proceed all actions and all passions. The first appears to be the doctrine of the authors of the system of Occasional Causes, and especially of the very ingenious Malebranche; the latter is received (and as I believe rightly) as the most true.

6. And in truth since this past decree does not exist at present, it can produce nothing now unless it then left after it some perduring effect, which now still continues and operates. And he who thinks otherwise renounces, if I judge rightly, all distinct explanation of things; and it can be said that anything is, by an equal title, the result of anything, if that which is absent in space and time can without intermedium operate here and now. Thus it is not sufficient to say that in creating things in the beginning God willed that they should observe a certain law in their progress, if his will is conceived to have been so inefficacious that things were not affected by it and no lasting effect was produced in them. And assuredly it is contrary to the notion of the divine power and will, which is pure and absolute, that God should will and nevertheless in willing produce or change nothing; that he is always acting and never effecting; that in a word he *leaves no work* or ἀποτελεσμα. Without doubt, if nothing was impressed on creatures by this divine word, "Let the earth bring forth, let the animals multiply"; if after it things were not affected otherwise than if no command intervened, it follows

(since there must be between the cause and the effect a certain connection, either immediate or mediate), either that nothing takes place now conformally to this mandate or that this mandate effecting so much in the present must be always renewed in the future, a consequence which the learned author, with reason, repels. But if, on the contrary, the law decreed by God left some trace of itself impressed on things; if things were so formed by the mandate as to render them fit to accomplish the will of the legislator, then it must be admitted that a certain efficacy, form or force, such as we are accustomed to call by the name of nature, is impressed on things, whence proceeds the series of phenomena according to the prescription of the first command.

7. But this indwelling force may indeed be conceived distinctly but not explained by images; nor, certainly, ought it to be so explained any more than the nature of the soul, for force is one of those things which are not to be grasped by the imagination but by the understanding. Thus, when the author of the apologetic dissertation (Chap. 4, § 6) asks that the manner in which indwelling law operates in bodies ignorant of this law be explained to him by the imagination, I understand him to desire to have an explanation of it through the understanding; for otherwise, it might be believed that he demanded that sounds be painted and colors heard. Furthermore, if the difficulty of explaining things is sufficient for rejecting them, he therefore merits the imputation which he himself (Chap. 1, § 2) repels as unjust, of preferring to decide that everything is moved merely by a divine virtue rather than to admit, under the name of nature, something the nature of which is unknown to him. And certainly even Hobbes and others could claim with equal right that all things are corporeal, because they are persuaded that only bodies can be explained distinctly and

by the imagination. But they themselves are justly refuted by the very fact that there is in things a power of acting which is not derived from imageable things, but merely to trace this to a mandate of God, which once given, in no wise affects things nor leaves any effect after it, so far from clearing up the difficulty, is rather to renounce the rôle of the philosopher and to cut the Gordian knot with the sword. For the rest, a more distinct and correct explanation of active force than has up to this time been given, may be drawn from our *Dynamics,* in which we give an interpretation of the laws of nature and of motion, which is true and in accordance with things.

8. But if some defender of the new philosophy which introduces the inertia and torpor of things, goes so far as to take away from the commands of God all durable effect and all efficacy for the future, and has no scruples in requiring of God incessantly renewed efforts (that which Sturm prudently declares he is averse to), he himself may see how worthy he thinks this of God; moreover, he could not be excused unless he offered an explanation of why things themselves can last some time but the attributes of things which we understand under the name of nature cannot be lasting; why it may not be, furthermore, according to reason that just as the word *fiat* left something after it, namely, the persisting thing itself, so the not less admirable word of *blessing* has left also after it in things a certain fecundity or virtue of producing their acts and of operating, whence, if there is no obstacle, the operation results. That which I have explained elsewhere might be added to this if perchance it is not yet perfectly clear to all, that the very substance of things consists in their power of acting and suffering, whence it follows that not even durable things can be produced if a force of some permanence cannot be im-

printed upon them by the divine power. Thus it would
follow that no created substance, no soul, would remain
numerically the same; that nothing would be preserved
by God, and consequently that all things would be only
certain passing or evanescent modifications, and, so to
speak, apparitions, of one permanent divine substance;
and, what amounts to the same thing, that nature itself
or the substance of all things, would be God; a pernicious
doctrine, recently introduced into the world or renewed
by a subtle but profane author [Spinoza]. If corporeal
things contained nothing but matter it would be quite
true to say that they are in a flux and have nothing
substantial, as the Platonists formerly very well recognized.

9. Another question is whether we must say that creatures properly and truly act. This question is included in
the first if we once understand that the indwelling nature
does not differ from the power of acting and suffering.
For there cannot be action without the power of acting,
and on the other hand that potency is worthless which
can never be exercised. Since, however, action and potency are none the less different things, the first successive, the second lasting, let us consider the action.
Here, I confess, I find no little difficulty in explaining
the thought of the learned Sturm. For he denies that
created things act properly and of themselves, and,
nevertheless soon after, while admitting that they act,
he does not wish that the comparison of creatures to an
ax moved by a wood-cutter be attributed to him. I cannot draw from this anything certain nor do I find explained with sufficient clearness to what extent he recedes
from the received opinions, or what distinct notion he
has conceived in his mind of action, which, as the debates
of the metaphysicians attest, is far from being obvious
and simple. As for me, as far as I seem to have grasped

the notion of action, the doctrine generally received in philosophy, that *actions belong to subjects,* follows from it and is established by it; and I think that this principle is so true that it may be inverted; so that not only is everything which acts a particular substance, but also every particular substance acts without cessation, not even excepting body itself, in which no absolute rest is ever found.

10. But let us now examine a little more attentively the opinion of those who take away from created things true and individual action; a thing which Robert Fludd, author of the *Philosophia Mosaica,* formerly did, and also now some Cartesians do who think that it is not at all the things which act, but indeed God, on occasion of things and according to the aptitude of things; and thus things are occasions not causes; they receive, but do not effect any action. After Cordemoi, de La Forge and other Cartesians had proposed this doctrine, Malebranche, with his superior mind, lent it the lustre of his style; but no one, in my opinion, has presented solid proofs. Certainly if this doctrine is pushed to the point of suppressing even the *immanent actions* of substances (a view which the illustrious Sturm in his *Select Physics,* Bk. I, ch. iv, Epilo., § 11, p. 176, rightly rejects, and in this he gives proof of much circumspection), then nothing in the world appears to be more contrary to reason. In truth, who will question that the mind thinks and wills, and that many thoughts and volitions in us are elicited from ourselves, and that we are endowed with spontaneity? This would be not only to deny human liberty and to make God the cause of evil, but also to contradict the testimony of our inmost experience and of our conscience; through which we feel that those things are ours, which, without any kind of reason, our adversaries would transfer to God. But if we attribute to our

soul the indwelling power of producing immanent actions, or, what is the same thing, of acting immanently, then nothing hinders, on the contrary, it is comfortable to reason, that this same power should reside in other animated beings or forms, or, if you prefer, in the nature of substances; but if some one should think that in the nature of things as known to us only our souls are active, or that all power of acting immanently, and so to speak *vitally,* is joined with intellect, such assertions certainly rest on no ground, and can be defended only in opposition to the truth. As to what is to be believed concerning the *transient actions of creatures,* that will be explained better in another place, and has, in part, already been explained by us elsewhere: that is to say, the *communication of substances* or of monads has its source not in influx but in a concord proceeding from divine preformation: each substance, at the same time, that it follows the indwelling power and laws of its own nature, being accommodated to the others; and it is in this that the union of the soul and body consists.

11. Moreover, that bodies are of themselves inert is true if it is rightly understood, to this extent, namely, that what is, for any reason, once assumed to be at rest cannot set itself in motion or allow itself without resistance to be set in motion by another body; any more than it can of itself change the rate of velocity or the direction which it once has, or allow it easily and without resistance to be changed by another body. And also it must be confessed that extension, or what is geometrical in body if taken simply, has nothing in it which can give rise to action and to motion; on the contrary, matter rather resists motion by a certain *natural inertia,* as Kepler has well called it, so that it is not indifferent to motion and rest, as is generally thought, but it needs in order to move an active force proportionate to its size.

Wherefore I make the very notion of *materia prima,* or
of mass, which is always the same in body and proportioned to its size, consist in this very passive force of
resistance (involving impenetrability and something
more); and hence, I show that entirely different laws
of motion follow than if there were in body and in matter
itself only impenetrability together with extension; and
that, as there is in matter a natural *inertia* opposed to
motion, so in body itself, and what is more, in every substance, there is a natural *constancy* opposed to *change.*
But this doctrine does not defend, but rather opposes,
those who deny action to things; for just as certain as
it is that matter of itself does not begin motion, so certain is it (as very fine experiments on the motion communicated by a moving body show) that body retains of
itself the impetus which it has once acquired, and that
it is *constant* in its mobility or makes an effort to persevere in that very series of changes which it has entered
on. As these activities and entelechies cannot be modifications of primary matter or of *mass,* a thing essentially
passive, as was recognized by the very judicious Sturm
himself (as we shall see in the following paragraph), it
may be inferred that there must be found in corporeal
substance a *first entelechy* or πρῶτον δεκτικόν for activity; that is, a primitive moving force which being joined
to extension (or what is purely geometrical) and to mass
(or what is purely material) always indeed acts but
nevertheless, in consequence of the meeting of bodies,
is variously modified through efforts and impetus. And it
is this same substantial principle which is called *soul* in
living beings, and *substantial form* in others; and so far
as by its union with matter it constitutes a substance
truly *one,* or one *per se,* it forms what I call a *monad:*
since if these true and real unities are taken away only
beings by aggregation will remain; nay, rather, it follows

from this, that there will be no real entities in bodies. For although there are atoms of substance given, that is, our monads without parts, there are no atoms of mass, i.e., of the smallest extension, or ultimate elements, since the continuous cannot be formed of points. In short, no being is given which is the greatest in mass or infinite in extension, although there may always be some larger than others: but a being is given which is the greatest by *intension* of perfections or infinite in power.

12. I see, however, that in this same apologetic dissertation, Ch. IV, § 7 et seq., the celebrated Sturm has undertaken to attack by certain arguments the moving force residing in bodies. "I shall abundantly here prove," he says, "that corporeal substance is not even capable of any *actively* moving potency." But I do not understand what a power not actively moving can be. Moreover, he says that he will employ two arguments, one drawn from the nature of matter and of body, the other from the nature of motion. The first amounts to this, that matter, in its nature and essentially, is a passive substance; and that thus it is no more possible to give it active force than it is for God to will that a stone, as long as it remains a stone, shall be living and rational, that is, not a stone; further, whatever qualities are posited in bodies are but modifications of matter, moreover (what I acknowledge is well said), a modification of a thing essentially passive cannot render this thing active. But it is easy to reply with the received and true philosophy that *matter* is to be understood as secondary or as primary; the secondary is a certain complete but not purely passive substance; the primary is purely passive but not complete, and consequently there must be added to it a soul, or form analogous to the soul, a primary ἐντελέχεια, that is, a certain effort or primitive power of acting, which is itself the indwelling law imprinted by

divine decree. I do not think that such a view is repugnant to the illustrious and ingenious man who lately maintained that body is composed of matter and of spirit; provided that *spirit* is taken not for an intelligent thing (as in other cases is done) but for a soul or form analogous to the soul; not for a simple modification, but for something constituent, substantial and perduring, which I am accustomed to call *monad,* and which possesses a sort of perception and desire. Therefore this received doctrine, agreeing with the favorably explained dogma of the schoolmen, must be first refuted, in order that the argument of this illustrious man may have any weight. Whence also it is evident that we cannot admit, what he assumes, that whatever is in corporeal substance is but a modification of matter. For it is well known that according to received philosophy there are in the bodies of living beings souls which assuredly are not modifications. For although the illustrious man appears to maintain the contrary and to take away from the brutes all feeling, in the true meaning of the word, and soul, properly speaking, nevertheless, he cannot assume this opinion as the foundation of his demonstration until it itself has been proved. And I believe, on the contrary, that it is consistent neither with the order nor the beauty nor the reason of things, that this vital or immanently active principle should be only in a small part of matter, when greater perfection demands that it be in all. Nor does aught hinder souls, or at least forms analogous to souls, from being everywhere, although the dominant, and hence intelligent, souls, like the human, cannot be everywhere.

13. The second argument, which the illustrious Sturm draws from the nature of motion, does not appear to me to be necessarily conclusive. He says that *motion* is only the successive existence of the thing in different places. Let us grant this provisionally, although we are not at

all satisfied with it, and although it expresses rather the
result of motion than its so-called formal reason; nevertheless moving force is not thus excluded. For a body is
not only at the actual moment of its motion in a place
commensurate to it, but it has also a tendency or effort
to change its place so that the succeeding state follows of
itself from the present by the force of nature; otherwise
at the actual moment, and hence at any moment, a body
A, which is in motion, would in no wise differ from a
body B, which is at rest; and from the opinion of the
illustrious man, were it contrary to ours on this point,
it would follow that there would be no difference whatever in bodies, because in the fullness of a mass in itself
uniform no other difference can be assumed than that
which respects the motion. Finally, it would further follow that·there would be absolutely no variation in bodies,
and that they would remain always in the same state. For
if any portion of matter does not differ from another
equal to and like it (which the illustrious Sturm must
admit, since he does away with active forces, impulses,
and all other qualities and modifications, except existence
in this place, which would be successively another and
another); if moreover the state at one instant does not
differ from the state at another instant except by the
transposition of portions of matter, equal and similar,
and at every point fitting to each other, it evidently follows that, on account of the perpetual substitution of
indiscernible things, it will be absolutely impossible to
distinguish the states in the world of bodies at different
moments. In truth, it would only be an *extrinsic denomination* by which one part of matter would be distinguished from another, that is, by the future, namely,
that it would be later in another and still another place;
but for the present state, there is no difference; and
not even from the future could a well founded difference

be drawn, because we could even later never arrive at any true present difference, since by no mark can one place be distinguished from another place, nor (on the hypothesis of the perfect uniformity in matter itself) matter from other matter of the same place. In vain also would we after motion have resort to *figure*. In a mass perfectly similar, indistinguishable and full, there arises no figure, nor limit and distinction of various parts, except from the motion itself. If then motion does not contain any mark of distinction it will impart none to figure; and as everything which is substituted for that which was, is perfectly equivalent, no one, even were he omniscient, could grasp the least indication of change, and consequently everything will be just as if no change and no distinction occurred in bodies: and we could never in this way account for the diverse appearances which we perceive. And it would bé as if we should imagine two perfect concentric spheres, perfectly similar in themselves and in all their parts, one of which should be enclosed in the other so that not the least aperture should be left: then, if we suppose that the inner sphere is either in motion or at rest, not even an angel, to say nothing more, will be able to perceive any difference between the states at different times, and will have no sign by which to distinguish whether the inner sphere is at rest or in motion and according to what law the motion is. Moreover, not even the boundary of the spheres can be defined, because of the want both of *aperture* and of difference; just as in this case motion cannot be noticed because of the lack of *difference*. Whence it must be considered as certain (although those who have not sufficiently penetrated into these things have little noticed it) that such things are foreign to the nature and order of things, and that (what is among the number of my new and greater axioms) there is *nowhere*

any perfect similarity; whence it follows also that we
find in nature neither corpuscles of an extreme hardness,
nor a fluid of an extreme tenuity, nor subtile matter universally diffused, nor ultimate elements, called by some
by the name of primary or secondary. It is, I believe,
because he had understood something of this, that Aristotle, more profound in my opinion than many think,
judged that in addition to local change there was need
of alteration, and that matter would remain invariable.
Moreover, this dissimilarity or diversity of qualities, and
hence this ἀλλοίωσις or alteration, which Aristotle did
not sufficiently explain, comes from the diverse degrees
and directions of efforts, and so from the modifications
of indwelling monads. We can understand by this that
there must necessarily be posited in bodies something
besides a uniform mass. Certainly, those who hold to
atoms and a vacuum diversify matter at least in some
degree by making it here divisible, there indivisible, full
in one place, porous in another. But for a long time now
I have understood (by laying aside the prejudices of
youth) that atoms together with vacuum must be rejected. The celebrated author adds that the existence of
matter through diverse moments is to be attributed to the
divine will; why not then, he says, attribute to the same
its existence here and now? I reply, that this, like all
other things in so far as they involve some perfection,
must undoubtedly be attributed to God; but just as this
universal first cause which preserves all things does not
destroy, but rather produces, the natural permanence,
or once granted perseverance in existence, of the thing
which begins to exist; so it will not destroy but rather
strengthen the natural efficacy, or perseverance in action
once communicated, of the thing set in motion.

14. Many other things are met with in this apologetic dissertation which present difficulties, as what is

said in Chapter IV, § 11, concerning motion transmitted
from one ball to another through several intermediaries,
that the last ball is moved by the *same force* by which
the first is moved, whereas, it seems to me, it is moved by
an equivalent but not the same force; for (what may
appear surprising), each ball repelled by the next im-
pinging it is set in motion by its *own force,* viz., its elasticity. (I do not here discuss at all the cause of this
elasticity, nor do I deny that it ought to be explained
mechanically by the movement of an indwelling and unstable fluid.) So also it will rightly seem surprising when
he says, § 12, that a thing which cannot set itself in
motion cannot of itself continue the motion. For it is
evident rather that, as there is need of force to communicate motion, so, when the impulse is once given, so
far from there being need of a new force to continue
it there is rather need of a new force to stop it. For the
question here is not of that preservation of motion by
means of a universal cause necessary to things, which,
as we have remarked, could not destroy the efficiency of
things without taking away their existence.

15. By this it will be again perceived that the doctrine
of occasional causes defended by some (unless it be explained in such a way as to admit of modifications which
the illustrious Sturm has in part admitted and in part
seems disposed to admit), is subject to dangerous consequences which are certainly not agreeable to its very
learned defenders. For so far is it from augmenting the
glory of God by doing away with the *idola* of nature,
that on the contrary, by resolving all created things into
simple modifications of a single divine substance, it
seems, with Spinoza, to make of God the very nature of
things; since that which does not act, that which lacks
active force, that which is deprived of distinctive mark,
and finally, of all reason and ground of permanence, can

in no wise be a substance. I am thoroughly persuaded
that the illustrious Sturm, a man remarkable for his
piety and learning, is very far removed from these monstrosities. Thus there is no doubt but that he will either
have to show clearly that there remains in things
some substance, or even some variation, without prejudice to his doctrine, or he will have to accept the
truth.

16. I have many reasons for suspecting that I have
not sufficiently grasped his meaning, nor he mine. He has
somewhere admitted to me that a certain *portion of
divine power* (that is, I think, an expression, imitation,
proximate effect; for the divine force itself can certainly not be divided into parts) can and even in a way
must be regarded as possessed by and attributed to
things. What he has transmitted to me and what he has
repeated in his *Select Physics,* may be seen in the passage which I quoted at the beginning of this essay. If
this be interpreted (as the terms seem to imply) in the
sense in which we speak of the soul as a portion of the
divine breath, then there is no longer any controversy
between us. But what prevents me from affirming that
such is his meaning, is that nowhere else do I see him
propounding anything like it, nor advancing any deductions from it. I notice on the contrary, that his general
views are little in harmony with this opinion, and that
his apologetic dissertation goes into everything else.
When indeed my views concerning indwelling force were
first published in the month of March, 1694, in the *Acta
Eruditorum* of Leipzig (views which my *Essay on Dynamics* published in the same in April, 1695,* farther
developed), he addressed to me by letter certain objections; but after having received my reply, he decided in

* See preceding selection, *Specimen Dynamicum* which was
Part I of Leibniz's *Essay on Dynamics.*

a very friendly way that the only difference between us was in the manner of expressing ourselves. When I, remarking this, had brought some other things to his attention, he turning about declared there were many differences between us, which I recognized: and finally, these having been removed, he wrote me anew that there was no difference between us except in terms, a thing very agreeable to me. I have, therefore, wished, on the occasion of the recent apologetic dissertation, to so explain the matter that finally the opinion of each one of us and the truth of the same may the more easily be established. For the illustrious author possesses, moreover, such rare penetration and clearness of exposition, that I hope that no little light will be thrown by his zeal on this great subject. And consequently this work of mine will not be useless because it furnishes him the opportunity, with his wonted talent and force of judgment, to examine and to explain some things of importance in the present subject, which have up to this time been omitted by authors and by me. But these things will be supplemented, if I am not mistaken, by new, more profound, and more comprehensive principles, whence perhaps may come, some day, a reconstructed and amended system of philosophy midway between the formal and the material (and properly uniting and preserving both).

7. ON SUBSTANCE AS ACTIVE FORCE RATHER THAN MERE EXTENSION
(Leibniz to De Volder, Mar. 24/April 3, 1699)

Your remarkable and exceptionally friendly letters have furnished me with so brilliant an example of your penetration of mind and its pure devotion to the quest

for truth that it can scarcely be matched. Would that I
could answer you on all the points you raise as satis-
factorily as I should wish to. But it is something to
speak forth boldly, and though what I say may not be
supported here by a strict demonstration, it may meanwhile be submitted to you for consideration as a clear
hypothesis which is quite consistent with itself and in
closest agreement with phenomena. I believe that for the
most part it will appear as certain to an attentive ob-
server. Now this is the axiom which I utilize, *namely,
that "no event takes place by a leap."* This proposition
flows, in my view, from the laws of order and rests on
the same rational ground by virtue of which it is generally recognized that *motion does not occur by leaps,*
that is, that a body in order to go from one place to
another must pass through definite intermediate places.
Now we can, of course, exclude peremptorily all discontinuities if we have once decided to accept as certain the
continuity of motion and the Author of things, but how
can we prove all this if not by means of experience or
the rational grounds of order? For since all things proceed from God by virtue of a perpetual generation, or
as people say, by virtue of a constant act of creation,
why then might he not have produced bodies in one place,
so to speak, from a distance and left open a hole in time
or in space, so that he could make a body, for example,
act in A and at the same time in B, etc. Experience
teaches that this does not happen, but it is equally demonstrable through a rational principle of order according
to which *the further we analyze things the more do they
have to satisfy the understanding.* Our understanding
will not put up with gaps, since analysis aims finally at
ἄρρητα, at something ultimate and indissoluble. This
holds, I believe, not only for transitions from place to
place, but also for those from form to form or from state

to state. For here also experience rejects all discontinuous changes; otherwise it would come into conflict, so far as I can see, with that *a priori* reason against letting a jump occur from one place to another as well as from one state to another.

I do not believe extension alone constitutes substance, since its conception is incomplete. Nor to my mind can extension be conceived in itself; rather it is a further analyzable and relative conception. For we can analyze it into plurality, continuity and co-existence (that is, simultaneous existence of parts). Plurality has to do with number, and continuity with time and motion; co-existence, on the contrary, is the only thing that approaches extension. Accordingly, there must always be presupposed something which continually acts or spreads out, as the white color of milk, the glitter, malleability and weight of gold, the resistance of matter. For continuity in itself—extension is, namely, nothing but a continuum with the character of simultaneity—is no more capable of constituting a complete substance than plurality or number requires the presence necessarily of the things counted, repeated and continued. Hence I believe that our thought of substance is perfectly satisfied in the conception of force and not in that of extension. Besides, there should be no need to seek any other explanation for the conception of power or force than that it is the attribute from which change follows and its subject is substance itself. I fail to see what is inconceivable here. The Nature of things does not reveal any more adequate illumination. I am convinced that any unity of extended things exists only in abstraction, so long as we neglect the inner motions of the parts through which each and every part of matter is actually analyzed into different parts. The fact that everything is filled does not stand in the way. Also, material parts are distinguishable not only ex-

ternally, for they are also contrasted with eternally existing animal souls and entelechies.

I have noticed that Descartes (in one of his letters),
following the example of Kepler, also recognized inertia
in matter. They wished to derive this inertia from the
power which each object has to persevere in its own
state and to admit nothing external to its nature. Thus
they believe that the simple conception of extension
extends also to this phenomenon. However, the axiom
concerning the conservation of state must be construed
differently; namely, it preserves (to give an example) in
the case of curvilinear motion not its curvature but its
direction. But it is self-evident that a force present in
matter and preserving its state cannot be derived in any
way from extension. I admit that every object perseveres
in its state until some sufficient reason for change arises.
That is a principle approaching metaphysical necessity; but it is not the same thing whether we assert that
something simply preserves its state until something
happens to change it—a case which also arises when the
subject is quite indifferent in regard to both states—or
whether, on the other hand, we assert that it is not indifferent but possesses a power accompanied by an inclination to preserve its own state and thus to resist actively
causes that would change it. I myself previously, in a
youthful work, started from the assumption that matter
was inherently indifferent to motion and rest; and then
have demonstrated as a consequence of the laws of
motion holding for such a system the hypothesis that a
very large body at rest must be set into motion by the
push of another body no matter how small that other
body is without the least diminution of the latter's
motion.

The case of such a world in which matter at rest
offers no resistance to being moved, might be conceived

as possible, but it would be a pure chaos. Two grounds,
to which I always refer in such reflections as these,
namely, success in experiment and considerations of a
rational order, have led me to the view that matter has'
been so constituted by God that it has a sort of inherent
aversion to motion and that this peculiarity is, in a word,
a *resistance;* whence a body as such opposes motion, so
that when at rest it resists motion, but when in motion
resists any stronger motion in the same direction, in
such a way that the force of the colliding body is diminished. Since therefore matter inherently opposes motion
through a universal passive force of resistance and is
driven to motion through a particular force of activity
or entelechy, it follows that its inertia during the whole
duration of the motion which is brought about through
the entelechy or the dynamic force, constantly offers
resistance. From this I have, in previous letters, deduced
that the single force is stronger or that the force is twice
as great when two units of velocity are added to a pound-
weight than when they are divided between two pounds,
and that, accordingly, the force of one with the double
velocity given to the pound-weight is double the force
which two single-pound weights have with the single
velocity. For if the velocity were equal in both situations,
the inertia in one pound of matter would offer half as
great a resistance as that of two pounds. The inequality
of the forces in both cases may be shown also in other
ways on the basis of our principle concerning the measure of force, but on the other hand it is also best deriv-
able from the consideration of inertia; so perfectly in
harmony is everything with everything else. The resistance of matter, accordingly, includes two aspects: impenetrability or antitype and resistance or inertia. In
this I place the essence of the passive principle or of
matter, since it is everywhere present in bodies or pro-

portional to their extension, just as I acknowledge in the case of active force, which externalizes itself in different ways by means of motion, an original entelechy and, in a word, something akin to the soul. For its nature consists in the fact that it constitutes an *enduring law* for a progressive series of changes which it undergoes with external impulsion. Nor can we dispense with this active principle or this original source of activity, for accidental or variable active forces and motion itself are definite, changing states of a substantial thing, but forces and activity cannot be states of a merely passive thing like matter. From this it therefore follows that a primary activity or substantial thing is given which varies according to the disposition of passive matter. Hence, it must be attributed to the secondary moving forces as well as to the motion itself of the secondary matter or to the complete bodies combining the active and the passive.

And so I come now to the connection between the souls or entelechies of organic bodies and the organic machine itself. In this I rejoice that so acute and judicious a man like you has not wholly mistaken my hypothesis. You explain it in fact quite excellently when you attribute to the soul an adequate idea of the organic machine, and my theory purports also to show that the essence of the soul is to represent bodies. Everything which follows from the laws of bodies must be represented to the soul in order and, indeed, very clearly; other things, on the contrary—whatever is involved in a plurality of bodies outside of one's own—are confused. The former is called understanding, the latter feeling.

I think you agree with me that the soul and the idea of the body do not signify the same thing. For the soul remains one and the same, while the idea of the body perpetually changes as the body itself, whose present state it represents, changes. In any case, the idea of the present bodily state constantly resides in the soul, but this idea is neither simple nor yet completely passive, but connected with a tendency of a new idea to arise from the previous one, so that consequently the soul is the source and foundation of all the manifold ideas of the same body, which successively arise according to definite laws. Now, when you construe adequate ideas so that they signify not the singular, variable state but the persisting law of the change itself, I have no objections, and I grant you that in the soul the idea of the body and the phenomena it offers are present. In addition to all this, we must discuss some still deeper problems, which I will not forbear to do in the given circumstances. For if it is also not easy—even in questions where I personally recognize necessary reasons—to deduce everything *a priori* with geometrical certainty or to explain everything completely, so I yet venture to promise that no objection can be raised which I shall not know how to meet. This, to my way of thinking, means not to despise things which are far removed from the senses, especially because among the most powerful indications of truth belongs the fact that scientific propositions agree with one another as well as with phenomena. However, objections which have some weight always serve to make clearer the nature of things. Hence, I recognize that I and all friends of the truth are exceptionally indebted to you: through your objections so much light is thrown on my thoughts that the result is that I now understand the latter better. If with the help which you, Bernouilli and other men offer (may it not be too sparing), I succeed in supporting what I have now been defending with convincing *demonstrations*, then I shall not withhold from anybody the fact that I owe so much to you. At least when I am assured by your judgment, I need not fear at all the opinions of others.

(Leibniz to De Volder, June 23, 1699)

. . . Your discussions of the concept of substance are, as was to be expected from you, both penetrating and highminded. In any case it is arbitrary which names one wishes to give to concepts, though the concepts which are formed in such a fashion do not always correspond to actually existing things or to customary linguistic usage.

We obtain the idea of substance, as you say, not from things but from concepts—but do we not form concepts themselves from things? The idea of substance is, according to you, a conception of the mind or, as the expression used to go, a "thing of reason" (*ens rationis*). This may be asserted indeed of every conception, and yet we can divide the *objects* to which the concepts refer, though not the concepts themselves, into two classes: real things and things of reason. Substance, however, must be a real, in fact, the most real thing. You distinguish further two kinds of concepts: one represents an essentially simple content from which no character can be abstracted without losing the whole itself; to this kind belong the substance *and* concept of extension, as you make it out. On the other hand, the second kind permits a concept to represent a duality or plurality of determinations. That is not entirely understandable to me: for *every* concept or definition is so formed that we cannot abstract from it without losing the whole defined content, though there can arise an other content that way. That happens if we abstract from a square the character of being equilateral, thus losing the square and leaving rectangularity to remain. In any case, a concept from which we cannot abstract must be simple and original; however, I do not believe that substance must be consti-

tuted by such a concept, no more than that the concept
of extension is of that kind. Furthermore, according to
your explanation a duality or plurality must be present
when one ingredient can be conceived quite independently of the others; so, for example, thought and extension are related in such a way that neither one includes
the other; on the other hand, motion includes extension,
whereas the converse is not true. Whence, motion is
either an accident or a mode. Now, in all of this I am
of quite another mind and hold that extension as well
as thought involves and presupposes motion, and that,
furthermore, substance and accident condition one another. Extension is an attribute, the extended, however,
or matter is not *a* substance but a plurality of *substances*. Extension and place are related to extended
things exactly as duration and time are to temporal
things. That things can be given which have no common
attributes at all is not evident. Also I cannot believe
that the concept of extension is original or of such a
sort that nothing can be abstracted from it, for it is
analyzed into *plurality* which extension has in common
with number, *continuity* which it shares with time, and
coexistence which it shares with unextended things. I
cannot believe that anybody would oppose the admission
of plurality in extension, especially since we grant parts
in what is actually given; otherwise we should have to
deny it in a crowd, in an army—in a word, in all things
generally. The continuity of motion does not coincide with
that of place, since the former comprehends the continuity of time as well as of any change of velocity. Time
is no more nor less a thing of reason than space is. Simultaneity, precedence and succession in existence are *real*
determinations, which they would not be, of course, if
the customary conception of matter and of substances
was binding. However, it is easier to indicate what these

concepts are *not* than to exhibit in words and to corroborate with reasons what they are.

According to you, the subject of extension is only a *logical* concept, understood, however, as a true concept. You might have with as much justification characterized it as a metaphysical concept. We easily neglect a truth that is evident even though it has in the meantime many consequences, nevertheless, which are not so evident. We must begin with nominal definitions, and this is what I meant when I said that there was no other explanation to seek for "force" than the one I adduced. The other consideration is of a causal kind and seeks to make intelligible the kind of way in which a change ensues; and here, of course, there is a great deal which may not be understandable to us. The unity of the extended is, according to you, also then to be assumed when it is differentiated into parts moving in different ways, since none of these can either exist or be conceived without the others. You assume therefore two things which I cannot admit: namely, that a part of the extended can neither exist nor be conceived without the other parts, and secondly, that everything of this kind forms a unity. From this you derive the *impossibility of empty space.* The proof of this impossibility is not brought forth by your school; and even if your opinion were accepted, it would only follow that a material part cannot exist without *something other,* but it does not have to be one of the specifically *chosen others*; for then this argument, it seems to me, proves too much, since it will also make what is diffused and remotely related a unity. As I understand unity, such things more properly indicate a plurality; they are *one* only in the same sense as an aggregate which is comprehended in an instant of consciousness. In a genuine single substance there is no plurality of substances. To extension I attribute neither inertia nor motion, determinations which I recognize in *matter* generally, but which are not contained in it by virtue of extension.

You observe quite correctly and in agreement with my own view that it goes contrary to the laws of force, of cause and effect, to have a large body suffer a push by a small one which goes on unpunished, so to speak, or unaffected. But just because of this I show that there is a dynamic principle by virtue of which the laws of force are observed, and that it consequently contains something else besides extension and impenetrability, since from these two hypotheses alone nothing like it can be demonstrated. I have imparted the same answer many years ago to an adversary in the *Journal de Paris*. That resistance signifies more than a merely passive state, I admit: but that secondary forces of motion cannot be corresponding states of a merely passive thing, and that consequently there is an active substantial principle, that is what I wanted to recall to those who still do not believe that every substance is active.

An extended body which should happen to be completely at rest belongs, I believe, to the same impossible category as the fastest motion and ought not be conceived as a distinct thing. You ask whether the active principle, on my view of extension, is a mode of extension, or a substance different from extension. I answer that it appears to me this active principle is the substantial and constitutive basis of extended things themselves or of matter, that is, of that whose nature sustains not only extension and impenetrability but also action and resistance. Extension itself is for me an attribute which results from a plurality of co-existing and constantly interdependent substances: The original force can consequently be neither extension itself nor a mode of the same. It also acts not on extension but on extended things. When you ask further whether a body full of souls has its own entelechy different from those of the souls in it, I answer that it has innumerable ones, since it consists again of parts which are besouled or as good as besouled. Though there is present in the soul an adequate idea of matter, the soul for me is still not the idea of matter itself, but the source of a multiplicity of ideas which arise internally from its own nature and which represent the different material states in accordance with an order. The idea is, so to speak, something dead and inherently immutable as the pattern; the soul, on the contrary, is something alive and active. In this sense I do not believe that there is some individual idea which strives by itself to bring about external changes, but I say that a multiplicity of ideas conforms to it from which any one of them can be inferred from the others. In another sense of the word, I could in any case say with assurance that the soul is the living or substantial idea, or better, that it is the substance which shapes ideas (*substantia ideans*). That is all you will be affirming when you say that ideas affect one another, in so far as they represent one another, for I believe that for you also ideas are not substances which support each other like bodies.

(Leibniz to De Volder, July 6, 1701)

. . . Substance should be, according to you, something whose conception has such a simple content that nothing can be taken away from the object conceived without destroying the whole. But is it not possible for a substance to add new realities to those of other substances? Surely every new reality serves, if I am not mistaken, as a foundation for new subjects of thought. Thus the Democriteans conceive space as a substance—this illustration is drawn on only for clarification, since, as you quite rightly observe, truth does not require it—and they conceive bodies as another more perfect substance which adds to mere extension the force of resistance. Some take as a case of novelty the fact that to certain bodies, a new reality and perfection can be added, namely, the capacity for *consciousness,* and the scholastic philosophy long ago regarded among bodies with souls the one with feeling as more perfect, and the one gifted with reason as the most perfect of all. I bring this up in order to observe that your conception of substance does not appear to agree with customary linguistic usage, but pertains only to simple substances. The same holds for the explanation that substance is that which is conceived through itself: * a proposition to which I have replied that an effect cannot be conceived better than through its cause, and that all substances have a cause with the exception of the first substance, God. Whereupon, you reply that a cause is required in order to know the existence but not the essence of a substance. Thereupon I make the following rejoinder: in order to know its essence the concept of a *possible* cause is required; for its existence an *actual* cause is required. I now foresee on your part a nice objection which rests on a geometrical example, for—you might say something of this sort—the concept of the ellipse, for example, does not depend on any one cause, since there are many possible causes for the same ellipse: viz., the cross-section of a cone, the section of a cylinder, and the motion of a string. The existence of an ellipse, however, cannot be conceived except by stipulating a determinate cause. And I reply further, *in the first place,* that if it is not necessary for the knowledge of the essence of an ellipse to conceive a determinate

* This is Spinoza's definition which De Volder had been defending in his letter to Leibniz. See Leibniz's Refutation of Spinoza in selection III-8, below.

cause, then neither the ellipse nor any other object, for that matter, can be perfectly conceived without its *a priori* possibility being demonstrated through a formal cause immanent in every particular mode of production of a thing. This necessarily requires simpler lines to be drawn. Secondly, I return to my previous argument, namely, that we obtain incomplete objects with lines and figures yielding objects similar to one another though produced through different causes, as, for example, the ellipse produced by a cross-section of a cone is similar to the one produced by a motion in a plane. However, in the concrete domain of completely determinate objects, this is impossible, and consequently, a *substance* can neither be perfectly similar to another nor can the same substance be produced in various ways. From this, apart from other grounds of proof, I have thence drawn the conclusion that atoms do not exist, that space is no substance, and that primary matter itself which is destitute of any activity should not be counted among substances.

I come now to modes which you and I distinguish from the remaining predicates, i.e., attributes and properties. If we find in the essence of modes only the fact that in order to be understood they need a concept outside their nature, then modes also become properties. Modes and properties share the common character of residing in an other thing. Because of this, their definition would also agree perfectly with those elements among which there does not subsist that relation of *inherence;* this is the case, as I have already shown, with cause and effect for effects need to be understood through their causes. In this way, then, all effects are modes of causes, and there can exist one and the same character in the mode of several things, for it can be the effect of several co-operative causes. Furthermore, who would deny that a substance is modified through the effect of another substance, for example, when a body is thrown back by an opposing obstacle? We shall therefore have to use the concept of *both* bodies in order to know distinctly the recoil of one of the bodies, and nevertheless the recoil is only a mode of that body insofar as it is possible for the other body to advance its course instead of throwing it back. Thus there.is still something more which belongs to modes, and the relation of inherence, which is common to properties and modes, affirms more than that the concept of another thing, outside their nature, is required. For in my view, there is nothing in the whole realm of created things which does not require the concept of other things in the totality of things, since all things exercise a reciprocal effect on one another, and we can consequently think nothing moved or modified without thinking the whole present state of the universe transformed. Besides, were A and B two absolutely simple substances of the kind you define them to be, I submit they could not really have any predicate in common. Nevertheless, it does not necessarily follow that there may not be a third, C, whose concept they both need. For just as relations come out of a plurality of absolute elements, so properties and activities may result from a plurality of substances. And as a relationship is not composed out of as many single relations as the objects and subjects of the relation present to us, so modes, which depend on several things, are not dissolved into several modes. Whence it follows not that a mode which needs several things cannot be a unity, but that it must be composed of a plurality of things. Besides, your concept of the origin of modes is not a correct explanation. For substance, as you define it, that is, whatever includes in itself only a simple apprehended content in relation to a single attribute, will have only *one* mode; for it is not evident whence different kinds of things could arise, since from the one only one can arise. Accordingly, a mode becomes immutable, contrary to hypothesis. Even further, in general no mode will have an existence of its own, since it is not evident how a mode can have a different status than an attribute. If it is assumed, as is commonly done, that bodies are identical with extension, and if extension is made out to be a simple and original attribute, then it is in no way explicable how in general a multiplicity will arise in bodies or how a plurality of bodies can exist. Indeed, I have shown in another place (in my reply to Sturm, published in the *Acta Eruditorum*) that if matter were not differentiated—as it is primarily through the entelechies—no manifold of phenomena could arise, that furthermore, then, only uniform states of extension would ever differentiate one another. In addition, I make no distinction here between the general concept of substance and the concept of determined substance; for every substance is determined, although different substances are determined in different ways. So far as *my* concept of substance is concerned, I should prefer to see it come out of our mutual deliberation—for I see that at least the beginnings are promising—than that I alone should bring it to light and also expound it.

As I take up again the next to the last letter of yours in order to have everything before me, I come across some things worthy of comment. It is difficult to bring up an example of a concept of such a kind that none of its given characters can be taken away from it. The original concepts always lie concealed in the results of reasoning, although they may clearly be lifted out and distinguished with patience. I doubt whether a body without motion can be understood, but I submit that motion without a body may be conceived. The concept of motion, however, includes not only bodies and changes,

but also the ground and determination of motion which
cannot be discovered in matter—if we assume its essence
to consist in merely passive determination, that is, in
extension alone or in extension and impenetrability. In
extension I already understand a plurality, namely, for
one thing, continuity—which it shares with time and
motion—and coexistence. Whence it is not necessary that
extension be considered as a whole or as nothing. Evidently one thing more is required for the existence of
extension, which is continually repeated, or a plurality
of things whose continual existence it is. You ask, what
we still assume in things which corresponds to extension
apart from extension itself? I answer that to mere extension the objective content of experience adds action and
passion. Then, you reply, extension is a mode of extended
things. I answer again that extension, as I understand
it, is not formed as a mode of the substances from which
it results, because it is itself immutable and indicates
a numerical determination of things which always remains one and the same in any arbitrary modification of
things. And surely you admit that modes are variable.
In addition, I submit that not only extension but also
action and passion cannot be conceived through themselves alone, and that in fact, as I have already remarked, it is not necessary or easy to arrive at concepts
of the highest simplicity. Consequently, if we demand
that sort of concept for substance, I fear that we would
be led to the denial of all created substances, with which
the knot would not be untied but cut through.

(Leibniz to De Volder, Dec. 27, 1701)

To return to your remarks, I do not believe any example can be given of a reality which has nothing whatsoever in common with another thing, and so might make
a substance out of itself.

For if the general concept of substance had to conform to the simplest or original substance, it becomes the *one and only* substance. Now I admit that it is within your power to define the word "substance" so that God alone becomes substance and everything else has another character. However, I fail to see how it is a suitable concept for the remainder of things or agrees with that of the general manner of speaking according to which all persons including yourself or myself are called substances. You will not dispute that this usage is permissible and that it is useful, as things go. Moreover, not everything which holds for a single unique substance fits the general concept of substance, no more than it is true that everything which holds for a square fits the general concept of parallelogram. I admit that every substance is in a certain sense simple; yet this holds for substance and not for an aggregate of substances.

If one now also supposes that every substance exists eternally, nevertheless all things, except the original first cause, must have causes, namely, objective grounds why they should exist rather than not exist.

If the properties B and C are conceived to be different from one another and from the essence A, then there must still be posited in their concepts something other than A.

If extended things are conceived through themselves alone, then nothing can be thought to exist except in space.

. . . Similarly, I hold that two subjects A and B which have no predicate in common are an impossibility. Also untrue is the consequence that a concept C cannot form a unity if two different predicates which help to constitute it are separable from one another. So, for example, a square is an equilateral rectangle, but we can separate the concept of rectangularity from that of equi-laterality—as in the figures called ἑτερομηκες—and the concept of equilaterality from that of rectangularity—as in the triangle, pentagon, etc.—and despite that, the square remains a *unique* figure having a unitary concept.

. . . You admit that existence and continuity, which are united in the *concept* of extension, are "formally" different from it, and I wish nothing more: if I make a concept merely by combining different formal concepts, the result is nothing original. Among the principal errors of the Cartesians is their view that extension is some-thing original and absolute, and constitutive of substance. This error must be discarded if we are to arrive at a correct philosophy, for only after this is done can we, so far as I can see, succeed in obtaining the right insight into the essence of bodies and of substance. The assump-tion of such an original property makes philosophy stag-nant, as can be seen among the defenders of occult quali-ties. That some have also nowadays occasionally sinned in this respect I have shown, not long ago in the Parisian *Journal des Savans;* I argued against the occasionalists who do not wish to refer sensations of heat, cold, etc., to states of motion but regard them as indefinable arbitrary qualities with which God impresses the mind on the occasion of the motions.

However, to return to our subject, extension never appears to us other than as a plurality of things whose togetherness is continuous, and we find nothing more pre-supposed in it than just this fact. Also the connection of these things is not a necessary one; for we can take away something and substitute something else for it without this making much difference. If we distinguish extension from extended things, then it is something abstract like duration or like number considered detached from things, in which the connection of the parts is just as necessary as with extension. So in the trinity three intelligible unities are held together through an eternal bond, although the connection of three *things* is perhaps not a necessary one. If we think of removing these determined things, then others always remain behind and number never lacks objects that can be counted; also there is just as little emptiness among them as there is in space or time or other orders of relationship—if we do not assume the universe annihilated so that only pure possibility remains. So that is what extension, duration, and number are without things, if we also regard their common substance as a kind of Platonic idea. Extension is furthermore a relative concept, for it is related to a determined nature whose spread it represents; duration is related to a continually persisting subject. Extension then has the peculiarity that different extended things are found successively in one and the same place, that is, they can enter into the same relation in the order of coexistence, whereas time is peculiar in that several elements can exist together at the same instant.

(Leibniz to De Volder, April 1702)

. . . I am not of the opinion that in the general concept of substance a single reality and perfection is to be assumed. In fact, it appears that your substance has to possess no more than a single attribute as a consequence of your concept of substance. For let a substance have the attributes A and B; since there can now be, according to you, another substance which possesses only the attribute A, so obviously the substance AB which cannot be conceived through itself but only through the substance A, would no longer be a substance on your explanation. Also if an absolutely simple attribute by itself alone can constitute a substance, there is no reason why another attribute cannot also do the same. Should we presuppose that every substance has only a single attribute, then the origin of modes and of changes in the nature of things is utterly inconceivable, for where else can they come from if not from substances? I hold to the contrary view that there is no substance which does not stand in relation to the realities of all other substances. A substance with only *one* attribute is consequently inconceivable; indeed, we cannot, so far as I see, grasp as such any simple and absolute attribute or predicate. I know well that the Cartesians on the first point and Spinoza on the second point have a different opinion, but I also know that that comes from an insufficiently penetrating analysis. The peculiar touchstone here consists in the demonstrative derivation of predicates from the subject. For in every proposition demonstrable in and by itself but not yet demonstrated there must be contained an insufficiently analyzed term.

When I say that every substance is simple, I understand by that, that it lacks parts. Were there *one* substance, contrary to everything that exists in necessary association with one another, then it would follow, if we exclude empty space, that all parts of matter, since they are necessarily connected with one another, would constitute *one* substance. As a result, however, substance would be equivalent to the aggregate of substances, whereas you yourself on this matter often call attention to the fact that it is a question here of the *concept* of substance and not of the *aggregate* made out of substances. The proposition which you apparently oppose to me as an impossible consequence, I suppose to be "that the extended, if it were conceived through itself alone, would no longer be the extended"; for that kind of extended things contains a contradiction. Also I hold as certain that whatever is conceived through itself alone cannot be felt at a place, for "to be felt at a place" is no merely external determination, as there is in general no external determination which does not presuppose an internal one as a foundation—a proposition which belongs also to first principles.

. . . The Cartesians are of the opinion that a substance may be constituted by extension, because they regard extension as something original. But if they would go into an analysis of this concept, they would see that mere extension does not furnish extended things any more than number yields things counted. I grant you that as the concept of triad does not suffice for the understanding of these three things, so also the concept of extension or of being spread out does not suffice for the understanding of the subject which is spread out. Furthermore, it is precisely this nature into which, to my mind, we must inquire from the start. And I leave you to judge whether it can be something other than a dynamical principle, that is, one from which action and passion follow.

Even if I cannot furnish the *a priori* proof which you especially wish, would my hypothesis on that account be finally less in agreement with things? If the proof were also capable of being made only *a posteriori,* the proposition in question would nevertheless be raised above the status of a mere hypothesis. And can anything more serious be brought against that other concept of substance than the objection that no modes or changes can arise from it, as you yourself admit? If then this impossibility were not also actually proven, we could still be content with creating concepts which would agree with experience, which are practically useful, and which solve its difficulties, and as a result of which the way is opened to higher grounds. Should someone then raise any doubts at all about my statements, I shall take the trouble frankly and publicly to satisfy him, as I have always been in the habit of doing while one expects to give up this hypothesis for some other one perhaps.

(Leibniz to De Volder, June 20, 1703)

To both of your letters filled with deep reflections I reply with this one writing. And I really hope that from the answer I gave Bayle my opinion on most points has also become clearer to you; so at least your letter appears to me to testify distinctly. Bayle also himself writes that he has now taken a deeper look into my hypothesis; it appears that he has difficulties only with the possibility of the continual progression of thoughts in the soul. For me there is no difficulty in this, either on the side of experience—for why should we not consider such a progression which we observe so frequently to be also possible—or on the side of *a priori* rational grounds, since it proceeds necessarily, in my judgment, in accordance with the individual essence of the substance involved, or has a tendency to do so. Hence it further comes about that everywhere—or at least in the domain of concrete, perfectly determinate things— the present conceals the future in its womb, so that all future states are predetermined by the present.

The difficulties you raise stem from another source. First of all, I return to your earlier letters in which you ask for a necessary connection between matter—or resistance—and active force, since they do not appear to be merely inconsequentially and superficially related. The cause of the connection, however, lies in the fact that though every substance is active and every finite substance is acted on, resistance is necessarily tied up with the state of being acted on. This kind of connection helps the nature of things to be maintained: they are not so destitute as to be wanting in the active principle and put up with a void in forms as well as in contents, not to mention anything at present of the common sources of activity and *unity*.

I do not approve of the theory of attributes on which people lean nowadays, for how can a simple absolute predicate, as an attribute is defined today, constitute substance? I, for one, do not find in any concepts any completely absolute predicate, that is, a predicate which contains no relation to other things. At least, thought and extension which are commonly adduced as examples, are certainly not such attributes, as I have frequently shown. But furthermore, a predicate is not identical with its subject, unless concretely labelled so; consequently, the mind belongs to the thinking subject and not to the objects of thought. For the subject has the property of containing past and future states of consciousness in addition to present states.

Those who explain all the differences of bodies only by what they call modes of extension, and, as you say, nowadays nearly everybody does so—if we continue to exclude empty space—do not doubt that bodies are to be distinguished from each other only as modes. But I maintain that two individual substances must be different for reasons deeper than that they are different modes. Even as things are commonly made out, you will find that they are never distinguished as modes. Namely, if we take two equal bodies A and B having the same figure and motion, it follows from the sort of concept of bodies which makes them presumably modes of extension that bodies in general have no internal, distinctive characteristics. Are not A and B distinct individuals? Or is it possible for things to be different even though they cannot in any way be distinguished from one another? This and innumerable other similar questions show sufficiently that the true conception of things is completely turned upside down by this new philosophy which makes substances out of merely material or passive subjects. Things which are distinguishable must differ from each other with respect to some character or possess some assignable difference, and we wonder only why this most clear of all basic principles and so many others have not generally been elaborated. Men, however, commonly are more concerned to satisfy their sensory imagination than to seek first principles; whence, the many monstrosities which have made inroads to the injury of true philosophy. So people apply only imperfectly abstract or mathematical concepts which may appeal to thought but which does not come to grips with the nature of things as specific existences. Illustrations of such abstractions are the concept of time as well as of space or merely mathematical extension, purely passive masses, motion in the mathematical sense, etc. In such cases we can handle diversities easily without individual diversification; for example, two parts of a straight line, because indeed the straight line is something incomplete and abstract and definable merely by theory. However, in nature itself any straight line you may take is individually different from any other straight line you may find. Accordingly, it cannot come about that two bodies are perfectly equal and alike. Even if they differ only in position, their individual relations to the environment must be taken into account, so that more is involved in their distinguishability than just position or just the force of some *external* determination, as is generally believed. Bodies cannot exist in nature as they are commonly conceived—as something like the atoms of the Democriteans or the perfect globules of the Cartesians; these are nothing but the imperfect conceptual constructions of philosophers who have not penetrated deeply into the essence of things. Besides this, I have shown (in another unanswered argument in my last reply to Sturm) in my rejection of empty space that matter so long as it is commonly thought to be determined by mere modifications of extension does not suffice to fill the universe, and that further we must assume in matter something necessarily quite different, amounting to a principle of change and diversity in phenomena, so that along with the expansion, contraction, and motion of the several parts of matter, a principle is required for its consilience and diversification. Consequently, I insist on assuming that no substance can be created or annihilated.

7a. FURTHER DISCUSSION OF *VIS VIVA*
(From letter to M. Bayle, 1702)

. . . You remark, Sir, that good minds are stumped by the difficulties of the free will of man, and that they say they cannot understand how if the soul of man is a created substance it can have its own true and internal force of acting. I would wish to understand more clearly why created substance cannot have such a force, for I would rather believe that without that force it would not be a substance. For the nature of substance consists, in my opinion, in that regulated tendency with which phenomena arise in an orderly fashion, a tendency which it received from the start and which is conserved in it by the author of things from whom all realities or perfections emanate constantly through a manner of continual creation.

Concerning free will I am of the sentiment of the Thomists and other philosophers who believe that everything is predetermined, and I see no ground for doubting it. However, that does not prevent us from having a

freedom not only exempt from constraint but even from
necessity, and in that we are like God himself who is
always determined in his actions for he cannot fail to
choose the best. But if he had nothing from which to
choose, and if what he does were the only thing possible,
he would be subjected to necessity. The more perfect
one is, the more one is determined to the good, and so is
more free at the same time. For our power and knowledge are so much the more extended and our will so
much the more limited within the bounds of perfect
reason.

If my thought about force can offer any satisfaction
to you, Sir, as well as to any small number of persons
like you, I should be quite content. Perhaps, the explanation I am going to put forward here will satisfy you
even more. My first consideration had been formerly
that there ought to be conserved in nature something
that would constantly produce an equal effect; for example, several bodies meeting one another, if you will,
on a horizontal plane, and no part of the force being
absorbed by friction, by the medium, or by the minute
parts of the bodies, I judged that it was necessary that
all of them together should be capable by their impetus
to raïse the same weight to the same height, or tighten
some springs to certain determinate degrees of torsion,
or impart certain velocities to certain bodies. But examining the matter more closely, I found that this conservation of force did not agree with that of the quantity
of motion. . . .

However, it is not the quantity of this movement, but
that of the force which I conserve; very nearly as when
two globes are put one into the other, the sum of the
surfaces is not conserved but that of the solidities
[masses], although the latter are never without corresponding surfaces. But now here is what will bring the

difficulty to a resolution. It is by way of a new approach which has taught me that not only is the force conserved but also the very quantity of kinetic action which is different from that of the motion [momentum], as you are going to see through a line of reasoning by which, I was myself surprised, seeing that nobody had made so easy an observation on so well worn a subject. Here is my argument: In the uniform motion of a single body (1) the action of traversing two leagues in two hours is double the action of traversing one league in one hour (for the first action contains the second exactly twice), (2) the action of traversing one league in one hour is double the action of traversing one league in two hours (for the actions producing the same effect are to each other as their speeds). Therefore, (3) the action of traversing two leagues in two hours is four times the action of traversing one league in two hours. This demonstration shows that a moving body receiving a double or triple speed in order to be able to produce a double or triple effect in the same time, receives an action four or nine times as great. Whence actions are to one another as the squares of the speeds. Now that happens most fortunately to agree with my estimate of the force obtained from experiment or from the principle of avoiding perpetual mechanical motion. For according to my estimate forces are to one another as the heights from which heavy bodies might descend in order to acquire their speeds. And as the force is always conserved in order to raise something finally to the same height or to produce some other effect, it follows that there is also conserved the same quantity of kinetic action in the world; that is to say, in order to get it straight, there is in one hour as much kinetic action in the universe as there is in any other hour whatsoever. So the purpose of our philosophers, and particularly of the late M. Descartes, was good in conserving action and in estimating the force by the action; but they have taken a *quid pro quo* by taking what they call the quantity of motion [momentum] for the quantity of kinetic action [energy]. There are very few persons to whom I have divulged this line of reasoning, not wishing to prostitute it before those who have no taste for abstract thoughts. I am not speaking here of the forces and actions which are also respectively conserved and have their own estimated values; and there are many other marvelous equalities or conservations which indicate not only the constancy but also the perfection of the Author of nature.

Sir, your immense factual researches, which are with great justification admired, have in no way injured your beautiful reflections on what are the profounder parts of philosophy. I cannot myself always dispense with that sort of discussion, having been even obliged to come to genealogical questions which would be most frivolous were not the interests of states often dependent on them. I have often worked on the history of Germany in so far as it has a relation to these countries, and this has furnished me with a few observations belonging to universal history. Thus I have learned not to neglect the knowledge of facts. But if I had the choice, I should prefer natural history to civil, and study the habits and laws that God has established in nature rather than those observed among men.

8. ON THE PRINCIPLE OF CONTINUITY
(From a Letter to Varignon, 1702)

. . . You ask me for some elucidation of my Principle of Continuity. I certainly think that this Principle is a general one and holds good not only in Geometry but also in Physics. Since Geometry is but the science of the Continuous, it is not surprising that that law is observed everywhere in it, for Geometry by its very nature cannot admit any sudden break in its subject-matter. In truth we know that everything in that science is perfectly interconnected and that no single instance can be adduced of any property suddenly vanishing or arising without the possibility of our determining the intermediate transition, the points of inflection and singular points, with which to render the change explicable, so that an algebraic equation which represents one state exactly virtually represents all the other states which may properly occur in the same subject. The universality of this principle in geometry soon informed me that it could not fail to apply also to physics, since I see that in order for there to be any regularity and order in Nature, the physical must be constantly in harmony with the geometrical, and that the contrary would happen if wherever geometry requires some continuation physics would allow a sudden interruption. To my mind everything is interconnected in the universe by virtue of metaphysical reasons so that *the present is always pregnant with the future,* and no given state is explicable naturally without reference to its immediately preceding state. If this be denied, the world will have hiatuses which would upset the Principle of Sufficient Reason and will compel recourse to miracles or to pure chance in the explanation of phenomena. I maintain then (to explain myself in algebraic fashion) that if, in imitation of Mr. Hudde who claimed he could give an algebraic curve for the profile of a given face, we could express by a formula of a higher Characteristic some essential property of the universe, we could read from it all the successive states of every part of the Universe at all assigned times.

Also it happens to be the case that we do not find a single natural event which belies this great Principle; on the contrary, all those events we do know exactly justify the principle perfectly. It has been recognized that the Laws of the Collision of Bodies left to us by Descartes are false; but I can show that they are false only because they would allow hiatuses in events by violating the Law of Continuity, and that as soon as we make the corrections which restore that Law, we come upon those very laws which Messrs. Huyghens and Wren have found and which experiments have confirmed. Continuity being therefore a necessary prerequisite or a distinctive character of the true laws of the communication of motion, can we doubt that all phenomena are subject to it or become intelligible except by means of the true laws of the communication of motions? But as, according to my view, there is a perfect continuity reigning in the order of successive things, so there is a similar order in simultaneous things, which fact establishes the plenum as real, and consigns empty spaces to imaginary realms. In things existing simultaneously there may be continuity even though the imagination perceives only breaks; because many things appear to our eyes to be completely dissimilar and disunited which nevertheless turn out to be perfectly similar and unified internally if we could get to know them distinctly. If we consider just the external shape of parabolas, ellipses, and hyperbolas, we should be tempted to believe that there was an immense gap between any two of these kinds of curves. However, we know that they are intimately connected so that it is impossible to insert between two of them some other intermediate kind which may enable us to go from one to the other by more imperceptible nuances. Therefore I think I have good reasons for believing that all the different classes of beings whose assemblage forms the universe are, in the ideas of God who knows distinctly their essential gradations, only like so many ordinates of the same curve whose unity does not allow us to place some other ordinates between two of them because that would be a mark of disorder and imperfection. Men are therefore related to animals, these to plants, and the latter directly to fossils which will be linked in their turn to bodies which the senses and the imagination represent to us as perfectly dead and formless. Now the Law of Continuity demands that *when the essential determinations of one being approximate those of another, as a consequence, all the properties of the former should also gradually approximate those of the latter.* Hence it is necessary that all the orders of natural beings form but a single chain in which different kinds like so many links clasp one another so firmly that it is impossible for the senses and imagination to fix the exact point where one begins or ends; all the species which border on or dwell, so to speak, in regions of inflection or singularity are bound to be ambiguous and endowed with characters related equally well to neighboring species. Thus, for example, the existence of Zoophytes, or as Buddaeus calls them *Plant-Animals,* is nothing freakish, but it is even befitting the order of nature that there should be such.

So great is the force of the Principle of Continuity in my philosophy, that I should not be surprised to learn that creatures might be discovered which in respect to several properties, for example, nutrition or reproduction, could pass for either vegetables or animals, and that would upset the commonly accepted rules based on the assumption of a perfect and absolute separation of the different orders of simultaneous creatures that fill the universe. I say I should not be greatly surprised, but I am even persuaded that there ought to be such beings which Natural History will some day come to know when it will have studied more that infinity of living beings whose small size hides them from ordinary observation and which are buried in the entrails of the earth and in the abyss of its waters. We have only yesterday begun to observe things, and how can we justly deny to reason what we have not yet had an opportunity to see? The Principle of Continuity is therefore beyond doubt to me, and might help establish several important truths in a genuine philosophy which rises above the imagination to seek the origin of phenomena in intellectual regions. I flatter myself for having some ideas on this score, but this century is not ripe to receive them.

8a. FURTHER DISCUSSION OF CONTINUITY
(Excerpts from a Letter to Remond de Montmort, 1715)

I. As to metempsychosis, I believe that the order of things makes it inadmissible, for that order requires everything to be distinctly explicable and nothing done by leaps. But the passage of the soul from one body into another would be a strange and inexplicable leap. There is always a presentiment in animals of what is to happen because the body is in a continual stream of change, and what we call birth or death is only a greater and more sudden change than usual, like the drop of a river or of a waterfall. But these leaps are not absolute and not the sort I disapprove of; e.g., I do not admit a body going from one place to another without passing through a medium. Such leaps are not only precluded in motions, but also in the whole order of things or of truths. That is why I showed Mr. Hartsoeker in some Letters inserted not long ago in the *Mémoires de Trévoux* that the assumption of the vacuum and atoms would lead us to such discontinuities. Now as in a geometric line there are certain special points called maxima, points of inflection, points of singularity, etc., and as there are lines which have an infinite number of such points, we must in like manner conceive in the animal's or person's life periods of extraordinary changes which are not outside general law, just as the special points on a curve may be determined by its general nature or its equation. . . .

III. There are doubtless a thousand irregularities, a thousand disorders, in particulars. But it is impossible that there should be any in the whole, or even in each Monad, because each Monad is a living mirror of the Universe, according to its point of view. Now it is impossible that the entire Universe should not be well regulated, the prevailing perfection being the reason for the existence of this system of things in preference to any other possible system. Thus disorders can appear only in the parts. In like manner there are geometric lines in which there are irregular parts, but when we consider the entire line, we find it perfectly ordered according to its equation or general nature. Whence all these particular disorders are straightened out advantageously to the whole, even in the case of each Monad.

IV. . . . Moreover, as the Monads are subject to passions, excepting the prime Monad, they are not pure forces; Monads are the grounds not only of actions but also of resistances or passivities, and their passions reside in their confused perceptions. This also comprehends matter or the infinite in numbers. . . . I have always been very pleased, ever since my youth, with the Morals of Plato and to some extent with his Metaphysics: also these two sciences go together as Mathematics and Physics.

9. CONSIDERATIONS ON THE PRINCIPLES OF LIFE, AND ON PLASTIC NATURES; BY THE AUTHOR OF THE SYSTEM OF PRE-ESTABLISHED HARMONY

(Histoire des Ouvrages des Savans, 1705)

As the dispute which has arisen on *plastic natures* and on the *principles of life* has given celebrated persons who are interested in it occasion to speak of my system, of which some explanation seems to be demanded (see *Biblioth. Chois.*, vol. 5, art. 5, p. 301, and also *l'Histoire des Ouvrages des Savans,* of 1704, art. 7, p. 393), I have thought it would be in place to add something on the subject to what I have already published in various passages of the Journals quoted by Bayle in his Dictionary, article *Rorarius.* I really admit principles of life diffused throughout all nature, and immortal since they are indivisible substances, or UNITIES; just as bodies are multitudes liable to perish by dissolution of their parts. These principles of life, or these souls, have perception and desire. When I am asked if they are substantial forms, I reply by making a distinction. For if this term is taken as Descartes takes it, when he maintains against Regis that the rational soul is the substantial form of man, I will answer, Yes. But I answer, No, if the term is taken as those take it who imagine that there is a substantial form of a piece of stone, or of any other non-organic body; for principles of life belong only to organic bodies. It is true (according to my system) that there is no portion of matter in which there are not innumerable organic and animated bodies, under which I include not only animals and plants, but perhaps also other kinds which are entirely unknown to us. But for all this, it must not be said that each portion of matter is animated, just as we do not say that a pond full of fishes is an animated body, although a fish is.

However, my opinion on the *principles of life* is in certain points different from that hitherto taught. One of these points is that all have believed that these principles of life change the course of the motion of bodies, or at least give occasion to God to change it, whereas, according to my system, this course is not changed at all in the order of nature, God having pre-established it as it ought to be. The Peripatetics believed that souls had an influence on bodies and that will or desire could have some influence on bodies. And the celebrated authors who have been responsible for the present dispute, by their principles of life and their plastic natures, have held the same view, although they are not Peripatetics. We cannot say as much of those who have employed ἀρχαί, or *hylarchic principles,* or other immaterial principles under different names. Descartes having well recognized that there is a law of nature, according to which the same quantity of force is preserved (although he was deceived in its application by confounding quantity of force with quantity of motion), believed that we ought not to ascribe to the soul the power of increasing or diminishing the force of bodies, but simply that of changing their direction, by changing the course of the animal spirits. And those Cartesians, who have introduced the doctrine of Occasional Causes, believed that the soul not being able to exert any influence on body, it was necessary that God should change the course or direction of the animal spirits according to the volitions of the soul. But if at the time of Descartes the new law of nature, which I have demonstrated, had been known, which affirms that not only the same quantity of total force of bodies which are in communication, but also their total direction, is preserved, he would probably

have discovered my system of Pre-established Harmony.
For he would have recognized that it is as reasonable
to say that the soul does not change the quantity of the
direction of bodies, as it is reasonable to deny to the
soul the power of changing the quantity of their force,
both being equally contrary to the order of things and
to the laws of nature, as both are equally inexplicable.
Thus, according to my system, souls or the principles
of life, do not change anything in the ordinary course of
bodies, and do not even give to God *occasion* to do so.
Souls follow their laws, which consist in a certain development of perceptions, according to goods and evils;
and bodies also follow their laws, which consist in the
laws of motion; and nevertheless these two beings of
entirely different kind are in perfect accord, and correspond like two clocks perfectly regulated on the same
basis, although perhaps of an entirely different construction. This is what I call Pre-established Harmony, which
removes any notion of miracles from purely natural
actions, and makes things run their course regulated in
an intelligible manner; whereas the common system has
recourse to absolutely inexplicable influences, and in that
of Occasional Causes, God, by a sort of general law and
as if by agreement, is obliged to change at each moment
the natural course of the thoughts of the soul to accommodate them to the impressions of the body, and to disturb the natural course of the motions of bodies according to the volitions of the soul; that which can only be
explained by a perpetual miracle, while I explain it quite
intelligibly by the natures which God has established
in things.

My system of Pre-established Harmony furnishes a
new proof, hitherto unknown, of the existence of God,
since it is quite manifest that the agreement of so many
substances, of which the one has no influence upon the

other, could only come from a general cause, on which
all of them depend, and that this must have infinite
power and wisdom to pre-establish all these harmonies.
M. Bayle himself has thought that there never has
been an hypothesis which so sets in relief the knowledge
which we have of the divine wisdom. The system has
moreover the advantage of preserving in all its rigor and
generality the great principle of physics, that a body
never receives change in its motion except by another
body in motion which impels it. *Corpus non moveri nisi
impulsum a corpore contiguo et moto.* This law has been
violated hitherto by all those who have admitted souls
or other immaterial principles, all Cartesians even included. The followers of Democritus, Hobbes, and some
other thoroughgoing materialists, who have rejected all
immaterial substance, having alone up to this time preserved this law, have believed that they found therein
ground for insulting other philosophers, as if they thus
maintained a very irrational opinion. But the ground of
their triumph has been but apparent and *ad hominem;*
and far from serving them, it serves to confound them.
And now, their illusion being discovered and their advantage turned against them, it seems that it may be said
that it is the first time that the better philosophy shows
itself also most in conformity in all respects to reason,
nothing remaining which can be opposed to it. This general principle, although it excludes particular prime
movers, by making us deny this quality to souls, or to
immaterial created principles, leads us so much the more
surely and clearly to the universal Prime Mover, from
whom comes the succession as well as the harmony of
perceptions and motions. There are, as it were, two
kingdoms, the one of efficient causes, the other of final;
each of which separately suffices in detail for explaining
all as if the other did not exist. But the one does not

suffice without the other in the general nature of their origin, for they both emanate from one source in which the power which constitutes efficient causes and the wisdom which regulates final causes are found united. This maxim also, that there is no motion which has not its origin in another motion, according to laws of mechanics, leads us again to the Prime Mover; because matter being indifferent in itself to all motion or rest, and nevertheless always possessing motion with all its force and direction, it could not have been put in motion except by the author himself of matter.

There is still another difference between the opinions of other authors who favor the principles of life, and mine. It is that I believe at the same time both that these principles of life are immortal and that they are everywhere; whereas according to the common opinion the souls of brutes perish, and according to the Cartesians, man only really has a soul and even perception and desire; an opinion which will never be approved, and which has only been embraced because it was seen that it was necessary either to accord to brutes immortal souls or to avow that the soul of man might be mortal. But it ought rather to have been said that, every simple substance being imperishable and every soul being consequently immortal, that which could not be reasonably refused to brutes, cannot fail also to subsist always, although in a way very different from our own, since brutes, as far as can be judged, are lacking in that reflection which makes us think of ourselves. And we do not see why men have been so loath to accord to the bodies of other organic creatures immaterial, imperishable substances, since the defenders of atoms have introduced material substances which do not perish, and since the soul of the brute has no more reflection than an atom. For there is a broad difference between feeling which is common to these souls and the reflection which accompanies reason, since we have a thousand feelings without reflecting upon them; and I do not think that the Cartesians have ever proved or can prove that every perception is accompanied by consciousness. It is reasonable also that there may be substances capable of perception below us as there are above; and that our soul far from being the last of all is in a middle position from which one may descend and ascend; otherwise there would be a want of order which certain philosophers call a gap of the forms (*vacuum formarum*). Thus reason and nature lead men to the opinion I have just propounded; but prejudices have turned them aside from it.

This view leads us to another in which I am again obliged to diverge from the received opinion. Those who are of my opinion will be asked, what the souls of brutes will do after the death of the animal, and the dogma of Pythagoras, who believed in the transmigration of souls, will be imputed to us, which not only the late M. Van Helmont, the younger, but also an ingenious author of certain Metaphysical Meditations, published at Paris, have wished to revive. But it must be known that I am far from this opinion, because I believe that not only the soul but also the animal itself subsists. Persons very accurate in experiments have already in our day perceived that it may be doubted whether an altogether new animal is ever produced, and whether animals wholly alive as well as plants are not already in miniature in germs before conception. This doctrine being granted, it will be reasonable to think that what does not begin to live also does not cease to live, and that death, like generation, is only the transformation of the same animal, which is sometimes augmented and sometimes diminished. This again reveals to us hitherto unthought-of marvels of divine contrivance. This is, that the mechanisms of nature being mechanisms even to their smallest parts, are indestructible, by reason of the envelopment of one little mechanism in a greater *ad infinitum*. Thus one finds one's self obliged at the same time to maintain the pre-existence of the soul as well as of the animal, and the substance of the animal as well as of the soul.

I have insensibly been led on to explain my view of the formation of plants and animals, since it appears from what I have just said that they are never formed altogether anew. I am therefore of the opinion of Cudworth (the greater part of whose excellent work pleases me extremely) that the laws of mechanics alone could not form an animal where there is nothing yet organized; and I find that, with reason, he is opposed to what some of the ancients have imagined on this subject, and even Descartes in his conception of man the formation of which costs him so little, but which is also very far from being a real man. And I reinforce this opinion of Cudworth by presenting for consideration the fact that matter arranged by divine wisdom must be essentially organized throughout, and that thus there is mechanism in the parts of the natural mechanism *ad infinitum,* and so many enfolded one within another, that an organic body never could be produced altogether new and without any preformation; nor could an animal already existing be entirely destroyed. Thus I have no need to resort with Cudworth to certain immaterial *plastic natures,* although I remember that Julius Scaliger and other Peripatetics, and also certain partisans of the Helmontian doctrine of Archæi, have believed that the soul manufactures its own body. I may say of it *non mi bisogna, e non mi basta,* for the very reason that preformation and organisms *ad infinitum* will furnish me the material plastic natures suited to the requirements of the case; whereas the immaterial plastic principles are as little necessary as they are little capable of satisfying the case. For since animals are never formed naturally of a non-organic mass, the mechanism incapable of producing *de novo* these infinitely varied organs can very well derive them through the development and through the transformation of a pre-existing organic body. Meanwhile those who employ plastic natures, whether material or immaterial, in no wise weaken the proof of the existence of God drawn from the marvels of nature, which appear particularly in the structure of animals, provided that these defenders of immaterial plastic natures add a particular direction from God, and provided that those who with me make use of a material cause in assenting to plastic mechanism, maintain not only a continual preformation, but also an original divine pre-establishment. Thus whatever view we take, we cannot overlook the divine existence in wishing to explain these marvels, which have always been admired, but which have never been more apparent than in my system.

We see by this, that not only the soul but also the animal must subsist always, in the ordinary course of things. But the laws of nature are made and applied with so much order and so much wisdom that they serve more than one end, and God, who occupies the position of inventor and architect as regards the mechanism and works of nature, occupies the position of king and father to substances possessing intelligence; and of these the soul is a spirit formed after his image. And as regards spirits, his kingdom, of which they are the citizens, is the most perfect monarchy which can be discovered; in which there is no sin which does not bring upon itself some punishment, and no good action without some recompense; in which everything tends finally to the glory of the monarch and the happiness of the subjects, by the most beautiful combination of justice and goodness which can be desired. Nevertheless I dare not assert anything positively either as regards pre-existence or as regards the details of the future condition of human souls, since God, as regards this, might make use of extraordinary ways in the kingdom of grace; nevertheless that which natural reason favors ought to be preferred, at least if Revelation does not teach us the contrary, a point which I do not here undertake to decide.

Before ending, it will perhaps be well to note, among the other advantages of my system, that of the universality of the laws which I employ, which are always without exception in my general philosophy: and it is just the opposite in other systems. For example, I have already said that the laws of mechanics are never violated in natural motions, that the same force is always preserved as also the same direction, and that everything takes place in souls as if there were no body, and that everything takes place in bodies as if there were no souls; that there is no part of space which is not full; that there is no particle of matter which is not actually divided, and which does not contain organic bodies; that there are also souls everywhere, as there are bodies everywhere; that souls and animals even, always subsist; that organic bodies are never without souls, and that souls are never separated from all organic body; although it is nevertheless true that there is no portion of matter of which it can be said that it is always affected by the same soul. I do not admit then that there are naturally souls entirely disembodied, nor that there are created spirits entirely detached from all body; in which I am of the opinion of several ancient Church Fathers. God only is above all matter, since he is its author; but creatures, free or freed from matter, would be at the same time detached from the universal concatenation, and like deserters from the general order. This universality of laws is confirmed by its great facility of explanation, since the uniformity, which I think is observed in all nature, brings about that everywhere else, in all time and in every place, it can be said that *all is as it is here,* to the degrees of greatness and of perfection nearly; and that thus those things which are farthest removed and most concealed are perfectly explained by the analogy of what is visible and near to us.

[The last paragraph, omitted here from this letter, refers to Leibniz's work on the History of the House of Brunswick and the medieval manuscripts he was using and reprinting in his History.]

10. ON BIOLOGY AND GEOLOGY
(From Letter to Bourguet, 1714)

I wish indeed that there were a more thorough investigation of the big question of the generation of animals which should be analogous to that of plants. Camerarius of Tübingen believed that the seed was like the ovary, and the pollen (though in the same plant) like the sperm of the male. But even if that were true, the question would still remain whether the basis of the transformation, the preformed organism, is in the ovary, according to Vallisnieri, or in the sperm, according to Leeuwhenhoek. For I maintain that a preformed living thing must always be the basis of the transformation whether it be in an animal or in a plant, and that the same dominant monad be in it. Nobody is more qualified to clear up this doubt than Vallisnieri and I hope very much to see his dissertation soon; its dedication would be giving me more honor than I deserve.

When I hold that there is no chaos, I do not mean that

our globe or other bodies have never been in a state of
external confusion; for experience would belie that. The
mass that Mt. Vesuvius throws up, for example, is such
a chaos. What I mean is that whoever would have sensitive organs penetrating enough to perceive the small parts
of things would find everything organized, and if he
could continually augment his penetration to the degree
needed, he would always see new organs which were imperceptible previously. For it is impossible for a creature
to be capable of penetrating everything simultaneously
in the smallest parts of matter, since the actual subdivision goes to infinity. Thus the apparent chaos is seen
only in a sort of distant perspective, as in looking at
a reservoir full of fish; or else, as in an army seen afar
where one cannot distinguish the order which it deploys.
I therefore believe that our globe was once in a state
similar to that of a burning mountain; and that it was
then that the minerals were discovered which are discovered today and can be imitated in our furnaces. You
will find my hypothesis explained more amply in an old
off-hand tract of mine published in the *Acts* of Leipzig
under the title *Protogaea*; I should like to learn your and
also Mr. Vallisnieri's opinion of it. Rocks which are, so
to speak, the bones of the earth are *scoriae* or vitrifica-
tions of this ancient fusion: sand is but the glass of this
vitrification, pulverized by motion. Sea-water is like an
Oleum per deliquium made by cooling after calcination.
There are three sorts of matter spread out all over the
surface of our globe (namely, the sea, rocks, and sand)
explained quite naturally by fire, which are not easily
explained by any other hypothesis. This water once covered the whole globe and caused many changes in it even
before Noah's flood. I incline therefore to the thought
of Descartes who judges our globe to have once been a
fixed star; or towards one of my own doctrine, that it

might have been a molten mass or big spot (*macule*) thrown out of the sun and into which it is still trying to fall back. . . .

11. METAPHYSICAL FOUNDATIONS OF MATHEMATICS
[1715]

The distinguished mathematician Christian Wolff in his Latin lectures on Mathematics has briefly mentioned and explicated in accord with his method a few of my thoughts on the analysis of axioms and on the mathematical concept of similarity (cf. *Acta Eruditorum,* 1714). Hence, I should like to present here, in order that they may not go lost, some reflections pertaining to these matters, which I have been harboring for a long time as proof that there is an art of Analysis which is more inclusive than Mathematics. The latter, in fact, borrows its most perfect methods from this art, which I must take up again and discuss somewhat more extensively than Wolff.

Given the existence of a multiplicity of concrete circumstances which are not mutually exclusive, we designate them as *contemporaneous* or *co-existing*. Hence, we regard the events of past years as not co-existing with those of this year, because they are qualified by incompatible circumstances.

When one of two non-contemporaneous elements contains the ground for the other, the former is regarded as the *antecedent,* and the latter as the *consequent*. My earlier state of existence contains the ground for the existence of the later. And since, because of the connection of all things, the earlier state in me contains also the earlier state of the other thing, it also contains the ground of the later state of the other thing, and is thereby prior to it. All existing elements may be thus ordered either by the relation of *contemporaneity* (co-existence) or by that of being *before or after in time* (succession).

Time is the order of non-contemporaneous things. It is thus the *universal* order of change in which we ignore the specific kind of changes that have occurred.

Duration is the quantity of time. If the quantity of time is continuously and uniformly diminished, the time passes into an *instant* which has no magnitude.

Space is the order of co-existing things, or the order of existence for all things which are contemporaneous. In each of both orders—in that of time as that of space— we can speak of a *propinquity* or *remoteness* of the elements *according to whether fewer or more connecting links are required to discern their mutual order.* Two points, then, are nearer to one another when the points between them and the structure arising out of them with the utmost definiteness, present something relatively simpler. Such a structure which unites the points between the two points is the simplest, i.e., the shortest and also the most uniform, *path* from one to the other; in this case, therefore, the straight line is the shortest one between two neighboring points.

Extension is the quantity of space. It is false to confound extension, as is commonly done, with extended things, and to view it as substance. If the quantity of space is continuously and uniformly diminished, then it becomes a *point* which has no magnitude.

Position is a determination of togetherness. It includes, therefore, not only quantity, but also quality.

Quantity or magnitude is that determination of things which *can be known in things only through their immediate contemporaneous togetherness (or through their simultaneous observation).* For example, it is impossible to know what the foot and yard are if there is not available an actually given object applied as a standard to compare different objects. What "a foot" is can, therefore, not be explained completely by a definition, i.e., by one which does not contain a determination of the same sort. For we may always say that a foot consists of 12 inches, but the same question arises again concerning the inch, and we have made no progress. Also we cannot say whether the concept of an inch is logically prior to that of a foot, for the choice of a fundamental unit lies entirely within our will.

Quality, however, is that determination of things which may be known in them *when we consider them individually and for themselves, hence without any necessity for their being given together.* To it belong all attributes which can be explained through a definition or through a group of characters which they entail.

We call *equal* whatever has the same quantity. We call *similar* whatever has the same *quality.* Hence, two similar things are different only if we consider them simultaneously together in order to distinguish one from the other.

From this it appears clearly that two equiangular triangles have proportional sides, and *vice versa.* Since the sides are proportional to one another, the triangles are necessarily similar, for their determining elements and the form in which they arise out of them, are similar. Furthermore, since in both triangles the sum of the angles is the same, i.e., two right angles, then the ratio of the corresponding angle to the sum of the angles in both figures, must be the same; for clearly one angle may be distinguished from the others simply by regarding it in itself as an individual. In this way it becomes easy to prove directly what we can now prove only indirectly.

Two elements are *homogeneous,* when we can produce two others of the kind which are equal to the first pair and similar to each other. For example, given A and B, if we can find an element L = A and another M = B such that L and M are similar to each other, then A and B are homogeneous.

Hence, I generally say also that elements are homogeneous when they can be made similar through a transformation of one into the other, as, e.g., a curve and a straight line. Through the fact that A is transformed into another equal magnitude L, it can be made similar to B or to M (into which B by hypothesis is transformed).

We say of an element that it is *contained* in a determinate structure or constitutes an *ingredient* of it, when through the determination of the structure the element is immediately determined without need of further reasoning. Thus, for example, we determine at once in the case of a finite line-segment that both of the end-points belong to it.

A structure which is contained in another homogeneous to it, is called *a part*—the other in which it is contained is called the *whole*. The part is, in other words, a homogeneous ingredient of the whole.

By the *common boundaries* of two structures we mean something contained in both, yet without their having a common part. If here both structures are viewed as parts of one and the same whole, then we designate their common boundary as a *cut* or *cross-section* of the whole.

From this it is clear that the boundary and what is bounded, the cross-section and what is cut, are not homogeneous.

Time and an instant, space and a point, boundary and the bounded, are not homogeneous, but nevertheless cognate or "homogonous"—*insofar as through a continuous change one can be transformed into the other.*

A spatial structure said to be contained within another is thought of as homogonous with it, but if a part of it is formed or is equal to one of its parts, then it is not only homogonous but also homogeneous. The *angle* though situated at a point is nonetheless not contained in that point, but might describe a magnitude at the point.

If a part of a quantity is equal to the whole of another quantity, then the first is called the *greater,* the second the *smaller.*

Whence *the whole is greater than the part.* Let A be the whole, B the part, then I judge A to be greater than B because a part of A (namely, that equal to B) is equal to the whole of B. We can also express this by means of a syllogism with the definition of "less than" as a major premise and an identity as the minor premise, to wit:

Whatever is equal to a part of A is less than A.

Now, B is by hypothesis identical with a part of A.

Therefore, B is less than A.

From this we see that all proofs may be reduced to two indemonstrable foundations: to the definitions of the ideas and to the original identical propositions, e.g., that B is the same as B, that every element is equal to itself, and innumerable other propositions of the same sort.

Motion is change of position.

We say that an object is *self-moved* when it alters its position and at the same time contains within itself the ground for this change.

The movable is homogonous with extension; for the point is also viewed as movable.

A *path* is the locus of the continuous, successive positions of a movable object.

Place is the position which the movable object occupies at a fixed instant. The limiting place or boundary of a movable object is therefore given by the cross-section of the path which the boundary prescribes, assuming that the object has a path and does not move in one and the same place.

We say that an object *moves in one and the same place* when every one of its points except its boundary occupies continually one or another position of the points belonging to the object itself.

Assuming that a movable thing does not move in this way, a *line* originates as the path of the point.

A *surface* is the path of a line.

The whole *volume of space* or, as is commonly said, the space of three-dimensional bodies is the path of a surface.

The magnitudes of the paths in which a point describes a line, the line a surface, and the surface a volume, are called *length, breadth,* and *depth,* or *dimensions.* It is proved in geometry that there are only three dimensions.

"Breadth" is ascribed to a structure when its cross-section or, in other words, its boundary has extension.

"Depth" belongs to a structure when it cannot be viewed as the boundary or cross-section of another structure; that is to say, in depth we have something new over and above the structures which can serve as boundaries.

The *line* is the ultimate boundary of extension.

Bodies of three dimensions are the ultimate extended and bounded structures.

The similarity or dissimilarity of two spatial wholes results from their boundaries; hence, three-dimensional space, since it is boundless, i.e., cannot be constituted by means of structures which can serve as boundaries, must itself essentially be universally uniform. *Volumes* whose ends or surfaces touch, cover, or resemble one another, belong themselves to a class of congruent, similar things. The same holds for the *plane,* which is an essentially uniform surface, similar in all its parts, and for the *straight line* which is essentially a uniform line.

The boundary on all sides of a given structure, extended with breadth, is called its *periphery.* Thus the periphery of a circle is its circumference, that of a sphere is the surface of the sphere.

A point, i.e., a spatial point, is the simplest locus, or the locus of no other locus.

Absolute space is the completely filled locus, or the locus of all loci.

From a single point nothing results.

From two points a new structure results, viz., the class of all the points whose places in relation to the two given points are uniquely determined, i.e., the straight line which goes through the two given points.

From three points the *plane* results, i.e., the locus of all the points whose places in relation to the three points, not lying in the same straight line, are uniquely determined.

From four points not lying in the same plane, *absolute space* results. For every point in relation to the given four not lying in the same plane, has its place uniquely determined.

I use the word "results" in order to indicate the origination of a new content, that is, insofar as a new structure is determined through the fixing of defined original elements, and stands to these elements in a unique *relationship.* In our case, being in a *place* is the kind of relationship involved.

Time is an infinite process. Since every temporal whole is *similar* to its parts, the same is true for the remaining time which is also a part capable of being thought as proceeding into a greater duration of time.

Likewise, also, the periphery of three-dimensional space proceeds to infinity insofar as every one of its parts can be taken as similar to the whole; and so for the plane and the straight line which may extend to infinity. Thus it is shown that space, as well as the straight line and time, and in general, every continuous structure, can be subdivided infinitely. Even those extended structures whose parts are not similar to the whole may yet be so subdivided in case they are transformed and put into the same relationship.

It also follows from the above that for every given motion there can be found another which is definitely related to it as faster or slower: if we, for example, move a straight line around a fixed midpoint, the motions of individual points are in proportion to their distances from the mid-point, so that velocities can vary in magnitude as straight lines.

There are two kinds of *measurement,* imperfect and perfect: imperfect, when we set up a relation of greater and less between two elements even though they are not homogeneous, nor stand in a numerical relation to one another, as when we say that a line is greater than a point, or a surface greater than a line. In this manner Euclid called the tangent angle (made by a curve and a tangent to the curve at a specified point) smaller than the rectilinear angle, although in truth between two such different kinds of construction we can scarcely find any comparison since they are neither homogeneous nor can one lead to the other by any continuous transformation. For the characteristically perfect measurement of homogeneous content the rule required is that we actually cover in a continuous transition from one end-point to the other all the intermediate links. This rule is not therefore applicable to the imperfect kind of comparison, because here the element we call intermediate is in fact heterogeneous in relation to the beginning and end-point. Thus, for example, we never arrive by a continuous transition from a given acute or right angle to the angle which the radius makes with the circumference of the circle, even if the latter angle, according to the customary designation, is "smaller than" a right angle and "larger than" any arbitrarily chosen acute angle, the expression "larger than" is used here only in a rough and borrowed sense in order to indicate that one figure lies *within* the region of the other.

Among quantities there are many different sorts of relations, e.g., the relation between two straight lines which makes their sum exactly equal to a constant length. Thus there are infinitely many pairs of straight lines, x and y, which satisfy the condition $x + y = a$. E.g., if $a = 10$, then x and y respectively may be 1 and 9, 2 and 8, 3 and 7, 4 and 6, 5 and 5, 6 and 4, 7 and 3, 8 and 2, 9 and 1. We can, however, also state infinitely many fractions, smaller than 10, which satisfy the equation of the problem. Further, between two straight lines there can exist a relation such that the square root of the sum of their squares is equal to a constant line: $x^2 + y^2 = a^2$; here there are also infinitely many pairs of values which satisfy the equation. A case of the latter relation is found in the circle if we let x equal the sine of an angle and y the sine of the complement; then a will equal the radius of the given circle. We can think up an infinite number of such relations—in fact, as many as there are lines that can be described in a plane. If we let the x's be the abscissae drawn on the horizontal co-ordinate axis, then the y's become the corresponding vertical ordinates of all the points lying in the line a, which goes through the origin.

We should further observe that all of Algebra is
merely an application of a *Combinatorial Science* of quantities, an application of the abstract doctrine of forms
or universal characteristic belonging to Metaphysics.
For example, the product of $a + b + c + \ldots$ and
$l + m + n + \ldots$ is none other than the sum of all the
different kinds of binomials which can be formed from
the letters in both factors. The product of three factors
$(a+b+c+\ldots)$, $(l+m+n+\ldots)$, $(s+t+u+\ldots)$
is the sum of all the different kinds of trinomials formed
from the letters; while through other operations, still
other forms result. Whence in calculation we perceive not
only the law of homogeneity but also the law of harmonious correspondence (*lex justitiae*) which consists
in the fact that the same kinds of relations given in the
data or hypotheses of a problem hold correspondingly
for similar relations in the *results* derived from the former; to the extent practically permitted by the particular
case, the operations of calculation can be manipulated
(and formed) with corresponding agreement and uniformity. The proposition holds generally that a definitely
governed order within the conditions corresponds to a
similar order within the series of things conditioned.
From this there results the *Law of Continuity,* first formulated by me, by virtue of which the law for bodies at
rest is in a certain sense only a special case of the
universal rule for moving bodies, the law for equality is
in a certain sense a case of the law of inequality, the
law for curves is likewise a subspecies of the law for
straight lines. This holds quite generally as often as a
transition is made from elements belonging to a common
species of a conceived class to a contrary species of the
class conceived. To this also belongs that method of
proof, long famous in geometry, by means of which
from any hypothetical assumption which is first made a

contrary notion will immediately emerge, so that what was first viewed as a subclass of the defined general class is shown to be contrary and disparate to it. And indeed this is the prerogative of the continuous. *Continuity* is present in time as well as in extension, in qualities as well as in motions; above all, however, it lurks in *every process in Nature,* since such a process never takes place by sudden jumps.

Place is a relation of coexistence among a plurality of elements. For a knowledge of place, we have to refer to other co-existing elements which serve as connecting links, i.e., we have to refer to the original elements which are in the simple relation of co-existence.

We know, therefore, not only the objects of our immediate awareness, but also whatever we make out as co-existing along with them, provided only that during the transition from one object to another, (1) the first object does not become annihilated, and (2) the second object is not created. If the latter of these two conditions alone holds, it follows that both terms exist together in the immediate present; if the former condition holds, then the result is that both terms have existed together at the instant we grasped the first term in our thought.

The transition from term to term pursues, furthermore, a definite *order,* insofar as it proceeds through determined connecting links. We may designate this order as a *path*: since it may vary in infinitely many ways, there must necessarily be conceived *one* simplest form of the transition in which through the nature of the thing itself the series of connecting terms is determined, whereby, therefore, in other words, the connecting terms show the *simplest* conceivable relationship going from the first through to the last term. For if this were not the case we could not possibly find any distinctions in the togetherness of things, since one could effect a transition from one element to another in any arbitrary form or manner. This unique order of transition then is the shortest path from one element to another—its magnitude may be caled the *distance* of the elements.

In order to analyze this concept, we shall now disregard all of the different properties of the elements whose "distance" is under discussion, and regard them as though they had no room for any plurality of determinations, that is, we wish to regard them just as points. An element is specifically called a "point" in that it is posited that nothing else in the element co-exists with it, so that everything in it is identical with it.

Then the path of the point will be a *line* which has no breadth, because its cross-section, viz., the point, has no length.

By means of *one* given point no further structure can be determined. Through *two* given points, the simplest path from one to the other determines what we call a *straight line*.

1) From this it follows *first* that the straight line is the shortest line from one point to the other, or that its magnitude is the distance between the points.

2) Secondly, the straight line between the end points is uniform. For there is nothing posited in it from which any heterogeneity might be derived.

3) Consequently, when we think of a point moving in a straight line, we can distinguish its different successive positions only through their different relations to the end-points.

Furthermore, every part of the straight line is itself a straight line; the latter is, accordingly, internally similar to itself throughout, and we cannot distinguish two of its parts except through their end-points.

4) If the end points are assumed as similar, congruent or coincident, then the straight lines themselves are re-

spectively similar, congruent and coincident. The end-points, however, are always similar to one another; hence, any two arbitrary straight lines are similar, and so again, every part of the line is similar to the whole.

5) Thirdly, it follows from its definition that the straight line goes through those points which stand in a unique relation to the position of the end-points, a relation which entails the highest degree of determination. However, there must not be any points which acquire any new determinations in relation to the two given elements. If there were still another point which was related to A and B as the points under consideration, then there would no longer be any reason why the formerly defined, simplest path should not go through this point rather than through the others. It is also clear, from what we have demonstrated above, that the straight line is completely determined by its end-points, so that when the latter are fixed, the straight line comes into existence.

6) Fourthly, it follows that the straight line is uniform on all sides, i.e., that it does not like a curved line possess a concave and a convex side; for from the hypothesis of two points A and B there arises no reason for such diversification.

7) If we further suppose situated outside the straight line two arbitrary points L and M which stand in the same relation to a pair of points (A and B) on the straight line, such that L is related to A and B as M is to A and B—then will their relation to the whole straight line also be identical, i.e., L will have exactly the same relation as M to the straight line through A and B.

8) It is clear, in addition, that a *fixed* straight line, that is, one whose points do not alter their diverse positions, cannot be moved if two points in it are fixed. For then there would be a diversity of points which would

all stand in the same relation to the two fixed points, namely, the places in which the movable point found itself from the beginning as well as those places through which it passed during its motion.

9) Conversely, it follows that all other points not lying on the straight line between A and B or in the direction AB, are movable without changing their situation in relation to the fixed points A and B. Since the straight line is the locus of all points which stand in a unique relation to A and B, all the remaining points may therefore vary, and in fact may do so all around the straight line, since it has the same relations in all directions.

10) Consequently, if a rigidly extended structure is moved in such a way that two points in it remain fixed, all its stationary points fall collectively on the straight line or axis through the fixed points, but every movable point describes a circle around the axis.

If three points are given not lying in the same straight line, then the structure that is determined by them is the *plane*. Given the points *A,B,C* not lying in the same straight line, then the straight line *AB* going through the points *A* and *B* is determined, as is the straight line *CB* through *C* and *B*. Every point of *AB*, furthermore, coupled with each point of *CB* determines a new straight line, and thus there results from the three given points *A,B,C* infinitely many straight lines whose locus is called the plane.

1) Whence, *first*, the plane is the smallest surface of all those which are possible within a given boundary. Its periphery does not consist in a straight line because the straight line does not bound or enclose any space, for then one of its parts would be dissimilar to the whole. Hence, if a perimeter is given, thereby three points not lying on the same straight line are also given; the perim-

eter accordingly alone determines the plane which it encloses, and therefore the plane is a minimum.

2) *Secondly,* the plane within its boundary is uniform because from the nature of its origin (three points) there is no ground for deriving any sort of diversity.

3) It follows from this that the plane is everywhere similar to itself so that the momentary position of a point which moves about in it is distinguishable from every other position only through the relation to the boundaries. It is also only through the relation to the boundaries of the plane that one of its parts can be distinguished from any other.

4) Furthermore, it follows that planes whose perimeters are similar or congruent, or coincide, are themselves similar or congruent, or coincide.

5) *Thirdly,* from the previous definition of the plane we see that it is the locus of all points whose positions in relation to the three given points are determined.

6) *Fourthly,* it follows that the plane is so uniform in its relations on both sides that it has neither a concave nor convex side.

7) If, therefore, there exists a point (outside the plane) in an arbitrary relation to A,B,C and consequently to the plane determined by them, then there is always another arbitrary point which shows the same relation to these three points, since no reason exists for any diverse form of relationship.

8) The plane possesses *breadth*; for it can be cut by a straight line which passes through any two given points. Whence, the cut has length; but whatever has length in its cut, itself possesses breadth.

If four points not lying in the same plane are given, then we obtain *depth* or a structure in which something appears which cannot be treated as a boundary, and which, therefore, cannot itself have a boundary in common with another structure unless the latter is included in it as a part.

12. ON NEWTON'S MATHEMATICAL PRINCIPLES OF PHILOSOPHY

LETTERS TO SAMUEL CLARKE * (1715–1716)

MR. LEIBNIZ'S FIRST PAPER: Being an Extract of a Letter written in November, 1715.

1. *Natural religion itself* seems to be declining [*in England*] very much. Many will have human *souls* to be material: others make *God himself* a corporeal Being.

2. Mr. *Locke,* and his followers, are *uncertain* at least, whether the *soul* is not *material,* and naturally perishable.

3. Sir *Isaac Newton* says, that space is an *organ,* which God makes use of to perceive things by. But if God stands in need of any *organ* to perceive things by, it will follow, that they do not depend altogether upon him, nor were produced by him.

4. Sir *Isaac Newton,* and his followers, have also a very odd opinion concerning the work of God. According to their doctrine, God Almighty needs to *wind up* his watch from time to time: otherwise it would cease to move. He had not, it seems, sufficient foresight to make it a perpetual motion. Nay, the machine of God's making is so imperfect, according to these gentlemen, that he is obliged to *clean* it now and then by an extraordinary concourse, and even to *mend* it, as a clockmaker mends his work; who must consequently be so much the more unskillful a workman, as he is oftener obliged to mend

* Translated into English by Clarke himself. Some of Clarke's phrases have been altered here when inaccurate or too outmoded.

his work and to set it right. According to *my* opinion, the *same* force and vigor remains always in the world, and only passes from one part of matter to another, agreeably to the laws of nature, and the beautiful *pre-established* order. And I hold, that when God works miracles, he does not do it in order to supply the wants of nature, but those of *grace*. Whoever thinks otherwise, must needs have a very mean notion of the wisdom and power of God.

MR. LEIBNIZ's SECOND PAPER: Being an Answer to
Dr. Clarke's First Reply.

1. It is rightly observed in the paper delivered to the *Princess of Wales*, which her *Royal Highness* has been pleased to communicate to me, that, next to corruption of manners, *the principles of the materialists* do very much contribute to keep up impiety. But I believe the author had no reason to add, that *the mathematical principles of philosophy are opposed to those of the materialists*. On the contrary, they are the same; only with this difference, that the *materialists,* in imitation of *Democritus, Epicurus,* and *Hobbes,* confine themselves altogether to *mathematical* principles, and admit only *bodies;* whereas the *Christian mathematicians* admit also immaterial substances. Wherefore, not *mathematical* principles (according to the usual sense of that word) but *metaphysical* principles ought to be opposed to those of the *materialists. Pythagoras, Plato,* and *Aristotle* in some measure, had a knowledge of these principles; but I do claim to have established them demonstratively in my *Theodicy,* although I have done it in a popular manner. The great foundation of *mathematics* is *the principle of contradiction or identity,* that is, that a proposition cannot be *true and false* at the same time; and that therefore *A* is *A*, and cannot be *not A*. This single prin-

ciple is sufficient to demonstrate every part of arithmetic
and geometry, that is, all *mathematical* principles. But
in order to proceed from *mathematics* to *natural philosophy,* another principle is requisite, as I have observed
in my *Theodicy:* I mean, *the principle of a sufficient
reason, viz.:* that nothing happens without a *reason* why
it should be *so,* rather than *otherwise.* And therefore
Archimedes being desirous to proceed from *mathematics*
to *natural philosophy,* in his book *De Aequilibrio,* was
obliged to make use of a particular case of the great
principle of *a sufficient reason.* He takes it for granted,
that if there be a *balance,* in which every thing is alike
on both sides, and if equal weights are hung on the two
ends of that balance, the whole will be at rest. It is because no *reason* can be given, why one side should weigh
down, rather than the other. Now, by that single principle, *viz.:* that *there ought to be a sufficient reason why
things should be so, and not otherwise,* one may demonstrate the being of a *God,* and all the other parts of
metaphysics or *natural theology;* and even, in some
measure those principles of *natural philosophy* that are
not exclusively *mathematical:* I mean, the *dynamic* principles, or the *principles of force.*

2. The author proceeds and says, that according to the
mathematical principles, that is, according to Sir *Isaac
Newton's philosophy* (for *mathematical principles* determine nothing in the present case), *matter is the most
inconsiderable part of the universe.* The reason is, because he admits *empty space,* besides *matter;* and because,
according to *his* notions, *matter* fills up only a very small
part of *space.* But *Democritus* and *Epicurus* maintained
the same thing: they differed from Sir *Isaac Newton,*
only as to the *quantity* of matter; and perhaps they believed there was *more* matter in the world than Sir
Isaac Newton will allow: wherein I think their opinion

ought to be preferred; for, the *more* matter there is, the *more* God has *occasion* to exercise his wisdom and power. Which is one reason, among others, why I maintain that there is *no vacuum* at all.

3. I find, in express words, in the *Appendix* to Sir *Isaac Newton's Optics,* that *space* is the *sensorium* of *God.* But the word *sensorium* hath always signified the *organ* of sensation. He, and his friends, may *now,* if they think fit, explain themselves quite otherwise: I shall not be against it.

4. The author supposes that the *presence* of the soul is sufficient to make it perceive what passes in the brain. But this is the very thing which Father *Malebranche,* and all the *Cartesians* deny; and they *rightly* deny it. More is requisite besides *bare presence,* to enable one thing to perceive what passes in another. Some communication that may be explained; some sort of *influence* is requisite for this purpose. *Space,* according to Sir *Isaac Newton,* is intimately present to the body contained in it, and commensurate with it. Does it follow from thence, that space *perceives* what passes in a body; and *remembers* it, when that body is gone away? Besides, the soul being *indivisible,* its immediate *presence,* which may be imagined in the body, would only be in *one point.* How then could it perceive what happens *outside* that point? I claim to be the first who has shown *how* the soul perceives what passes in the body.

5. The reason why God perceives every thing, is not his only *presence,* but also his *operation.* It is because he preserves things by an action, which *continually produces* whatever is good and perfect in them. But the *soul* having no immediate *influence* over the *body,* nor the *body* over the *soul,* their mutual correspondence cannot be explained by their being *present* to each other.

6. The true and principal reason why we commend a

machine, is rather grounded upon the *effects* of the machine, than upon its *cause*. We don't enquire so much about the *power* of the artist, as we do about his *skill* in his workmanship. And therefore the reason alleged by the author for extolling the machine of God's making, grounded upon his having *made it entirely,* without wanting any materials to make it of; that reason, I say, is not sufficient. It is a mere shift the author has been forced to have recourse to: and the reason why God exceeds any other artist is *not only* because he makes the *whole,* whereas all other artists must seek material to work upon. This excellency in God would be *only* on the account of *power*. But God's excellency arises also from *another* cause, *viz.: wisdom,* whereby his machine *lasts longer,* and moves *more regularly,* than those of any other artist whatsoever. He who buys a watch does not mind whether the *workman* made every part of it *himself,* or whether he got the several parts made by *others,* and did only put them together; provided the watch goes right. And if the workman had received from God even the gift of *creating* the material of the wheels; yet the buyer of the watch would not be satisfied, unless the workman had also received the gift of *putting them well together*. In like manner, he who will be pleased with *God's* workmanship, cannot be so, without some *other* reason than that which the author has here alleged.

7. Thus the *skill* of *God* must not be inferior to that of a workman; nay, it must go infinitely beyond it. The bare *production* of every thing would indeed show the *power* of God; but it would not sufficiently show his *wisdom*. They who maintain the contrary, will fall exactly into the error of the *materialists,* and of *Spinoza,* from whom they profess to differ. They would, in such case, acknowledge *power,* but not sufficient wisdom, in the principle or cause of all things.

8. I do not say, the material world is a machine, or watch, that goes *without* God's *interposition;* and I have sufficiently insisted, that the creation wants to be continually influenced by its *Creator.* But I maintain it to be a watch, that goes *without* wanting to be *mended* by him: otherwise we must say, that God *wishes to improve upon his own work again.* No; God has *foreseen* everything; he has provided a remedy for everything *beforehand;* there is in his works a harmony, a beauty, already *pre-established.*

9. This opinion does not exclude God's *providence,* or his *government* of the world: on the contrary, it makes it *perfect.* A true *providence* of God requires a perfect *foresight.* But then it requires, moreover, not only that he should have foreseen everything; but also that he should have *provided* for everything *beforehand,* with proper remedies: otherwise, he must want either *wisdom* to *foresee* things, or *power* to *provide* against them. He will be like the God of the *Socinians,* who *lives only from day to day,* as Mr. *Jurieu* says. Indeed God, according to the *Socinians,* does not so much as *foresee* inconveniences; whereas, the gentlemen I am arguing with, who put him upon *mending* his work, say only, that he *does not provide against* them. But this seems to me to be still a very great *imperfection.* According to this doctrine, God must want either *power,* or *good will.*

10. I don't think I can be rightly blamed, for saying that God is *intelligentia supramundana.* Will they say, that he is *intelligentia mundana;* that is, *the soul of the world?* I hope not. However, they will do well to take care not to fall into that notion unawares.

11. The comparison of a king, under whose reign everything should go on without his interposition, is by no means to the present purpose; since God preserves everything continually, and nothing can subsist without

him. His kingdom therefore is not a *nominal* one. It is just as if one should say, that a king, who should originally have taken care to have his subjects so well educated, and should, by his care in providing for their substance, preserve them so well in their fitness for their several stations, and in their good affection towards him, as that he should have no occasion ever to be amending anything amongst them, would be only a *nominal* king.

12. To conclude. If God is obliged to mend the course of nature from time to time, it must be done either *supernaturally* or *naturally*. If it be done *supernaturally*, we must have recourse to *miracles*, in order to explain natural things: which is reducing an hypothesis *ad absurdum*: for, everything may easily be accounted for by *miracles*. But if it be done *naturally*, then God will not be *intelligentia supramundana*: he will be comprehended under the nature of things; that is, he will be *the soul of the world*.

Mr. Leibniz's Third Paper: Being an Answer to Dr. Clarke's Second Reply.

1. According to the usual way of speaking, *mathematical* principles concern only mere *mathematics*, viz.: numbers, figures, arithmetic, geometry. But *metaphysical* principles concern *more general notions*, such as are cause and effect.*

2. The author grants me this important *principle;* that *nothing happens without a sufficient reason, why it should be so, rather than otherwise*. But he grants it only in *words* and *in reality* denies it. Which shows that he does not fully perceive the strength of it. And therefore he makes use of an instance, which exactly falls in with

* This is Leibniz's reply to Clarke's claim that Newton's mathematical principles were a sufficient metaphysical basis to refute materialism.

one of my demonstrations against *real absolute space,* which is an *idol* of some modern *Englishmen.* I call it an *idol,* not in a theological sense, but in a philosophical one; as Chancellor *Bacon* says, that there are *idols of the tribe, idols of the cave.*

3. These gentlemen maintain, therefore, that *space* is a *real absolute being.* But this involves them in great difficulties; for such a *being* must needs be *eternal* and *infinite.* Hence some have believed it to be *God himself,* or, one of his attributes, his *immensity.* But since space consists of *parts,* it is not a thing which can belong to God.

4. As for my own opinion, I have said more than once, that I hold *space* to be something *merely relative,* as *time* is; that I hold it to be an *order of co-existences,* as *time* is an *order of successions.* For *space* denotes, in terms of possibility, *an order* of things which exist at the same time, considered as existing *together;* without inquiring into their particular manner of existing. And when many things are seen *together,* one perceives *that order of things among themselves.*

5. I have many demonstrations, to confute the fancy of those who take *space* to be a *substance,* or at least an absolute *being.* But I shall only use, at the present, one demonstration, which the author here gives me occasion to insist upon. I say then, that if *space* were an absolute *being,* there would happen something, for which it would be impossible there should be a *sufficient reason.*

Which is against my Axiom. And I can prove it thus. *Space* is something absolutely *uniform;* and, without the things placed in it, *one point* of space does not absolutely differ in any respect whatsoever from *another point* of space. Now from hence it follows (supposing space to be something in itself, besides the *order of bodies among themselves,*) that it is impossible there should be a *reason,* why God, preserving the same situations of bodies among themselves, should have placed them in space in *one certain particular manner,* and not *otherwise;* why everything was not placed the *quite contrary way,* for instance, by changing *east* into *west.* But if space is nothing else but that *order* or *relation;* and is nothing at all without bodies but the possibility of placing them; then those two states, the *one* such as it now is, the *other* supposed to be the quite contrary way, would not at all differ from one another. *Their difference* therefore is only to be found in our *chimerical* supposition of the *reality* of space in itself. But in truth the *one* would exactly be the same thing as the *other,* they being absolutely *indiscernible;* and consequently there is no room to inquire after a reason for the preference of the one to the other.

6. The case is the same with respect to *time.* Supposing any one should ask, why God did not create everything *a year sooner;* and the same person should infer from thence, that God has done something, concerning which it is *not possible* there should be a *reason,* why he did it *so,* and not *otherwise:* the answer is, that his inference would be right, if *time* were any thing distinct from things existing in time. For it would be *impossible* there should be any *reason,* why things should be applied to such *particular instants,* rather than to *others,* their succession continuing the same. But then the same argument proves, that *instants,* considered without the things, are *nothing at all;* and that they consist only in the successive *order* of things: which order remaining the same, *one* of the two states, *viz.* that of a supposed anticipation, would not at all differ, nor could be discerned from, the *other* which now is.

7. It appears from what I have said, that my axiom has not been well understood; and that the author denies

it, though he seems to grant it. *It is true,* says he, *that there is nothing without a sufficient reason why it is, and why it is thus, rather than otherwise:* but he adds, that *this sufficient reason,* is often the *simple or mere will of God:* as, when it is asked why matter was not placed *otherwise* in space; the same situations of bodies among themselves being preserved. But this is plainly maintaining, that God *wills* something, without any *sufficient reason* for his will: against the axiom, or the general rule of whatever happens. This is falling back into the *loose indifference,* which I have confuted at large, and showed to be absolutely *chimerical* even in creatures, and contrary to the wisdom of God, as if he could operate without acting by reason.

8. The author objects against me, that if we don't admit this *simple and mere will,* we take away from God the power of *choosing,* and bring in a fatality. But quite the contrary is true. I maintain that God has the power of choosing, since I ground that power upon the *reason of a choice* agreeable to his wisdom. And 'tis not *this fatality* (which is only the wisest order of Providence) but a *blind fatalism* or *necessity* void of all wisdom and choice, which we ought to avoid.

9. I had observed, that by lessening the *quantity of matter,* the quantity of objects, upon which God may exercise his goodness, will be lessened. The author answers, that instead of *matter,* there are other things in the void space, on which God may exercise his goodness. Be it so: though I don't grant it; for I hold that every created substance is attended with matter. However, let it be so: I answer, that *more matter* was consistent with those same things; and consequently the said objects will still be lessened. The instance of a greater number of *men,* or *animals,* is not to the purpose; for they would *fill up* place, in exclusion of other things.

10. It will be difficult to make me believe that *sensorium* does not, in its *usual* meaning, signify an *organ* of sensation. See the words of *Rudolphus Goclenius,* in his *Dictionarium Philosophicum; v.* sensiterium. *Barbarum Scholasticorum,* says he, *qui interdum sunt Simiæ Græcorum. Hi dicunt* Ἀιθητήριον. *Ex quo illi fecerunt* sensiterium *pro* sensorio, *id est, órgano sensationis.**

11. The *mere presence* of a substance, even an animated one, is not sufficient for perception. A blind man, and even a man whose thoughts are wandering, does not *see.* The author must explain, how the soul perceives what is *outside* itself.

12. God is not present in things by *situation,* but by *essence:* his presence is manifest by his immediate *operation.* The presence of the *soul* is quite of another nature. To say that it is diffused all over the body, is to make it extended and divisible. To say it is, the whole of it, in every part of the body, is to make it divided from itself. To fix it to a *point,* to diffuse it all over *many points,* are only abusive expressions, *idols of the tribe.*

13. If *active force* should *diminish* in the universe, by the natural laws which God has established; so that there should be need for him to give a *new impression* in order to restore that force, like an artisan's mending the imperfections of his machine; the disorder would not only be with respect to *us,* but also with respect to *God himself.* He *might have* prevented it, and taken better measures to avoid such an inconvenience: and therefore, indeed, he has *actually* done it.

14. When I said that God has provided remedies beforehand against such disorders, I did not say that God

---

* *Sensiterium:* a barbarism of the Scholastics who sometimes ape the Greeks. The latter say αἰσθητήριον from which the former make the word *sensiterium* for *sensorium,* that is, the organ of sensation.

suffers disorders to happen, and then finds remedies for them; but that he has found a way beforehand to prevent any disorders happening.

15. The author strives in vain to criticize my expression, that God is *intelligentia supramundana*. To say that God is above the world, is not denying that he is in the world.

16. I never gave any occasion to doubt, but that God's conservation is an actual preservation and continuation of the beings, powers, orders, dispositions, and motions of all things: and I think I have perhaps explained it better than many others. But, says the author, *this is all that I contended for*. To this I answer: *your humble servant for that, sir*. Our dispute consists in many other things. The question is, whether God does not act in the most *regular* and most *perfect* manner, whether his machine is liable to *disorder*, which he is obliged to mend by extraordinary means, whether the will of God can act *without reason*, whether space is an *absolute being*, also concerning the nature of *miracles*; and many such things, which make a wide difference between us.

17. *Divines* will not grant the author's position against me, viz. that there is no difference, with respect to *God*, between *natural* and *supernatural*: and it will be still less approved by most *philosophers*. There is a vast difference between these two things; but it plainly appears, it has not been duly considered. That which is *supernatural* exceeds *all the powers of creatures*. I shall give an instance, which I have often made use of with good success. If God would cause a body to move free in the *æther* round about a certain fixed center, without any other creature acting upon it: I say, it could not be done without a *miracle*; since it cannot be explained by the nature of bodies. For, a free body does naturally recede from a curve in the tangent. And therefore I maintain,

that the *attraction* of bodies, properly so called, is a *miraculous* thing, since it cannot be explained by the nature of bodies.

Mr. Leibniz's Fourth Paper; Being an Answer to Dr. Clarke's Third Reply.

1. In things *absolutely indifferent,* there is no [foundation for] choice; and consequently no election, nor will; since choice must be founded on some *reason,* or principle.

2. *A mere will* without any motive, is a fiction, not only contrary to God's perfection, but also chimerical and contradictory; inconsistent with the definition of the *will,* and sufficiently confuted in my *Theodicy.*

3. 'Tis a thing *indifferent,* to place three bodies, equal and perfectly alike, in any order whatsoever; and consequently they will *never be placed in any order,* by him who does nothing without wisdom. But then, he being the author of things, no such things will be *produced by him* at all; and consequently there *are no such things* in nature.

4. There is no such thing as two individuals *indiscernible* from each other. An ingenious gentleman of my acquaintance, discoursing with me, in the presence of her *Electoral Highness the Princess* Sophia, in the garden of *Herrenhausen,* thought he could find two leaves perfectly alike. The princess defied him to do it, and he ran all over the garden a long time to look for some; but it was to no purpose. Two drops of water, or milk, viewed with a microscope, will appear distinguishable from each other. This is an argument against *atoms;* which are confuted, as well as a *vacuum,* by the principles of true metaphysics.

5. Those great principles of a *sufficient reason* and of the *identity of indiscernibles,* change the state of

metaphysics. That science becomes real and demonstrative by means of these principles; whereas before, it did generally consist in empty words.

6. To suppose *two* things *indiscernible,* is to suppose the *same thing* under *two names.* And therefore to suppose that the universe could have had at first *another* position of *time* and *place,* than that which it actually had; and yet that all the parts of the universe should have had the same situation among themselves, as that which they actually had; such a supposition, I say, is an *impossible* fiction.

7. The same reason, which shows that *extramundane* space is *imaginary,* proves that *all empty space* is an *imaginary* thing; for they differ only as greater and less.

8. If *space* is a *property* or attribute, it must be the property of some *substance.* But *what substance* will that *bounded* empty space be an affection or property of, which the persons I am arguing with, suppose to be between two bodies?

9. If *infinite space* is *immensity, finite space* will be the opposite to immensity, that is, 'twill be *mensurability,* or *limited extension.* Now extension must be the affection of some thing extended. But if that space be empty, it will be an attribute *without a subject,* an extension without any thing extended. Wherefore by making space a *property,* the author falls in with my opinion, which makes it an order of things, and not any thing absolute.

10. If space is an absolute *reality;* far from being a *property* or an accident opposed to substance, it will have a *greater reality* than *substances* themselves. God cannot destroy it, nor even change it in any respect. It will be not only immense in the whole, but also *immutable* and *eternal* in every part. There will be an infinite number of eternal things *besides God.*

11. To say that *infinite space* has no *parts,* is to say that it does not consist of *finite spaces;* and that infinite space might subsist, though all finite space should be reduced to nothing. It would be, as if one should say, in the *Cartesian* hypothesis of a material, extended, unlimited world, that such a world might subsist, though all the bodies of which it consists, should be reduced to nothing.

12. The author ascribes *parts* to space, *p. 19 of the 3d edition of his Defense of the Argument against Mr. Dodwell;* and makes them *inseparable* one from another. But, *p. 30 of his Second Defense,* he says they are *parts improperly so-called:* which may be understood in a good sense.

13. To say that God can cause the whole universe to *move forward* in a straight line, or in any other line, without making otherwise any alteration in it, is another *chimerical* supposition. For, *two states indiscernible* from each other, are the *same* state; and consequently, 'tis a change without any change. Besides, there is neither *rhyme* nor *reason* in it. But God does nothing without *reason;* and 'tis *impossible* there should be any here. Besides, it would be acting without doing anything (*agendo nihil agere*), as I have just now said, because of the indiscernibility.

14. These are *idols of the tribe,* mere chimeras, and superficial imaginations. All this is only grounded upon the supposition, that imaginary space is real.

15. It is a like fiction, (that is) an *impossible* one, to suppose that God might have created the world some millions of years sooner. They who run into such kind of fictions, can give no answer to one that should argue for the *eternity* of the world. For since God does nothing without reason, and no reason can be given why he did not create the world sooner; it will follow, either that he has created nothing at all, or that he created the

world before any assignable time, that is, that the world is *eternal*. But when once it has been shown, that the beginning, *whenever* it was, is always the *same thing;* the question, why it was not otherwise ordered, becomes needless and insignificant.

16. If *space* and *time* were anything absolute, that is, if they were anything else, besides certain *orders* of things; then indeed my assertion would be a *contradiction*. But since it is not so, the hypothesis [*that space and time are anything absolute*] is contradictory, that is, 'tis an *impossible* fiction.

17. And the case is the same as in *geometry;* where by the very supposition that a figure *is* greater than it really is, we sometimes prove that it *is not* greater. This indeed is a *contradiction;* but it lies in the hypothesis, which appears to be false for that very reason.

18. Space being *uniform,* there can be neither any *external* nor *internal* reason, by which to distinguish its parts, and to make any choice among them. For, any *external* reason to discern between them, can only be grounded upon some *internal* one. Otherwise we should discern what is indiscernible, or choose without discerning. A will without reason, would be the *chance* of the *Epicureans*. A God, who should act by such a will, would be a God only in name. The cause of these errors proceeds from want of care to avoid what derogates from the divine perfections.

19. When *two* things which cannot both be together, are *equally good;* and neither in themselves, nor by their combination with other things, has the one any advantage over the other; God will produce *neither of them.*

20. God is never determined by *external* things, but always by what is *in himself;* that is, by his knowledge of things, before any thing exists *outside* himself.

21. There is no *possible* reason, that *can limit* the quantity of matter; and therefore such limitation can have no place.

22. And supposing an arbitrary limitation of the quantity of matter is the fittest for the present constitution of things. And from the perfection of those things which do already exist; and consequently something must always be added, in order to act according to the principle of the perfection of the divine operations.

23. And therefore it cannot be said, that the present quantity of matter is the fittest for the present constitution of things. And supposing it were, it would follow that this present constitution of things would not be the fittest absolutely, if it hinders God from using more matter. It were therefore better to choose another constitution of things, capable of something more.

24. I should be glad to see a passage of any philosopher, who takes *sensorium* in any other sense than *Goclenius* does.

25. If *Scapula* says that *sensorium* is the *place* in which the understanding resides, he means by it the *organ* of internal sensation. And therefore he does not differ from *Goclenius*.

26. *Sensorium* has always signified the *organ* of sensation. The *glandula penealis* would be, according to *Cartesius,* the *sensorium,* in the above-mentioned sense of *Scapula.*

27. There is hardly any expression less proper upon this subject, than that which makes God to have a sensorium. It seems to make God the *soul of the world.* And it will be a hard matter to put a justifiable sense upon this word, according to the use Sir *Isaac Newton* makes of it.

28. Though the question be about the sense put upon that word by Sir *Isaac Newton,* and not by *Goclenius;*

yet I am not to blame for quoting the philosophical dictionary of that author, because the design of dictionaries is to show the use of words.

29. God perceives things in himself. Space is the place of *things*, and not the place of God's *ideas:* unless we look upon space as something that makes a union between God and things, in imitation of the imagined union between the soul and the body; which would still make God the *soul of the world.*

30. And indeed the author is much in the wrong, when he compares *God's* knowledge and operation, with the knowledge and operation of *souls.* The *soul* knows things, because God has put into it a *principle representative* of *external things.* But *God* knows things, because he *produces* them continually.

31. The soul does not *act* upon things, according to my opinion, any otherwise than because the body adapts itself to the desires of the soul, by virtue of the *harmony,* which God has *pre-established* between them.

32. But they who fancy that the soul can give a *new force* to the body; and that God does the same in the world, in order to mend the imperfections of his machine; make God too much like the soul, by ascribing too much to the soul, and too little to God.

33. For, none but God can give a *new force* to nature; and *he* does it only *supernaturally.* If there was need for him to do it in the *natural* course of things; he would have made a very imperfect work. At that rate, *he* would be with respect to the *world,* what the *soul* is commonly held to be with respect to the body.

34. Those who undertake to defend the common opinion concerning the soul's *influence* over the body, by illustrating it in God's operating on things external, make God still too much like a soul of the world. To which I add, that the author's affecting to find fault

with the words, *intelligentia supramundana,* seems also to incline that way.

35. The images, with which the soul is immediately affected, are within itself; but they correspond to those of the body. The presence of the soul is imperfect, and can only be explained by that correspondence. But the presence of God is perfect, and manifested by his operation.

36. The author wrongly supposes against me, that the presence of the soul is connected with its *influence* over the body; for he knows, I reject that *influence.*

37. The soul's being *diffused through the brain,* is no less inexplicable, than its being diffused through the whole body. The difference is only in *more* and *less.*

38. They who fancy that *active force* lessens of itself in the world,* do not well understand the principal laws of nature, and the beauty of the works of God.

39. How will they be able to prove, that this *defect* is a consequence of the dependence of things?

40. The imperfection of our machines, which is the reason why they want to be mended, proceeds from this very thing, that they do not sufficiently depend upon the workman. And therefore the dependence of nature upon God, far from being the cause of such an imperfection, is rather the reason why there is no such imperfection in nature, because it depends so much upon an artist, who is too perfect to make a work that wants to be mended. 'Tis true that every particular machine of nature, is, in some measure, liable to be disordered; but not the whole *universe,* which *cannot diminish in perfection.*

* Clarke had quoted from Newton's *Optics:* "Since therefore all the various motions that are in the world are perpetually *decreasing,* 'tis absolutely necessary in order to preserve and renew those motions, that we have recourse to some *active* principles."

41. The author contends, that *space* does not depend upon the *situation* of *bodies*. I answer: 'Tis true, it does not depend upon *such* or *such* a situation of bodies; but it is *that order,* which renders bodies capable of being situated, and by which they have a situation among themselves when they *exist together;* as *time* is *that order,* with respect to their *successive* position. But if there were no creatures, space and time would be only in the ideas of God.

42. The author seems to acknowledge here, that his notion of a miracle is not the same with that which divines and philosophers *usually* have. It is therefore sufficient for my purpose, that my adversaries are obliged to have recourse to what is *commonly called* a miracle.

43. I am afraid the author, by altering the sense *commonly put* upon the word *miracle,* will fall into an inconvenient opinion. The nature of a miracle does not at all consist in *usualness or unusualness:* for then *monsters* would be *miracles.*

44. There are *miracles* of an *inferior* sort, which an *angel* can work. He can, for instance, make a man walk upon the water without sinking. But there are miracles, which none but God can work; they exceeding all natural powers. Of which kind, are *creating* and *annihilating.*

45. It is also a supernatural thing, that bodies should *attract* one another at a distance, without any intermediate means; and that a body should move around, without following the tangent, though nothing hinder it from so moving. For these effects cannot be explained by the nature of things.

46. Why should it be impossible to explain the motion of animals by *natural* forces? Though indeed, the *beginning* of animals is no less inexplicable by natural forces, than the beginning of the world.

P. S.—All those who maintain a *vacuum,* are more

influenced by imagination than by reason. When I was a young man, *I* also gave in to the notion of a *vacuum* and *atoms;* but reason brought me into the right way from what had been pleasing to the imagination. The atomists carry their inquiries no farther than those two things: they (as it were) nail down their thoughts to them: they fancy, they have found out the first elements of things, a *non plus ultra.* We would have nature to go no farther; and to be finite, as our minds are: but this is to overlook the greatness and majesty of the author of things. The least corpuscle is actually subdivided *in infinitum,* and contains a world of other creatures, which would be lacking in the universe, if that corpuscle were an *atom,* that is, a body of one entire piece without subdivision. In like manner, to admit a *vacuum* in nature, is ascribing to God a very imperfect work: it is violating the great principle of the necessity of a *sufficient reason,* which many have talked of, without understanding its true meaning, as I have lately shown, in proving, by that principle, that *space* is only an *order* of things as *time* also is, and not at all an absolute being. To omit many other arguments against a *vacuum* and *atoms,* I shall here mention those which I ground upon *God's perfection,* and upon the *necessity of a sufficient reason.* I lay it down as a principle, that every perfection, which God *could* impart to things without derogating from their other perfections, has actually been imparted to them. Now, let us fancy a *space* wholly empty. God *could* have placed some matter in it, without derogating in any respect from all other things: therefore he hath actually placed some matter in that space: therefore, there is no space wholly *empty:* therefore all is full. The same argument proves that there is no corpuscle, but what is subdivided. I shall add another argument, grounded upon the necessity of a *sufficient reason.* It is *impossible* there should be any principle to determine what proportion of matter there ought to be, out of all the possible degrees from a *plenum* to a *vacuum,* or from a *vacuum* to a *plenum.* Perhaps it will be said, that the one should be equal to the other: but, because matter is more perfect than a *vacuum,* reason requires that a geometrical proportion should be observed, and that there should be as much more matter than vacuum, as the former deserves to have the preference before the latter. But then there must be *no vacuum* at all; for the perfection of matter is to that of a *vacuum,* as *something* to *nothing.* And the case is the same with *atoms:* What reason can any one assign for *confining* nature in the progression of subdivision? These are fictions merely arbitrary, and unworthy of true philosophy. The reasons alleged for a *vacuum* are mere sophisms.

MR. LEIBNIZ'S FIFTH PAPER: Being an answer to Dr. Clarke's Fourth Reply.

To § 1 and 2, of the foregoing paper [Clarke's Fourth Reply].

1. I shall at this time make a *larger* answer; to clear the difficulties; and to try whether the author be willing to hearken to reason, and to show that he is a lover of truth; or whether he will only cavil, without clearing anything.

2. He often endeavors to impute to me *necessity and fatalism;* though perhaps no one has better and more fully explained, than I have done in my *Theodicy,* the true difference between *liberty, contingency, spontaneity,* on the one side; and *absolute necessity, chance, coaction,* on the other. I know not yet, whether the author does this, because he *will* do it, whatever I may say; or whether he does it (supposing him sincere in those imputations), because he has *not yet* duly *con-*

sidered my opinions. I shall soon find what I am to think of it, and I shall take my measures accordingly.

3. It is true, that *reason* in the *mind* of a wise being, and *motives* in any mind whatsoever, do that which answers to the effect produced by *weights* in a *balance*. The author objects, that this notion leads to *necessity* and *fatalism*. But he says so without proving it and without taking notice of the explanations I have formerly given in order to remove the difficulties that may be raised upon that head.

4. He seems also to play with *equivocal* terms. There are *necessities*, which ought to be admitted. For we must distinguish between an *absolute* and an *hypothetical necessity*. We must also distinguish between a *necessity*, which takes place because the opposite implies a contradiction (which necessity is called *logical, metaphysical,* or *mathematical*); and a *necessity* which is *moral*, whereby a wise being chooses the best, and every mind follows the strongest inclination.

5. *Hypothetical necessity* is that, which the supposition or *hypothesis* of God's *foresight* and *pre-ordination* lays upon *future contingents*. And this must needs be admitted, unless we deny, as the *Socinians* do, God's *foreknowledge of future contingents*, and his *providence* which regulates and governs every particular thing.

6. But neither that *foreknowledge*, nor that *pre-ordination*, derogate from *liberty*. For God, being moved by his supreme reason to choose, among many series of things or worlds possible, that, in which free creatures should take such or such resolutions, though not without his concourse, has thereby rendered every event certain and determined once for all; he has not derogated thereby from the liberty of those creatures: that simple decree of choice, not at all changing, but only *actualizing* their free natures, which he saw in his ideas.

7. As for *moral* necessity, this also does not derogate from *liberty*. For when a wise being, and especially God, who has supreme wisdom, chooses what is best, he is not the less free upon that account: on the contrary, it is the most perfect liberty, not to be hindered from acting in the best manner. And when anyone else chooses according to the most apparent and the most strongly inclining good, he imitates therein the liberty of a truly wise being, in proportion to his disposition. Without this, the choice would be a blind chance.

8. But the good, either true or apparent, in a word, the motive, inclines without necessitating; that is, without imposing an *absolute necessity*. For when God (for instance) chooses the best; what he does not choose, and is inferior in perfection, is nevertheless possible. But if what he chooses, were absolutely necessary; any other way would be impossible: which is against the hypothesis. For God chooses among possibles, that is, among many ways, none of which implies a contradiction.

9. But to say, that God can only choose what is *best;* and to infer from thence, that what he does not choose, is impossible; this, I say, is a confusion of terms; it is blending *power* and *will, metaphysical necessity* and *moral necessity, essences* and *existences.* For what is *necessary,* is so by its essence, since the opposite implies a contradiction; but a contingent which exists, owes its existence to the *principle of what is best,* which is a *sufficient reason* for the existence of things. And therefore I say, that motives incline without necessitating; and that there is a certainty and infallibility, but not an absolute necessity in contingent things. Add to this, what will be said hereafter, *Nos. 73 and 76.*

10. And I have sufficiently shown in my *Theodicy,* that this *moral necessity* is a good thing, agreeable to the divine perfection; agreeable to the great principle or

ground of *existences,* which is that of *the need of a sufficient reason:* whereas *absolute and metaphysical necessity,* depends upon the other great principle of our reasoning, *viz.,* that of *essences,* that is, the principle of identity or contradiction: for what is absolutely necessary is the only possible way, and its contrary implies a contradiction.

11. I have also shown that our *will* does *not* always exactly *follow* the *practical understanding;* because it may have or find *reasons* to *suspend* its resolution till a further examination.

12. To impute to me after this, the notion of an *absolute necessity,* without having anything to say against the *reasons* which I have just now alleged, and which go to the bottom of things, perhaps beyond what is to be seen elsewhere; this, I say, will be an unreasonable obstinacy.

13. As to the notion of *fatalism,* which the author lays also to my charge; this is another ambiguity. There is a *fatum Mahometanum,* a *fatum Stoicum,* and a *fatum Christianum.* The *Turkish fate* will have an effect to happen, even though its cause should be avoided; as if there were an *absolute necessity.* The *Stoical fate* will have a man to be quiet, because he must have patience whether he will or not, since it is impossible to resist the course of things. But it is agreed, that there is *fatum Christianum,* a *certain destiny* of every thing, regulated by the foreknowledge and providence of God. *Fatum* is derived from *fari;* that is *to pronounce, to decree;* and in its right sense, it signifies the decree of providence. And those who submit to it through a knowledge of the divine perfections, whereof the love of God is a consequence, have not only patience, like the heathen philosophers, but are also contented with what is ordained by God, knowing he does every thing for the best; and not

only for the greatest good in general, but also for the greatest particular good of those who love him.

14. I have been obliged to enlarge, in order to remove ill-grounded imputations once for all; as I hope I shall be able to do by these explanations, so as to satisfy equitable persons. I shall now come to an *objection* raised here, against my comparing the *weights* of a *balance* with the *motives* of the *will*. It is objected, that a *balance* is merely *passive* and moved by the weights; whereas agents intelligent, and endowed with will, are *active*. To this I answer, that the *principle of the need of a sufficient reason* is common both to *agents* and *patients*: they need a *sufficient reason* for their *action*, as well as for their *passion*. A *balance* does not only act, when it is equally *pulled* on both sides; but the *equal weights* likewise do not act when they are in an *equilibrium*, so that one of them cannot go down without the other's rising up as much.

15. It must also be considered, that, properly speaking, motives do not act upon the mind, as weights do upon a balance; but it is rather the mind that acts by virtue of the motives, which are *its dispositions* to act. And therefore to pretend, as the author does here, that the mind prefers sometimes weak motives to strong ones, and even that it prefers that which is *indifferent* before *motives:* this, I say, is to divide the *mind* from the *motives,* as if they were *outside the mind,* as the weight is distinct from the balance; and as if the *mind* had, besides *motives*, other *dispositions* to act, by virtue of which it could reject or accept the *motives.* Whereas, in truth, the *motives* comprehend *all the dispositions,* which the mind can have to act voluntarily; for they *include* not only the *reasons,* but also the *inclinations* arising from passions, or other preceding impressions. Wherefore, if the mind should prefer a weak *inclination* to a strong

one, it would act against itself, and otherwise than it is disposed to act. Which shows that the author's notions, contrary to mine, are superficial, and appear to have no solidity in them, when they are well considered.

16. To assert also, that the *mind may have good reasons to act,* when it has *no motives,* and *when things are absolutely indifferent,* as the author explains himself here; this, I say, is a manifest contradiction. For if the mind has *good reasons* for taking the *part* it takes, then the things are not *indifferent* to the mind.

17. And to affirm that the mind will act, when it has *reasons* to act, *even though the ways of acting were absolutely indifferent:* this, I say, is to speak again very superficially, and in a manner that cannot be defended. For a man never has a sufficient reason to *act,* when he has not also a sufficient reason to act *in a certain particular manner;* every action being individual, and not general, nor abstract from its circumstances, but always needing some particular way of being put in execution. Wherefore, when there is a sufficient reason to do any particular thing, there is also a sufficient reason to do it in a certain particular manner; and consequently, several manners of doing it are not *indifferent.* As often as a man has sufficient reasons for a single action, he has also sufficient reasons for all its requisites. See also what I shall say below, *No.* 66.

18. These arguments are very obvious: and it is very strange to charge me with advancing my principle of *the need of a sufficient reason* without any proof drawn either from the nature of things or from the divine perfections. For the *nature of things* requires that every event should have beforehand its proper conditions, requisites, and dispositions, the existence whereof makes the sufficient reason of such event.

19. And *God's perfection* requires that all his actions

should be agreeable to his wisdom; and that it may not be said of him, that he has acted without reason; or even that he has preferred a weaker reason before a stronger.

20. But I shall speak more largely at the conclusion of this paper, concerning the solidity and importance of this great principle of the *need of a sufficient reason* in order to every event; the overthrowing of which principle, would overthrow the best part of all philosophy. It is therefore very strange that the author should say I am herein guilty of a *petitio principii;* and it plainly appears he is desirous to maintain indefensible opinions, since he is reduced to deny that great principle, which is one of the most essential principles of reason.

To § 3 and 4.

21. It must be confessed that though this great principle has been acknowledged, yet it has not been sufficiently made use of. Which is, in great measure, the reason why metaphysics (*prima philosophia*) has not been hitherto so fruitful and demonstrative, as it should have been. I infer from that principle, among other consequences, that there are not in nature *two* real, absolute beings, *indiscernible* from each other; because if there were, God and nature would act without reason, in ordering the one otherwise than the other; and that therefore God does not produce *two* pieces of matter perfectly *equal* and *alike*. The author answers this conclusion without confuting the reason of it; and he answers with a very weak objection. *That argument,* says he, *if it was good, would prove that it would be impossible for God to create any matter at all. For, the perfectly solid parts of matter, if we take them of equal figure and dimensions (which is always possible in supposition), would be exactly alike.* But 'tis a manifest *petitio principii* to suppose *that perfect likeness,* which,

according to me, cannot be admitted. This supposition of two *indiscernibles*, such as two pieces of matter perfectly alike, seems indeed to be *possible* in abstract terms; but is it not consistent with the order of things, nor with the divine wisdom, by which nothing is admitted without reason. The vulgar fancy such things, because they content themselves with incomplete notions. And this is one of the faults of the *atomists*.

22. Besides I do not admit in matter parts perfectly *solid* or that are the same throughout, without any variety or particular *motion* in their parts, as the pretended atoms are imagined to be. To suppose such bodies, is another popular opinion ill-grounded. According to my demonstrations, every part of matter is *actually* subdivided into parts differently *moved,* and no one of them is perfectly *like* another.

23. I said, that in sensible things, *two* that are *indiscernible* from each other, can never be found; that (for instance) two *leaves* in a garden, or two *drops* of water, perfectly alike, are not to be found. The author acknowledges it as to *leaves*, and *perhaps* as to *drops* of water. But he might have admitted it, without any hesitation, without a *perhaps* (an *Italian* would say, *senzà forse*), as to *drops* of water likewise.

24. I believe that these general observations in things *sensible,* hold also in proportion in things *insensible,* and that one may say, in this respect, what *Harlequin* says in the *Emperor of the Moon; 'tis there, just as 'tis here.* And it is a great objection against *indiscernibles,* that no instance of them is to be found. But the author opposes this consequence, because (says he) *sensible* bodies are *compounded*; whereas he maintains there are *insensible* bodies which are *simple.* I answer again that I don't admit *simple* bodies. There is nothing *simple,* in my opinion, but true *monads,* which have neither parts

nor extension. Simple bodies, and even perfectly similar ones, are a consequence of the false hypothesis of a *vacuum* and of *atoms,* or of *lazy* philosophy, which does not sufficiently carry on the *analysis* of things, and fancies it can attain to the first material elements of nature, because our imagination would be thus satisfied.

25. When I deny that there are two drops of water perfectly alike, or any two other bodies *indiscernible* from each other; I don't say, it is absolutely *impossible* to suppose them; but that it is a thing contrary to the divine *wisdom,* and which consequently does not exist.

To § 5 and 6.

26. I own, that if two things perfectly *indiscernible* from each other did exist, they would be *two;* but that supposition is false, and contrary to the great principle of reason. The vulgar philosophers were mistaken, when they believed that there are things different *solo numero,* or only because they are *two;* and from this error have arisen their perplexities about what they called *the principles of individuation.* Metaphysics have generally been handled like a science of mere *words,* like a philosophical dictionary, without entering into the discussion of *things.* Superficial philosophy, such as is that of the *atomists* and *vacuists,* forges things, which superior reasons do not admit. I hope my demonstrations will change the face of philosophy, notwithstanding such weak objections as the author raises here against me.

27. The *parts* of *time* or *place,* considered *in themselves,* are *ideal* things; and therefore they perfectly resemble one another, like two *abstract units.* But it is not so with two *concrete ones,* or with two *real times,* or two *spaces filled up,* that is, truly *actual.*

28. I don't say that *two* points of space are *one and the same* point, nor that *two* instants of time are *one and*

the same instant, as the author seems to charge me with saying. But a man may fancy, for want of knowledge, that there are two different instants, where there is but one: in like manner as I observed in the 17th paragraph of the foregoing answer, that frequently in geometry we suppose *two*, in order to show up the error of an adversary, when there is really but *one*. If any man should suppose that a straight line cuts another in *two* points; it will be found after all, that those *two* pretended points must coincide, and make but *one* point. This happens also when a straight line becomes a tangent to a curve instead of cutting it.

29. I have demonstrated that *space* is nothing else but an *order* of the existence of things, observed as existing together; and therefore the fiction of a material finite universe, moving forward in an infinite empty space, cannot be admitted. It is altogether unreasonable and *impracticable*. For, besides that there is *no real space* out of the material universe; such an action would be without any design in it; it would be working without doing anything, *agendo nihil agere*. There would happen *no change*, which could be observed by any person whatsoever. These are imaginations of *philosophers who have incomplete notions*, who make space an absolute reality. Mere mathematicians, who are only taken up with the conceits of imagination, are apt to forge such notions; but they are destroyed by superior reasons.

30. Absolutely speaking, it appears that God *can* make the material universe *finite* in extension; but the contrary appears more agreeable to his wisdom.

31. I don't grant that *every finite* is *movable*. According to the hypothesis of my adversaries themselves, a *part* of *space*, though *finite*, is not movable. What is movable must be capable of changing its situation with respect to *something else*, and to be in a new state *dis-*

cernible from the first: otherwise the change is but a fiction. A *movable finite*, must therefore be part of *another* finite, in order that any change may happen which can be *observed*.

32. *Cartesius* maintains that *matter* is *unlimited*; and I *don't* think he has been sufficiently *refuted*. And though this be granted him, yet it does not follow that matter would be *necessary*, nor that it would have existed from all *eternity;* since that unlimited diffusion of matter, would only be an effect of God's *choice* judging that to be the better.

To § 7.

33. Since *space* in itself is an *ideal* thing, like *time;* space *out of the world* must needs be imaginary, as the *schoolmen* themselves have acknowledged. The case is the same with empty space *within* the world; which I take also to be imaginary, for the reasons before alleged.

34. The author objects against me the *vacuum* discovered by Mr. *Guericke* of *Magdeburg,* which is made by pumping the air out of a *receiver;* and he pretends that there is truly a perfect *vacuum,* or a space without matter (at least in part), in that *receiver.* The *Aristotelians* and *Cartesians,* who do not admit a true *vacuum,* have said in answer to that experiment of Mr. *Guericke,* as well as to that of *Torricellius* of *Florence* (who emptied the air out of a glass-tube by the help of quicksilver), that there is no *vacuum* at all in the tube or in the receiver: since glass has small pores, which the beams of light, the *effluvia* of the loadstone, and other very thin fluids may go through. I am of their opinion: and I think the receiver may be compared to a box full of holes in the water, having fish or other gross bodies shut up in it; which being taken out, their place would nevertheless be filled up with water. There is only this dif-

ference; that though water be fluid and more yielding than those gross bodies, yet it is as heavy and massive, if not more, than they: whereas the matter which gets into the receiver in the room of the air, is much more subtle. The new sticklers for a *vacuum* allege in answer to this instance, that it is not the *grossness* of matter, but its mere *quantity,* that makes resistance; and consequently that there is of necessity *more vacuum,* where there is *less resistance.* They add, that the *subtleness* of matter has nothing to do here; and that the particles of *quicksilver* are as *subtle* and *fine* as those of *water;* and yet that *quicksilver* resists above *ten times more.* To this I reply, that it is not so much the *quantity* of matter, as its *difficulty of giving place,* that makes *resistance.* For instance; *floating timber* contains *less* of heavy matter, than an equal bulk of *water* does; and yet it makes *more resistance* to a boat, than the water does.

35. And as for *quicksilver;* it is true, it contains about fourteen times more of *heavy* matter, than an equal bulk of *water* does; but it does not follow, that it contains fourteen times more matter absolutely. On the contrary, *water* contains as much matter; if we include both its own matter, which is heavy; and the extraneous matter void of heaviness, which passes through its pores. For, both *quicksilver* and *water* are masses of heavy matter, full of pores, through which there passes a great deal of matter void of heaviness [and which does not sensibly resist]; such as is probably that of the rays of light, and other insensible fluids; and especially that which is itself the cause of the gravity of gross bodies, by receding from the center towards which it drives those bodies. For, it is a strange imagination to make all matter gravitate, and that towards all other matter, as if each body did equally *attract* every other body according to their masses and distances; and this by an *attrac-*

tion properly so called, which is not derived from an occult impulse of bodies: whereas the gravity of sensible bodies towards the center of the earth, ought to be produced by the motion of some fluid. And the case must be the same with other gravities, such as is that of the planets towards the sun or towards each other. (A body is never moved naturally except by another body which impels it by touching it; and afterwards it advances until it is stopped by another body which touches it. Every other operation on bodies is either miraculous or imaginary.)

To § 8 and 9.

36. I objected that space, taken for something real and absolute without bodies, would be a thing eternal, impassable, and not dependent on God. The author endeavors to elude this difficulty, by saying that space is a property of God. In answer to this, I have said, in my foregoing paper, that the property of God is *immensity;* but that *space* (which is often commensurate with bodies), and God's immensity, are not the same thing.

37. I objected further that if space be a property, and *infinite space* be the *immensity* of *God; finite space* will be the *extension* or *measurability* of something *finite.* And therefore the *space* taken up by a *body,* will be the *extension of that body.* Which is an absurdity; since a body can change *space,* but cannot leave its *extension.*

38. I asked also: if space is a *property,* what thing will an empty *limited space* (such as that which my adversary imagines in an exhausted receiver), be the property of? It does not appear reasonable to say that this empty space either round or square, is a property of God. Will it be then perhaps the property of some immaterial, extended, imaginary substances, which the author seems to fancy in the imaginary spaces?

39. If space is the property or affection of the substance, which is in space; the *same space* will be sometimes the *affection* of *one body,* sometimes of *another body,* sometimes of an *immaterial* substance, and sometimes perhaps of *God* himself, when it is void of all other substance material or immaterial. But this is a strange property or *affection,* which *passes from one subject to another.* Thus subjects will leave off their accidents, like clothes; that other subjects may put them on. At this rate, how shall we distinguish accidents and substances?

40. And if *limited spaces* are the *affections* of *limited substances,* which are in them; and *infinite space* be a property of *God;* a property of God must (which is very strange) be made up of the affections of creatures; for all finite spaces taken together make up infinite space.

41. But if the author denies that *limited space* is an *affection* of *limited things;* it will not be reasonable either, that *infinite space* should be the *affection* or property of an *infinite thing.* I have suggested all these difficulties in my foregoing paper; but it does not appear that the author has endeavored to answer them.

42. I have still other reasons against this strange imagination, that space is a property of God. If it be so, space belongs to the *essence* of God. But space has *parts:* therefore there would be *parts* in the *essence* of God. *Spectatum admissi.*

43. Moreover, spaces are sometimes empty, and sometimes filled up. Therefore there will be in the essence of God, parts sometimes empty and sometimes full, and consequently liable to a perpetual *change.* Bodies, filling up space, would fill up part of God's essence, and would be commensurate with it; and in the supposition of a *vacuum,* part of God's essence will be within the *receiver.* Such a *God having parts,* will very much resemble the

Stoic's God, which was the whole universe considered as a divine animal.

44. If infinite *space* is God's *immensity,* infinite *time* will be God's *eternity;* and therefore we must say, that what is in space, is in God's immensity, and consequently in his essence; and that what is in time, is also in the essence of God. *Strange* expressions; which plainly show, that the author makes a wrong use of terms.

45. I shall give another instance of this. God's immensity makes him actually present in all spaces. But now if God is *in* space, how can it be said that space is *in* God, or that it is a property of God? We have often heard, that a property is in its subject; but we never heard, that a subject is in its property. In like manner, God exists *in* all time. How then can time be *in* God; and how can it be a property of God? These are perpetual abuses of words.

46. It appears that the author confounds immensity, or the *extension of things,* with the *space* according to which that extension is taken. Infinite space is not the immensity of God; finite space is not the extension of bodies: as time is not their duration. Things keep their extension, but they do not always keep their space. Everything has its own extension, its own duration; but it has not its own time, and does not keep its own space.

47. I will here show *how* men come to form to themselves the notion of *space.* They consider that many things exist at once, and they observe in them a certain *order* of co-existence, according to which the relation of one thing to another is more or less simple. This order is their *situation* or distance. When it happens that one of those co-existent things changes its *relation* to a multitude of others, which do not change their relation among themselves; and that another thing, newly come, acquires the same relation to the others, as the former

had; we then say it is come into the *place* of the former; and this change, we call a *motion* in that body, wherein is the immediate cause of the change. And though many, or even all the co-existent things, should change according to certain known rules of direction and swiftness; yet one may always determine the relation of situation, which every co-existent acquires with respect to every other co-existent; and even that relation, which any other co-existent would have to this, or which this would have to any other, if it had not changed, or if it had changed any otherwise. And supposing, or feigning, that among those co-existents there is a sufficient number of them, which have undergone no change; then we may say, that those which have such a *relation* to those fixed existents, as others had to them before, have now the same *place* which those others had. And that which comprehends *all those places*, is called *space*. Which shows, that in order to have an idea of *place*, and consequently of space, it is sufficient to consider these *relations*, and the rules of their changes, without needing to fancy any absolute reality *outside* the things whose situation we consider, and, to give a kind of definition: *place* is that which we say is the same to *A*, and to *B*, when the *relation* of the co-existence of *B*, with *C*, *E*, *F*, *G*, &c., agrees perfectly with the relation of the co-existence, which *A* had with the same *C*, *E*, *F*, *G*, &c., supposing there has been no cause of change in *C*, *E*, *F*, *G*, &c. It might be said also, without entering into any further particularity, that *place* is that, which is the same in different moments to different existent things, when their *relations of co-existence* with certain other existents, which are supposed to continue fixed from one of those moments to the other, agree entirely together. And *fixed existents* are those, in which there has been no cause of any change of the *order* of their co-existence with others;

or (which is the same thing), in which there has been no *motion*. Lastly, *space* is that which results from *places taken together*. And here it may not be amiss to consider the difference between *place*, and the *relation of situation*, which is in the body that fills up the place. For, the *place* of *A* and *B*, is the *same;* whereas the *relation* of *A* to fixed bodies, is not precisely and individually the *same*, as the relation which *B* (that comes into its place) will have to the same fixed bodies; but these relations *agree* only. For two different subjects, as *A* and *B*, cannot have precisely the *same* individual affection; it being impossible, that the same individual accident should be in two subjects, or pass from one subject to another. But the mind not contented with an agreement, looks for an identity, for something that should be truly the same; and conceives it as being extrinsic to the subject: and this is what we here call *place* and *space*. But this can only be an ideal thing; containing a certain *order*, wherein the mind conceives the application of relations. In like manner, as the mind can fancy to itself an *order* made up of *genealogical lines*, whose bigness would consist only in the number of generations, wherein every person would have his place: and if to this one should add the fiction of a *metempsychosis*, and bring in the *same* human souls again; the persons in those lines might change place; he who was a father, or a grand-father, might become a son, or a grand-son, &c. And yet those genealogical *places*, *lines*, and *spaces*, though they should express real truths, would only be ideal things. I shall allege another example, to show how the mind uses, upon occasion of accidents which are *in* subjects, to fancy to itself something answerable to those accidents, *outside* the subjects. The *ratio* or *proportion* between two lines *L* and *M*, may be conceived three several ways; as a *ratio* of the greater *L* to the lesser

M; as a ratio of the lesser *M* to the greater *L;* and lastly, as something abstracted from both, that is, the *ratio* between *L* and *M,* without considering which is the antecedent, or which the consequent; which the subject, and which the object. And thus it is, that proportions are considered in music. In the first way of considering them, *L* the greater; in the second, *M* the lesser, is the subject of that accident, which philosophers call *relation.* But, which of them will be the subject, in the third way of considering them? It cannot be said that both of them, *L* and *M* together, are the subject of such an accident; for if so, we should have an accident in two subjects, with one leg in one, and the other in the other; which is contrary to the notion of accidents. Therefore we must say that this relation, in this third way of considering it, is indeed *outside* the subjects; but being neither a substance, nor an accident, it must be a mere ideal thing, the consideration of which is nevertheless useful. To conclude: I have here done much like *Euclid,* who not being able to make his readers well understand what *ratio* is absolutely in the sense of geometricians; defines what are the *same ratios.* Thus, in like manner, in order to explain what *place* is, I have been content to define what is the *same place.* Lastly; I observe, that the traces of movable bodies, which they leave sometimes upon the immovable ones on which they are moved; have given men occasion to form in their imagination such an idea, as if some trace did still remain, even when there is nothing unmoved. But this is a mere ideal thing, and imports only, that *if there was any unmoved thing there, the trace might be marked out upon it.* And it is this analogy, which makes men fancy *places, traces,* and *spaces;* though these things consist only in the truth of *relations,* and not at all in any absolute reality.

48. To conclude. If the space (which the author fancies) void of all bodies, is not altogether empty; what is it then full of? Is it full of extended spirits perhaps, or immaterial substances, capable of extending and contracting themselves; which move therein, and penetrate each other without any inconvenience, as the shadows of two bodies penetrate one another upon the surface of a wall? Methinks I see the revival of the *odd* imaginations of Dr. *Henry More* (otherwise a learned and well-meaning man), and of some others, who fancied that those spirits can make themselves impenetrable whenever they please. Nay, some have fancied, that *man* in the state of innocence, had also the gift of penetration; and that he became solid, opaque, and impenetrable by his fall. Is it not overthrowing our notions of things, to make God have parts, to make spirits have extension? The principle of the *need of a sufficient reason* does alone drive away all these spectres of imagination. Men easily run into fictions, for want of making a right use of that great principle.

To § 10.

49. It cannot be said, that (a certain) *duration* is eternal; but that *things,* which continue always, are eternal (by gaining always new duration). Whatever exists of time and of duration (being successive) perishes continually: and how can a thing exist eternally, which (to speak exactly) does never exist at all? For, how can a thing exist, whereof no part does ever exist? Nothing of time does ever exist, but instants; and an instant is not even itself a part of time. Whoever considers these observations, will easily apprehend that time can only be an ideal thing. And the analogy between time and space, will easily make it appear, that the one is as merely ideal as the other. (However, if by saying

that the duration of a thing is eternal, is merely understood that it lasts eternally, I have no objection.)

50. If the reality of space and time is necessary to
the immensity and eternity of God; if God must be in
space; if being in space, is a property of God; he will,
in some measure, depend upon time and space, and stand
in need of them. For I have already prevented that sub-
terfuge that space and time are (in God and as it were)
properties of God. (Could the opinion which should
affirm that bodies move about in the parts of the divine
essence be maintained?)

To § 11 and 12.

51. I objected that space cannot be in God, because
it has *parts*. Hereupon the author seeks another subter-
fuge, by departing from the received sense of words;
maintaining that space has no parts, because its parts
are not separable, and cannot be removed from one another by severance. But it is sufficient that space has
parts, whether those parts be separable or not; and they
may be assigned in space, either by the bodies that are
in it, or by lines and surfaces that may be drawn and
described in it.

To § 13.

52. In order to prove that space, without bodies, is an
absolute reality; the author objected, that a finite material universe might *move forward* in space. I answered,
it does not appear *reasonable* that the material universe
should be *finite;* and, though we should suppose it to be
finite; yet it is *unreasonable* it should have *motion* any
otherwise, than as its parts change their situation among
themselves; because such a motion would produce *no
change* that could be observed, and would be without

design. It is another thing, when its parts change their situation among themselves; for then there is a *motion in space;* but it consists in the *order of relations* which are changed. The author replies now, that the reality of motion does not depend upon being *observed;* and that a ship may go forward, and yet a man, who is in the ship, may not perceive it. I answer, motion does not indeed depend upon being *observed;* but it does depend upon it being *possible to be observed.* There is no *motion,* when there is no *change that can be observed.* And when there is no *change that can be observed,* there is *no change at all.* The contrary opinion is grounded upon the supposition of a real absolute space, which I have demonstratively refuted by the principle of the *necessity of a sufficient reason* of things.

53. I find nothing in the *eighth definition of the Mathematical Principles of Nature,* nor in the *scholium belonging to it,* that proves, or can prove, the reality of space in itself. However, I grant there is a *difference* between *an absolute true motion of a body,* and a *mere relative change of its situation with respect to another body.* For when the immediate cause of the change is in the body, that body is truly in motion; and then the situation of other bodies, with respect to it, will be changed consequently, though the cause of that change be not in them. It is true that, exactly speaking, there is not any one body, that is perfectly and entirely at rest; but we will frame an abstract notion of rest, by considering the thing mathematically. Thus have I left nothing unanswered, of what has been alleged for the absolute reality of space. And I have demonstrated the falsehood of that reality, by a fundamental principle, one of the most certain both in reason and experience; against which, no exception or instance can be alleged. Upon the whole, one may judge from what has been said,

that I ought not to admit a *movable universe;* nor any *place* outside the material universe.

To § 14.

54. I am not sensible of any objection but what I think I have sufficiently answered. As for the objection that *space* and *time* are *quantities,* or rather things *endowed with quantity*; and that *situation* and *order* are not so: I answer, that *order* also has its quantity; there is in it, that which goes before, and that which follows; there is distance or interval. *Relative* things have their *quantity,* as well as *absolute* ones. For instance, *ratios* or *proportions* in mathematics, have their *quantity,* and are *measured* by *logarithms;* and yet they are *relations.* And therefore though *time* and *space* consist in *relations,* yet they have their *quantity.*

To § 15.

55. As to the question whether God could have created the world *sooner;* it is necessary here to understand each other rightly. Since I have demonstrated that *time,* without things is nothing else but a mere ideal possibility; it is manifest, if any one should say that this same world, which has been actually created, might have been created *sooner,* without any other change; he would say *nothing that is intelligible.* For there is no mark or difference, whereby it would be possible to know, that this world was created *sooner.* And therefore (as I have already said), to suppose that God created the same world *sooner,* is supposing a chimerical thing. It is making *time* a thing absolute, independent of God; whereas *time* must co-exist with creatures, and is only conceived by the *order* and *quantity* of their changes.

56. But yet absolutely speaking, one *may conceive*

that a universe began *sooner,* than it actually did. Let us suppose our universe, or any other, to be represented by the figure *A F;* and that the ordinate *A B* represents its first state; and the ordinates *C D, E F,* its following states: I say, one *may conceive* that such a world began *sooner,* by conceiving the figure prolonged backwards, and by adding to it *S R A B S.* For thus, *things* being increased, *time* will be also increased. But whether such an augmentation be *reasonable* and agreeable to God's wisdom, is another question, to which we answer in the negative; otherwise God *would* have made such an augmentation. It would be as

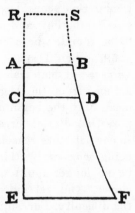

> *Humano capiti cervicem pictor equinam*
> *Jungere si velit.*

The case is the same with respect to the *destruction* (duration—*Ger.*) of the universe. As one *might conceive* something added to the beginning, so one *might also conceive* something taken off towards the end. But such a retrenching from it, would be also *unreasonable.*

57. Thus it appears how we are to understand that God created things at what *time* he *pleased;* for this depends upon the *things,* which he resolved to create. But *things* being once resolved upon, together with their *relations;* there remains no longer any choice about the *time* and the *place,* which of themselves have nothing in them real, nothing that can distinguish them, nothing that is at all discernible.

58. One cannot therefore say, as the author does here,

that the wisdom of God may have *good reasons* to create this world at *such* or *such a particular time:* that particular time, considered without the *things,* being an *impossible* fiction; and *good reasons* for a choice, being not to be found, where everything is indiscernible.

59. When I speak of this *world,* I mean the whole *universe* of material and immaterial creatures taken together, from the beginning of things. But if any one mean only the beginning of the *material* world, and suppose *immaterial* creatures before it; he would have somewhat more reason for his supposition. For *time* then being *marked* by things that existed already, it would be no longer indifferent; and there might be room for choice. And yet indeed, this would be only putting off the difficulty. For, supposing the whole universe of immaterial and material creatures together, to have a beginning; there is no longer any choice about the *time,* in which God would place that beginning.

60. And therefore one must not say, as the author does here, that God created things in what particular *space,* and at what particular *time* he *pleased.* For, all time and all spaces being in themselves perfectly uniform and indiscernible from each other, one of them cannot *please* more than another.

61. I shall not enlarge here upon my opinion explained elsewhere, that there are no created substances wholly destitute of matter. For I hold with the ancients, and according to reason, that angels or intelligences, and souls separated from a gross body, have always ethereal bodies, though they themselves be incorporeal. The vulgar philosophy easily admits all sorts of fictions: mine is more strict.

62. I don't say that matter and space are the same thing. I only say, *there is no space, where there is no matter;* and that space in itself is not an absolute reality.

Space and matter differ, as time and motion. However, these things, though different, are *inseparable*.

63. But yet it does not at all follow that matter is eternal and necessary; unless we suppose *space* to be eternal and necessary; a supposition ill-grounded in all respects.

To § 16 and 17.

64. I think I have answered everything; and I have particularly replied to that objection that *space* and *time* have *quantity,* and that *order* has none. *See above, Number* 54.

65. I have clearly shown that the contradiction lies in the hypothesis of the opposite opinion, which looks for a difference where there is none. And it would be a manifest iniquity to infer from thence, that I have acknowledged a contradiction in my own opinion.

To § 18.

66. Here I find again an argument which I have overthrown above, *Number* 17. The author says, God may have *good reasons* to make two cubes perfectly equal and alike: and then (says he) God must needs assign them to their places, though every other respect be perfectly equal. But things ought not to be separated from their circumstances. This argument consists in incomplete notions. God's resolutions are never abstract and imperfect: as if God decreed, first, to create the two cubes; and then, made another decree where to place them. Men, being such limited creatures as they are, may act in this manner. They may resolve upon a thing, and then find themselves perplexed about means, ways, places, and circumstances. But God never takes a resolution about the ends, without resolving at the same time about the means, and all the circumstances. Nay, I have shown

in my *Theodicy,* that properly speaking, there is but one decree for the whole universe, whereby God resolved to bring it out of possibility into existence. And therefore God will not choose a cube, without choosing its place at the same time; and he will *never choose* among *indiscernibles.*

67. The parts of space are not determined and distinguished, but by the things which are in it: and the diversity of things in space, determines God to act differently upon different parts of space. But space without things, has nothing whereby it may be distinguished; and indeed not anything *actual.*

68. If God is resolved to place a certain cube of matter at all, he is also resolved in which particular place to put it. But it is with respect to other parts of matter; and not with respect to bare space itself, in which there is nothing to distinguish it.

69. But wisdom does not allow God to place at the same time *two cubes perfectly equal and alike;* because there is no way to find any *reason* for assigning them different places. At this rate, there would be *a will without a motive.*

70. A *will without motive* (such as superficial reasoners suppose to be in God), I compared to *Epicurus's chance.* The author answers: *Epicurus's chance* is a blind necessity, and not a choice of will. I reply that *Epicurus's chance* is not a necessity, but something indifferent. *Epicurus* brought it in on purpose to avoid necessity. It is true, chance is blind; but a *will without motive* would be no less blind, and no less owing to mere chance.

To § 19.

71. The author repeats here what has been already confuted above, *Number* 21; that matter cannot be cre-

ated, without God's choosing among indiscernibles. He
would be in the right, if matter consisted of atoms, similar particles, or other the like fictions of superficial
philosophy. But that great principle, which proves there
is no choice among indiscernibles, destroys also these
ill-contrived fictions.

To § 20.

72. The author objected against me in his *third paper*
(*Numbers 7 and 8*) that God would not have in himself a principle of acting, if he was determined by things
external. I answered, that the ideas of external things
are in him: and that therefore he is determined by
internal reasons, that is, by his wisdom. But the author
here will not understand, to what end I said it.

To § 21.

73. He frequently confounds, in his objections against
me, what God *will not* do, with what he *cannot* do. *See
above, Number 9 [and below Number 76]*. For example;
God *can* do everything that is possible, but he *will* do
only what is best. And therefore I don't say, as the
author here will have it, that God *cannot* limit the extension of matter; but it is likely he *will not* do it,
and that he has thought it better to set no bounds to
matter.

74. From extension to duration, the consequent does
not hold. Though the *extension* of matter were unlimited,
yet it would not follow that its *duration* would be also
unlimited; nay even it would not follow, that it had no
beginning. If it is the nature of things in the whole, to
grow uniformly in perfection, the universe of creatures
must have had a beginning. And therefore, there will be
reasons to limit the *duration* of things, even though there
were none to limit their extension. Besides, the world's

having a beginning, does not derogate from the infinity
of its duration *a parte post;* but bounds of the universe
would derogate from the infinity of its extension. And
therefore it is more reasonable to admit a beginning of
the world, than to admit any bounds of it; that the character of its infinite author, may be in both respects preserved.

75. However, those who have admitted the *eternity*
of the world, or, at least (as some famous divines have
done), the *possibility* of its eternity; did not, for all that,
deny its dependence upon God; as the author here lays
to their charge, without any ground.

To § 22, 23.

76. He here further objects without any reason that,
according to my opinion, whatever God *can* do, he *must
needs* have done. As if he was ignorant that I have
solidly confuted this notion in my *Theodicy;* and that
I have overthrown the opinion of those, who maintain
that there is nothing possible but what really happens;
as some ancient philosophers did, and among others *Dio-
dorus* in *Cicero.* The author confounds *moral necessity,*
which proceeds from the choice of what is *best,* with
absolute necessity: he confounds the *will* of God with
his *power.* God *can* produce everything that is possible,
or whatever does not imply a contradiction; but he *wills*
only to produce what is the *best* among things possible.
*See what has been said above, Number 9 (and Number
74.)*

77. God is not therefore a *necessary agent* in producing creatures, since he acts with choice. However, what
the author adds here, is ill-grounded, *viz.,* that a *necessary agent* would not be an agent at all. He frequently
affirms things boldly, and without any ground; advancing (against me) notions which cannot be proved.

To § 24–28.

78. The author alleges, it was not affirmed that space is God's *sensorium,* but only *as it were* his *sensorium.* The latter seems to be as improper, and as little intelligible, as the former.

To § 29.

79. *Space* is not the place of all things; for it is not the place of *God.* Otherwise there would be a thing coeternal with God, and not dependent on him; nay, he himself would depend upon *it,* if he has need of *place.*

80. Nor do I see how it can be said that *space* is the *place of ideas;* for *ideas* are in the *understanding.*

81. It is also very strange to say that the *soul of man* is the *soul of the images* it perceives. The *images,* which are in the understanding, are in the mind: but if the mind was the *soul of the images,* they would then be extrinsic to it. And if the author means *corporeal images,* how then will he have a *human mind* to be the *soul of those images,* they being only transient impressions in a body belonging to that soul?

82. If it is by *means* of a *sensorium* that God perceives what passes in the world; it seems that things act upon him; and that therefore he is what we mean by *a soul of the world.* The author charges me with repeating objections without taking notice of the answers; but I don't see that he has answered this difficulty. They had better *wholly lay aside* this pretended *sensorium.*

To § 30.

83. The author speaks as if he did not understand how, according to my opinion, the *soul* is a *representative principle.* This is as if he had never heard of my *preestablished harmony.*

84. I do not assent to the vulgar notions that the *images of things are conveyed* by the *organs* (of sense) to the *soul*. For, it is not conceivable by what passage, or by what means of conveyance, these images can be carried from the organ to the soul. This vulgar notion in philosophy is not intelligible, as the new *Cartesians* have sufficiently shown. It cannot be explained, how *immaterial* substance is affected by *matter:* and to maintain an unintelligible notion thereupon, is having recourse to the scholastic chimerical notion of I know not what inexplicable *species intentionales,* passing from the organs to the soul. Those *Cartesians* saw the difficulty; but they could not explain it. They had recourse to a (certain wholly special) concourse of God, which would really be miraculous. But, I think, *I have given* the *true solution* of that *enigma.*

85. To say that God perceives what happens in the world, because he is *present* to the things, and not by [the dependence which the continuation of their existence has upon him and which may be said to involve] a *continual production* of them; is saying something unintelligible. A mere *presence* or proximity of co-existence, is not sufficient to make us understand, how that which happens in one being, should answer to what happens in another.

86. Besides; this is exactly falling into that opinion, which makes God to be the *soul of the world;* seeing it supposes God to perceive things, not by their dependence upon him, that is, by a *continual production* of what is good and perfect in them; but by a kind of perception, such as that by which men fancy our soul perceives what happens in the body. This is a degrading of God's knowledge very much.

87. In truth and reality, this way of perception is wholly chimerical, and has no place even in *human souls.*

They prehend what happens *outside* them, by what happens *within* them answering to the things without; in virtue of the *harmony,* which God has pre-established by the most beautiful and the most admirable of all his productions; whereby *every simple substance* is by its nature (if one may so say) a *concentration* and a *living mirror* of the *whole universe,* according to its *point of view.* Which is likewise one of the most beautiful and most undeniable proofs of the existence of God; since none but God, *viz.,* the universal cause, can produce such a harmony of things. But God himself cannot perceive things by the same means whereby he makes other beings perceive them. He perceives them because he is able to produce that means. And other beings would not be caused to perceive them, if he himself did not produce them all *in harmony,* and had not therefore in himself a representation of them; not as if that representation came from the things, but because the things proceed from him, and because he is the efficient and exemplary cause of them. He perceives them, because they proceed from him; if one may be allowed to say, that he *perceives* them: which ought not to be said, unless we divest that word of its imperfection; for else it seems to signify that things act upon him. They exist, and are known to him, because he understands and wills them; and because what he wills is the same as what exists. Which appears so much the more, because he makes them to be perceived by one another; and makes them perceive one another in consequence of the natures which he has given them once for all, and which he keeps up only according to the laws of every one of them severally; which, though different one from another, yet terminate in an exact correspondence of the results of the whole. This surpasses all the ideas which men have generally framed concerning the divine perfections and the works of God;

and raises [*our notion of*] them, to the highest degree;
as Mr. *Bayle* has acknowledged, though he believed,
without any ground, that it exceeded possibility.

88. To infer from that passage of Holy Scripture,
wherein God is said to have rested from his works, that
there is no longer a *continual production* of them; would
be to make a very ill use of that text. It is true, there is
no production of *new* simple substances: but it would be
wrong to infer from thence, that God is now in the world,
only as the soul is conceived to be in the body, *governing
it merely* by his presence, without any concourse being
necessary to continue its existence.

To § 31.

89. The *harmony*, or correspondence between the *soul*
and the *body*, is not a perpetual *miracle;* but the effect
or consequence of an original miracle worked at the creation of things; as all natural things are. Though indeed
it is a perpetual *wonder*, as many natural things are.

90. The word, *pre-established harmony*, is a term of
art, I confess; but it is not a term that explains nothing, since it is made out very intelligibly; and the author alleges nothing that shows there is any difficulty
in it.

91. The nature of *every simple substance, soul,* or
true monad being such that its following state is a
consequence of the preceding one; here now is the cause
of the *harmony* found out. For God needs only to make
a *simple substance* become *once* and from the beginning,
a *representation of the universe,* according to its *point of
view;* since from thence alone it follows, that it will be
so *perpetually;* and that *all simple substances* will
always have a *harmony* among themselves, because they
always *represent* the same *universe.*

To § 32.

92. It is true that, according to me, the *soul* does not disturb the laws of the *body,* nor the *body* those of the *soul;* and that the *soul* and *body* do *only agree* together; the one acting freely according to the rules of final causes; and the other acting *mechanically,* according to the laws of efficient causes. But this does not derogate from the liberty of our souls, as the author here will have it. For, every agent which acts (with choice—*Ger.*) according to final causes, is free, though it happens to agree with an agent acting only by efficient causes without knowledge, or *mechanically;* because God, foreseeing what the free cause would do, did from the beginning regulate the *machine* in such manner, that it cannot fail to *agree* with that free cause. Mr. *Jaquelot* has very well resolved this difficulty, in one of his books against Mr. *Bayle;* and I have cited the passage, in my *Theodicy,* Part I, § 63. I shall speak of it again below, *Number* 124.

To § 33.

93. I do not admit that every *action* gives a *new force* to the *patient.* It frequently happens in the concourse of bodies, that each of them preserves its *force;* as when two equal hard bodies meet directly. Then the direction only is changed, without any change in the *force;* each of the bodies receiving the direction of the other, and going back with the same *swiftness* it came.

94. However, I am far from saying that it is *supernatural* to give a *new force* to a body; for I acknowledge that one body does frequently receive a new *force* from another, which loses as much of its own. But I say only, it is *supernatural* that the whole *universe of bodies* should receive a *new force;* and consequently that one

body should acquire any new *force,* without the loss of as much in others. And therefore I say likewise, it is an indefensible opinion to suppose the *soul* gives *force* to the *body;* for then the whole universe of bodies would receive a *new force.*

95. The author's *dilemma* here is ill-grounded; *viz.,* that according to me, either a man must act supernaturally, or be a mere *machine,* like a watch. For, man does not act supernaturally: and his body is truly a *machine,* acting only *mechanically;* and yet his *soul* is a free cause.

To § 34 and 35.

96. I here refer to what has been or shall be said in this paper, *Numbers* 82, 86, (88) *and* 111: concerning the comparison between *God* and a *soul of the world;* and how the opinion contrary to mine, brings the one of these too near to the other.

To § 36.

97. I here also refer to what I have before said, concerning the *harmony* between the *soul* and the *body, Number* 89, &c.

To § 37.

98. The author tells us that the soul is not in the brain, but in the *sensorium;* without saying what that *sensorium* is. But supposing that *sensorium* to be extended, as I believe the author understands it; the same difficulty still remains, and the question returns, whether the soul be diffused through that whole extension, be it great or small. For, more or less, in bigness, is nothing to the purpose here.

To § 38.

99. I don't undertake here to establish my *Dynamics,* or my doctrine of *forces:* this would not be a proper

place for it. However, I can very well answer the objection here brought against me. I have affirmed that *active forces* are preserved in the world (*without diminution*). The author objects, that two *soft* or inelastic bodies meeting together, lose some of their *force*. I answer, no. It is true, their *wholes* lose it with respect to their total motion; but their *parts* receive it, being shaken (internally) by the force of the concourse. And therefore that loss of *force,* is only in appearance. The *forces* are not destroyed, but scattered among the small parts. The bodies do not *lose* their *forces;* but the case here is the same, as when men change great money into small. However, I agree that the *quantity of motion* does not remain the same; and herein I approve what Sir *Isaac Newton* says, *page* 341 of his *Optics,* which the author here quotes. But I have shown elsewhere, that there is a difference between the quantity of *motion,* and the quantity of *force.*

To § 39.

100. The author maintained against me that *force* does naturally *lessen* in the material universe; and that this arises from the dependence of things (*Third Reply,* § 13 *and* 14). In my *third answer,* I desired him to prove that this imperfection is a consequence of the dependence of things. He avoids answering my demand; by falling upon an incident, and denying this to be an imperfection. But whether it be an imperfection or not, he should have proved that it is a consequence of the dependence of things.

101. However; that which would make the machine of the world as imperfect as that of an unskillful watchmaker surely must needs be an imperfection.

102. The author says now that it is a consequence of the *inertia* of matter. But this also, he will not prove.

That *inertia,* alleged here by *him,* mentioned by *Kepler,* repeated by *Descartes* (in his letters), and made use of by *me* in my *Theodicy,* in order to give a notion (and at the same time an example) of the natural imperfection of creatures, has no other effect than to make the velocities diminish, when the quantities of matter are increased: but this is without any *diminution of the forces.*

To § 40.

103. I maintained that the dependence of the machine of the world upon its divine author, is rather a reason why there can be no such imperfection in it; and that the work of God does not want to be set right again; that it is not liable to be disordered; and lastly, that it cannot lessen in perfection. Let any one guess now, how the author can hence infer against me, as he does, that, if this be the case, then the material world must be *infinite* and *eternal,* without any beginning; and that God must always have created *as many* men and other kinds of creatures, as *can possibly* be created.

To § 41.

104. I do not say that space is an *order* or *situation* which makes things capable of being *situated:* this would be nonsense. Any one needs only consider my own words, and add them to what I said above (*Number* 47), in order to show how the mind comes to form to itself an idea of *space,* and yet that there need not be any real and absolute being answering to that idea, distinct from the mind, and from all relations. I don't say therefore, that *space* is an *order or situation,* but an *order of situations;* or an order according to which, situations are disposed; and that *abstract space is that order of situations,*

when they are conceived as being possible. Space is therefore something *merely* ideal. But, it seems the author will not understand me. I have already, in this paper (*Number 54*), answered the objection, that *order* is not capable of *quantity*.

105. The author objects here that *time* cannot be an *order of successive things,* because the *quantity of time* may become *greater* or *less,* and yet the *order of successions* continues the *same.* I answer: this is not so. For if the *time* is *greater,* there will be *more* successive and like states interposed; and if it be *less,* there will be *fewer;* seeing there is no *vacuum,* or condensation, or penetration (if I may so speak), in *times,* any more than in *places.*

106. It is true, I maintain that the immensity and eternity of God would subsist, though there were no creatures; but those attributes would have no dependence either on *times* or *places.* If there were no creatures, there would be neither *time* nor *place,* and consequently no actual *space.* The immensity of God is independent of *space,* as his eternity is independent of *time.* These attributes signify only in respect to these two orders of things, that God would be present and coexistent with all the things that should exist. And therefore I don't admit what's here alleged, that if God existed alone, there would be *time* and *space* as there is now; whereas then, in my opinion, they would be only in the ideas of God as mere possibilities. The immensity and eternity of God are things more *transcendent* than the duration and extension of creatures; not only with respect to the *greatness,* but also to the *nature* of the things. Those divine attributes do not imply the supposition of things extrinsic to God, such as are actual *places* and *times.* These truths have been sufficiently acknowledged by *divines* and *philosophers.*

To § 42.

107. I maintained that an operation of God, by which
he should mend the machine of the material world, tending in its nature (as this author pretends) to lose all
its motion, would be a *miracle*. His answer was that it
would not be a miraculous operation, because it would
be *usual*, and must frequently happen. I replied; that
it is not *usualness* or *unusualness*, that makes a *miracle*
properly so called, or a miracle of the highest sort; but
its *surpassing the powers of creatures;* and that this is
the *general* opinion of *divines* and *philosophers:* and
that therefore the author acknowledges *at least,* that the
thing he introduces, and I disallow, is, according to the
received notion, a miracle of the highest sort, that is,
one which surpasses all created powers: and that this is
the very thing which all men endeavor to avoid in
philosophy. He answers now that this is appealing from
reason to *vulgar opinion.* But I reply again that this
vulgar opinion, according to which we ought in philosophy to avoid, as much as possible, what surpasses the
natures of creatures; is a very reasonable opinion. Otherwise nothing will be easier than to account for anything
by bringing in the Deity, *Deum ex machina,* without
minding the natures of things.

108. Besides, the *common* opinion of *divines,* ought
not to be looked upon merely as *vulgar opinion.* A man
should have *weighty reasons,* before he ventures to contradict it; and I see no such reasons here.

109. The author seems to depart from his own notion,
according to which miracle ought to be unusual; when,
in § 31, he objects to me (though without any ground),
that the *pre-established harmony* would be a perpetual
miracle. Here, I say, he seems to depart from his own

notion; unless he had a mind to argue against me *ad hominem.*

To § 43.

110. If a *miracle* differs from what is *natural,* only in appearance and with *respect to us;* so that we call that only a *miracle,* which we seldom see; there will be no *internal real difference,* between a *miracle* and what is *natural;* and at the bottom, every thing will be either equally *natural,* or equally *miraculous.* Will *divines* like the former, or *philosophers* the latter?

111. Will not this doctrine, moreover, tend to make *God* the *soul of the world;* if all his operations are *natural,* like those of our souls upon our bodies? And so *God* will be a part of *nature.*

112. In good philosophy, and sound theology, we ought to distinguish between what is explicable by the *natures* and *powers* of *creatures,* and what is explicable only by the *powers* of the *infinite substance.* We ought to make an infinite difference between the *operation of God,* which goes beyond the extent of *natural powers;* and the *operations* of things that follow the law which God has given them, and which he has enabled them to follow *by their natural powers,* though not without his assistance.

113. This overthrows *attractions,* properly so called, and other operations inexplicable by the natural powers of creatures; which kinds of operations, the assertors of them must suppose to be effected by *miracle;* or else have recourse to absurdities, that is, to the *occult qualities* of the schools; which some men begin to revive under the specious name of *forces;* but they bring us back again into the kingdom of darkness. This is, *inventa fruge, glandibus vesci.*

114. In the time of Mr. *Boyle,* and other excellent

men, who flourished in *England* under *Charles* II, nobody would have ventured to publish such chimerical notions. I hope that happy time will return under so good a government as the present and that minds a little too much carried away by the misfortune of the times will betake themselves to the better cultivation of sound learning. Mr. *Boyle* made it his chief business to inculcate that everything was done *mechanically* in natural philosophy. But it is men's misfortune to grow, at last, out of enjoyment of reason itself, and to be weary of light. *Chimeras* begin to appear again, and they are pleasing because they have something in them that is wonderful. What has happened in *poetry,* happens also in the *philosophical world.* People are grown weary of rational *romances,* such as were the *French Clelia,* or the *German Aramene;* and they are become fond again of the *tales of fairies.*

115. As for the *motions of the celestial bodies,* and even the *formation of plants and animals;* there is nothing in them that looks like a *miracle,* except their *beginning.* The *organism* of *animals* is a *mechanism,* which supposes a divine *pre-formation.* What follows upon it, is purely natural, and entirely *mechanical.*

116. *Whatever* is performed in the *body of man,* and of every *animal,* is no less *mechanical,* than what is performed in a *watch.* The difference is only such, as ought to be between a *machine* of *divine* invention, and the workmanship of such a limited artist as *man* is.

To § 44.

117. There is no difficulty among divines about the *miracles of angels.* The question is only about the use of that word. It may be said that *angels* work *miracles;* but less properly so called, or of an inferior order. To dispute about this would be a mere question about a

word. It may be said that the *angel,* who carried *Habak-kuk* through the air, and he who troubled the water of the pool of *Bethesda,* worked a *miracle.* But it was not a miracle of the highest order; for it may be explained by the natural powers of angels, which surpass those of man.

To § 45.

118. I objected that an *attraction* properly so called, or in the *scholastic* sense, would be an operation at a distance, without any *means* intervening. The author answers here that an *attraction* without any *means* intervening, would be indeed a contradiction. Very well! But then what does he mean, when he will have the sun to attract the globe of the earth through an empty space? Is it God himself that performs it? But this would be a *miracle,* if ever there was any. This would surely exceed the powers of creatures.

119. Or, are perhaps some immaterial substances, or some spiritual rays, or some accident without a substance, or some kind of *species intentionalis,* or some other *I know not what,* the *means* by which he claims this to be performed? Of which sort of things the author seems to have still a good stock in his head, without explaining himself sufficiently.

120. *That means* of communication (says he) is invisible, intangible, not mechanical. He might as well have added, inexplicable, unintelligible, precarious, groundless, and unexampled.

121. But it is *regular* (says the author), it is *constant,* and consequently *natural.* I answer; it cannot be regular, without being reasonable; nor natural, unless it can be explained by the natures of creatures.

122. If the *means,* which causes an *attraction* properly so called, be constant, and at the same time inex-

plicable by the powers of creatures, and yet be true, it must be a perpetual *miracle:* and if it is not miraculous, it is false. It is a chimerical thing, a scholastic *occult quality.*

123. The case would be the same as in a body going round without moving in the tangent, though nothing that can be explained hindered it from so moving. Which is an instance I have already alleged; and the author has not thought fit to answer it, because it shows too clearly the difference between what is truly *natural* on the one side, and a *chimerical occult quality* of the schools on the other.

To § 46.

124. All the natural forces of *bodies* are subject to *mechanical laws;* and all the natural powers of *spirits,* are subject to *moral laws.* The former follow the order of efficient causes; and the latter follow the order of final causes. The former operate without liberty, like a watch; the latter operate with liberty, though they exactly agree with that machine, which another cause, free and superior, has adapted to them beforehand. I have already spoken of this, *above, No.* 92.

125. I shall conclude with what the author objected against me at the beginning of this fourth reply: to which I have already given an answer above (*Numbers* 18, 19, 20). But I deferred speaking more fully upon that head to the conclusion of this paper. He pretended, that I have been guilty of a *petitio principii.* But, of *what* principle, I beseech you? Would to God, less clear principles had never been laid down. The principle in question, is the principle of the *need of a sufficient reason* in order to establish any thing's existing, any event's happening, any truth's taking place. Is this a principle, that *needs* to be *proved?* The author granted it, or pretended to

grant it, *Number* 2, *of his third paper;* possibly, because
the denial of it would have appeared too unreasonable.
But either he has done it only in words, or he contradicts
himself, or retracts his concession.

126. I dare say that without this great principle one
cannot prove the existence of God, nor account for many
other important truths.

127. Has not everybody made use of this principle,
upon a thousand occasions? It is true, it has been neglected, out of carelessness, on many occasions: but that
neglect has been the true cause of *chimeras;* such as are
(for instance), an absolute real *time* or *space,* a *vacuum,
atoms, attraction* in the scholastic sense, a *physical
influence of the soul over the body,* and a thousand other
fictions, either derived from erroneous opinions of the
ancients, or lately invented by modern philosophers.

128. Was it not on account of *Epicurus's* violating
this great principle, that the ancients derided his groundless *declination* of atoms? And I dare say, the scholastic
attraction, revived in our days, and no less derided about
thirty years ago, is not at all more reasonable.

129. I have often defied people to allege an instance
against that great principle, to bring any one uncontested
example wherein it fails. But they have never done it,
nor ever will. It is certain, there is an infinite number
of instances, wherein it succeeds, or rather, it succeeds
in all the known cases in which it has been made use of.
From whence one may reasonably judge, that it will
succeed also in unknown cases, or in such cases as can
only by its means become known: according to the method
of experimental philosophy, which proceeds *a posteriori;*
though the principle were not perhaps otherwise justified
by bare reason, or *a priori.*

130. To deny this great principle is likewise to do as
Epicurus did, for he was reduced to deny that other great

principle, *viz.*, the *principle of contradiction;* which is, that every intelligible enunciation must be either true or false. *Chrysippus* undertook to prove that principle against *Epicurus;* but I think I need not imitate him. I have already said what is sufficient to justify mine: and I might say something more upon it; but perhaps it would be too abstruse for this present dispute. And, I believe, reasonable and impartial men will grant me, that having forced an adversary to deny that principle, is reducing him to absurdity.

III. THEORY OF KNOWLEDGE AND METAPHYSICS

1. WHAT IS AN IDEA?
[c. 1676]

By the term *Idea* we mean, first of all, *something which is in our mind;* traces of brain-impressions, therefore, are not ideas, for I take it to be certain that the mind is something else than the brain or some ethereal substance in the brain.

But there are many things in our mind, for example, opinions, perceptions, emotions, etc., which we know well enough are not simply ideas though they would not be produced without ideas. What I mean by an idea is *not a certain act of thinking, but a power or faculty* such that we have an idea of a thing even if we are not actually thinking about it but know that we can think it when the occasion arises.

However, there is a certain difficulty here for we have the power of thinking about remote things of which we may not have any ideas, in so far as we have the power of recalling things; *an idea, therefore, requires a certain power or faculty of thinking things near at hand.*

But even this will not suffice, for whoever has a method to follow in order to understand a thing, does not yet have an idea of it. For example, if I should go through all the sections of a cone in order, I am bound to come across a pair of hyperbolas although until I do so I may not yet have an idea of them. Therefore, there must be something in me *which not only leads to the thing but also expresses it.*

The means of expression must include conditions corresponding to the conditions of the thing to be expressed.

But these means of expression are varied; for example, the model of a machine expresses the machine itself, a perspective drawing in a plane expresses a solid, a speech expresses opinions and truths, letters express numbers, an algebraic equation expresses a circle or some other figure; and it is because these means of expression have something in common with the conditions of the thing expressed and studied, that we can come to know the corresponding properties of the thing expressed. Hence, evidently the means of expression need not be similar to the thing expressed, so long as a certain analogy holds among the conditions in both.

It is also evident that some means of expression have a natural basis and others are at least partly arbitrary, for example, those due to sounds or written characters. Those based on nature require either some similarity such as there is between a large and a small circle, or between a region and its map; or at least a relationship such as there is between a circle and an ellipse which represents it in perspective, for there is a one-to-one correspondence between every point of the ellipse and every point of the circle, determined by a certain law. To use any figure similar to the circle in such a case would give a bad representation. Likewise, every complete effect represents a complete cause, for from the knowledge of the effect I can always infer its cause. Thus every person's action represents his mind, and the world itself in a sense represents God. It is also possible for the same cause to express itself in alternative effects, for example, speech and gesture. So some deaf people understand those who speak not by the sound but by the motion of the mouth.

Thus the idea of things which exists in us is exclusively due to the fact that God, the author of both things and the mind, has endowed our mind with this power to infer from its own internal operations the truths which correspond perfectly to those of external things. Whence, although the idea of a circle is not exactly like the circle, we may yet infer from the idea truths which experience would undoubtedly confirm concerning the true circle.

2. REFLECTIONS ON KNOWLEDGE, TRUTH, AND IDEAS
[1684]

Since questions concerning the truth and falsity of ideas are being discussed and argued today by eminent men, and since Descartes himself did not ever give a thoroughly satisfactory solution to this problem, a subject of the greatest significance for the knowledge of truth, I propose here to explain briefly my understanding of the necessary distinctions and criteria of ideas and knowledge. Knowledge is either *obscure* or *clear;* clear ideas again are either *indistinct or distinct;* distinct ideas are either *adequate* or *inadequate, symbolic* or *intuitive;* perfect knowledge, finally, is that which is both *adequate* and *intuitive.*

An idea is *obscure* when it does not suffice for the recognition of things after they have been experienced, for example, when my vague idea of a flower or animal which I once previously saw, does not suffice to enable me, when I am confronted with a new instance, to recognize it or *distinguish* it from anything similar to it. Should I reflect somewhat on some term not clearly defined in the schools, e.g., Aristotle's entelechy, the four *causes* lumped together as material, formal, efficient, and final causes, and other similar terms of which we have no clear definitions, I should call the judgment which includes such a notion *obscure.*

On the other hand, knowledge is *clear* when it is sufficient to enable me to recognize the things represented; and again, such knowledge is either *indistinct* or *distinct*. It is *indistinct* as soon as I am not able to enumerate separately the characteristics required to distinguish the thing from others, even though such characteristics and distinctions are really in the thing itself and in the data which enable us to analyze the notion. Thus it is that we can recognize clearly enough colors, smells, tastes, and other particular sensory objects, and distinguish them by the simple testimony of the senses, rather than by characters we can formulate. That is why we cannot explain to a blind man what "red" is, nor can we convey to others similar qualities except as they are led to see, smell, or taste qualities actually already experienced, or at least recall something similar to them in their previous experience. Nevertheless, the ideas of these qualities are surely composite, and must be further analyzable, since the qualities themselves have causes. In similar fashion, we often observe that painters and other artists judge quite correctly what is good or defective in works of art, but are frequently not able to account for their judgment, and if asked, can only answer that they somehow missed something in the things which displeased them but what it was they themselves did not know. A *distinct idea,* however, is like the one the goldsmiths have of gold, namely, one based on distinctive characters and results of assayers' tests which suffice to distinguish gold from all other similar bodies. Usually these characters are obtained from notions common to several senses, e.g., number, size, and shape, and the same holds for many affections of the soul, e.g., fear and hope—in a word, everything of which we have a *nominal definition,* which is nothing more than an enumeration of the sufficient distinguishing characters. There is also distinct knowledge of an indefinable term when it is *primitive,* i.e., when it is unanalyzable, and knowable only through itself, and so does not show the marks of its elements. In composite ideas the individual elements are still clear but known in confused fashion, e.g., weight, color, solubility in aqua regia, and other characteristics of gold; such a knowledge of gold is *distinct* all right but nevertheless *inadequate.* On the other hand, if every element included in a distinct concept is again distinctly known, and if the analysis is carried through to the end, then the knowledge is *adequate.* Of course, our human knowledge reveals perhaps no perfect example of this kind of knowledge, but the knowledge of numbers comes pretty close to it. In most cases, however, particularly in a more lengthy analysis, we do not perceive all at once the whole nature of the objects, but we substitute for the objects themselves defined signs, whose explanation we can omit for the sake of brevity, assuming that we could, if necessary, give one. If I think of a regular polygon with a thousand equal sides, I do not have to consider always the nature of a side, of equality, and of the number 1000—i.e., the third power of 10—but I use that word, whose meaning for me is the least obscure and immediately present, for the idea itself, since my mind having once attested to its meaning I do not now have to consider any explanation as necessary. I usually designate such knowledge as *blind* or also as *symbolic;* we make use of it to a great extent in Algebra, in Arithmetic and nearly everywhere. And surely we cannot, when an idea is very complex, think at once of all its constituent characters; however, when it is possible to do so, and to the extent that it is possible, I call that knowledge *intuitive.* Only intuitive knowledge can give us distinct, primitive ideas, whereas we can have only symbolic knowledge of complex ideas.

From this it already becomes clear that in order to have distinct knowledge, we need some intuitive awareness of its content. It frequently happens that we *erroneously* believe we have *ideas* in us; this happens when we falsely assume that we have already explained certain terms we are using. It is false, or at least ambiguous to say as some do, that we necessarily must have the idea of a thing in order to be able to express it in speech, and understand what we are saying. For indeed we often understand the individual words or recall vaguely that we previously understood each one of them; but since we nevertheless are content with this blind knowledge and do not pursue the analysis of ideas far enough, we can easily fall into a contradiction which may be contained in the composite idea. I was once instigated to make a more exact investigation of this question by the famous scholastic argument for the existence of God, which Descartes recently revived. Whatever follows from the idea or the definition of a thing—so the argument runs—is predicable of the thing itself. Now existence follows from the idea of God as the most perfect or greatest possible being. For the most perfect being includes all perfections within himself, and existence is one of them. Therefore, we can predicate existence of God. In truth, however, this argument permits us only to conclude that God's existence follows if his *possibility* is already proven. For we cannot use a definition in an argument without first making sure that it is a *real* definition, or that it contains no contradiction. From concepts which contain a contradiction, we can draw conclusions contrary to one another, which is absurd. I used to explain this with the illustration that the fastest motion contained an absurdity: Let us assume a wheel is turning with the fastest motion; then it is easy to see that if one of the wheel's spokes were lengthened to extend beyond the rim, its end-point would be moving faster than a nail lying on the rim, whose motion is therefore not the fastest, which contradicts the hypothesis. At first glance, it might appear we had the idea of the fastest motion, for we understand what we are saying, and yet the fact is that we cannot have an idea of impossible things. So it is not enough to say we think the most perfect being in order to certify that we can have an idea of such a being and in the aforementioned proof the validity of the argument depends on proving or presupposing the *possibility* of the most perfect being. In this case it is absolutely true that the most perfect being is possible and even necessary; yet the proof given is not conclusive, and had already been rejected by Thomas Aquinas.

We also insist here on a distinction between *nominal definitions,* which contain only characters enabling us to distinguish one thing from another, and *real definitions* from which the possibility of things can be shown. In this way we may refute the view of Hobbes, according to whom all truths are arbitrary because they depend on nominal definitions, for he did not consider that the very reality of the definition is not a matter of our choice, and that not all arbitrary concepts can be consistently connected together. Finally, all of this makes clear the distinction between *true* and *false* ideas. An idea is true if what it represents is possible; false if the representation contains a contradiction. The *possibility* of a thing, however, is known either *a priori* or *a posteriori:* the former, when we analyze the idea into its elements, that is, into other ideas whose possibility is known, and know that it contains nothing which is incompatible. For example, this is the case when we perceive the manner in which an object is produced, whence *causal definitions* are of such paramount significance. On the other hand, we recognize the *a posteriori* possibility of a thing when its actuality is known to us through experience. For whatever exists or has existed must in any case be possible. In any case of adequate knowledge we have at the same time an *a priori* knowledge of the possibility; to wit, if we have carried the analysis through to the end and no contradiction is visible, the possibility of the idea is demonstrated. But whether human knowledge will ever attain to a perfect analysis of ideas, hence, to the *first possibility* and to unanalyzable concepts—in other words, whether it will be able to reduce all thoughts to the absolute attributes of God himself,—to first causes and the final reason of things that is a question which I do not care to consider or decide just now. Usually we are content to ascertain the reality of certain concepts by means of experience in order then to synthesize them according to the model of nature.

As a result, we may conclude that the appeal to ideas is not always free from objections, and that many of these ideas with glittering names are abused in order to convert their conceits into currency. The example of the fastest motion has already shown that we do not always have the idea of everything brought to our consciousness. Nowadays there is much abuse of the famous principle: "Everything I clearly and distinctly conceive of a thing must be true or may be asserted about it." Frequently, for example, something clear and distinct appears in a premature judgment, and it turns out to be really obscure and indistinct. This axiom is therefore useless so long as we have not drawn up the *criteria* of the clear and distinct, such as we have given, and demonstrated the truth of the ideas. Furthermore, the rules of *common logic* are worthy of consideration as criteria of truth and falsity; the geometer makes use of them. One of these, for example, is the precept, to accept as certain only what is confirmed by exact experience or strong proof.

But a proof is strong when it conforms to the prescriptions of logical form. Indeed it does not always have to be the traditional, classroom syllogisms—such as Christian Herlinus and Konrad Dasypodius have used for demonstrating the first six books of Euclid—but all that is required is that the proof by virtue of its form alone should establish the conclusion. An example of such a proof, carried out in regular form, may be found in any sound system of calculation. No necessary premises are omitted, and all premises must have previously been demonstrated or been assumed as hypotheses; in the latter case, the conclusion is also hypothetical. By observing this rule carefully, we shall know how to avoid deceptive ideas. It was in accord with this that the penetrating Pascal (in his famous treatise on the geometrical spirit, a fragment of which is contained in the distinguished book of the celebrated Antoine Arnauld on the art of thinking), indicated that the problem of geometers is to define all obscure terms and to demonstrate all doubtful truths agreed upon. I only wish he had defined the means of knowing when an idea or a proposition is no longer obscure or doubtful. The necessity for doing this appears clearly in the detailed reflections we have offered above.

As to *whether we see all things in God* (an old view which should not be completely dismissed, if properly understood), or whether all ideas are our own, we must realize that even if we do see all things in God, it is still necessary for the ideas through which we see to be our own at the same time; that is, our ideas are not little replicas, so to speak, but affections or modifications corresponding to what we perceive in God. This is because our thoughts in their continual succession contain whatever change occurs in our mind; and of the things we are not actually conceiving, we have ideas lying in our mind as the statue of Hercules is dormant in the rough marble. But in God, on the other hand, there must actually exist the idea not only of absolute, infinite extension, but also of each configuration which is a modification of absolute extension. Furthermore, in perceiving colors and smells, we perceive nothing but certain kinds of configurations and motions so complex and subtle, however, that our mind is unable at the moment to consider distinctly each one of them, and hence does not notice that the immediate perception is composed of very small configurations and motions. Thus, after mixing yellow with blue powder we perceive a green color, imagining it to be a new entity, though we have been perceiving nothing but a mixture of the yellow and blue.

3. DISCOURSE ON METAPHYSICS
[1686]

I. Concerning the divine perfection and that God does everything in the most desirable way.

The conception of God which is the most common and the most full of meaning is expressed well enough in the words: God is an absolutely perfect being. The implications, however, of these words fail to receive sufficient consideration. For instance, there are many different kinds of perfection, all of which God possesses, and each one of them pertains to him in the highest degree.

We must also know what perfection is. One thing which can surely be affirmed about it is that those forms or natures which are not susceptible of it to the highest degree, say the nature of numbers or of figures, do not permit of perfection. This is because the number which is the greatest of all (that is, the sum of all the numbers), and likewise the greatest of all figures, imply contradictions.* The greatest knowledge, however, and omnipotence contain no impossibility. Consequently power and knowledge do admit of perfection, and in so far as they pertain to God they have no limits.

Whence it follows that God who possesses supreme and infinite wisdom acts in the most perfect manner not only metaphysically, but also from the moral standpoint. And with respect to ourselves it can be said that the more we are enlightened and informed in regard to the works of God the more will we be disposed to find them excellent and conforming entirely to that which we might desire.

II. Against those who hold that there is in the works of God no goodness, or that the principles of goodness and beauty are arbitrary.

Therefore I am far removed from the opinion of those who maintain that there are no principles of goodness or perfection in the nature of things, or in the ideas which God has about them, and who say that the works of God are good only through the formal reason that God has made them. If this position were true, God, knowing that he is the author of things, would not have to regard them afterwards and find them good, as the Holy Scripture witnesses. Such anthropological expressions are used only to let us know that excellence is recognized in regarding the works themselves, even if we do not consider their evident dependence on their author. This is confirmed by the fact that it is in reflect-

* See Sec. II, 2c above, "On the Actual Infinite," which Leibniz imputes to God and the infinitely divisible parts of matter, despite contradictions in our idea of infinity.

ing upon the works that we are able to discover the one who wrought. They must therefore bear in themselves his character. I confess that the contrary opinion seems to me extremely dangerous and closely approaches that of recent innovators * who hold that the beauty of the universe and the goodness which we attribute to the works of God are chimeras of human beings who think of God in human terms. In saying, therefore, that things are not good according to any standard of goodness, but simply by the will of God, it seems to me that one destroys, without realizing it, all the love of God and all his glory; for why praise him for what he has done, if he would be equally praiseworthy in doing the contrary? Where will be his justice and his wisdom if he has only a certain despotic power, if arbitrary will takes the place of reasonableness, and if in accord with the definition of tyrants, justice consists in that which is pleasing to the most powerful? Besides it seems that every act of willing supposes some reason for the willing and this reason, of course, must precede the act. This is why, accordingly, I find so strange those expressions of certain philosophers who say that the eternal truths of metaphysics and Geometry, and consequently the principles of goodness, of justice, and of perfection, are effects only of the will of God. To me it seems that all these follow from his understanding, which does not depend upon his will any more than does his essence.

III. Against those who think that God might have made things better than he has.

Neither am I able to approve of the opinion of certain modern writers who boldly maintain that that which

---

* E.g., Spinoza, who is criticized further by Leibniz in selection below (III. 8).

God has made is not perfect in the highest degree, and that he might have done better. It seems to me that the consequences of such an opinion are wholly inconsistent with the glory of God. *Uti minus malum habet rationem boni, ita minus bonum habet rationem mali.* I think that one acts imperfectly if he acts with less perfection than he is capable of. To show that an architect could have done better is to find fault with his work. Furthermore this opinion is contrary to the Holy Scriptures when they assure us of the goodness of God's work. For if comparative perfection were sufficient, then in whatever way God had accomplished his work, since there is an infinitude of possible imperfections, it would always have been good in comparison with the less perfect; but a thing is little praiseworthy when it can be praised only in this way.

I believe that a great many passages from the divine writings and from the holy fathers will be found favoring my position, while hardly any will be found in favor of that of these modern thinkers. Their opinion is, in my judgment, foreign to the writers of antiquity and is a deduction based upon the too slight acquaintance which we have with the general harmony of the universe and with the hidden reasons for God's conduct. In our ignorance, therefore, we are tempted to decide audaciously that many things might have been done better.

These modern thinkers insist upon certain hardly tenable subtleties, for they imagine that nothing is so perfect that there might not have been something more perfect. This is an error. They think, indeed, that they are thus safeguarding the liberty of God. As if it were not the highest liberty to act in perfection according to the sovereign reason. For to think that God acts in anything without having any reason for his willing, even if we overlook the fact that such action seems impossible, is an opinion which conforms little to God's glory. For example, let us suppose that God chooses between A and B, and that he takes A without any reason for preferring it to B. I say that this action on the part of God is at least not praiseworthy, for all praise ought to be founded upon reason which *ex hypothesi* is not present here. My opinion is that God does nothing for which he does not deserve to be glorified.

IV. That love for God demands on our part complete satisfaction with and acquiescence in that which he has done.

The general knowledge of this great truth that God acts always in the most perfect and most desirable manner possible, is in my opinion the basis of the love which we owe to God in all things; for he who loves seeks his satisfaction in the felicity or perfection of the subject loved and in the perfection of his actions. *Idem velle et idem nolle vera amicitia est.* I believe that it is difficult to love God truly when one, having the power to change his disposition, is not disposed to wish for that which God desires. In fact those who are not satisfied with what God does seem to me like dissatisfied subjects whose attitude is not very different from that of rebels. I hold, therefore, that on these principles, to act conformably to the love of God it is not sufficient to force oneself to be patient, we must be really satisfied with all that comes to us according to his will. I mean this acquiescence in regard to the past; for as regards the future one should not be a quietist with the arms folded, open to ridicule, awaiting that which God will do; according to the sophism which the ancients called λόγον ἄεργον, the lazy reason. It is necessary to act conformably to the pre-

sumptive will of God as far as we are able to judge of
it, trying with all our might to contribute to the general
welfare and particularly to the ornamentation and the
perfection of that which touches us, or of that which is
nigh and so to speak at our hand. For if the future shall
perhaps show that God has not wished our good intention to have its way, it does not follow that he has not
wished us to act as we have; on the contrary, since he
is the best of all masters, he ever demands only the right
intentions, and it is for him to know the hour and the
proper place to let good designs succeed.

*V. In what the principles of the divine perfection
consist, and that the simplicity of the means counter-
balances the richness of the effects.*

It is sufficient, therefore, to have this confidence in
God, that he has done everything for the best and that
nothing will be able to injure those who love him. To
know in particular, however the reasons which have
moved him to choose this order of the universe, to permit
sin, to dispense his salutary grace in a certain manner—
this passes the capacity of a finite mind, above all when
such a mind has not come into the joy of the vision
of God. Yet it is possible to make some general remarks
touching the course of providence in the government of
things. One is able to say, therefore, that he who acts
perfectly is like an excellent Geometer who knows how
to find the best construction for a problem; like a good
architect who utilizes his location and the funds destined
for the building in the most advantageous manner, leaving nothing which shocks or which does not display that
beauty of which it is capable; like a good householder
who employs his property in such a way that there shall

be nothing uncultivated or sterile; like a clever machin-
ist who makes his production in the least difficult way
possible; and like an intelligent author who encloses the
most of reality in the least possible compass.

Of all beings those which are the most perfect and
occupy the least possible space, that is to say those
which interfere with one another the least, are the spirits
whose perfections are the virtues. That is why we may
not doubt that the felicity of the spirits is the principal
aim of God and that he puts this purpose into execution,
as far as the general harmony will permit. We will recur
to this subject again.

When the simplicity of God's way is spoken of, reference is specially made to the means which he employs,
and on the other hand when the variety, richness and
abundance are referred to, the ends or effects are had
in mind. Thus one ought to be proportioned to the other,
just as the cost of a building should balance the beauty
and grandeur which is expected. It is true that nothing
costs God anything, just as there is no cost for a philosopher who makes hypotheses in constructing his imaginary world, because God has only to make decrees in
order that a real world come into being; but in matters
of wisdom the decrees or hypotheses meet the expenditure in proportion as they are more independent of one
another. Reason wishes to avoid multiplicity in hypotheses or principles very much as the simplest system is
preferred in Astronomy.

*VI. That God does nothing which is not orderly, and
that it is not even possible to conceive of events which
are not regular.*

The activities or the acts of will of God are commonly divided into ordinary and extraordinary. But it

is well to bear in mind that God does nothing out of order. Therefore, that which passes for extraordinary is so only with regard to a particular order established among the created things, for as regards the universal order, everything conforms to it. This is so true that not only does nothing occur in this world which is absolutely irregular, but it is even impossible to conceive of such an occurrence. Because, let us suppose for example that some one jots down a quantity of points upon a sheet of paper helter skelter, as do those who exercise the ridiculous art of Geomancy; now I say that it is possible to find a geometrical line whose concept shall be uniform and constant, that is, in accordance with a certain formula, and which line at the same time shall pass through all of those points, and in the same order in which the hand jotted them down; also if a continuous line be traced, which is now straight, now circular, and now of any other description, it is possible to find a mental equivalent, a formula or an equation common to all the points of this line by virtue of which formula the changes in the direction of the line must occur. There is no instance of a face whose contour does not form part of a geometric line and which can not be traced entire by a certain mathematical motion. But when the formula is very complex, that which conforms to it passes for irregular. Thus we may say that in whatever manner God might have created the world, it would always have been regular and in a certain order. God, however, has chosen the most perfect, that is to say the one which is at the same time the simplest in hypotheses and the richest in phenomena, as might be the case with a geometric line, whose construction was easy, but whose properties and effects were extremely remarkable and of great significance. I use these comparisons to picture a certain imperfect resemblance to the divine wisdom, and to point out that which may at least raise our minds to conceive in some sort what cannot otherwise be expressed. I do not pretend at all to explain thus the great mystery upon which the whole universe depends.

VII. That miracles conform to the regular order although they go against the subordinate regulations; concerning that which God desires or permits and concerning general and particular intentions.

Now since nothing is done which is not orderly, we may say that miracles are quite within the order of natural operations. We use the term natural of these operations because they conform to certain subordinate regulations which we call the nature of things. For it can be said that this nature is only a custom of God's which he can change on the occasion of a stronger reason than that which moved him to use these regulations. As regards general and particular intentions, according to the way in which we understand the matter, it may be said on the one hand that everything is in accordance with his most general intention, or that which best conforms to the most perfect order he has chosen; on the other hand, however, it is also possible to say that he has particular intentions which are exceptions to the subordinate regulations above mentioned. Of God's laws, however, the most universal, i. e., that which rules the whole course of the universe, is without exceptions.

It is possible to say that God desires everything which is an object of his particular intention. When we consider the objects of his general intentions, however, such as are the modes of activities of created things and especially of the reasoning creatures with whom God wishes to co-operate, we must make a distinction; for if the

action is good in itself, we may say that God wishes it
and at times commands it, even though it does not take
place; but if it is bad in itself and becomes good only
by accident through the course of events and especially
after chastisement and satisfaction have corrected its
malignity and rewarded the ill with interest in such a
way that more perfection results in the whole train of
circumstances than would have come if that ill had not
occurred,—if all this takes place we must say that God
permits the evil, and not that he desired it, although he
has co-operated by means of the laws of nature which
he has established. He knows how to produce the greatest good from them.

*VIII. In order to distinguish between the activities
of God and the activities of created things we must
explain the conception of an individual substance.*

It is quite difficult to distinguish God's actions from
those of his creatures. Some think that God does everything; others imagine that he only conserves the force
that he has given to created things. How far can we say
either of these opinions is right?

In the first place since activity and passivity pertain
properly to individual substances (*actiones sunt sup-
positorum*) it will be necessary to explain what such a
substance is. It is indeed true that when several predicates are attributes of a single subject and this subject
is not an attribute of another, we speak of it as an individual substance, but this is not enough, and such an
explanation is merely nominal. We must therefore inquire what it is to be an attribute in reality of a certain
subject. Now it is evident that every true predication
has some basis in the nature of things, and even when
a proposition is not identical, that is, when the predicate

is not expressly contained in the subject, it is still necessary that it be virtually contained in it, and this is what the philosophers call *in-esse,* saying thereby that the predicate is in the subject. Thus the content of the subject must always include that of the predicate in such a way that if one understands perfectly the concept of the subject, he will know that the predicate appertains to it also. This being so, we are able to say that this is the nature of an individual substance or of a complete being, namely, to afford a conception so complete that the concept shall be sufficient for the understanding of it and for the deduction of all the predicates of which the substance is or may become the subject. Thus the quality of king, which belonged to Alexander the Great, an abstraction from the subject, is not sufficiently determined to constitute an individual, and does not contain the other qualities of the same subject, nor everything which the idea of this prince includes. God, however, seeing the individual concept, or hæcceity, of Alexander, sees there at the same time the basis and the reason of all the predicates which can be truly uttered regarding him; for instance that he will conquer Darius and Porus, even to the point of knowing *a priori* (and not by experience) whether he died a natural death or by poison,—facts which we can learn only through history. When we carefully consider the connection of things we see also the possibility of saying that there was always in the soul of Alexander marks of all that had happened to him and evidences of all that would happen to him and traces even of everything which occurs in the universe, although God alone could recognize them all.

IX. *That every individual substance expresses the whole universe in its own manner and that in its full*

*concept are included all its experiences together with all
the attendant circumstances and the whole sequence of
exterior events.*

There follow from these considerations several noticeable paradoxes; among others that it is not true that
two substances may be exactly alike and differ only
numerically, *solo numero,* and that what St. Thomas
says on this point regarding angels and intelligences
(*quod ibi omne individuum sit species infima*) is true
of all substances, provided that the specific difference is
understood as Geometers understand it in the case of
figures; again that a substance will be able to commence
only through creation and perish only through annihilation; that a substance cannot be divided into two nor can
one be made out of two, and that thus the number of
substances neither augments nor diminishes through natural means, although they are frequently transformed.
Furthermore every substance is like an entire world
and like a mirror of God, or indeed of the whole world
which it portrays, each one in its own fashion; almost
as the same city is variously represented according to the
various viewpoints from which it is regarded. Thus the
universe is multiplied in some sort as many times as
there are substances, and the glory of God is multiplied
in the same way by as many wholly different representations of his works. It can indeed be said that every
substance bears in some sort the character of God's
infinite wisdom and omnipotence, and imitates him as
much as it is able to; for it expresses, although confusedly, all that happens in the universe, past, present
and future, deriving thus a certain resemblance to an
infinite perception or power of knowing. And since all
other substances express this particular substance and
accommodate themselves to it, we can say that it exerts

its power upon all the others in imitation of the omnipotence of the creator.

X. *That the belief in substantial forms has a certain basis in fact, but that these forms effect no changes in the phenomena and must not be employed for the explanation of particular events.*

It seems that the ancients, able men, who were accustomed to profound meditations and taught theology and philosophy for several centuries and some of whom recommend themselves to us on account of their piety, had some knowledge of that which we have just said and this is why they introduced and maintained the substantial forms so much decried to-day. But they were not so far from the truth nor so open to ridicule as the common run of our new philosophers imagine. I grant that the consideration of these forms is of no service in the details of physics and ought not to be employed in the explanation of particular phenomena. In regard to this last point, the schoolmen were at fault, as were also the physicists of times past who followed their example, thinking they had given the reason for the properties of a body in mentioning the forms and qualities without going to the trouble of examining the manner of operation; as if one should be content to say that a clock had a certain amount of clockness derived from its form, and should not inquire in what that clockness consisted. This is indeed enough for the man who buys it, provided he surrenders the care of it to someone else. The fact, however, that there was this misunderstanding and misuse of the substantial forms should not bring us to throw away something whose recognition is so necessary in metaphysics. Since without these we will not be able, I hold, to know the ultimate principles nor to lift our minds to the knowledge of the incorporeal natures and of the marvels of God. Yet as the geometer does not need to encumber his mind with the famous puzzle of the composition of the continuum, and as no moralist, and still less a jurist or a statesman has need to trouble himself with the great difficulties which arise in conciliating free will with the providential activity of God (since the geometer is able to make all his demonstrations and the statesman can complete all his deliberations without entering into these discussions which are so necessary and important in Philosophy and Theology), so in the same way the physicist can explain his experiments, now using simpler experiments already made, now employing geometrical and mechanical demonstrations without any need of the general considerations which belong to another sphere, and if he employs the co-operation of God, or perhaps of some soul or animating force, or something else of a similiar nature, he goes out of his path quite as much as that man who, when facing an important practical question, would wish to enter into profound argumentations regarding the nature of destiny and of our liberty; a fault which men quite frequently commit without realizing it when they cumber their minds with considerations regarding fate, and thus they are even sometimes turned from a good resolution or from some necessary provision.

XI. That the opinions of the theologians and of the so-called scholastic philosophers are not to be wholly despised.

I know that I am advancing a great paradox in pretending to resuscitate in some sort the ancient philosophy, and to recall *postliminio* the substantial forms almost banished from our modern thought. But perhaps

I will not be condemned lightly when it is known that I have long meditated over the modern philosophy and that I have devoted much time to experiments in physics and to the demonstrations of geometry and that I, too, for a long time was persuaded of the baselessness of those "beings" which, however, I was finally obliged to take up again in spite of myself and as though by force. The many investigations which I carried on compelled me to recognize that our moderns do not do sufficient justice to Saint Thomas and to the other great men of that period and that there is in the theories of the scholastic philosophers and theologians far more solidity than is imagined, provided that these theories are employed *à propos* and in their place. I am persuaded that if some careful and meditative mind were to take the trouble to clarify and direct their thoughts in the manner of analytic geometers, he would find a great treasure of very important truths, wholly demonstrable.

XII. That the conception of the extension of a body is in a way imaginary and does not constitute the substance of the body.

But to resume the thread of our discussion, I believe that he who will meditate upon the nature of substance, as I have explained it above, will find that the whole nature of bodies is not exhausted in their extension, that is to say, in their size, figure and motion, but that we must recognize something which corresponds to soul, something which is commonly called substantial form, although these forms effect no change in the phenomena, any more than do the souls of beasts, that is if they have souls. It is even possible to demonstrate that the ideas of size, figure and motion are not so distinctive as is imagined, and that they stand for something imaginary relative to our perceptions as do, although to a greater extent, the ideas of color, heat, and the other similar qualities in regard to which we may doubt whether they are actually to be found in the nature of the things outside of us. This is why these latter qualities are unable to constitute "substance" and if there is no other principle of identity in bodies than that which has just been referred to a body would not subsist more than for a moment.

The souls and the substance-forms of other bodies are entirely different from intelligent souls which alone know their actions, and not only do not perish through natural means but indeed always retain the knowledge of what they are; a fact which makes them alone open to chastisement or recompense, and makes them citizens of the republic of the universe whose monarch is God. Hence it follows that all the other creatures should serve them, a point which we shall discuss more amply later.

XIII. As the individual concept of each person includes once for all everything which can ever happen to him, in it can be seen the a priori evidences or the reasons for the reality of each event, and why one happened sooner than the other. But these events, however certain, are nevertheless contingent, being based on the free choice of God and of his creatures. It is true that their choices always have their reasons, but they incline to the choices under no compulsion of necessity.

But before going further it is necessary to meet a difficulty which may arise regarding the principles which we have set forth in the preceding. We have said that the concept of an individual substance includes once for all everything which can ever happen to it and that in

considering this concept one will be able to see everything which can truly be said concerning the individual,
just as we are able to see in the nature of a circle all
the properties which can be derived from it. But does
it not seem that in this way the difference between contingent and necessary truths will be destroyed, that
there will be no place for human liberty, and that an
absolute fatality will rule as well over all our actions as
over all the rest of the events of the world? To this I
reply that a distinction must be made between that
which is certain and that which is necessary. Every one
grants that future contingencies are assured since God
foresees them, but we do not say just because of that
that they are necessary. But it will be objected, that if
any conclusion can be deduced infallibly from some definition or concept, it is necessary; and now since we
have maintained that everything which is to happen to
anyone is already virtually included in his nature or
concept, as all the properties are contained in the definition of a circle, therefore, the difficulty still remains. In
order to meet the objection completely, I say that the
connection or sequence is of two kinds: the one, absolutely necessary, whose contrary implies contradiction,
occurs in the eternal verities like the truths of geometry;
the other is necessary only *ex hypothesi,* and so to speak
by accident, and in itself it is contingent since the contrary is not implied. This latter sequence is not founded
upon ideas wholly pure and upon the pure understanding
of God, but upon his free decrees and upon the processes
of the universe. Let us give an example. Since Julius
Caesar will become perpetual Dictator and master of
the Republic and will overthrow the liberty of Rome,
this action is contained in his concept, for we have supposed that it is the nature of such a perfect concept of
a subject to involve everything, in fact so that the predi-

cate may be included in the subject *ut possit inesse subjecto*. We may say that it is not in virtue of this concept or idea that he is obliged to perform this action, since it pertains to him only because God knows everything. But it will be insisted in reply that his nature or form responds to this concept, and since God imposes upon him this personality, he is compelled henceforth to live up to it. I could reply by instancing the similar case of the future contingencies which as yet have no reality save in the understanding and will of God, and which, because God has given them in advance this form, must needs correspond to it. But I prefer to overcome a difficulty rather than to excuse it by instancing other difficulties, and what I am about to say will serve to clear up the one as well as the other. It is here that must be applied the distinction in the kind of relation, and I say that that which happens conformably to these decrees is assured, but that it is not therefore necessary, and if anyone did the contrary, he would do nothing impossible in itself, although it is impossible *ex hypothesi* that that other happen. For if anyone were capable of carrying out a complete demonstration by virtue of which he could prove this connection of the subject, which is Caesar, with the predicate, which is his successful enterprise, he would bring us to see in fact that the future dictatorship of Caesar had its basis in his concept or nature, so that one would see there a reason why he resolved to cross the Rubicon rather than to stop, and why he gained instead of losing the day at Pharsalus, and that it was reasonable and by consequence assured that this would occur, but one would not prove that it was necessary in itself, nor that the contrary implied a contradiction, almost in the same way in which it is reasonable and assured that God will always do what is best although that which is less perfect is not thereby implied. For it would be found that this demonstration of this predicate as belonging to Caesar is not as absolute as are those of numbers or of geometry, but that this predicate supposes a sequence of things which God has shown by his free will. This sequence is based on the first free decree of God which was to do always that which is the most perfect and upon the decree which God made following the first one, regarding human nature, which is that men should always do, although freely, that which appears to be the best. Now every truth which is founded upon this kind of decree is contingent, although certain, for the decrees of God do not change the possibilities of things and, as I have already said, although God assuredly chooses the best, this does not prevent that which is less perfect from being possible in itself. Although it will never happen, it is not its impossibility but its imperfection which causes him to reject it. Now nothing is necessitated whose opposite is possible. One will then be in a position to satisfy these kinds of difficulties, however great they may appear (and in fact they have not been less vexing to all other thinkers who have ever treated this matter), provided that he considers well that all contingent propositions have reasons why they are thus, rather than otherwise, or indeed (what is the same thing) that they have proof *a priori* of their truth, which render them certain and show that the connection of the subject and predicate in these propositions has its basis in the nature of the one and of the other, but he must further remember that such contingent propositions have not the demonstrations of necessity, since their reasons are founded only on the principle of contingency or of the existence of things, that is to say, upon that which is, or which appears to be the best among several things equally possible. Necessary truths, on the other hand, are founded upon the principle of contradiction, and upon the possibility or impossibility of the essences themselves, without regard here to the free will of God or of creatures.

XIV. God produces different substances according to the different views which he has of the world, and by the intervention of God, the appropriate nature of each substance brings it about that what happens to one corresponds to what happens to all the others, without, however, their acting upon one another directly.

After having seen, to a certain extent, in what the nature of substances consists, we must try to explain the dependence they have upon one another and their actions and passions. Now it is first of all very evident that created substances depend upon God who preserves them and can produce them continually by a kind of emanation just as we produce our thoughts, for when God turns, so to say, on all sides and in all fashions, the general system of phenomena which he finds it good to produce for the sake of manifesting his glory, and when he regards all the aspects of the world in all possible manners, since there is no relation which escapes his omniscience, the result of each view of the universe as seen from a different position is a substance which expresses the universe conformably to this view, provided God sees fit to render his thought effective and to produce the substance, and since God's vision is always true, our perceptions are always true and that which deceives us are our judgments, which are of us. Now we have said before, and it follows from what we have just said that each substance is a world by itself, independent of everything else excepting God; therefore, all our phenomena that is all things which are ever able to happen to us, are only consequences of our being. Now as the phenomena maintain a certain order conformably to our nature, or so to speak to the world which is in us (from whence it follows that we can, for the regulation of our conduct, make useful observations which are justified by the outcome of the future phenomena) and as we are thus able often to judge the future by the past without deceiving ourselves, we have sufficient grounds for saying that these phenomena are true and we will not be put to the task of inquiring whether they are outside of us, and whether others perceive them also.

Nevertheless it is most true that the perceptions and expressions of all substances intercorrespond, so that each one following independently certain reasons or laws which he has noticed meets others which are doing the same, as when several have agreed to meet together in a certain place on a set day, they are able to carry out the plan if they wish. Now although all express the same phenomena, this does not bring it about that their expressions are exactly alike. It is sufficient if they are proportional. As when several spectators think they see the same thing and are agreed about it, although each one sees or speaks according to the measure of his vision. It is God alone (from whom all individuals emanate continually, and who sees the universe not only as they see it, but besides in a very different way from them) who is the cause of this correspondence in their phenomena and who brings it about that that which is particular to one, is also common to all, otherwise there would be no relation. In a way, then, we might properly say, although it seems strange, that a particular substance never acts upon another particular substance nor is it acted upon by it. That which happens to each one is only the consequence of its complete idea or concept, since this idea already includes all the predicates and expresses the whole universe. In fact nothing can happen to us except thoughts and perceptions, and all our thoughts and perceptions are but the consequence, contingent it is true, of our precedent thoughts and perceptions, in such a way that were I able to consider directly all that happens or appears to me at the present time, I should be able to see all that will happen to me or that will ever appear to me. This future will not fail me, and will surely appear to me even if all that which is outside of me were destroyed, save only that God and myself were left.

Since, however, we ordinarily attribute to other things an action upon us which brings us to perceive things in a certain manner, it is necessary to consider the basis of this judgment and to inquire what there is of truth in it.

XV. The action of one finite substance upon another consists only in the increase in the degrees of the expression of the first combined with a decrease in that of the second, in so far as God has in advance fashioned them so that they shall act in accord.

Without entering into a long discussion it is sufficient for reconciling the language of metaphysics with that of practical life to remark that we preferably attribute to ourselves, and with reason, the phenomena which we express the most perfectly, and that we attribute to other substances those phenomena which each one expresses the best. Thus a substance, which is of an infinite extension in so far as it expresses all, becomes limited in proportion to its more or less perfect manner of expression. It is thus then that we may conceive of substances as interfering with and limiting one another, and hence we are able to say that in this sense they act upon one

another, and that they, so to speak, accommodate themselves to one another. For it can happen that a single
change which augments the expression of the one may
diminish that of the other. Now the virtue of a particular
substance is to express well the glory of God, and the
better it expresses it, the less is it limited. Everything
when it expresses its virtue or power, that is to say, when
it acts, changes to better, and expands just in so far as
it acts. When therefore a change occurs by which several
substances are affected (in fact every change affects them
all) I think we may say that those substances, which by
this change pass immediately to a greater degree of perfection, or to a more perfect expression, exert power and
act, while those which pass to a lesser degree disclose
their weakness and suffer. I also hold that every activity
of a substance which has perception implies some pleasure, and every passion some pain, except that it may
very well happen that a present advantage will be even-
tually destroyed by a greater evil, whence it comes that
one may sin in acting or exerting his power and in finding pleasure.

*XVI. The extraordinary intervention of God is not
excluded in that which our particular essences express,
because their expression includes everything. Such intervention, however, goes beyond the power of our natural
being or of our distinct expression, because these are
finite, and follow certain subordinate regulations.*

There remains for us at present only to explain how
it is possible that God has influence at times upon men
or upon other substances by an extraordinary or miraculous intervention, since it seems that nothing is able to
happen which is extraordinary or supernatural in as
much as all the events which occur to the other sub-

stances are only the consequences of their natures. We must recall what was said above in regard to the miracles in the universe. These always conform to the universal law of the general order, although they may contravene the subordinate regulations, and since every person or substance is like a little world which expresses the great world, we can say that this extraordinary action of God upon this substance is nevertheless miraculous, although it is comprised in the general order of the universe in so far as it is expressed by the individual essence or concept of this substance. This is why, if we understand in our natures all that they express, nothing is supernatural in them, because they reach out to everything, an effect always expressing its cause, and God being the veritable cause of the substances. But as that which our natures express the most perfectly pertains to them in a particular manner, that being their special power, and since they are limited, as I have just explained, many things there are which surpass the powers of our natures and even of all limited natures. As a consequence, to speak more clearly, I say that the miracles and the extraordinary interventions of God have this peculiarity that they cannot be foreseen by any created mind however enlightened. This is because the distinct comprehension of the fundamental order surpasses them all, while on the other hand, that which is called natural depends upon less fundamental regulations which the creatures are able to understand. In order then that my words may be as irreprehensible as the meaning I am trying to convey, it will be well to associate certain words with certain significations. We may call that which includes everything that we express and which expresses our union with God himself, nothing going beyond it, our essence. But that which is limited in us may be designated as our nature or our power, and in accordance

with this terminology that which goes beyond the natures
of all created substances is supernatural.

*XVII. An example of a subordinate regulation in
the law of nature which demonstrates that God always
preserves the same amount of force but not the same
quantity of motion:—against the Cartesians and many
others.*

I have frequently spoken of subordinate regulations,
or of the laws of nature, and it seems that it will be
well to give an example. Our new philosophers are unani-
mous in employing that famous law that God always
preserves the same amount of motion in the universe.
In fact it is a very plausible law, and in times past I
held it as indubitable. But since then I have learned
in what its fault consists. Monsieur Descartes and many
other clever mathematicians have thought that the quantity of motion, that is to say the velocity multiplied by
the bulk of the moving body, is exactly equivalent to the
moving force, or to speak in mathematical terms that the
force varies as the velocity multiplied by the bulk. Now
it is reasonable that the same force is always preserved
in the universe. So also, looking to phenomena, it will
be readily seen that a mechanical perpetual motion is
impossible, because the force in such a machine, being
always diminished a little by friction and so ultimately
destined to be entirely spent, would necessarily have to
recoup its losses, and consequently would keep on increasing of itself without any new impulsion from without; and we see furthermore that the force of a body is
diminished only in proportion as it gives up force, either
to a contiguous body or to its own parts, in so far as
they have a separate movement. The mathematicians to
whom I have referred think that what can be said of

force can be said of the quantity of motion. In order, however, to show the difference I make two suppositions: in the first place, that a body falling from a certain height acquires a force enabling it to remount to the same height, provided that its direction is turned that way, or provided that there are no hindrances. For instance, a pendulum will rise exactly to the height from which it has fallen, provided the resistance of the air and of certain other small particles do not diminish a little its acquired force.

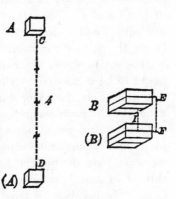

I suppose in the second place that it will take as much force to lift a body A weighing one pound to the height CD, four feet, as to raise a body B weighing four pounds to the height EF, one foot. These two suppositions are granted by our new philosophers. It is therefore manifest that the body A falling from the height CD acquires exactly as much force as the body B falling from the height EF, for the body B at F, having by the first supposition sufficient force to return to E, has therefore the force to carry a body of four pounds to the distance of one foot, EF. And likewise the body A at D, having the force to return to C, has also the force required to carry a body weighing one pound, its own weight, back to C, a distance of four feet. Now by the second supposition the force of these two bodies is equal. Let us now see if the quantity of motion is the same in each case. It is here that we will be surprised to find a very great difference, for it has been proved by Galileo that the velocity acquired by the fall CD is

double the velocity acquired by the fall EF, although the
height is four times as great. Multiplying, therefore, the
body A, whose bulk is 1, by its velocity, which is 2,
the product or the quantity of movement will be 2, and
on the other hand, if we multiply the body B, whose
bulk is 4, by its velocity, which is 1, the product or
quantity of motion will be 4. Hence the quantity of the
motion of the body A at the point D is half the quantity
of motion of the body B at the point F, yet their forces
are equal, and there is therefore a great difference between the quantity of motion and the force. This is what
we set out to show. We can see therefore how the force
ought to be estimated by the quantity of the effect which
it is able to produce, for example by the height to which
a body of certain weight can be raised. This is a very
different thing from the velocity which can be imparted
to it, and in order to impart to it double the velocity
we must have double the force. Nothing is simpler than
this proof and Monsieur Descartes has fallen into error
here, only because he trusted too much to his thoughts
even when they had not been ripened by reflection. But
it astonishes me that his disciples have not noticed this
error, and I am afraid that they are beginning to imitate
little by little certain Peripatetics whom they ridicule,
and that they are accustoming themselves to consult
rather the books of their master, than reason or nature.

*XVIII. The distinction between force and the quan-
tity of motion is, among other reasons, important as
showing that we must have recourse to metaphysical
considerations in addition to discussions of extension if
we wish to explain the phenomena of matter.*

This consideration of the force, distinguished from
the quantity of motion, is of importance, not only in

physics and mechanics for finding the real laws of nature
and the principles of motion, and even for correcting
many practical errors which have crept into the writings
of certain able mathematicians, but also in metaphysics
it is of importance for the better understanding of principles. Because motion, if we regard only its exact and
formal meaning, that is, change of place, is not something really absolute, and when several bodies change
their places reciprocally, it is not possible to determine by
considering the bodies alone to which among them movement or repose is to be attributed, as I could demonstrate
geometrically, if I wished to stop for it now. But the
force, or the proximate cause of these changes is something more real, and there are sufficient grounds for
attributing it to one body rather than to another, and
it is only through this latter investigation that we can
determine to which one the movement must appertain.
Now this force is something different from size, from
form or from motion, and it can be seen from this consideration that the whole meaning of a body is not exhausted in its extension together with its modifications
as our moderns persuade themselves. We are therefore
obliged to restore certain beings or forms which they
have banished. It appears more and more clear that
although all the particular phenomena of nature can be
explained mathematically or mechanically by those who
understand them, yet nevertheless, the general principles
of corporeal nature and even of mechanics are metaphysical rather than geometric, and belong rather to certain indivisible forms or natures as the causes of the
appearances, than to the corporeal mass or to extension.
In this way we are able to reconcile the mechanical philosophy of the moderns with the circumspection of those
intelligent and well-meaning persons who, with a certain
justice, fear that we are becoming too far removed from

immaterial beings and that we are thus prejudicing piety.

XIX. *The utility of final causes in Physics.*

As I do not wish to judge people in ill part I bring no accusation against our new philosophers who pretend to banish final causes from physics, but I am nevertheless obliged to avow that the consequences of such a banishment appear to me dangerous, especially when joined to that position which I refuted at the beginning of this treatise. That position seemed to go the length of discarding final causes entirely as though God proposed no end and no good in his activity, or as if good were not to be the object of his will. I hold on the contrary that it is just in this that the principle of all existences and of the laws of nature must be sought, hence God always proposes the best and most perfect. I am quite willing to grant that we are liable to err when we wish to determine the purposes or councils of God, but this is the case only when we try to limit them to some particular design, thinking that he has had in view only a single thing, while in fact he regards everything at once. As for instance, if we think that God has made the world only for us, it is a great blunder, although it may be quite true that he has made it entirely for us, and that there is nothing in the universe which does not touch us and which does not accommodate itself to the regard which he has for us according to the principle laid down above. Therefore when we see some good effect or some perfection which happens or which follows from the works of God we are able to say assuredly that God has purposed it, for he does nothing by chance, and is not like us who sometimes fail to do well. Therefore, far from being able to fall into error in this respect as do the extreme statesmen who postulate too much foresight in the designs of Princes, or as do commentators who seek for too much erudition in their authors, it will be impossible to attribute too much reflection to God's infinite wisdom, and there is no matter in which error is less to be feared provided we confine ourselves to affirmations and provided we avoid negative statements which limit the designs of God. All those who see the admirable structure of animals find themselves led to recognize the wisdom of the author of things and I advise those who have any sentiment of piety and indeed of true philosophy to hold aloof from the expressions of certain pretentious minds who instead of saying that eyes were made for seeing, say that we see because we find ourselves having eyes. When one seriously holds such opinions which hand everything over to material necessity or to a kind of chance (although either alternative ought to appear ridiculous to those who understand what we have explained above) it is difficult to recognize an intelligent author of nature. The effect should correspond to its cause and indeed it is best known through the recognition of its cause, so that it is reasonable to introduce a sovereign intelligence ordering things, and in place of making use of the wisdom of this sovereign being, to employ only the properties of matter to explain phenomena. As if in order to account for the capture of an important place by a prince, the historian should say it was because the particles of powder in the cannon having been touched by a spark of fire expanded with a rapidity capable of pushing a hard solid body against the walls of the place, while the little particles which composed the brass of the cannon were so well interlaced that they did not separate under this impact,—as if he should account for it in this way instead of making us see how the foresight of the conqueror brought him to choose the time and the proper means and how his ability surmounted all obstacles.

XX. A noteworthy disquisition in Plato's Phaedo against the philosophers who were too materialistic.

This reminds me of a fine disquisition by Socrates in Plato's Phaedo, which agrees perfectly with my opinion on this subject and seems to have been uttered expressly for our too materialistic philosophers. This agreement has led me to a desire to translate it although it is a little long. Perhaps this example will give some of us an incentive to share in many of the other beautiful and well balanced thoughts which are found in the writings of this famous author.

XXI. If the mechanical laws depended upon Geometry alone without metaphysical influences, the phenomena would be very different from what they are.

Now since the wisdom of God has always been recognized in the details of the mechanical structures of certain particular bodies, it should also be shown in the general economy of the world and in the constitution of the laws of nature. This is so true that even in the laws of motion in general, the plans of this wisdom have been noticed. For if bodies were only extended masses, and motion were only a change of place, and if everything ought to be and could be deduced by geometric necessity from these two definitions alone, it would follow, as I have shown elsewhere, that the smallest body on contact with a very large one at rest would impart to it its own velocity, yet without losing any of the velocity that it had. A quantity of other rules wholly contrary to the formation of a system would also have to be admitted. But the decree of the divine wisdom in preserving always the same force and the same total direction has provided for a system. I find indeed that many of the effects of nature can be accounted for in a twofold way, that is to say by a consideration of efficient causes, and again independently by a consideration of final causes. An example of the latter is God's decree always to carry out his plan by the easiest and most determined way. I have shown this elsewhere in accounting for the catoptric and dioptric laws, and I will speak more at length about it in what follows.

XXII. Reconciliation of the two methods of explanation, the one using final causes, and the other efficient causes, thus satisfying both those who explain nature mechanically and those who have recourse to incorporeal natures.

It is worth while to make the preceding remark in order to reconcile those who hope to explain mechanically the formation of the first tissue of an animal and all the interrelation of the parts, with those who account for the same structure by referring to final causes. Both explanations are good; both are useful not only for the admiring of the work of a great artificer, but also for the discovery of useful facts in physics and medicine. And writers who take these diverse routes should not speak ill of each other. For I see that those who attempt to explain beauty by the divine anatomy ridicule those who imagine that the apparently fortuitous flow of certain liquids has been able to produce such a beautiful variety and that they regard them as overbold and irreverent. These others on the contrary treat the former as simple and superstitious, and compare them to those ancients who regarded the physicists as impious when they maintained that not Jupiter thundered but some ma-

terial which is found in the clouds. The best plan would
be to join the two ways of thinking. To use a practical
comparison, we recognize and praise the ability of a
workman not only when we show what designs he had
in making the parts of his machine, but also when we
explain the instruments which he employed in making
each part, especially if these instruments are simple and
ingeniously contrived. God is also a workman able enough
to produce a machine still a thousand times more ingenious than is our body, by employing only certain quite
simple liquids purposely composed in such a way that
ordinary laws of nature alone are required to develop
them so as to produce such a marvellous effect. But it is
also true that this development would not take place if
God were not the author of nature. Yet I find that the
method of efficient causes, which goes much deeper and
is in a measure more immediate and *a priori,* is also
more difficult when we come to details, and I think that
our philosophers are still very frequently far removed
from making the most of this method. The method of
final causes, however, is easier and can be frequently
employed to find out important and useful truths which
we should have to seek for a long time, if we were confined to that other more physical method of which anatomy is able to furnish many examples. It seems to me
that Snellius, who was the first discoverer of the laws
of refraction, would have waited a long time before finding them if he had wished to seek out first how light was
formed. But he apparently followed that method which
the ancients employed for Catoptrics, that is, the method
of final causes. Because, while seeking for the easiest
way in which to conduct a ray of light from one given
point to another given point by reflection from a given
plane (supposing that that was the design of nature)
they discovered the equality of the angles of incidence

and reflection, as can be seen from a little treatise by
Heliodorus of Larissa and also elsewhere. This principle
Mons. Snellius, I believe, and afterwards independently
of him, M. Fermat, applied most ingeniously to refraction. For since the rays while in the same media always
maintain the same proportion of sines, which in turn
corresponds to the resistance of the media, it appears
that they follow the easiest way, or at least that way
which is the most determinate for passing from a given
point in one medium to a given point in another medium.
That demonstration of this same theorem which M. Descartes has given, using efficient causes, is much less satisfactory. At least we have grounds to think that he would
never have found the principle by that means if he had
not learned in Holland of the discovery of Snellius.

*XXIII. Returning to immaterial substances we ex-
plain how God acts upon the understanding of spirits
and ask whether one always keeps the idea of what he
thinks about.*

I have thought it well to insist a little upon final
causes, upon incorporeal natures and upon an intelligent
cause with respect to bodies so as to show the use of
these conceptions in physics and in mathematics. This
for two reasons, first to purge from mechanical philosophy the impiety that is imputed to it, second, to elevate
to nobler lines of thought the thinking of our philosophers who incline to materialistic considerations alone.
Now, however, it will be well to return from corporeal
subtances to the consideration of immaterial natures and
particularly of spirits, and to speak of the methods which
God uses to enlighten them and to act upon them. Although we must not forget that there are here at the
same time certain laws of nature in regard to which I

can speak more amply elsewhere. It will be enough for now to touch upon ideas and to inquire if we see everything in God and how God is our light. First of all it will be in place to remark that the wrong use of ideas occasions many errors. For when one reasons in regard to anything, he imagines that he has an idea of it and this is the foundation upon which certain philosophers, ancient and modern, have constructed a demonstration of God that is extremely imperfect. It must be, they say, that I have an idea of God, or of a perfect being, since I think of him and we cannot think without having ideas; now the idea of this being includes all perfections and since existence is one of these perfections, it follows that he exists. But I reply, inasmuch as we often think of impossible chimeras, for example of the highest degree of swiftness, of the greatest number, of the meeting of the conchoid with its base or determinant, such reasoning is not sufficient. It is therefore in this sense that we can say that there are true and false ideas according as the thing which is in question is possible or not. And it is when he is assured of the possibility of a thing, that one can boast of having an idea of it. Therefore, the aforesaid argument proves that God exists, if he is possible. This is in fact an excellent privilege of the divine nature, to have need only of a possibility or an essence in order to actually exist, and it is just this which is called self-sufficient being, *ens a se*.

XXIV. What clear and obscure, distinct and confused, adequate and inadequate, intuitive and assumed knowledge is, and the definition of nominal, real, causal and essential.

In order to understand better the nature of ideas it is necessary to touch somewhat upon the various kinds of knowledge. When I am able to recognize a thing among others, without being able to say in what its differences or characteristics consist, the knowledge is confused. Sometimes indeed we may know clearly, that is without being in the slightest doubt, that a poem or a picture is well or badly done because there is in it an "I know not what" which satisfies or shocks us. Such knowledge is not yet distinct. It is when I am able to explain the peculiarities which a thing has, that the knowledge is called distinct. Such is the knowledge of an assayer who discerns the true gold from the false by means of certain tests or marks which make up the definition of gold. But distinct knowledge has degrees, because ordinarily the conceptions which enter into the definitions will themselves be in need of definition, and are only known confusedly. When at length everything which enters into a definition or into distinct knowledge is known distinctly, even back to the primitive conception, I call that knowledge adequate. When my mind understands at once and distinctly all the primitive ingredients of a conception, then we have intuitive knowledge. This is extremely rare as most human knowledge is only confused or indeed assumed. It is well also to distinguish nominal from real definition. I call a definition nominal when there is doubt whether an exact conception of it is possible; as for instance, when I say that an endless screw is a line in three dimensional space whose parts are congruent or fall one upon another. Now although this is one of the reciprocal properties of an endless screw, he who did not know by other means what an endless screw was could doubt if such a line were possible, because the other lines whose ends are congruent (there are only two: the circumference of a circle and the straight line) are plane figures, that is to say they can be described *in plano*. This instance enables us to

see that any reciprocal property can serve as a nominal
definition, but when the property brings us to see the
possibility of a thing it makes the definition real, and as
long as one has only a nominal definition he cannot be
sure of the consequences which he draws, because if it
conceals a contradiction or an impossibility he would be
able to draw the opposite conclusions. That is why truths
do not depend upon names and are not arbitrary, as some
of our new philosophers think. There is also a considerable difference among real definitions, for when the
possibility proves itself only by experience, as in the
definition of quicksilver, whose possibility we know because such a body, which is both an extremely heavy
fluid and quite volatile, actually exists, the definition is
merely real and nothing more. If, however, the proof of
the possibility is *a priori,* the definition is not only real
but also causal as for instance when it contains the possible generation of a thing. Finally, when the definition,
without assuming anything which requires a proof *a priori* of its possibility, carries the analysis clear to the
primitive conception, the definition is perfect or essential.

*XXV. In what cases knowledge is added to mere con-
templation of the idea.*

Now it is manifest that we have no idea of a conception when it is impossible. And in case the knowledge,
where we have the idea of it, is only assumed, we do not
visualize it because such a conception is known only in
like manner as conceptions internally impossible. And
if it be in fact possible, it is not by this kind of knowledge that we learn its possibility. For instance, when
I am thinking of a thousand or of a chiliagon, I frequently do it without contemplating the idea. Even if I
say a thousand is ten times a hundred, I frequently do

not trouble to think what ten and a hundred are, because I assume that I know, and I do not consider it necessary to stop just at present to conceive of them. Therefore it may well happen, as it in fact does happen often enough, that I am mistaken in regard to a conception which I assume that I understand, although it is an impossible truth or at least is incompatible with others with which I join it, and whether I am mistaken or not, this way of assuming our knowledge remains the same. It is, then, only when our knowledge is clear in regard to confused conceptions, and when it is intuitive in regard to those which are distinct, that we see its entire idea.

XXVI. Ideas are all stored up within us. Plato's doctrine of reminiscence.

In order to see clearly what an idea is, we must guard ourselves against a misunderstanding. Many regard the idea as the form or the differentiation of our thinking, and according to this opinion we have the idea in our mind, in so far as we are thinking of it, and each separate time that we think of it anew we have another idea although similar to the preceding one. Some, however, take the idea as the immediate object of thought, or as a permanent form which remains even when we are no longer contemplating it. As a matter of fact our soul has the power of representing to itself any form or nature whenever the occasion comes for thinking about it, and I think that this activity of our soul is, so far as it expresses some nature, form or essence, properly the idea of the thing. This is in us, and is always in us, whether we are thinking of it or no. (Our soul expresses God and the universe and all essences as well as all existences.) This position is in accord with my principles that naturally nothing enters into our minds from outside.

It is a bad habit we have of thinking as though our minds receive certain messengers, as it were, or as if they had doors or windows. We have in our minds all those forms for all periods of time because the mind at every moment expresses all its future thoughts and already thinks confusedly of all that of which it will ever think distinctly. Nothing can be taught us of which we have not already in our minds the idea. This idea is as it were the material out of which the thought will form itself. This is what Plato has excellently brought out in his doctrine of reminiscence, a doctrine which contains a great deal of truth, provided that it is properly understood and purged of the error of pre-existence, and provided that one does not conceive of the soul as having already known and thought at some other time what it learns and thinks now. Plato has also confirmed his position by a beautiful experiment. He introduces [*Meno*] a boy, whom he leads by short steps, to extremely difficult truths of geometry bearing on incommensurables, all this without teaching the boy anything, merely drawing out replies by a well arranged series of questions. This shows that the soul virtually knows those things, and needs only to be reminded (animadverted) to recognize the truths. Consequently it possesses at least the idea upon which those truths depend. We may say even that it already possesses those truths, if we consider them as the relations of the ideas.

XXVII. In what respect our souls can be compared to blank tablets and how conceptions are derived from the senses.

Aristotle preferred to compare our souls to blank tablets prepared for writing, and he maintained that nothing is in the understanding which does not come through the senses. This position is in accord with the popular conceptions, as Aristotle's approach usually is. Plato thinks more profoundly. Such tenets or practicologies are nevertheless allowable in ordinary use somewhat in the same way as those who accept the Copernican theory still continue to speak of the rising and setting of the sun. I find indeed that these usages can be given a real meaning containing no error, quite in the same way as I have already pointed out that we may truly say particular substances act upon one another. In this same sense we may say that knowledge is received from without through the medium of the senses because certain exterior things contain or express more particularly the causes which determine us to certain thoughts. Because in the ordinary uses of life we attribute to the soul only that which belongs to it most manifestly and particularly, and there is no advantage in going further. When, however, we are dealing with the exactness of metaphysical truths, it is important to recognize the powers and independence of the soul which extend infinitely further than is commonly supposed. In order, therefore, to avoid misunderstandings it would be well to choose separate terms for the two. These expressions which are in the soul whether one is conceiving of them or not may be called ideas, while those which one conceives of or constructs may be called conceptions, *conceptus*. But whatever terms are used, it is always false to say that all our conceptions come from the so-called external senses, because those conceptions which I have of myself and of my thoughts, and consequently of being, of substance, of action, of identity, and of many others come from an inner experience.

XXVIII. The only immediate object of our perceptions which exists outside of us is God, and in him alone is our light.

In the strictly metaphysical sense no external cause acts upon us excepting God alone, and he is in immediate relation with us only by virtue of our continual dependence upon him. Whence it follows that there is absolutely no other external object which comes into contact with our souls and directly excites perceptions in us. We have in our souls ideas of everything, only because of the continual action of God upon us, that is to say, because every effect expresses its cause and therefore the essences of our souls are certain expressions, imitations or images of the divine essence, divine thought and divine will, including all the ideas which are there contained. We may say, therefore, that God is for us the only immediate external object, and that we see things through him. For example, when we see the sun or the stars, it is God who gives to us and preserves in us the ideas and whenever our senses are affected according to his own laws in a certain manner, it is he, who by his continual concurrence, determines our thinking. God is the sun and the light of souls, *lumen illuminans omnem hominem venientem in hunc mundum,* although this is not the current conception. I think I have already remarked that during the scholastic period many believed God to be the light of the soul, *intellectus agens animæ rationalis,* following in this the Holy Scriptures and the fathers who were always more Platonic than Aristotelian in their mode of thinking. The Averroists misused this conception, but others, among whom were several mystic theologians, and William of Saint Amour also, I think, understood this conception in a manner which assured the dignity of God and was able to raise the soul to a knowledge of its welfare.

XXIX. Yet we think directly by means of our own ideas and not through God's.

Nevertheless I cannot approve of the position of certain able philosophers who seem to hold that our ideas themselves are in God and not at all in us. I think that in taking this position they have neither sufficiently considered the nature of substance, which we have just explained, nor the complete purview and independence of the soul which includes all that happens to it, and expresses God, and with him all possible and actual beings in the same way that an effect expresses its cause. It is indeed inconceivable that the soul should think using the ideas of something else. The soul when it thinks of anything must be affected dynamically in a certain manner, and it must needs have in itself in advance not only the passive capacity of being thus affected, a capacity already wholly determined, but it must have besides an active power by virtue of which it has always had in its nature the marks of the future production of this thought, and the disposition to produce it at its proper time. All of this shows that the soul already includes the idea which is comprised in any particular thought.

XXX. How God inclines our souls without necessitating them; that there are no grounds for complaint; that we must not ask why Judas sinned because this free act is contained in his concept, the only question being why Judas the sinner is admitted to existence, preferably to other possible persons; concerning the original imperfection or limitation before the fall and concerning the different degrees of grace.

Regarding the action of God upon the human will there are many quite different considerations which it would take too long to investigate here. Nevertheless the following is what can be said in general. God in co-operating with ordinary actions only follows the laws which he has established, that is to say, he continually preserves and produces our being so that the ideas come to us spontaneously or with freedom in that order which the concept of our individual substance carries with itself. In this concept they can be foreseen for all eternity. Furthermore, by virtue of the decree which God has made that the will shall always seek the apparent good in certain particular respects (in regard to which this apparent good always has in it something of reality expressing or imitating God's will), he, without at all necessitating our choice, determines it by that which appears most desirable. For absolutely speaking, our will as contrasted with necessity, is in a state of indifference, being able to act otherwise, or wholly to suspend its action, either alternative being and remaining possible. It therefore devolves upon the soul to be on guard against appearances, by means of a firm will, to reflect and to refuse to act or decide in certain circumstances, except after mature deliberation. It is, however, true and has been assured from all eternity that certain souls will not employ their power upon certain occasions.

But who could do more than God has done, and can such a soul complain of anything except itself? All these complaints after the deed are unjust, inasmuch as they would have been unjust before the deed. Would this soul shortly before committing the sin have had the right to complain of God as though he had determined the sin? Since the determinations of God in these matters cannot be foreseen, how would the soul know that it was preordained to sin unless it had already committed the sin? It is merely a question of wishing to or not wishing to, and God could not have set an easier or juster condition. Therefore all judges without asking the reasons which have disposed a man to have an evil will, consider only how far this will is wrong. But, you object, perhaps it is

ordained from all eternity that I will sin. Find your own
answer. Perhaps it has not been. Now then, without asking for what you are unable to know and in regard to
which you can have no light, act according to your duty
and your knowledge. But, some one will object; whence
comes it then that this man will assuredly do this sin?
The reply is easy. It is that otherwise he would not be
a man. For God foresees from all time that there will
be a certain Judas, and in the concept or idea of him
which God has, is contained this future free act. The
only question, therefore, which remains is why this certain Judas, the betrayer who is possible only because
of the idea of God, actually exists. To this question,
however, we can expect no answer here on earth excepting to say in general that it is because God has found
it good that he should exist notwithstanding that sin
which he foresaw. This evil will be more than overbal-
anced. God will derive a greater good from it, and it will
finally turn out that this series of events in which is
included the existence of this sinner, is the most perfect
among all the possible series of events. An explanation in
every case of the admirable economy of this choice cannot be given while we are sojourners on earth. It is
enough to know the excellence without understanding it.
It is here that we must recognize the unfathomable
depth of the divine wisdom, without hesitating at a detail
which involves an infinite number of considerations. It is
clear, however, that God is not the cause of ill. For not
only after the loss of innocence by men, has original sin
possessed the soul, but even before that there was an
original limitation or imperfection in the very nature of
all creatures, which rendered them open to sin and able
to fall. There is, therefore, no more difficulty in the
supralapsarian view than there is in the other views of
sin. To this also, it seems to me, can be reduced the opin-

ion of Saint Augustine and of other authors: that the
root of evil is in the privation, that is to say, in the lack
or limitation of creatures which God graciously remedies
by whatever degree of perfection it pleases him to give.
This grace of God, whether ordinary or extraordinary,
has its degrees and its measures. It is always efficacious
in itself to produce a certain proportionate effect and
furthermore it is always sufficient not only to keep one
from sin but even to effect his salvation, provided that
the man co-operates with that which is in him. It has not
always, however, sufficient power to overcome the inclination, for, if it did, it would no longer be limited in any
way, and this superiority to limitations is reserved to
that unique grace which is absolutely efficacious. This
grace is always victorious whether through its own self
or through the congruity of circumstances.

*XXXI. Concerning the motives of election; concern-
ing faith foreseen and the absolute decree and that it
all reduces to the question why God has chosen and resolved to admit to existence just such a possible person,
whose concept includes just such a sequence of free acts
and of free gifts of grace. This at once puts an end to
all difficulties.*

Finally, the grace of God is wholly unprejudiced and
creatures have no claim upon it. Just as it is not sufficient in accounting for God's choice in his dispensations
of grace to refer to his absolute or conditional prevision
of men's future actions, so it is also wrong to imagine
his decrees as absolute with no reasonable motive. As
concerns foreseen faith and good works, it is very true
that God has elected none but those whose faith and
charity he foresees, *quos se fide donaturum praescivit.*
The same question, however, arises again as to why God

gives to some rather than to others the grace of faith
or of good works. As concerns God's ability to foresee
not only the faith and good deeds, but also their content
and predisposition, or that which a man on his part contributes to them (since there are as truly diversities on
the part of men as on the part of grace, and a man
although he needs to be aroused to good and needs to
become converted, yet acts in accordance with his tem-
perament)—as regards his ability to foresee there are
many who say that God, knowing what a particular man
will do without grace, that is without his extraordinary
assistance, or knowing at least what will be the human
contribution, resolves to give grace to those whose natural dispositions are the best, or at any rate are the
least imperfect and evil. But if this were the case then
the natural dispositions in so far as they were good would
be like gifts of grace, since God would have given advantages to some over others; and therefore, since he would
well know that the natural advantages which he had
given would serve as motives for his grace or for his
extraordinary assistance, would not everything be reduced to his mercy? I think, therefore, that since we do
not know how much and in what way God regards natural dispositions in the dispensations of his grace, it
would be safest and most exact to say, in accordance with
our principles and as I have already remarked, that
there must needs be among possible beings the person
Peter or John whose concept or idea contains all that
particular sequence of ordinary and extraordinary manifestations of grace together with the rest of the accompanying events and circumstances, and that it has pleased
God to choose him among an infinite number of persons
equally possible for actual existence. When we have said
this there seems nothing left to ask, and all difficulties
vanish. For in regard to that great and ultimate question

why it has pleased God to choose him among so great a
number of possible persons, it is surely unreasonable to
demand more than the general reasons which we have
given. The reasons in detail surpass our ken. Therefore,
instead of postulating an absolute decree, which being
without reason would be unreasonable, and instead of
postulating reasons which do not succeed in solving the
difficulties and in turn have need themselves of reasons,
it will be best to say with St. Paul that there are for
God's choice certain great reasons of wisdom and congruity which he follows, which reasons, however, are
unknown to mortals and are founded upon the general
order, whose goal is the greatest perfection of the world.
This is what is meant when the motives of God's glory
and of the manifestation of his justice are spoken of, as
well as when men speak of his mercy, and his perfection
in general; that immense vastness of wealth, in fine, with
which the soul of the same St. Paul was to be thrilled.

*XXXII. Usefulness of these principles in matters of
piety and of religion.*

In addition it seems that the thoughts which we have
just explained and particularly the great principle of
the perfection of God's operations and the concept of
substance which includes all its changes with all its
accompanying circumstances, far from injuring, serve
rather to confirm religion, serve to dissipate great difficulties, to inflame souls with a divine love and to raise
the mind to a knowledge of incorporeal substances much
more than the present-day hypotheses. For it appears
clearly that all other substances depend upon God just
as our thoughts emanate from our own substances; that
God is all in all and that he is intimately united to all

created things, in proportion however to their perfection; that it is he alone who determines them from without by his influence, and if to act is to determine directly, it may be said in metaphysical language that God alone acts upon me and he alone causes me to do good or ill, other substances contributing only because of his determinations; because God, who takes all things into consideration, distributes his bounties and compels created beings to accommodate themselves to one another. Thus God alone constitutes the relation or communication between substances. It is through him that the phenomena of the one meet and accord with the phenomena of the others, so that there may be a reality in our perceptions. In common parlance, however, an action is attributed to particular causes in the sense that I have explained above because it is not necessary to make continual mention of the universal cause when speaking of particular cases. It can be seen also that every substance has a perfect spontaneity (which becomes liberty with intelligent substances). Everything which happens to it is a consequence of its idea or its being and nothing determines it except God only. It is for this reason that a person of exalted mind and revered saintliness may say that the soul ought often to think as if there were only God and itself in the world. Nothing can make us hold to immortality more firmly than this independence and vastness of the soul which protects it completely against exterior things, since it alone constitutes our universe and together with God is sufficient for itself. It is as impossible for it to perish save through annihilation as it is impossible for the universe to destroy itself, the universe whose animate and perpetual expression it is. Furthermore, the changes in this extended mass which is called our body cannot possibly affect the soul nor can the dissipation of the body destroy that which is indivisible.

XXXIII. Explanation of the relation between the soul and the body, a matter which has been regarded as inexplicable or else as miraculous; concerning the origin of confused perceptions.

We can also see the explanation of that great mystery "the union of the soul and the body," that is to say how it comes about that the passions and actions of the one are accompanied by the actions and passions or else the appropriate phenomena of the other. For it is not possible to conceive how one can have an influence upon the other and it is unreasonable to have recourse at once to the extraordinary intervention of the universal cause in an ordinary and particular case. The following, however, is the true explanation. We have said that everything which happens to a soul or to any substance is a consequence of its concept; hence the idea itself or the essence of the soul brings it about that all of its appearances or perceptions should be born out of its nature and precisely in such a way that they correspond of themselves to that which happens in the universe at large, but more particularly and more perfectly to that which happens in the body associated with it, because it is in a particular way and only for a certain time according to the relation of other bodies to its own body that the soul expresses the state of the universe. This last fact enables us to see how our body belongs to us, without, however, being attached to our essence. I believe that those who are careful thinkers will decide favorably for our principles because of this single reason, viz., that they are able to see in what consists the relation between the soul and the body, a parallelism which appears inexplicable in any other way. We can also see that the perceptions of our senses even when they are clear must necessarily contain certain confused elements, for as all the bodies in the universe are in sympathy, ours receives the impressions of all the others, and while our senses respond to everything, our soul cannot pay attention to every particular. That is why our confused sensations are the result of a variety of perceptions. This variety is infinite. It is almost like the confused murmuring which is heard by those who approach the shore of a sea. It comes from the continual beatings of innumerable waves. If now, out of many perceptions which do not at all fit together to make one, no particular one perception surpasses the others, and if they make impressions about equally strong or equally capable of holding the attention of the soul, they can be perceived only confusedly.

XXXIV. Concerning the difference between spirits and other substances, souls or substantial forms; that the immortality which men desire includes memory.

Supposing that the bodies which constitute a *unum per* se, as human bodies, are substances, and have substantial forms, and supposing that animals have souls, we are obliged to grant that these souls and these substantial forms cannot entirely perish, any more than can the atoms or the ultimate elements of matter, according to the position of other philosophers; for no substance perishes, although it may become very different. Such substances also express the whole universe, although more imperfectly than do spirits. The principal difference, however, is that they do not know that they are, nor what they are. Consequently, not being able to reason, they are unable to discover necessary and universal truths. It is also because they do not reflect regarding themselves that they have no moral qualities, whence it follows that they undergo myriad transformations—as we see a caterpillar change into a butterfly; the result from a moral or practical standpoint is the same as if we said that they perished in each case, and we can indeed say it from the physical standpoint in the same way that we say bodies perish in their dissolution. But the intelligent soul, knowing that it exists, having the ability to say that word "I" so full of meaning, not only continues and exists, metaphysically far more certainly than do the others, but it remains the same from the moral standpoint, and constitutes the same personality, for it is its memory or knowledge of this ego which renders it open to punishment and reward. Also the immortality which is required in morals and in religion does not consist merely in this perpetual existence, which pertains to all substances, for if in addition there were no remembrance of what one had been, immortality would not be at all desirable. Suppose that some individual could suddenly become King of China on condition, however, of forgetting what he had been, as though being born again, would it not amount to the same practically, or as far as the effects could be perceived, as if the individual were annihilated, and a king of China were the same instant created in his place? The individual would have no reason to desire this.

XXXV. The excellence of spirits; that God considers them preferable to other creatures; that the spirits express God rather than the world, while other simple substances express the world rather than God.

In order, however, to prove by natural reasons that God will preserve forever not only our substance, but also our personality, that is to say the recollection and knowledge of what we are (although the distinct knowledge is sometimes suspended during sleep and in swoons) it is necessary to join to metaphysics moral considerations. God must be considered not only as the principle and the cause of all substances and of all existing things, but also as the chief of all persons or intelligent substances, as the absolute monarch of the most perfect city or republic, such as is constituted by all the spirits together in the universe, God being the most complete of all spirits at the same time that he is greatest of all beings. For assuredly the spirits are the most perfect of substances and best express the divinity. Since all the nature, purpose, virtue and function of substances is, as has been sufficiently explained, to express God and the universe, there is no room for doubting that those substances which give the expression, knowing what they are doing and which are able to understand the great truths about God and the universe, do express God and the universe incomparably better than do those natures which are either brutish and incapable of recognizing truths, or are wholly destitute of sensation and knowledge. The difference between intelligent substances and those which are not intelligent is quite as great as between a mirror and one who sees. As God is himself the greatest and wisest of spirits it is easy to understand that the spirits with which he can, so to speak, enter into conversation and even into social relations by communicating to them in particular ways his feelings and his will so that they are able to know and love their benefactor, must be much nearer to him than the rest of created things which may be regarded as the instruments of spirits. In the same way we see that all wise persons consider far more the condition of a man than of anything else however precious it may be; and it seems that the greatest satisfaction which a soul, satisfied in other respects, can have is to see itself loved by others. However, with respect to God there is this difference that his glory and our worship can add nothing to his satisfaction, the recognition of creatures being nothing but a consequence of his sovereign and perfect felicity and being far from contributing to it or from causing it even in part. Nevertheless, that which is reasonable in finite spirits is found eminently in him and as we praise a king who prefers to preserve the life of a man before that of the most precious and rare of his animals, we should not doubt that the most enlightened and most just of all monarchs has the same preference.

XXXVI. God is the monarch of the most perfect republic composed of all the spirits, and the happiness of this city of God is his principal purpose.

Spirits are of all substances the most capable of perfection and their perfections are different in this that they interfere with one another the least, or rather they aid one another the most, for only the most virtuous can be the most perfect friends. Hence it follows that God who in all things has the greatest perfection will have the greatest care for spirits and will give not only to all of them in general, but even to each one in particular the highest perfection which the universal harmony will permit. We can even say that it is because he is a spirit that God is the originator of existences, for if he had lacked the power of will to choose what is best, there would have been no reason why one possible being should exist rather than any other. Therefore God's being a spirit himself dominates all the consideration which he may have toward created things. Spirits alone are made in his image, being as it were of his blood or as children in the family, since they alone are able to serve him of free will, and to act consciously imitating the divine nature. A single spirit is worth a whole world, because it not only expresses the whole world, but it also knows

it and governs itself as does God. In this way we may
say that though every substance expresses the whole
universe, yet the other substances express the world
rather than God, while spirits express God rather than
the world. This nature of spirits, so noble that it enables
them to approach divinity as much as is possible for
created things, has as a result that God derives infinitely
more glory from them than from the other beings, or
rather the other beings furnish to spirits the material
for glorifying him. This moral quality of God which constitutes him Lord and Monarch of spirits influences him
so to speak personally and in a unique way. It is through
this that he humanizes himself, that he is willing to
suffer anthropologies, and that he enters into social relations with us; and this consideration is so dear to him
that the happy and prosperous condition of his empire
which consists in the greatest possible felicity of its
inhabitants, becomes supreme among his laws. Happiness
is to persons what perfection is to beings. And if the
dominant principle in the existence of the physical world
is the decree to give it the greatest possible perfection, the primary purpose in the moral world or in the
city of God which constitutes the noblest part of the universe ought to be to extend the greatest happiness possible. We must not therefore doubt that God has so ordained everything that spirits not only shall live forever,
because this is unavoidable, but that they shall also preserve forever their moral quality, so that his city may
never lose a person, quite in the same way that the world
never loses a substance. Consequently they will always
be conscious of their being, otherwise they would be
open to neither reward nor punishment, a condition
which is the essence of a republic, and above all of
the most perfect republic where nothing can be neglected.
In fine, God being at the same time the most just and

the most debonnaire of monarchs, and requiring only a
good will on the part of men, provided that it be sincere
and intentional, his subjects cannot desire a better condition. To render them perfectly happy he desires only
that they love him.

*XXXVII. Jesus Christ has revealed to men the mys-
tery and the admirable laws of the kingdom of heaven,
and the greatness of the supreme happiness which God
has prepared for those who love him.*

The ancient philosophers knew very little of these
important truths. Jesus Christ alone has expressed them
divinely well, and in a way so clear and simple that the
dullest minds have understood them. His gospel has entirely changed the face of human affairs. It has brought
us to know the kingdom of heaven, or that perfect republic of spirits which deserves to be called the city of God.
He it is who has discovered to us its wonderful laws.
He alone has made us see how much God loves us and
with what care everything that concerns us has been
provided for; how God, inasmuch as he cares for the
sparrows, will not neglect reasoning beings, who are
infinitely more dear to him; how all the hairs of our
heads are numbered; how heaven and earth may pass
away but the word of God and that which belongs to the
means of our salvation will not pass away; how God has
more regard for the least one among intelligent souls
than for the whole machinery of the world; how we ought
not to fear those who are able to destroy the body but
are unable to destroy the soul, since God alone can render the soul happy or unhappy; and how the souls of
the righteous are protected by his hand against all the
upheavals of the universe, since God alone is able to act
upon them; how none of our acts are forgotten; how

everything is to be accounted for; even careless words and even a spoonful of water which is well used; in fact how everything must result in the greatest welfare of the good, for then shall the righteous become like suns and neither our sense nor our minds have ever tasted of anything approaching the joys which God has laid up for those that love him.

4. ON THE ULTIMATE ORIGIN OF THINGS
[1697]

In addition to the world or aggregate of finite things, there is some unity which dominates, not only like the soul in me, or rather like the Ego itself in my body, but in a much higher sense. For the unity dominating the universe, not only rules the world but creates and fashions it, is superior to the world, and, so to speak, extramundane, and is thus the ultimate reason of things. For the sufficient reason of existence can not be found either in any particular thing or in the whole aggregate or series. Suppose a book on the elements of geometry to have been eternal and that others had been successively copied from it, it is evident that, although we might account for the present book by the book which was its model, we could nevertheless never, by assuming any number of books whatever, reach a perfect reason for them; for we may always wonder why such books have existed from all time; that is, why books exist at all and why they are thus written. What is true of books is also true of the different states of the world, for in spite of certain laws of change a succeeding state is in a certain way only a copy of the preceding, and to whatever anterior state you may go back you will never find there a complete reason why there is any world at all, and why this world rather than some other. And even if you imagine the world eternal, nevertheless since you posit nothing but a succession of states, and as you find a sufficient reason for them in none of them whatsoever, and as any number of them whatever does not aid you in giving a reason for them, it is evident that the reason must be sought elsewhere. For in eternal things even where there is no cause there must be a reason which, in permanent things, is necessity itself or essence, but in the series of changing things, if it were supposed that they succeed each other eternally, this reason would be, as will soon be seen, the prevailing of *inclinations* where the reasons are not necessitating (*i. e.*, of an absolute or metaphysical necessity the opposite of which would imply contradiction), but inclining. From which it follows that even by supposing the eternity of the world, an ultimate extramundane reason of things, or God, cannot be escaped.

The reasons of the world, therefore, lie hidden in something extramundane different from the chain of states or series of things, the aggregate of which constitutes the world. We must therefore pass from physical or hypothetical necessity, which determines the later states of the world by the prior, to something which is of absolute or metaphysical necessity, the reason for which cannot be given. For the present world is necessary, physically or hypothetically, but not absolutely or metaphysically. It being granted, indeed, that the world such as it is, is to be, it follows that things must happen in it just as they do. But as the ultimate origin must be in something which is metaphysically necessary, and as the reason of the existing can only be from the existing, there must exist some one being metaphysically necessary, or whose essence is existence; and thus there exists something which differs from the plurality of beings or from the world, which, as we have recognized and shown, is not metaphysically necessary.

But in order to explain a little more clearly how, from eternal or essential or metaphysical truths, temporary, contingent or physical truths arise, we ought first to recognize that from the very fact that something exists rather than nothing, there is in possible things, that is, in the very possibility or essence, a certain exigent need of existence, and, so to speak, some claim to existence; in a word, that essence tends of itself towards existence. Whence it further follows that all possible things, whether expressing essence or possible reality, tend by equal right toward existence, according to their quantity of essence or reality, or according to the degree of perfection which they contain, for perfection is nothing else than quantity of essence.

Hence it is most clearly understood that among the infinite combinations of possibles and possible series, that one actually exists by which the most of essence or of possibility is brought into existence. And indeed there is always in things a principle of determination which is based on consideration of maximum and minimum, such that the greatest effect is obtained with the least, so to speak, expenditure. And here the time, place, or in a word, the receptivity or capacity of the world may be considered as the expenditure or the ground upon which the world can be most easily built, whereas the varieties of forms correspond to the commodiousness of the edifice and the multiplicity and elegance of its chambers. And the matter itself may be compared to certain games where all the spaces on a table are to be filled according to determined laws, and where, unless a certain skill be employed, you will be finally excluded by unfavorable spaces and forced to leave many more places empty than

you intended or wished. But there is a certain way of
filling most easily the most space. Just as, therefore, if
we have to make a triangle, there being no other determining reason, it will be an equilateral one; and if we
have to go from one point to another, without any further determination as to the way, the easiest and shortest
path will be chosen; so it being once posited that being
is better than not being, or that there is a reason why
something rather than nothing should be, or that we
must pass from the possible to the actual, it follows
that, even if nothing further is determined, the quantity
of existence must be as great as possible, regard being
had to the capacity of the time and of the place (or to
the possible order of existence), exactly as tiles are disposed in a given area in such a way that it shall contain
the greatest number of them possible.

From this it is now marvelously understood how in
the very origin of things a sort of divine mathematics
or metaphysical mechanics was employed, and how the
determination of the greatest quantity of existence takes
place. It is thus that of all angles the determinate
angle in geometry is the right angle, and that liquids
placed in heterogeneous positions take that form which
has the most capacity, or the spherical; but especially it
is thus that in ordinary mechanics itself, when several
heavy bodies act against each other the motion which
results constitutes, on the whole, the greatest descent.
For just as all possibles tend by equal right to exist in
proportion to their reality, so all weights tend by an
equal right to descend in proportion to their gravity;
and as here a motion is produced which contains the
greatest possible descent of heavy bodies, so there a world
is produced in which the greatest number of possibles
comes into existence.

And thus we now have physical necessity from metaphysical; for although the world be not metaphysically necessary, in the sense that its contrary implies a contradiction or a logical absurdity, it is nevertheless physically necessary, or determined in such a way that its contrary implies imperfection or moral absurdity. And as possibility is the principle of essence, so perfection or the degree of essence (through which the greatest possible number is at the same time possible) is the principle of existence. Whence at the same time it is evident that the author of the world is free, although he makes all things determinately; for he acts according to a principle of wisdom or of perfection. Indeed indifference arises from ignorance, and the wiser one is, the more determined one is to the highest degree of perfection.

But, you will say, however ingenious this comparison of a certain determining metaphysical mechanism with the physical mechanism of heavy bodies may appear, nevertheless it fails in this, that heavy bodies truly exist, whereas possibilities and essences prior to existence or outside of it are only fancies or fictions in which the reason of existence cannot be sought. I answer, that neither these essences nor the so-called eternal truths regarding them are fictions, but that they exist in a certain region of ideas, if I may thus speak, that is in God himself, the source of all essences and of the existence of all else. And the existence of the actual series of things shows sufficiently of itself that my assertion is not gratuitous. For since the reason of the series is not found in itself, as we have shown above, but must be sought in metaphysical necessities or eternal truths, and since that which exists can only come from that which exists, as we have remarked above, eternal truths must have their existence in a certain subject, absolutely and metaphysically necessary, that is in God, through whom those things which otherwise would be imaginary, are (to speak barbarously but significantly) realized.

And in truth we discover that everything takes place in the world according to the laws, not only geometrical but also metaphysical, of eternal truths; that is, not only according to material necessities but also according to formal necessities; and this is true not only generally in that which concerns the reason, which we have just explained, of a world existing rather than non-existing, and existing thus rather than otherwise (a reason which can only be found in the tendency of the possible to existence); but if we descend to the special we see the metaphysical laws of cause, of power, of action holding good in admirable manner in all nature, and prevailing over the purely geometrical laws themselves of matter, as I found in accounting for the laws of motion: a thing which struck me with such astonishment that, as I have explained more lengthily elsewhere, I was forced to abandon the law of the geometrical composition of forces which I had defended in my youth when I was more materialistic.

Thus, therefore, we have the ultimate reason of the reality of essences as well as of existences in one Being who is necessarily much superior and anterior to the world itself, since it is from him that not only the existences which this world contains, but also the possibles themselves derive their reality. And this reason of things can be sought only in a *single* source, because of the connection which they all have with one another. But it is evident that it is from this source that existing things continually emanate, that they are and have been its products, for it does not appear why one state of the world rather than another, the state of yesterday rather than that of to-day, should come from the world itself. We see, also, with the same clearness, how God acts, not only physically but freely; how both the efficient and final cause of things is in him, and how he manifests not only his greatness and his power in the mechanism of the world as constructed, but also his goodness and his wisdom in constructing it.

And in order that no one should think that we confound here moral perfection or goodness with metaphysical perfection or greatness, and that the former is denied while the latter is granted, it must be known that it follows from what has been said that the world is most perfect, not only physically, or, if you prefer, metaphysically, because that series of things is produced in which there is actually the most of reality, but also that it is most perfect morally, because real moral perfection is physical perfection for souls themselves. Thus the world is not only the most admirable mechanism, but in so far as it is composed of souls, it is also the best republic, through which as much happiness or joy is brought to souls as is possible, in which their physical perfection consists.

But, you will say, we experience the contrary in this world, for often good people are very unhappy, and not only innocent brutes but also innocent men are afflicted and even put to death with torture; finally, the world, if you regard especially the government of the human race, resembles a sort of confused chaos rather than the well ordered work of a supreme wisdom. This may appear so at the first glance, I confess, but if you examine the thing more closely, it evidently follows *a priori* from the things which have been adduced, that the contrary should be affirmed; that is, that all things, and consequently souls, attain to the highest degree of perfection possible.

And, in truth, as the jurisconsults say, it is not proper to judge before having examined the whole law. We know only a very small part of eternity which extends into immensity; for the memory of the few thousands of years which history transmits to us is indeed a very little thing. And yet from an experience so short we dare to judge of the immense and of the eternal, like men who, born and brought up in a prison, or, if you prefer in the subterranean salt mines of the Sarmatians, think that there is no other light in the world than the lamp whose feeble gleam hardly suffices to direct their steps. Let us look at a very beautiful picture, and let us cover it in such a way as to see only a very small part of it, what else will appear in it, however closely we may examine it and however near we may approach to it, except a certain confused mass of colors without choice and without art? And yet when we remove the covering and regard it from the proper point of view we will see that what appeared thrown on the canvas haphazardly has been executed with the greatest art by the author of the work. What the eyes discover in the picture, the ears discover in music. The most illustrious composers often mingle discords with their harmonies in order to excite and pique, so to speak, the listener, who, anxious as to the outcome, is all the more pleased when soon all things are restored to order. Just as we rejoice to have passed through slight dangers and experienced small ills, either because we have a sense of relief or because we find pleasure in the frightful images which tight-rope dances or leapings between swords (*sauts périlleux*) present; we playfully swing laughing children, pretending to throw them far away from us, like the ape which, having taken Christian, king of the Danes, while still an infant wrapped in swaddling clothes, carried him to the top of the roof, and when everybody was frightened brought him back laughing, safe and sound to his cradle. According to the same principle, it is insipid always to eat sweetmeats; we must mingle with them sharp, tart and even bitter things, which excite the taste. He who has not tasted bitter things has not merited sweet things and, indeed, will not appreciate them. It is the very law of joy, that pleasure be not uniform, for this engenders disgust and renders us stupid and not joyous.

As to what we said, that no part may be disturbed without prejudice to the general harmony, it must not be understood as meaning that no account is taken of the parts, or that it suffices that the entire world be in perfect harmony, despite the possibility that the human race should be unhappy, and that there should be in the universe no regard for justice, no heed taken of our lot, as some think who do not judge rightly enough of the whole of things. For it ought be known that as in a well-constituted republic as much care as possible is taken of the good of the individual, so the universe cannot be perfect if individual interests are not protected as much as the universal harmony will permit. And for this a better law could not be established than the very law of justice which declares that each one participate in the perfection of the universe and in a happiness of his own in proportion to his own virtue and to the good will he entertains toward the common good; by which that which we call charity and love of God is fulfilled, in which alone, according to the judgment of the wisest theologians, the force and power of the Christian religion itself consists. And it ought not appear astonishing that so large a part should be given to souls in the universe since they reflect the most faithful image of the supreme Author, and hold to him not only the relation of machine to artificer, but also that of citizen to prince; and they are to continue as long as the universe itself; and in a manner they express and concentrate the whole in themselves so that it can be said that minds are whole parts.

As regards especially the afflictions of good people, we must hold for certain that there results for them a greater good, and this is not only theologically but physically true. So grain cast into the ground suffers before producing its fruit. And we may affirm, generally, that afflictions, temporarily evil, are in effect good, since they are short cuts to greater perfections. So in physics, liquors which ferment slowly take more time also to improve; whereas those the agitation of which is greater, reject certain parts with more force and are more promptly improved. And we might say of this that it is retreating in order the better to leap forward (*qu'on recède, pour mieux sauter*). We should therefore regard these considerations not merely as agreeable and consoling, but also as most true. And, in general, I feel that there is nothing truer than happiness, and nothing happier or sweeter than truth.

And in addition to the general beauty and perfection of the works of God, we must recognize a certain perpetual and very free progress of the whole universe, such that it advances always to still greater improvement (*cultum*). It is thus that even now a great part of our earth has received cultivation and will receive more and more. And although it is true that sometimes certain parts of it grow up wild again or again suffer destruction and deterioration, this nevertheless must be understood as we interpreted affliction above, that is to say, this very destruction and deterioration leads to some greater result, so that we profit in some way by the loss itself.

And as to the possible objection, that if it were so the world ought long ago to have become a paradise, the reply is ready: Even if many substances have already reached great perfection, nevertheless on account of the infinite divisibility of the continuum, there always remain

in the depths of things slumbering parts which must yet
be awakened and become greater and better, and, in a
word, attain a better culture. And hence progress never
comes to an end.

5. ON THE SUPERSENSIBLE ELEMENT IN KNOWLEDGE, AND ON THE IMMATERIAL IN NATURE

(Letter to Queen Charlotte of Prussia, 1702)

Madame:

The letter written not long since from Paris to Osna-
bruck and which I recently read, by your order, at Hanover, seemed to me truly ingenious and beautiful. And
as it treats of the two important questions, *Whether
there is something in our thoughts which does not come
from the senses, and Whether there is something in
nature which is not material,* concerning which I acknowledge that I am not altogether of the opinion of the
author of the letter, I should like to be able to explain
myself with the same grace as he, in order to obey the
commands and to satisfy the curiosity of your Majesty.

We use the external senses as, to use the comparison
of one of the ancients, a blind man does a stick, and they
make us know their particular objects, which are colors,
sounds, odors, flavors, and the qualities of touch. But
they do not make us know what these sensible qualities
are or in what they consist. For example, whether red
is the revolving of certain small globules which it is
claimed cause light; whether heat is the whirling of a
very fine dust; whether sound is made in the air as
circles in the water when a stone is thrown into it, as
certain philosophers claim; this is what we do not see.
And we could not even understand how this revolving,

these whirlings and these circles, if they should be real, should cause exactly these perceptions which we have of red, of heat, of noise. Thus it may be said that *sensible qualities* are in fact *occult qualities,* and that there must be others *more manifest* which can render the former more explicable. And far from understanding only sensible things, it is exactly these which we understand the least. And although they are familiar to us we do not understand them the better for that; as a pilot understands no better than another person the nature of the magnetic needle which turns toward the north, although he has it always before his eyes in the compass, and although he does not admire it any the more for that reason.

I do not deny that many discoveries have been made concerning the nature of these occult qualities, as, for example, we know by what kind of refraction blue and yellow are formed, and that these two colors mixed form green; but for all this we cannot yet understand how the perception which we have of these three colors results from these causes. Also we have not even nominal definitions of such qualities by which to explain the terms. The purpose of nominal definitions is to give sufficient marks by which the thing may be recognized; for example, assayers have marks by which they distinguish gold from every other metal, and even if a man had never seen gold these signs might be taught him so that he would infallibly recognize it if he should some day meet with it. But it is not the same with these sensible qualities; and marks to recognize blue, for example, could not be given if we had never seen it. So that blue is its own mark, and in order that a man may know what blue is it must necessarily be shown to him.

It is for this reason that we are accustomed to say that the *notions* of these qualities are *clear,* for they serve to recognize them; but that these same notions are not *distinct,* because we cannot distinguish or develop that which they include. It is an *I know not what* of which we are conscious, but for which we cannot account. Whereas we can make another understand what a thing is of which we have some description or nominal definition, even although we should not have the thing itself at hand to show him. However, we must do the senses the justice to say that, in addition to these occult qualities, they make us know other qualities which are more manifest and which furnish more distinct notions. And these are those which we ascribe to the *common sense,* because there is no external sense to which they are particularly attached and belong. And here definitions of the terms or words employed may be given. Such is the idea of *numbers,* which is found equally in sounds, colors, and touches. It is thus that we perceive also *figures,* which are common to colors and to touches, but which we do not notice in sounds. Although it is true that in order to conceive distinctly numbers and even figures, and to form sciences of them, we must come to something which the senses cannot furnish, and which the understanding adds to the senses.

As therefore our soul compares (for example) the numbers and figures which are in colors with the numbers and figures which are found by touch, there must be an *internal sense,* in which the perceptions of these different external senses are found united. This is what is called the *imagination,* which comprises at once the *notions of the particular senses,* which are *clear* but *confused,* and the *notions of the common sense,* which are clear and distinct. And these clear and distinct ideas which are subject to the imagination are the objects of the *mathematical sciences,* namely of arithmetic and geometry, which are *pure* mathematical sciences, and of the application of these sciences to nature, forming mixed mathematics. It is evident also that particular sensible qualities are susceptible of explanations and of reasonings only in so far as they involve what is common to the objects of several external senses, and belong to the internal sense. For those who try to explain sensible qualities distinctly always have recourse to the ideas of mathematics, and these ideas always involve *size* or multitude of parts. It is true that the mathematical sciences would not be demonstrative, and would consist in a simple induction or observation, which would never assure us of the perfect generality of the truths there found, if something higher and which intelligence alone can furnish did not come to the aid of the *imagination* and the *senses.*

There are, therefore, objects of still other nature, which are not included at all in what is observed in the objects of the senses in particular or in common, and which consequently are not objects of the imagination either. Thus besides the *sensible* and *imageable,* there is that which is purely *intelligible,* as being the *object of the understanding alone,* and such is the object of my thought when I think of myself.

This thought of the *Ego,* which informs me of sensible objects, and of my own action resulting therefrom, adds something to the objects of the senses. To think a color and to observe that one thinks it, are two very different thoughts, as different as the color is from the Ego which thinks it. And as I conceive that other beings may also have the right to say *I,* or that it could be said for them, it is through this that I conceive what is called *substance* in general, and it is also the consideration of the Ego itself which furnishes other *metaphysical* notions, such as cause, effect, action, similarity, etc., and even those of *logic* and of *ethics.* Thus it can be said that there is nothing in the understanding which does not come from the senses, except the understanding itself, or that which understands.

There are then three grades of notions: the *sensible only,* which are the objects appropriate to each sense in particular; the *sensible and at the same time intelligible,* which pertain to the common sense; and the *intelligible only,* which belong to the understanding. The first and the second are both imageable, but the third are above the imagination. The second and third are intelligible and distinct; but the first are confused, although they are clear or recognizable.

Being itself and *truth* are not known wholly through the senses; for it would not be impossible for a creature to have long and orderly dreams, resembling our *life,* of such a sort that everything which it thought it perceived through the senses would be but mere *appearances.* There must therefore be something beyond the senses, which distinguishes the true from the apparent. But the truth of the demonstrative sciences is exempt from these doubts, and must even serve for judging of the truth of sensible things. For as able philosophers, ancient and modern, have already well remarked:—if all that I should think that I see should be but a dream, it would always be true that I who think while dreaming, would be something, and would actually think in many ways, for which there must always be some reason.

Thus what the ancient Platonists have observed is very true, and is very worthy of being considered, that the existence of sensible things and particularly of the *Ego* which thinks and which is called spirit or soul, is incomparably more sure than the existence of sensible things; and that thus it would not be impossible, speaking with metaphysical rigor, that there should be at bottom only these intelligible substances, and that sensible things should be but appearances. While on the other hand our lack of attention makes us take sensible things for the only true things. It is well also to observe that if I should discover any demonstrative truth, mathematical or other, while dreaming (as might in fact be), it would be just as certain as if I had been awake. This shows us how intelligible truth is independent of the truth or of the existence outside of us of sensible and material things.

This conception of *being* and of *truth* is found therefore in the Ego and in the understanding, rather than in the external senses and in the perception of external objects.

There we find also what it is to affirm, to deny, to doubt, to will, to act. But above all we find there the *force of the consequences* of reasoning, which are a part of what is called the *natural light*. For example, from this premise, that *no wise man is wicked,* we may, by reversing the terms, draw this conclusion, that *no wicked man is wise*. Whereas from this sentence, that *every wise man is praiseworthy,* we cannot conclude by converting it, that *every one praiseworthy is wise* but only that *some praiseworthy ones are wise*. Although we may always convert particular affirmative propositions, for example, if *some wise man is rich* it must also be that *some rich men are wise,* this cannot be done in particular negatives. For example, we may say that *there are charitable persons who are not just,* which happens when charity is not sufficiently regulated; but we cannot infer from this that *there are just persons who are not charitable;* for in justice are included at the same time charity and the rule of reason.

It is also by this *natural light* that the *axioms* of mathematics are recognized; for example, that *if from two equal things the same quantity be taken away the things which remain are equal;* likewise that *if in a balance everything is equal on the one side and on the other, neither will incline,* a thing which we foresee without ever having experienced it. It is upon such foundations that we construct arithmetic, geometry, mechanics and the other demonstrative sciences; in which, in truth, the senses are very necessary, in order to have certain ideas of sensible things, and experiments are necessary to establish certain facts, and even useful to verify reasonings as by a kind of proof. But the force of the demonstrations depends upon intelligible notions and truths, which alone are capable of making us discern what is necessary, and which, in the conjectural sciences, are even capable of determining demonstratively the degree of probability upon certain given suppositions, in order that we may choose rationally among opposite appearances, the one which is greatest. Nevertheless this part of the art of reasoning has not yet been cultivated as much as it ought to be.

But to return to *necessary truths,* it is generally true that we know them only by this natural light, and not at all by the experiences of the senses. For the senses can very well make known, in some sort, what is, but they cannot make known what *ought to be* or could not be otherwise.

For example, although we may have experienced numberless times that every massive body tends toward the centre of the earth and is not sustained in the air, we are not sure that this is necessary as long as we do not understand the reason of it. Thus we could not be sure that the same thing would occur in air at a higher altitude, at a hundred or more leagues above us; and there are philosophers who imagine that the earth is a magnet, and as the ordinary magnet does not attract the needle when a little removed from it, they think that the attractive force of the earth does not extend very far either. I do not say that they are right, but I do say that one cannot go very certainly beyond the experiences one has had, when one is not aided by reason.

This is why the geometricians have always considered that what is only proved by *induction* or by examples, in geometry or in arithmetic, is never perfectly proved. For example, experience teaches us that odd numbers continuously added together produce the square numbers, that is to say, those which come from multiplying a number by itself. Thus 1 and 3 make 4, that is to say 2 times 2. And 1 and 3 and 5 make 9, that is to say 3 times 3. And 1 and 3 and 5 and 7 make 16, that is 4 times 4. And 1 and 3 and 5 and 7 and 9 make 25, that is 5 times 5. And so on.

$$
\begin{array}{cccc}
1 & 1 & 1 & 1 \\
3 & 3 & 3 & 3 \\
- & 5 & 5 & 5 \\
4 & - & 7 & 7 \\
| & 9 & - & 9 \\
| & | & 16 & - \\
| & | & | & 25 \\
| & | & | & | \\
2 & 3 & 4 & 5 \\
\times & \times & \times & \times \\
2 & 3 & 4 & 5 \\
- & - & - & - \\
4 & 9 & 16 & 25
\end{array}
$$

However, if one should experience it a hundred thousand times, continuing the calculation very far, he may reasonably think that this will always follow; but he does not therefore have absolute certainty of it, unless he learns the demonstrative reason which the mathematicians found out long ago. And it is on this foundation of the uncertainty of inductions, but carried a little too far, that an Englishman has lately wished to maintain that we can avoid death. For (said he) the inference is not good: my father, my grandfather, my great-grandfather are dead and all the others who have lived before us; therefore we shall also die. For their death has no influence on us. The trouble is that we resemble them a little too much in this respect that the causes of their death subsist also in us. For the resemblance would not suffice to draw sure consequences without the consideration of the same reasons.

In truth there are *experiments* which succeed numberless times and ordinarily, and yet it is found in some extraordinary cases that there are *instances* where the experiment does not succeed. For example, if we should have found a hundred thousand times that iron put all alone on the surface of water goes to the bottom, we are not sure that this must always happen. And without recurring to the miracle of the prophet Elisha, who made iron float, we know that an iron pot may be made so hollow that it floats, and that it can even carry besides a considerable weight, as do boats of copper or of tin. And even the abstract sciences like geometry furnish cases in which what ordinarily occurs occurs no longer. For example, we ordinarily find that two lines which continually approach each other finally meet, and many people will almost swear that this could never be otherwise. And nevertheless geometry furnishes us with extraordinary lines, which are for this reason called *asymptotes*, which prolonged *ad infinitum* continually approach each other, and nevertheless never meet.

This consideration shows also that there is a *light born within us*. For since the senses and inductions could never teach us truths which are thoroughly universal, nor that which is absolutely necessary, but only that which is, and that which is found in particular examples;

and since we nevertheless know necessary and universal truths of the sciences, a privilege which we have above the brutes; it follows that we have derived these truths in part from what is within us. Thus we may lead a child to these by simple interrogations, after the manner of Socrates, without telling him anything, and without making him experiment at all upon the truth of what is asked him. And this could very easily be practiced in numbers and other similar matters.

I agree, nevertheless, that in the present state the external senses are necessary to us for thinking, and that, if we had none, we could not think. But that which is necessary for something does not for all that constitute its essence. Air is necessary for life, but our life is something else than air. The senses furnish us the matter for reasoning, and we never have thoughts so abstract that something from the senses is not mingled therewith; but reasoning requires something else in addition to what is from the senses.

As to the *second question,* whether there are *immaterial substances,* in order to solve it, it is first necessary to explain one's self. Hitherto by matter has been understood that which includes only notions purely passive and indifferent, namely, extension and impenetrability, which need to be determined by something else to some form or action. Thus when it is said that there are immaterial substances, it is thereby meant that there are substances which include other notions, namely, perception and the principle of action or of change, which could not be explained either by extension or by impenetrability. These beings, when they have feeling, are called *souls,* and when they are capable of reason, they are called spirits. Thus if one says that force and perception are essential to matter, he takes matter for corporeal substance which is complete, which includes form and mat-

ter, or the soul with the organs. It is as if it were said
that there were souls everywhere. This might be true, and
would not be contrary to the doctrine of immaterial substances. For it is not intended that these souls be separate from matter, but simply that they are something
more than matter, and are not produced nor destroyed
by the changes which matter undergoes, nor subject to
dissolution, since they are not composed of parts.

Nevertheless it must be avowed also that there is *substance separated from matter*. And to see this, one has
only to consider that there are numberless forms which
matter might have received in place of the series of variations which it has actually received. For it is clear, for
example, that the stars could move quite otherwise, space
and matter being indifferent to every kind of motion and
figure.

Hence the reason or universal determining cause
whereby things are, and are as they are rather than
otherwise, must be outside of matter. And even the existence of matter depends thereon, since we do not find in
its notion that it carries with it the reason of its existence.

Now this ultimate reason of things, which is common
to them all and universal by reason of the connection
existing between all parts of nature, is what we call
God, who must necessarily be an infinite and absolutely
perfect substance. I am inclined to think that all immaterial finite substances (even the genii or angels according to the opinion of the ancient Church Fathers) are
united to organs, and accompany matter, and even that
souls or active forms are everywhere found in it. And
matter, in order to constitute a substance which is complete, cannot do without them, since force and action are
found everywhere in it, and since the laws of force depend on certain remarkable metaphysical reasons or in-

telligible notions, and cannot be explained by notions which are merely material or mathematical or which belong to the sphere of the imagination.

Perception also could not be explained by any mechanism whatsoever. We may therefore conclude that there is in addition something immaterial everywhere in these creatures, and particularly in us, in whom this force is accompanied by a sufficiently distinct perception, and even by that light, of which I have spoken above, which makes us resemble in miniature the Divinity, as well by knowledge of the order, as by the ordering which we ourselves know how to give to the things which are within our reach, in imitation of that which God gives to the universe. It is in this also that our *virtue* and perfection consist, as our *felicity* consists in the pleasure which we take therein.

And since every time we penetrate into the depths of things, we find there the most beautiful order we could wish, even surpassing what we have therein imagined, as all those know who have fathomed the sciences; we may conclude that it is the same in all the rest, and that not only immaterial substances subsist always, but also that their lives, progress and changes are regulated for advance toward a certain end, or rather to approach more and more thereto, as do the asymptotes. And although we sometimes recoil, like lines which retrograde, advancement none the less finally prevails and wins.

The natural light of reason does not suffice for knowing the detail thereof, and our experiences are still too limited to catch a glimpse of the laws of this order. The revealed light guides us meanwhile through faith, but there is room to believe that in the course of time we shall know them even more by experience, and that there are spirits that know them already more than we do.

Meanwhile the philosophers and the poets, for want

of this, have betaken themselves to the fictions of metempsychosis or of the Elysian Fields, in order to give some
ideas which might strike the populace. But the consideration of the perfection of things or (what is the
same thing) of the sovereign power, wisdom and goodness of God, who does all for the best, that to say, in
the greatest order, suffices to render content those who
are reasonable, and to make us believe that the contentment ought to be greater, according as we are more disposed to follow order or reason.

6. EXTRACTS FROM THE *NEW ESSAYS ON THE HUMAN UNDERSTANDING*

[1704]

PREFACE

The essay on the human Understanding by an illustrious Englishman is one of the most beautiful and
esteemed works of the time. I have resolved to make some
Remarks on it, because, having sufficiently meditated for
a long time on the same subject and upon most of the
matters which are therein touched upon, I have thought
that it would be a good opportunity to put forth something under the title of *New Essays on the Understanding,* and to obtain a favorable reception for my thoughts
by putting them in such good company. I have thought
also that I should be able to profit by the work of another, not only to lessen my own (since in fact it is less
difficult to follow the thread of a good author than to
labor entirely *de novo*), but also to add something to
what he has given us, which is always easier than to
start from the beginning; for I think I have cleared up
some difficulties which he had left in their entirety. Thus

his reputation is advantageous to me; besides, being inclined to do justice, and far from wishing to lessen the esteem in which that work is held, I would increase it, if my approval was of any weight. It is true that I often differ from him; but far from denying the merit of celebrated writers, we bear witness to it, by making known in what and why we separate ourselves from their opinion, when we think it necessary to prevent their authority from prevailing over reason on certain points of importance; besides by satisfying such excellent men, we make truth more acceptable, and it must be supposed that it is principally for truth that they labor.

In fact, although the author of the *Essay* says a thousand fine things of which I approve, our systems differ very much. His has more relation to Aristotle, and mine to Plato, although we both diverge in many things from the doctrines of these two ancients. He is more popular, and I am forced at times to be a little more esoteric (*acromatic*) and more abstract, which is not an advantage to me, especially when I write in a living language. I think nevertheless that by making two persons speak, one of whom expounds the views taken from the *Essay* of the author and the other joins thereto my observations, the parallel will be more to the liking of the reader than wholly dry remarks, the reading of which would be constantly interrupted by the necessity of referring to his book to understand mine. It will nevertheless be well to compare our writings now and then and not to judge of his views except by his own work, although I have ordinarily preserved his expressions. It is true that owing to the limitation of following the discourse of another and in making Remarks about it, I was prevented from thinking of making the embellishments of which the dialogue is susceptible: but I hope that the matter will make up for the defect of style.

Our differences are on subjects of some importance. The question is to know whether the soul in itself is entirely empty, like the tablet on which nothing has yet been written (*tabula rasa*) according to Aristotle and the author of the *Essay,* and whether all that is traced thereon comes solely from the senses and from experience; or whether the soul contains originally the principles of several notions and doctrines which external objects merely awaken on occasions, as I believe, with Plato, and even with the schoolmen, and with all those who take with this meaning the passage of St. Paul (Romans, 2, 15) where he remarks that the law of God is written in the heart. The Stoics called these principles *prolepses,* that is to say, fundamental assumptions, or what is taken for granted in advance. The mathematicians call them *common notions* (κοιναὶ ἔννοιαι). Modern philosophers give them other beautiful names, and Julius Scaliger in particular named them *semina aeternitatis,* also *zopyra,* as meaning living fires, luminous rays, concealed within us, but which the encounter of the senses makes appear like the sparks which the blow makes spring from the steel. And it is not without reason that these flashes are believed to indicate something divine and eternal, which appears especially in necessary truths. Whence there arises another question, whether all truths depend on experience, that is to say, on induction and examples, or whether there are some which have still another basis. For if some events can be foreseen before any trial has been made of them, it is manifest that we contribute something of our own thereto. The senses, although necessary for all our actual knowledge, are not sufficient to give to us the whole of it, since the senses never give anything except examples, that is to say, particular or individual truths. Now all the examples which confirm a general truth, however numerous they be, do not suffice to establish the universal necessity of this same truth; for it does not follow that what has happened will happen in the same way. For example, the Greeks and Romans, and all other peoples of the earth known to the ancients, have always noticed that before the expiration of twenty-four hours day changes into night and the night into day. But we would be deceived if we believed that the same rule holds good everywhere else; for since then, the contrary has been experienced in the region of Nova Zembla. And he would still deceive himself who believed that, in our climates at least, it is a necessary and eternal truth which will last always; since we must think that the earth and the sun even do not exist necessarily, and that there will perhaps be a time when this beautiful star will no longer be, at least in its present form, nor all its system. Whence it would seem that necessary truths, such as are found in pure mathematics and especially in arithmetic and in geometry, must have principles the proof of which does not depend on examples, nor, consequently, on the testimony of the senses, although without the senses we would never take it into our heads to think of them. This ought to be well recognized, and this is what Euclid has so well understood that he often demonstrates by reason that which is sufficiently seen through experience and by sensible images. Logic also, together with metaphysics and ethics, one of which forms theology and the other jurisprudence, both natural, are full of such truths; and consequently their proof can only come from internal principles which are called innate. It is true that we must not imagine that these eternal laws of the reason can be read in the soul as in an open book, as the edict of the pretor is read upon his *album* without difficulty and without research; but it is enough that they can be discovered in us by force of attention, for which occasions are furnished by the senses; and the success of experiments serves also as confirmation to the reason, very much as proofs serve in arithmetic for better avoiding error of reckoning when the reasoning is long. It is also in this that human knowledge and that of the brutes differ: the brutes are purely empirics and only guide themselves by examples, for they never, as far as we can judge, come to form necessary propositions; whereas men are capable of demonstrative sciences. It is also for this reason that the faculty which brutes have of making associations [of ideas] is something inferior to the reason which is in man. The association [of ideas] of the brutes is merely like that of simple empirics, who claim that what has happened sometimes will happen also in a case where that which strikes them is similar, without being able to judge whether the same reasons hold good. This is why it is so easy for men to entrap brutes and so easy for simple empirics to make mistakes. This is why persons who have become skilled by age or by experience are not exempt from error when they rely too much upon their past experience, as has happened to many in civil and military affairs; because they do not sufficiently consider that the world changes and that men become more skilled by finding a thousand new dexterities, whereas deer and hares of the present day do not become more cunning than those of past time. The association [of ideas] of the brutes are only a shadow of reasoning, that is to say, they are but connections of the imagination and passages from one image to another, because in a new juncture which appears similar to the preceding they expect anew what they found conjoined with it before, as if things were linked together in fact because their images are connected in the memory. It is true that even reason counsels us to expect ordinarily to see that happen in the future which is conformed to a long past experience, but this is not for this reason a necessary

and infallible truth, and success may cease when we
expect it least, if the reasons which have sustained it
change. This is why the wisest do not so rely upon it as
not to try to discover something of the reason (if it is
possible) of this fact, in order to judge when it will be
necessary to make exceptions. For reason is alone capable of establishing reliable rules, and of supplying what
is lacking to those which were not such by inserting their
exceptions; and of finding, finally, certain connections
in the force of necessary consequences, which often
enables us to foresee the event without having to experience the sensible connections of images, to which the
brutes are reduced; so that that which justifies the internal principles of necessary truths, also distinguishes
man from the brutes.

Perhaps our able author will not differ entirely from
my opinion. For after having employed the whole of his
first book in rejecting innate knowledge (*lumières*),
taken in a certain sense, he nevertheless admits at the
beginning of the second and in what follows, that the
ideas which do not originate in sensation come from reflection. Now reflection is nothing else than attention to
what is in us, and the senses do not give us that which
we already carry with us. This being so, can it be denied
that there is much that is innate in our mind, since we
are innate, so to say, in ourselves, and since there is in
ourselves, being, unity, substance, duration, change, action, perception, pleasure, and a thousand other objects
of our intellectual ideas? And these objects being immediate to our understanding and always present (although
they cannot be always perceived on account of our distractions and wants), why be astonished that we say
that these ideas, with all which depends on them, are
innate in us? I have made use also of the comparison
of a block of marble which has veins, rather than of a

block of marble wholly even, or of blank tablets, that is to say, of what is called among philosophers *tabula rasa*. For if the soul resembled these blank tablets, truths would be in us as the figure of Hercules is in marble when the marble is entirely indifferent toward receiving this figure or some other. But if there were veins in the block which should mark out the figure of Hercules rather than other figures, the block would be more determined thereto, and Hercules would be in it as in some sort innate, although it would be necessary to labor in order to discover these veins and to cleanse them by polishing and by cutting away that which prevents them from appearing. It is thus that ideas and truths are innate in us, as inclinations, dispositions, habits, or natural capacities, and not as actions; although these capacities are always accompanied by some actions, often insensible, which correspond to them.

It seems that our able author claims that there is nothing *virtual* in us, and nothing even of which we are not always actually conscious; but this cannot be taken strictly, otherwise his opinion would be too paradoxical; since, moreover, acquired habits and the stores of our memory are not always consciously perceived and do not even come always to our aid at need, although we often easily bring them back to the mind on some slight occasion which makes us remember them, just as we need but the beginning of a song to remember it. He modifies his assertion also in other places, by saying that there is nothing in us of which we have not been at least formerly conscious. But in additon to the fact that no one can be sure, by reason alone, how far our past *apperceptions,* which we may have forgotten, may have gone, especially according to the doctrine of reminiscence of the Platonists, which, mythical as it is, has nothing in it incompatible, at least in part, with bare reason; in addition to this, I say, why is it necessary that all be acquired by us through the perceptions of external things, and that nothing can be unearthed in ourselves? Is our soul then such a blank that, besides the images imprinted from without, it is nothing? This is not an opinion (I am sure) which our judicious author can approve. And where are there found tablets which are not somewhat varied in themselves? For we never see a surface perfectly even and uniform. Why, then, could we not furnish also to ourselves some object of thought from our own depths, if we should dig therein? Thus I am led to believe that at bottom his opinion on this point is not different from mine, or rather from the common opinion, inasmuch as he recognizes two sources of our knowledge, the Senses and Reflection.

I do not know whether it will be as easy to bring him in accord with us and with the Cartesians, when he maintains that the mind does not always think, and particularly that it is without perception when we sleep without dreaming. And he objects that, since bodies may be without motion, souls may also well be without thought. But here I reply a little differently than is wont to be done, for I maintain that naturally a substance cannot be without activity, and even that there never is a body without motion. Experience already favors me, and one has only to consult the book of the illustrious Mr. Boyle against absolute rest, to be persuaded of it; but I believe that reason also favors it, and this is one of the proofs which I have for discarding atoms.

Furthermore, there are a thousand indications which lead us to think that there are at every moment numberless *perceptions* in us, but without apperception and without reflection; that is to say, changes in the soul itself of which we are not conscious, because the impressions are either too slight or in too great a number or too even, so that they have nothing sufficient to distinguish them one from the other; but joined to others, they do not fail to produce their effect and to make themselves felt at least confusedly in the mass. Thus it is that custom causes us not to take notice of the motion of a mill or of a waterfall when we have lived near them for some time. It is not that the motion does not always strike our organs, and that something does not enter the soul which responds to it, on account of the harmony of the soul and the body; but these impressions which are in the soul and in body, being destitute of the charms of novelty, are not strong enough to attract our attention and our memory, attached as they are to objects more engrossing. For all attention requires memory, and often when we are not admonished, so to speak, and advised to attend to some of our own present perceptions, we let them pass without reflection and even without being noticed; but if some one calls our attention to them immediately afterwards and makes us notice, for example, some noise which was just heard, we remember it and are conscious of having had at the time some feeling of it. Thus they were perceptions of which we were not immediately conscious, apperception only coming in this case from the warning received after some interval, small though it may be. And to judge still better of the *minute perceptions* which we are unable to distinguish in the crowd, I am accustomed to make use of the example of the roar or noise of the sea which strikes one when on the shore. To hear this noise as one does it would be necessary to hear the parts which compose the whole, that is to say, the noise of each wave, although each of these little noises only makes itself known in the confused collection of all the others together, that is to say, in the roar itself, and would not be noticed if the wave which makes it was alone. For it must be that we are affected a little by the motion of this wave and that we have some perception of each of these noises however small; otherwise we would not have that of a hundred thousand waves, since a hundred thousand nothings cannot make something. One never sleeps so profoundly but that he has some feeble and confused feeling, and he would never be awakened by the greatest noise in the world if he did not have some perception of its small beginning, just as one would never break a rope by the greatest effort in the world if it was not stretched and lengthened a little by smaller efforts, although the little extension which they produce is not apparent.

These *minute (petites) perceptions* are then of greater influence because of their consequences than is thought. It is they which form I know not what, these tastes, these images of the sensible qualities, clear in the mass but confused in the parts, these impressions which surrounding bodies make upon us, which embrace the infinite, this connection which each being has with all the rest of the universe. It may even be said that in consequence of these minute perceptions the present is big with the future and laden with the past, that all things conspire (σύμπνοια πάντα, as Hippocrates said); and that in the least of substances eyes as piercing as those of God could read the whole course of the things in the universe, *Quae sint, quae fuerint, quae mox futura trahantur.** These insensible perceptions indicate also and constitute the identity of the individual, who is characterized by the traces or expressions which they preserve of the preceding states of this individual, in making the connection with his present state; and these can be known by a superior mind, even if this individual himself should

* 'What things are, what they were, and what the future may soon bring forth' (Virgil, *Georgics,* iv, 393). Leibniz misquotes *futura* for *ventura.*

not be aware of them, that is to say, when a definite recollection of them will no longer be in him. But they (these perceptions, I say) furnish the means of recovering this recollection at need, by the periodic developments which may some day happen. It is for this reason that death can be but a sleep, and cannot indeed continue, the perceptions merely ceasing to be sufficiently distinguished and being, in animals, reduced to a state of confusion which suspends apperceptive consciousness, but which could not last always; not to speak here of man who must have in this respect great privileges in order to preserve his personality.

It is also through the insensible perceptions that the admirable pre-established harmony of the soul and the body, and indeed of all monads or simple substances, is to be explained; which supplies the place of the untenable influence of the one upon the others, and which, in the judgment of the author of the finest of Dictionaries [Bayle], exalts the greatness of the divine perfections above what has ever been conceived. After this I should add little, if I were to say that it is these minute perceptions which *determine* us in many a juncture without our thinking it, and which deceive people by the appearance of an *indifference of equilibrium,* as if we were entirely indifferent to turning (for example) to the right or to the left. It is not necessary also that I notice here, as I have done in the book itself, that they cause that *uneasiness* which I show consists in something which does not differ from pain except as the small from the great, and which nevertheless often constitutes our desire and even our pleasure, in giving to it a stimulating flavor. It is also the insensible parts of our sensible perceptions which produce a relation between the perceptions of colors, of heat and of other sensible qualities and the motions in bodies which correspond to them; whereas the Cartesians with our author, thoroughly penetrating as he is, conceive the perceptions which we have of these qualities as arbitrary, that is to say, as if God had given them to the soul according to his good pleasure without having regard to any essential relation between these perceptions and their objects: an opinion which surprises me, and which appears to me little worthy of the Author of things, who does nothing without harmony and without reason.

In a word, *insensible perceptions* are of as great use in psychology as insensible corpuscles are in physics, and it is equally as unreasonable to reject the one as the other under the pretext that they are beyond the reach of our senses. Nothing takes place all at once, and it is one of my great maxims, and one of the most verified, that *nature never makes leaps:* this is what I called the *Law of Continuity,* when I spoke of it in the first *Nouvelles de la République des Lettres* *; and the use of this law is very considerable in physics. It teaches that we pass always from the small to the great, and *vice versa,* through the intermediate magnitudes in degree as in quantity; and that motion never rises immediately from rest nor is reduced to it except through a smaller motion, just as one never completes running any line or length before having completed a shorter line; although hitherto those who have laid down the laws of motion have not observed this law, believing that a body can receive in an instant a motion contrary to the one immediately preceding. And all this leads us to conclude rightly that *noticeable perceptions* also come by degrees from those which are too minute to be noticed. To think otherwise is to understand little the immense subtlety of things

---

* See Letter to Bayle (1687), pp. 65 f. above. Bayle (1647–1706) was editor of the journal.

which always and everywhere embraces an actual infinite
[of gradations].

I have also noticed that in virtue of insensible variations, two individual things cannot be perfectly alike,
and that they must always differ more than numerically;
which destroys the blank tablets of the soul, a soul without thought, a substance without action, a void in space,
atoms and even particles not actually divided in matter,
absolute rest, entire uniformity in one part of time, of
space or of matter, perfect globes of the second element,
born of perfect and original cubes, and a thousand other
fictions of the philosophers which come from their incomplete notions, and which the nature of things does not
permit, and which our ignorance and the little attention
we give to the insensible, let pass, but which cannot be
tolerated, unless they are limited to abstractions of the
mind which protests that it does not deny what it puts
aside and what it thinks ought not enter into any present
consideration. Otherwise if we really meant this, namely,
that things of which we are not conscious, are not in the
soul nor in the body, we should be lacking in philosophy
as in politics, in neglecting τὸ μικρὸν, insensible progressions; whereas an abstraction is not an error, provided
we know that what we ignore is there. Just as mathematicians employ abstraction when they speak of perfect
lines which they propose to us, of uniform motions and of
other regulated effects, although *matter* (that is to say,
the medley of the effects of the surrounding infinite) always makes some exception. It is in order to distinguish
the various conditions, and to reduce, as far as is possible, the effects to reasons, and to foresee some of their
consequences, that we proceed thus: for the more careful
we are to neglect no condition which we are able to con-
trol, the more practice corresponds to theory. But it pertains only to the Supreme Reason, which nothing escapes,

to comprehend distinctly all the infinite and to see all the reasons and all the consequences. All that we can do as regards infinites is to recognize them confusedly, and to know at least distinctly that they are there; otherwise we judge very wrongly of the beauty and grandeur of the universe; so also we could not have a sound physics which should explain the nature of bodies in general, and still less a sound philosophy of soul which should comprise the knowledge of God, of souls and of simple substances in general.

This knowledge of unconscious (*insensible*) perceptions serves also to explain why and how two souls, human or otherwise, of the same kind, never come from the hands of the Creator perfectly alike, and each always has its original relation to the points of view which it will have in the universe. But this it is which already follows from what I have remarked of two individuals, namely, that their *difference* is always *more than numerical.* There is still another point of importance, on which I am obliged to differ not only from the opinions of our author but also from those of the greater part of modern philosophers; this is, that I believe, with most of the ancients, that all higher spirits (genii), all souls, all simple created substances are always joined to a body, and that there never are souls entirely disembodied. I have *a priori* reasons for this; but this advantage is also found in the doctrine, that it resolves all the philosophical difficulties as to the condition of souls, as to their perpetual preservation, as to their immortality and as to their action. The difference of one of their states from another never being and never having been anything but that of more sensible to less sensible, of more perfect to less perfect, or *vice versa,* this doctrine renders their past or future state as explicable as that of the present. One feels sufficiently, however little reflec-

tion one makes, that this is rational, and that a leap from
one state to another infinitely different state could not
be so natural. I am astonished that by quitting the natural
explanation without reason, the schoolmen have been willing to plunge themselves purposely into very great difficulties, and to furnish matter for apparent triumphs of
freethinkers, all of whose reasons fall at a single blow
by this explanation of things; according to which there
is no more difficulty in conceiving the preservation of
souls (or rather, according to me, of the animal) than
there is in conceiving the change of the caterpillar into
the butterfly, and the preservation of thought in sleep,
to which Jesus Christ has divinely well compared death.
I have already said, also, that sleep could not last always, and it will last least or almost not at all for
rational souls, who are destined always to preserve the
personality which has been given them in the City of
God, and consequently remembrance: and this in order
to be more susceptible to punishments and rewards. And
I add further that in general no derangement of the
visible organs is able to throw things into entire confusion in the animal or to destroy all the organs and to
deprive the soul of the whole of its organic body and
of the ineffaceable remains of all preceding impressions.
But the ease with which the ancient doctrine has been
abandoned of ethereal bodies united to the angels (which
was confounded with the corporeality of the angels themselves), and the introduction of pretended separated intelligences in creatures (to which those disembodied
intelligences which make the heavens of Aristotle revolve
have contributed much), and finally the ill-considered
opinion into which people have fallen that the souls of
brutes could not be preserved without falling into metempsychosis and conducting them from body to body, and
the embarrassment in which men have been placed by

not knowing what to do with them, have caused us, in my opinion, to neglect the natural way of explaining the preservation of the soul. This has done great injury to natural religion and has made many believe that our immortality was only a miraculous grace of God, of which also our celebrated author speaks with some doubt, as I shall presently remark. But it were to be desired that all who are of this opinion had spoken as wisely and with as good faith as he; for it is to be feared that many who speak of immortality through grace do it but to save appearances, and approximate at heart those Averroists and some erring Quietists who picture to themselves an absorption and the reunion of the soul with the ocean of divinity; a notion the impossibility of which perhaps my system alone makes evident.

It seems also that we differ further as regards matter, in that the author thinks a vacuum is here necessary for motion, because he thinks that the minute parts of matter are rigid. And I acknowledge that if matter were composed of such parts motion in the *plenum* would be impossible, just as if a room were full of a quantity of small pebbles without there being the least vacant space. But this supposition, for which there appears also no reason, is not admissible, although this able author goes to the point of believing that rigidity or cohesion of minute parts constitutes the essence of body. It is necessary rather to conceive space as full of an originally fluid matter, susceptible of all divisions, and even actually subjected to divisions and subdivisions *ad infinitum;* but nevertheless with this difference that it is divisible and divided unequally in different places, on account of the motions already there which more or less concur in producing division. This it is which causes it to have everywhere a degree of rigidity as well as of fluidity, and which causes no body to be hard or fluid to the highest degree, that is to say, no atom to be found of an insurmountable hardness nor any mass entirely indifferent to division. Thus the order of nature and particularly the law of continuity destroy both equally.

I have shown also that *cohesion,* which would not itself be the effect of impulse or of motion, would cause a *traction* taken strictly. For if there were a body originally inflexible, for example, an Epicurean atom, which should have a part projecting in the form of a hook (since we can conceive atoms of all sorts of shapes), this hook pushed would carry with it the rest of the atom; that is to say, the part which is not pushed and which does not fall in the line of impulsion. Nevertheless our able author is himself opposed to these philosophical tractions, such as were attributed formerly to the abhorrence of a vacuum; and he reduces them to *impulses,* maintaining, with the moderns, that one part of matter operates immediately upon another only by pushing it by contact. In which I think they are right, since otherwise there would be nothing intelligible in the operation.

It is, however, necessary not to conceal the fact that I have noticed a sort of retraction by our excellent author on this subject; whose modest sincerity in this respect I cannot refrain from praising as much as I have admired his penetrating genius on other occasions. It is in the reply to the second letter of the late Bishop of Worcester, printed in 1699, p. 408, where to justify the opinion which he had maintained in opposition to that learned prelate, namely, that matter might think, he says among other things: *I admit that I have said* (book 2 of the *Essay on the Understanding,* chap. 8, § 11) *that body acts by impulse and not otherwise. This also was my opinion when I wrote it, and still at present I cannot conceive in it another manner of acting. But since then I have been convinced by the incomparable book of the judicious Mr. Newton, that there is too much presumption in wishing to limit the power of God by our limited conceptions. The gravitation of matter towards matter, by ways which are inconceivable to me, is not only a demonstration that God can, when it seems good to him, put in bodies powers and ways of acting which transcend that which can be derived from our idea of body or explained by what we know of matter; but it is further an incontestable instance that he has really done so. I shall therefore take care that in the next edition of my book this passage be corrected.* I find that in the French version of this book, made undoubtedly according to the latest editions, it has been put thus in this § 11: *It is evident,* at least so far as we are able to conceive it, *that it is by impulse and not otherwise that bodies act on each other, for it is impossible for us to understand that body can act upon what it does not touch, which is as much as to imagine that it can act where it is not.*

I cannot but praise that modest piety of our celebrated author, which recognizes that God can do things beyond what we are able to understand, and that thus there may be inconceivable mysteries in the articles of faith; but I should not like to be obliged to resort to miracle in the ordinary course of nature, and to admit powers and operations absolutely inexplicable. Otherwise too much license will be given to bad philosophers, under cover of what God can do; and by admitting these *centripetal forces* [*vertus*] or these *immediate attractions* from a distance, without its being possible to render them intelligible, I see nothing to hinder our scholastics from saying that everything is done simply by their 'faculties,' and from maintaining their 'intentional species' which go from objects to us and find means of entering even into our souls. If this is so, *omnia jam fient, fieri quae* *posse negabam.** So that it seems to me that our author, quite judicious as he is, goes here a little too much from one extreme to the other. He is squeamish concerning the operations of *souls,* when the question merely is to admit that which is not *sensible;* and now, behold, he gives *to bodies* that which is not even intelligible; granting them powers and actions which surpass all that in my opinion a created spirit could do and understand, for he grants them attraction, and that even at great distances, without limiting them to any sphere of activity, and this to maintain an opinion which does not appear to me less inexplicable; namely, the possibility that in the order of nature matter may think.

The question which he discusses with the celebrated prelate who attacked him, is *whether matter can think;* and as this is an important point, even for the present work, I cannot exempt myself from entering upon it a little and from taking notice of their controversy. I will present the substance of it on this subject and will take the liberty of saying what I think of it. The late Bishop of Worcester, fearing (but in my opinion without good reason) that our author's doctrine of ideas was liable to some abuses prejudicial to the Christian faith, undertook to examine some passages of it in his *Vindication of the Doctrine of the Trinity;* and having done justice to this excellent writer by recognizing that he regards the existence of the mind as certain as that of body, although the one of these substances is as little known as the other, he asks (pp. 241 seqq.) how reflection can assure us of the existence of the mind, if God can give to matter the faculty of thinking, according to the opinion of our author, bk. 4, chap. 3, since thus the way of ideas which ought to enable us to discern what may be proper to the

* 'All the things will presently happen which I said could not happen' (Ovid, *Tristia,* bk. i, el. 8, ver. 7).

soul or to the body, would become useless; whereas he had said, bk. 2 of the *Essay on the Understanding,* ch. 23, § § 15, 27, 28, that the operations of the soul furnish us the idea of the mind, and that the understanding along with the will renders this idea as intelligible to us as the nature of body is rendered intelligible by solidity and impulse. This is how our author replies in the first letter (pp. 65 seqq.): *I think I have proved that there is a spiritual substance in us, for we experiment in ourselves thinking; now this action or this mode of thinking is inconsistent with the idea of self-subsistence, and therefore has a necessary connection with support or subject of inhesion, and the idea of that support is what we call substance.* . . . For since the general idea of substance is everywhere the same, *it follows that the modification, which is called thought or power of thinking, being joined to it, there results a mind without there being need of considering what other modification it has in addition; that is whether it has solidity or not. And on the other hand, the substance which has the modification called solidity will be matter, whether thought be joined to it or not. But if by a spiritual substance you understand an immaterial substance, I confess that I have not proved that there is one in us, and that it cannot be proved demonstratively on my principles. Although what I have said on the systems of matter* (bk. 4, ch. 10, § 16), *in demonstrating that God is immaterial, renders it extremely probable that the substance which thinks in us is immaterial.* . . . . *However I have shown* (adds the author, p. 68) *that the great ends of religion and of morals are assured by the immortality of the soul, without its being necessary to suppose its immateriality.*

The learned Bishop in his reply to this letter, in order to show that our author was of another opinion when he wrote his second book of the *Essay,* quotes, p. 51, the passage (taken from the same book, ch. 23, § 15) where it is said, *that by the simple ideas which we have deduced from the operations of our mind, we can form the complex idea of a mind. And that putting together the ideas of thought, of perception, of liberty and of power of moving our body, we have as clear a notion of immaterial substances as of material.* He quotes still other passages to show that the author opposed mind to body. And he says (p. 54) that the ends of religion and of morals are the better assured by proving that the soul is immortal by its nature, that is, immaterial. He quotes also (p. 70) this passage, *that all the ideas which we have of particular and distinct kinds of substances are nothing but different combinations of simple ideas;* and that thus the author believed that the idea of thinking and of willing presupposes another substance different from that which the idea of solidity and of impulse gives; and that (§ 17) he observes that these ideas constitute the body as opposed to mind.

The Bishop of Worcester might have added that from the fact that the *general idea* of substance is in the body and in the mind, it does not follow that their *differences* are *modifications* of one and the same thing, as our author has just said in the passage which I have adduced from his first letter. It is necessary to distinguish carefully between modifications and attributes. The faculties of having perception and of acting, extension, solidity, are attributes or perpetual and principal predicates; but thought, impulsion, figures, motions are modifications of these attributes. Furthermore, we must distinguish between *physical* (or rather real) genus, and *logical* or ideal genus. Things which are of the same physical genus, or which are *homogeneous,* are of the same *matter,* so to speak; and may often be changed the one into the other by the change of the modification, as circles and squares.

But two *heterogeneous* things may have a common logical genus, and then their *differences* are not simply accidental modifications of the same subject or of the same metaphysical or physical matter. Thus time and space are very heterogeneous things, and we should do wrong to imagine I know not what real common subject, which had but continuous quantity in general, and the modifications of which should make time or space to arise.

Perhaps some one will mock at these philosophical distinctions of two genera, the one merely logical, the other real; and of two matters, the one physical which is that of bodies, the other only metaphysical or general; as if some one said that two parts of space are of the same matter, or that two hours also are of the same matter among themselves. Nevertheless these distinctions are not merely of terms, but of things themselves, and seem to come in here very appropriately, where their confusion has given rise to a false conclusion. These two genera have a common notion, and the notion of the real genus is common to the two matters, so that their genealogy will be as follows:

Genus:
- *Logical* merely, varied by simple *differences*.
- *Real,* the *differences* of which are *modifications,* that is to say, *matter.*
  - *Metaphysical* only, where there is homogeneity.
  - *Physical,* where there is a solid homogeneous mass.

I have not seen the second letter from the author to the Bishop; and the reply which the prelate makes to it hardly touches on the point regarding the thinking of matter. But the *reply of our author* to this second answer, returns to it. *God* (he says, very nearly in these

words, p. 397) *adds to the essence of matter the quali-*
ties and perfections which he pleases, simple motion to
some parts, but to plants vegetation, and to animals feel-
ing. Those who agree up to this point, cry out as soon as
I take one more step and say that God can give to matter
thought, reason, will, as if this destroyed the essence of
matter. But to prove it, they allege that thought or rea-
son is not included in the essence of matter, a point of
no consequence, since motion and life are not included
in it either. They assert also that we cannot conceive that
matter thinks; but our conception is not the measure of
the power of God. After this he cites the example of the
attraction of matter, p. 99, but especially p. 408, where
he speaks of the gravitation of matter toward matter,
attributed to Mr. Newton (in the terms which I have
quoted above), confessing that we can never conceive the
manner of it. This is in reality to return to occult, or,
what is more, inexplicable, qualities. He adds, p. 401,
that nothing is more fit to favor the sceptics than to deny
what we do not understand; and, p. 402, that we do not
conceive even how the soul thinks. He thinks, p. 403,
that since the two substances, material and immaterial,
are capable of being conceived in their bare essence without any activity, it depends on God to give to the one
or to the other the power of thinking. And he wishes to
take advantage of the admission of his opponent, who
granted feeling to brutes, but who would not grant them
any immaterial substance. He claims that liberty and
consciousness (p. 408), and the power of making abstractions (p. 409), can be given to matter, not as matter, but
as enriched by a divine power. Finally he adduces the
remark (p. 434) of a traveller as important and as judicious as M. de la Loubère, that the pagans of the east
recognize the immortality of the soul without being able
to comprehend its immateriality.

On all this I will remark, before coming to the explanation of my opinion, that it is certain that matter is as
little capable of mechanically producing feeling as of
producing reason, as our author agrees; that in truth I
acknowledge that it is not right to deny what we do not
understand, but I add that we are right in denying (at
least in the natural order) what is absolutely neither
intelligible nor explicable. I maintain also that substances
(material or immaterial) cannot be conceived in their
bare essence without any activity; that activity belongs
to the essence of substance in general; that, finally, the
conception of creatures is not the measure of the power
of God, but that their conceptivity or force of conceiving
is the measure of the power of nature: for all this is
in accord with the natural order and is capable of being
conceived or understood by some creature.

Those who understand my system will think that I
cannot agree entirely with the one or the other of these
two excellent authors, whose controversy, however, is
highly instructive. But, to explain myself distinctly, before all else it is necessary to consider that the modifications which may belong naturally or without miracle to
a subject, must come to it from the limitations or variations of a real genus, or of a constant and absolute original nature. For it is thus that philosophers distinguish
the modes of an absolute being from that being itself;
as it is known that size, figure and motion are manifestly limitations and variations of corporeal nature. For
it is clear in what way a limited extension gives figures,
and that the change which takes place in it is nothing but
motion. And every time that we find some quality in a
subject, we must believe that if we understood the
nature of this subject and of this quality, we should conceive how this quality can result therefrom. Thus, in the
order of nature (miracles set aside), it is not optional

with God to give to substances indifferently such or such qualities, and he will never give them any but those which shall be natural to them; that is, which can be derived from their nature as explicable modifications. Thus it may be asserted that matter will not naturally have the above mentioned attraction, and will not move of itself in a curved line, because it is not possible to conceive how this takes place there; that is, to explain it mechanically; whereas that which is natural, must be able to become distinctly conceivable if we were admitted into the secrets of things. This distinction between what is natural and explicable and what is inexplicable and miraculous, removes all the difficulties; and by rejecting it, we should maintain something worse than occult qualities; and in this we would renounce philosophy and reason, by opening asylums of ignorance and idleness, through a moot system which admits not only that there are qualities which we do not understand, of which there are only too many, but also that there are some which the greatest mind, if God gave it all the compass possible, could not comprehend; that is, which would be either miraculous or without rhyme and reason; and also that God should make miracles ordinarily, would be without rhyme and reason, so that this useless hypothesis would destroy equally our philosophy which seeks reasons, and divine wisdom which furnishes them.

Now as to thought, it is certain, and the author recognizes it more than once, that it could not be an intelligible modification of matter or one which could be comprised therein and explained; that is to say, that the feeling or thinking being is not a mechanical thing like a clock or a mill, such that we might conceive sizes, figures and motions, the mechanical conjunction of which might produce something thinking and even feeling in a mass in which there was nothing of the sort, which thinking and

feeling should cease also in the same way by the derangement of this mechanism. It is not then natural for
matter to feel and to think; and this can only take place
within it in two ways, one of which will be that God
should join to it a substance, to which it is natural to
think, and the other that God should put thought in it
by miracle. In this, then, I am entirely of the opinion
of the Cartesians, except that I extend it even to brutes,
and that I believe that they have feeling and immaterial
souls (properly speaking), and are also as imperishable
as the atoms of Democritus or Gassendi; whereas the
Cartesians, groundlessly embarrassed by the souls of
brutes and not knowing what to do with them if they are
preserved (for want of having bethought themselves of
the preservation of the same animal reduced to miniature), have been forced, contrary to all appearances and
to the judgment of the human race, to deny even feeling
to brutes. But if some one should say that God at least
may add the faculty of thinking to the prepared mechanism, I would reply that if this were done and if God
added this faculty to matter, without depositing in it at
the same time a substance which was the subject of inhesion of this same faculty (as I conceive it), that is
to say, without adding to it an immaterial soul, it would
be necessary that matter should be miraculously exalted
in order to receive a power of which it is not naturally
capable; as some scholastics claim that God exalts fire
even to the point of giving it the power to burn immediately spirits separated from matter, a thing which
would be a miracle, pure and simple. And it is enough
that it cannot be maintained that matter thinks without
putting in it an imperishable soul, or rather a miracle,
and that thus the immortality of our souls follows from
that which is natural; since their extinction could be
effected only by a miracle, either by exalting matter or

by annihilating the soul. For we well know that the power
of God could render our souls mortal, however immaterial
(or immortal by nature alone) they may be, for he can
annihilate them.

Now this truth of the immateriality of the soul is undoubtedly of importance. For it is infinitely more advantageous to religion and to morals, especially in the times
in which we live (when many people hardly respect
revelation alone and miracles), to show that souls are
naturally immortal, and that it would be a miracle if they
were not, than to maintain that our souls ought naturally
to die, but that it is by virtue of a miraculous grace,
founded in the promise alone of God, that they do not
die. Also for a long time it has been known that those
who have wished to destroy natural religion and reduce
all to revealed religion, as if reason taught us nothing
concerning it, have been regarded with suspicion; and
not always without reason. But our author is not of this
number; he maintains the demonstration of the existence
of God, and he attributes to the immateriality of the soul
a *probability* in the *highest degree,* which could pass
consequently for a *moral certainty;* so that I imagine
that, having as much sincerity as penetration, he could
accommodate himself easily to the doctrine which I have
just stated and which is fundamental in every rational
philosophy; for otherwise I do not see how one can prevent himself from falling back into the *fanatical philosophy,* such as the *Philosophia Mosaica* of Fludd, which
saves all phenomena by attributing them to God immediately and by miracle, or into the *barbaric* philosophy,
like that of certain philosophers and physicians of the
past, which still bore the marks of the barbarousness of
their time, and which is to-day with reason despised. They
saved appearances by forging expressly occult qualities
or faculties which they imagined to be like little demons

or goblins capable of producing unceremoniously that which is demanded, just as if watches marked the hours by a certain horodeictic faculty without having need of wheels, or as if mills crushed grains by a fractive faculty without needing any thing resembling millstones. As to the difficulty which many people have had in conceiving an immaterial substance, it will easily cease (at least in good part) when they do not demand substances separated from matter; as indeed I do not believe there ever are any such substances naturally among created things.

BOOK I.—OF INNATE IDEAS.

CHAPTER I. [II IN LOCKE.]

Are there Innate Principles in the Mind of Man?

. . . It is necessary that I tell you,* as news, that I am no longer a Cartesian, and that, nevertheless, I am farther removed than ever from your Gassendi, whose knowledge and merit I otherwise recognize. I have been impressed by a new system, of which I have read something in the philosophical journals of Paris, of Leipsic, and of Holland, and in the marvellous Dictionary of M. Bayle, article *Rorarius;* and since then I believe I see a new aspect of the interior of things. This system appears to unite Plato with Democritus, Aristotle with Descartes, the scholastics with the moderns, theology and ethics with reason. It seems to take the best from every side, and then afterwards to go farther than any one has yet gone. I find in it an intelligible explanation of

* The dialogue form of argument between two protagonists of Locke's and Leibniz's views has been dropped in this translation and selection. The author of the article *Rorarius* was Leibniz. He speaks through Théophile in the *New Essays.*

the union of the soul and body, a thing of which I had
before despaired. I find the true principles of things in
the Unities of Substance which this system introduces,
and in their harmony preëstablished by the Primitive
Substance. I find in it a surprising simplicity and uniformity, so that it may be said that this substance is
everywhere and always the same thing, differing only in
degrees of perfection. I see now what Plato meant when
he took matter for an imperfect and transitory entity;
what Aristotle meant by his entelechy; what the promise
which Democritus himself made of another life is, as
recorded in Pliny; just how far the Sceptics were right
in inveighing against the senses; how the animals are in
reality automata according to Descartes, and how they
have, nevertheless, souls and feeling, according to the
opinion of the human race; how it is necessary to explain
rationally those who have lodged life and perception in
all things, like Cardan, Campanella, and better than
they, the late Countess of Con[na]way, a Platonist, and
our friend, the late M. François Mercure van Helmont
(although elsewhere bristling with unintelligible paradoxes), with his friend, the late Mr. Henry More. How
the laws of nature (a large part of which were unknown
before this system) have their origin in principles superior to matter, and how, nevertheless, everything takes
place mechanically in matter; in which respect the spiritualistic authors, whom I have just mentioned, had failed
with their Archæi, and even the Cartesians, in believing
that immaterial substances changed if not the force at
least the direction or determination of the motions of
bodies; whereas the soul and body perfectly retain their
laws, each its own, according to the new system, and yet
one obeys the other as far as is necessary. Finally, it is
since I have meditated on this system that I have found
out how the souls of brutes and their sensations are not

at all prejudicial to the immortality of human souls, or, rather how nothing is more adapted to establish our natural immortality than to conceive that all souls are imperishable (*morte carent animae*), without, however, there being any fear of metempsychoses, since not only souls but also animals remain and will remain living, feeling, acting. Reality is always and everywhere similar to what is within us, according to what I have already said to you; unless it be that the states of animals are more or less perfect and developed without there ever being need of souls altogether separate, while, nevertheless, we always have minds as pure as possible, notwithstanding our organs, which cannot disturb by any influence, the laws of our spontaneity. I find the vacuum and atoms excluded on grounds different from the sophism of the Cartesians, founded on the pretended coincidence between the idea of body and of extension. I see all things regulated and adorned, beyond anything conceived of up to this time; organic matter everywhere; no sterile, neglected vacuum; nothing too uniform, everything varied but with order; and, what surpasses the imagination, the whole universe in epitome, but with a different aspect in each of its parts and even in each of its unities of substance. In addition to this new analysis of things, I have better understood that of notions or ideas and of truths. I understand what is a true, clear, distinct, adequate idea, if I dare adopt this word. I understand what are primitive truths, and true axioms, the distinction between necessary truths and those of fact, between the reasoning of men and the association of ideas (*consécutions*) of brutes which are a shadow of it. Finally, you will be surprised, sir, to hear all that I have to say to you, and especially to understand how knowledge of the greatness and perfection of God is thereby exalted. For I cannot conceal from you, from whom I have had nothing secret, how much I am imbued now with admiration and (if we may venture to make use of this term) with love for this sovereign source of things and of beauties, having found that those which this system reveals, surpass everything hitherto conceived. You know that I had gone a little too far formerly, and that I began to incline to the side of the Spinozists, who leave only infinite power to God, without recognizing either perfection or wisdom as respects him, and, scorning the search after final causes, derive everything from brute necessity. But these new lights have cured me of this. . . . .

§ 1.* I have always favored, as I do still, the innate idea of God, which M. Descartes maintained, and consequently other innate ideas which cannot come to us from the senses. Now, I go still farther in conformity with the new system, and I even believe that all the thoughts and actions of our soul come from its own depths and cannot be given to it by the senses, as you shall see in the sequel. But at present I shall set aside this investigation, and accommodating myself to the received expressions, since in truth they are good and maintainable, and since in a sense it may be said that the external senses are in part causes of our thoughts, I shall examine how in my opinion it must be said, even in the common system (speaking of the action of bodies on the soul, as the Copernicans speak with other men of the motion of the sun, and with reason), that there are ideas and principles which do not come to us from the senses, and which we find in us without forming them, although the

* These numbers (given by Leibniz) refer to the sections in Locke's *Essay Concerning Human Understanding*, selected by Leibniz for comment in the form of a dialogue. Only Leibniz's spokesman is translated; Locke's topic is summarized here in bracketed italics whenever necessary.

senses give us occasion to become conscious of them. I
imagine that your able author [Locke] has remarked
that under the name of innate principles one often maintains his prejudices, and wishes to exempt himself from
the trouble of discussions, and that this abuse has animated his zeal against this supposition. He has wished
to combat the indolence and the superficial manner of
thinking of those who, under the specious pretext of
innate ideas and truths engraved naturally on the mind,
to which we easily give assent, do not concern themselves
with seeking and examining the sources, connections and
certainty of this knowledge. In this I am altogether of
his opinion, and I even go farther. I would that our
analysis should not be limited, that definitions of all
terms capable thereof should be given, and that all the
axioms which are not primitive, should be demonstrated
or the means of demonstrating them be given; without
distinguishing the opinion which men have thereof, and
without caring whether they give their consent thereto or
not. This would be more useful than is thought. But it
seems that the author has been carried too far on the
other side by his zeal, otherwise highly praiseworthy.
He has not sufficiently distinguished, in my opinion, the
origin of necessary truths whose source is in the understanding, from that of the truths of fact, drawn from
the experiences of the senses, and even from the confused
perceptions which are in us. You see, therefore, sir, that
I do not admit what you lay down as fact, that we can
acquire all our knowledge without having need of innate
impressions. And the sequel will show which of us is
right.

§ § 2, 3, 4. I do not base the certainty of innate principles on *universal consent,* for I have already told you
that my opinion is that we ought to labor to be able to
prove all the axioms which are not primitive. I grant

also that a consent very general, but which is not universal, may come from a tradition diffused throughout the human race, as the practice of smoking tobacco has been received by almost all nations in less than a century, although some islanders have been found who, not knowing even fire, were unable to smoke. Thus some able people, even among theologians, but of the party of Arminius, have believed that the knowledge of the Divinity came from a very ancient and general tradition; and I believe indeed, that instruction has confirmed and rectified this knowledge. It appears, however, that nature has aided in reaching it without instruction; the marvels of the universe have made us think of a superior power. A child born deaf and dumb has been seen to show veneration for the full moon, and nations have been found, who seemed not to have learned anything else of other people, fearing invisible powers. I grant that this is not yet the idea of God, such as we have it and as we demand; but this idea itself does not cease to be in the depths of our souls, without being placed there, as we shall see, and the eternal laws of God are in part engraved thereon in a way still more legible, and by a sort of instinct. But they are practical principles of which we shall also have occasion to speak. It must be admitted, however, that the inclination which we have to recognize the idea of God, lies in human nature. And even if the first instruction therein should be attributed to Revelation, the readiness which men have always shown to receive this doctrine comes from the nature of their souls. I conclude that a sufficiently general consent among men is an indication and not a demonstration of an innate principle; but that the exact and decisive proof of these principles consists in showing that their certainty comes only from what is in us. To reply again to what you say against the general approbation given to the two great speculative principles,

which are nevertheless the best established, I may say
to you that even if they were not known, they would
none the less be innate, because they are recognized as
soon as heard; but I will add further, that at bottom
everyone knows them and makes use at every moment of
the principle of contradiction (for example) without
examining it distinctly, and there is no barbarian, who,
in a matter which he considers serious, would not be
shocked at the conduct of a liar who contradicts himself.
Thus these maxims are employed without being expressly
considered. And it is very much so that we have virtually in the mind the propositions suppressed in enthymemes, which are set aside not only externally, but
also in our thought.

§ 5. [*Not on the mind naturally imprinted, because
not known to children, idiots, &c.*] If you are so prejudiced as to say that there are truths imprinted on the
soul which it does not perceive, I am not surprised that
you reject innate knowledge. But I am astonished that
it has not occurred to you that we have an infinity of
knowledge of which we are not always conscious, not
even when we have need of it. It is for memory to retain
it and for reminiscence to represent it to us, as it often
does, but not always when needed. This is very well
called remembrance (*subvenire*), for reminiscence requires some help. And it must be that in this multiplicity
of our knowledge we are determined by something to
renew one portion rather than another, since it is impossible to think distinctly and at once of *all that we
know*. . . .

In a sense it must be said that all arithmetic and all
geometry are innate and are in us virtually, so that they
may be found there if we consider attentively and arrange what is already in the mind, without making use
of any truth learned by experience or by the tradition

of others, as Plato has shown in a dialogue, where he
introduces Socrates leading a child to abstract truths by
mere questions, without telling him anything. We may
therefore invent these sciences in our libraries and even
with closed eyes, without learning by sight or even by
touch, the truths which we need; although it is true that
we would not consider the ideas in question if we had
never seen or touched anything. For by an admirable economy of nature we cannot have abstract thoughts which
do not need something sensible, were it only in the form
of characters like the shapes of letters or sounds, although there may be no connection between such arbitrary characters and such thoughts. . . .

Since an acquired knowledge may be concealed in the
soul by the memory, as you admit, why could not nature
have also hidden there some original knowledge? Must
everything which is natural to a substance which knows
itself, be known there actually in the beginning? Can
not and must not this substance (such as our soul) have
many properties and modifications, all of which it is
impossible to consider at first and altogether? It was the
opinion of the Platonists that all our knowledge was
reminiscence, and that thus the truths which the soul has
brought along at the birth of the man, and which are
called innate, must be the remains of an express anterior knowledge. But this opinion has no foundation.
And it is easy to judge that the soul must already have
innate knowledge in the preceding state (if pre-existence
were a fact), however distant it might be, just as here;
it, therefore, would have to come also from another preceding state, or it would be finally innate, or at least
concreate; or it would be necessary to go to infinity and
make souls eternal, in which case this knowledge would
be innate in truth, from the fact that it would never have
a beginning in the soul; and if someone claimed that each

anterior state has had something from another more
anterior, which it has not left to the succeeding, the
reply will be made, that it is manifest that certain evident truths must have been in all these states. And in
whatever way it may be taken, it is always clear in all
the states of the soul that necessary truths are innate,
and are proved by what is internal, it not being possible
to establish them by experiences as we establish truths
of fact. Why should it be necessary also that we could
possess nothing in the soul of which we had never made
use? And is to have a thing without making use of it
the same thing as to have merely the faculty of acquiring it? If it were so, we should never possess anything
except the things which we enjoy; whereas we know that
in addition to the faculty and the object, there must often
be some disposition in the faculty or in the object or in
both, in order that the faculty be exercised upon the
object. . . .

If the mind had only the simple capacity of receiving
knowledge or passive power for it, as indeterminate as
that which the wax has for receiving figures, and the
blank tablet for receiving letters, it would not be the
source of necessary truths, as I have just shown it to
be; for it is incontestable that the senses do not suffice
to show their necessity, and that thus the mind has a
disposition (as much active as passive) to draw them
itself from its depths; although the senses are necessary
in order to give it the occasion and attention for this,
and to carry it to some rather than to others. You see,
therefore, sir, that these people, otherwise very able,
who are of a different opinion, seem not to have sufficiently meditated on the consequences of the difference
which there is between necessary or eternal truths and
the truths of experience, as I have already remarked,
and as all our discussion shows. The original proof of

necessary truths comes from the understanding alone, and the other truths come from experiences or from the observations of the senses. Our mind is capable of knowing both, but it is the source of the former; and whatever number of particular experiences we may have of a universal truth, we could not be assured of it forever by induction, without knowing its necessity through the reason. . . .

§ 11. It is the particular relation of the human mind to these truths which renders the exercise of the faculty easy and natural as respects them, and which causes them to be called innate. It is not, therefore, a naked faculty which consists in the mere possibility of understanding them; it is a disposition, an aptitude, a preformation, which determines our soul and which brings it about that they may be derived from it. Just as there is a difference between the figures which are given to the stone or marble indifferently, and those which its veins already mark out, or are disposed to mark out, if the workman profits by them.

The intellectual ideas, which are the source of necessary truths, do not come from the senses; and you recognize that there are ideas which are due to the reflection of the mind when it reflects upon itself. For the rest, it is true that the express knowledge of truths is posterior (*tempore vel natura*) to the express knowledge of ideas; as the nature of truths depends on the nature of ideas, before we expressly form one or the other; and the truths, into which the ideas which come from the senses enter, depend on the senses, at least in part. But the ideas which come from the senses are confused, and the truths which depend upon them are confused also, at least in part; whereas the intellectual ideas and the truths which depend on them, are distinct, and neither the one class nor the other has its origin in the senses, although it may be true that we would never think of them without the senses. . . .

§ 18. [*If such an assent be a mark of innate, then, that one and two are equal to three, that sweetness is not bitterness, and a thousand the like, must be innate.*] I do not see how this: *what is the same thing is not different,* can be the origin of the principle of contradiction, and easier; for it seems to me that you give yourself more liberty by advancing that A is not B, than by saying that A is not non-A. And the reason which prevents A from being B, is that B includes non-A. For the rest, the proposition: *the sweet is not the bitter,* is not innate, according to the meaning which we have given to the term innate truth. For the sensations of sweet and of bitter come from the external senses. Thus it is a mixed conclusion (*hybrida conclusio*), where the axiom is applied to a sensible truth. But as for this proposition: *the square is not a circle,* it may be said to be innate, for, in considering it, you make a subsumption or application of the principle of contradiction to what the understanding itself furnishes as soon as you are conscious of innate thoughts.

§ 19. [*Such less general propositions known before these universal maxims.*] We build on these general maxims, as we build on unexpressed major premises when we reason by enthymemes; for although very often we do not think distinctly of what we do in reasoning, any more than of what we do in walking and jumping, it is always true that the force of the conclusion consists partly in what is unexpressed and could not come from elsewhere, as will be found if you should wish to prove it.

§ 20. [*One and one equal to two, &c., not general nor useful, answered.*] It is true that we begin sooner to perceive particular truths, when we begin with more composite and gross ideas; but this does not prevent the order of nature from beginning with the most simple, and the reason of more particular truths from depending on the more general, of which they are only examples. And when we wish to consider what is in us virtually, and before all *apperception,* we are right in beginning with the most simple. For the general principles enter into our thoughts, of which they form the soul and the connection. They are as necessary thereto as the muscles and sinews are for walking, although we do not think of them. The mind leans upon these principles at all times, but it does not so easily come to distinguish them and to represent them to itself distinctly and separately, because that requires great attention to what it does, and most people, little accustomed to meditate, have hardly any. Have not the Chinese, like ourselves, articulate sounds? and yet being attached to another way of writing, they have not yet thought of making an alphabet of these sounds. It is thus that one possesses many things without knowing it.

§ 21. [*These maxims not being known sometimes till proposed, proves them not innate.*] The nature of things and the nature of the mind agree. And since you oppose the consideration of the thing to the apperception of that which is engraved on the mind, this objection itself shows, sir, that those whose side you take, understand by *innate truths* only those which would be approved naturally as by *instinct,* and even without knowing it, unless confusedly. There are some of this nature, and we shall have occasion to speak of them. But that which is called *natural light* supposes a distinct knowledge, and very often the consideration of the nature of things is nothing else than the knowledge of the nature of our mind and of these innate ideas which we do not need to seek outside. Thus I call innate, those truths which need only this consideration in order to be verified. I have already replied, § 5, to the objection, § 22, which claimed that when it is said that innate ideas are implicitly in the mind, this must mean simply that it has the faculty of knowing them; for I have shown that in addition to this, it has the faculty of finding them in itself, and the disposition to approve them when it thinks of them as it should.

§ 23. [*The argument of assenting on first hearing, is upon a false supposition of no precedent teaching.*] . . . I would name as propositions whose ideas are innate, the propositions of arithmetic and geometry, which are all of this nature; and, as regards necessary truths, no others could be found.

§ 25. [*These maxims not the first known.*] . . . The apperception of that which is in us, depends upon attention and order. Now, it is not only possible, but it is also proper, that children pay more attention to the ideas of the senses, because the attention is regulated by the need. The result, however, shows in the sequel, that nature has not uselessly given herself the trouble of impressing upon us innate knowledge, since without it there would be no means of arriving at actual knowledge of the truths necessary in the demonstrative sciences, and at the reasons of facts; and we should possess nothing above the brutes.

§ 26. [*And so not innate.*] Not at all, for thoughts are activities; and knowledge or truths, in so far as they are in us, even when we do not think of them, are habits or dispositions; and we know very many things of which we hardly think.

[*It is very difficult to conceive that a truth be in the mind, if the mind has never thought of this truth.*]

It is as if someone said that it is difficult to conceive that there are veins in marble before they are discovered. This objection also seems to approach a little too much the *petitio principii.* All those who admit innate truths without basing them upon the Platonic reminis-cence, admit those of which they have not yet thought. Moreover, this reasoning proves too much; for if truths are thoughts, we should be deprived not only of the truths of which we have never thought, but also of those of which we have thought and of which we no longer actually think; and if truths are not thoughts but habits, and aptitudes, natural or acquired, nothing prevents there being some in us of which we have never thought, nor will ever think.

§ 27. [*Not innate, because they appear least where what is innate shows itself clearest.*] I believe that we must reason here very differently. Innate maxims appear only through the attention which is given them; but these persons [children, idiots, savages], have very little of it, or have it for entirely different things. They think of hardly anything except the needs of the body; and it is reasonable that pure and detached thoughts should be the prize of nobler pains. It is true that children and savages have the mind less altered by customs, but they also have it less exalted by the teaching which gives attention. It would not be very just that the brightest lights should burn better in minds which deserve them less, and which are enveloped in thicker clouds. I would not, then, that one give too much honor to ignorance and savagery, when one is as learned and as clever as you are; that would be to depreciate the gifts of God. Some one will say, that the more ignorant one is, the nearer he approaches to the advantage of a block of marble or of a piece of wood, which are infallible and sinless. But unfortunately, it is not in this way that one approaches thereto; and as far as we are capable of knowledge, we sin in neglecting to acquire it, and we shall fail so much the more easily as we are less instructed. . . .

BOOK II.—OF IDEAS.

Of Ideas in general and whether the soul always thinks.

§ 1. [*Idea is the object of thinking.*] I admit it, provided that you add that it is an immediate internal object, and that this object is an expression of the nature or of the qualities of things. If the idea were the *form* of thought, it would come into existence and would cease with the actual thoughts which correspond to it; but being its object it might exist anterior to and after the thoughts. External sensible objects are but *mediate,* because they cannot act immediately upon the soul. God alone is the *immediate external object.* It might be said that the soul itself is its own immediate *internal object;* but it is so in so far as it contains ideas or what corresponds to things; for the soul is a microcosm in which distinct ideas are a representation of God, and in which confused ideas are a representation of the universe.

§ 2. [*All ideas come from sensation or reflection.*] This *tabula rasa,* of which so much is said, is, in my opinion, only a fiction, which nature does not admit of, and which has its foundation in the incomplete notions of philosophers, like the vacuum, atoms, and rest, absolute or relative, of two parts of a whole, or like the primary matter (*materia prima*) which is conceived as without form. Uniform things and those which contain no variety, are never anything but abstractions, like time, space, and the other entities of pure mathematics. There is no body, the parts of which are at rest, and there is no substance which has nothing by which to distinguish it from every other. Human souls differ not only from other souls, but also among themselves, although the difference is not of the kind which is called specific. And according to the demonstrations, which I think I have, everything substantial, whether soul or body, has its own peculiar relation to each of the others; and the one must always differ from the other by *intrinsic characteristics;* not to mention that those who speak so much of this *tabula rasa,* after having taken away from it ideas, are not able to say what is left to it, like the scholastic philosophers who leave nothing to their *materia prima.* It may, perhaps, be answered that this *tabula rasa* of the philosophers means that the soul has naturally and originally only bare faculties. But faculties without some act, in a word, the pure powers of the school, are also but fictions unknown to nature, and which are obtained only by abstraction. For where in the world will there ever be found a faculty which confines itself to the mere power, without exercising any act? There is always a particular disposition to action, and to one action rather than to another. And besides the disposition, there is a tendency to action, of which tendencies there is always an infinity at once in each subject; and these tendencies are never without some effect. Experience is, I admit, necessary in order that the soul be determined to such or such thoughts, and in order that it take notice of the ideas which are in us; but by what means can experience and the senses give ideas? Has the soul windows? does it resemble tablets? is it like wax? It is evident that all who think of the soul thus, make it at bottom corporeal. This axiom received among the philosophers, will be opposed by me, *that there is nothing in the soul which does not come from the senses.* But the soul itself and its affections must be excepted. *Nihil est in intellectu, quod non fuerit in sensu, excipe: nisi ipse intellectus.* Now the soul comprises being, substance, unity, identity, cause, perception, reason, and many other notions which the

senses cannot give. This agrees somewhat with your
author [Locke] who finds (in his *Essay*) a good part of
our ideas proceeding from the mind's own reflections on
itself. . . .

In order to avoid a discussion upon what has delayed
us too long, I declare to you in advance, sir, that when
you say that ideas come to us from one or the other of
these causes [sensation or reflection], I understand it
of their *actual* perception, for I think that I have shown
that they are in us before they are perceived, so far as
they have anything distinct about them.

§ § 9 and 10. [*The soul begins to have ideas when it
begins to perceive. The soul thinks not always.*] Action
is no more connected with the soul than with body; a
state without thought in the soul and an absolute rest
in body, appear to me equally contrary to nature,
and without example in the world. A substance once
in action will be so always, for all the impressions
remain and are merely mixed with other new ones. By
striking a body we excite or rather determine an infinity
of vortices, as in a liquid, for at bottom every solid has
a degree of liquidity and every liquid a degree of solidity, and there is no means of ever arresting entirely
these internal vortices. Now we may believe that if the
body is never at rest, the soul, which corresponds to it,
will never be without perception either.

It is certain that we slumber and sleep, and that God
is exempt from this. But it does not follow that while
sleeping we are without perception. Rather just the opposite is found to be the case, if it is well considered.

Real powers are never simple possibilities. There is
always tendency and action.

[*That the soul always thinks is not self-evident.*]
I do not say that it is self-evident that the soul always
thinks. A little attention and reasoning is needed to dis-

cover it. The common people perceive it as little as the pressure of the air or the roundness of the earth.

It is decided as it is proved that there are imperceptible bodies and invisible movements, although certain persons ridicule them. There are likewise, numberless perceptions which are not sufficiently distinguished for them to be perceived or remembered, but they are made known by certain consequences.

I have not read the book which contains this objection [that it is an inference from Locke's position, that a thing is not, because we are not sensible of it in our sleep], but it would not have been wrong merely to object to you, that it does not follow because the thought is not perceived that it ceases for that reason; for otherwise it could be said, for the same reason, that there is no soul during the time when it is not perceived. And in order to refute this objection it is necessary to point out in particular the thought that it is essential to it that it be perceived.

§ 11. [*It is not always conscious of it.*] There [that it is not easy to conceive that a thing can think and not be conscious that it thinks] is, undoubtedly, the knot of the affair and the difficulty which has embarrassed able men. But here is the means of getting out of it. We must consider that we think of many things at once, but we attend only to the thoughts which are most important; and it could not be otherwise, for if we attend to all it would be necessary to think attentively of an infinity of things at the same time, all of which we feel and which make an impression upon our senses. I say even more: there remains something of all our past thoughts and none can ever be entirely effaced. Now when we sleep without dreaming and when we are stunned by some blow, fall, symptom or other accident, there is formed within us an infinite number of minute confused sensations; and death itself can produce no other effect upon the souls of animals who, without doubt, ought, sooner or later, to acquire important perceptions, for all goes on in an orderly manner in nature. I acknowledge, however, that in this state of confusion, the soul would be without pleasure and without pain, for these are noticeable perceptions.

§ 12. [*If a sleeping man thinks without knowing it, the sleeping and waking man are two persons.*] . . . I, in turn, will make you another supposition which appears more natural. Is it not true that it must always be admitted that after some interval or some great change, one may fall into a condition of general forgetfulness? Sleidan, it is said, before his death, forgot all that he knew; and there are numbers of other examples of this sad occurrence. Let us suppose that such a man became young again and learned all *de novo;* would he be another man for all that? It is not then memory which, properly, makes the same man. Nevertheless, the fiction of a soul which animates different bodies by turns, without what happens to it in one of these bodies interesting it in the other, is one of those fictions contrary to the nature of things, which come from the incomplete notions of the philosophers, like space without body, and body without motion, and which disappear when one penetrates a little farther; for it must be known that each soul preserves all its preceding impressions and cannot divide itself equally in the way just mentioned. The future in each substance has a perfect connection with the past. It is this which constitutes the identity of the individual. Moreover, memory is not necessary nor even always possible, on account of the multitude of present and past impressions which coöperate toward our present thoughts; for I do not believe there are in man thoughts of which there is not some effect at least confused, or some remnant mixed with subsequent thoughts. Many things can be forgotten, but they could also be remembered long afterward if they were recalled as they should be.

§ 13. [*Impossible to conceive those that sleep without dreaming, that they think.*] One is not without some feeble feeling while asleep, even when the sleep is dreamless. Waking itself shows it, and the easier it is to be awakened, the more feeling one has of what is going on externally, although this feeling is not always sufficiently strong to cause the awakening. . . .

§ 15. [*Upon this hypothesis, the thoughts of a sleeping man ought to be the most rational.*] All impressions have their effect, but all the effects are not always noticeable. When I turn to one side rather than to the other, it is very often through a series of minute impressions of which I am not conscious, and which render one movement a little more uncomfortable than the other. All our unpremeditated actions are the result of a concurrence of minute perceptions, and even our customs and passions, which have such influence in our deliberations, come therefrom; for these habits grow little by little, and, consequently, without the minute perceptions, we should not arrive at these noticeable dispositions. I have already remarked that he who would deny these effects in morals, would imitate the poorly instructed persons who deny insensible corpuscles in physics; and yet I see that there are, among those who speak of liberty, those who, taking no notice of these insensible impressions, capable of inclining the balance, imagine an entire indifference in moral actions, like that of the ass of Buridan divided equally between two meadows. And of this we shall speak more fully in what follows. I acknowledge, however, that these impressions incline without necessitating. . . .

§ 23. [*When does a man begin to have ideas?*] I am of the same opinion [namely, that it is when he has some sensation]; but it is by a principle a little peculiar, for I believe that we are never without thoughts and also never without sensation. I distinguish only between ideas and thoughts; for we have always all pure or distinct ideas independently of the senses; but thoughts always correspond to some sensation.

§ 25. [*In the perception of simple ideas the soul is for the most part passive.*] How can it be that it is merely passive with regard to the perception of all simple ideas, since, according to your own avowal, there are simple ideas the perception of which comes from reflection, and since the mind gives itself thoughts from reflection, for it is itself which reflects? Whether it can refuse them is another question; and it cannot do it undoubtedly without some reason which turns it aside from them, when there is some occasion for this. . . .

CHAPTER IV.
Of solidity.

§ 1. [*We receive this idea from touch.*] And at bottom solidity, in so far as the notion is distinct, is conceived by the pure reason, although the senses furnish to the reason the proof that it is in nature. . . .

CHAPTER V.
Of simple ideas of divers senses.

These ideas which are said to come from more than one sense, as those of space, figure, motion, rest, are given us rather by the common sense, that is to say, the mind itself, for these are ideas of the pure understanding, but which have relation to externality and which the senses make us perceive; also they are capable of definitions and demonstrations. . . . .

CHAPTER VII.

Of ideas which come from sensation and from reflection.

§ 1. [*Pleasure and pain, power, existence, etc.*] It seems to me that the senses could not convince us of the *existence* of sensible things without the aid of the reason. Thus I believe the consideration of existence comes from reflection. Those of *power* and of *unity* come also from the same source and are of an entirely different nature from the perceptions of pleasure and of pain.

CHAPTER VIII.

Other considerations concerning simple ideas.

§ 2. [*Privative qualities.*] I had not believed that the privative nature of rest could be doubted. It suffices for it that motion in body be denied; but it does not suffice for motion that rest be denied, and something more must be added in order to determine the degree of motion, since it receives essentially more or less, while all rest is equal. It is another thing when we speak of the cause of rest, which must be positive in secondary matter or mass. I should further believe that the very idea of rest is privative, that is, that it consists only in negation. It is true that the act of denying is a positive thing.

§ 10. [*Secondary qualities.*] I believe that it can be said that *power,* when it is intelligible and can be distinctly explained, ought to be counted among *primary qualities;* but when it is only sensible and gives but a confused idea, it ought to be put among *secondary qualities.* . . .

CHAPTER IX.
Of perception.

§ 1. [*Perception the first simple idea of reflection.*] It might, perhaps, be added that brutes have perception, and that it is not necessary that they have thought, that is to say, that they have reflection or what may be its object. Also we ourselves have minute *perceptions* of which we are not conscious in our present state. It is true that we could very well perceive them and reflect on them, if we were not turned aside by their multitude, which distracts our minds, or if they were not effaced or rather obscured by the greater ones.

§ 4. I should prefer to distinguish between *perception* and *apperception.* The perception of light or of color, for example, of which we are conscious, is composed of many minute perceptions of which we are not conscious; and a noise of which we have a perception but to which we do not attend, becomes *apperceptible* by a little addition or augmentation. For if what precedes made no impression on the soul, this small addition would also make none and the whole would make no more.

§ 8. [*"The problem of Molyneux."*] * . . . I think that supposing that the blind man knows that these two figures which he sees are those of the cube and of the

* Could a man born blind, who has learned to distinguish by touch a cube from a sphere, distinguish them without touch if he should come to enjoy vision? Molyneux and Locke gave a negative reply which Leibniz tries to amend.

globe, he would be able to distinguish them and to say without touching them, this is the globe, this is the cube.

Perhaps Molyneux and the author of the *Essay* are not so far from my opinion as at first appears, and that the reasons of their opinion, contained apparently in the letter of the former, who has employed them with success in order to convince people of their error, have been suppressed purposely by the latter in order to give more exercise to the mind of his readers. If you will weigh my answer, you will find that I have put a condition in it which can be considered as included in the question; it is, that the only thing in question is that of distinguishing, and that the blind man knows that the two figured bodies which he must distinguish are there, and that thus each of the appearances which he sees is that of the cube or that of the globe. In this case, it seems to me beyond doubt that the blind man who ceases to be blind, can distinguish them by the principles of reasoning joined to what touch has provided him with beforehand of sensible knowledge. For I do not speak of what he will do perhaps in fact and immediately, while stunned and confounded by the novelty, or also if he is little accustomed to drawing conclusions. The foundation of my opinion is that in the globe there are no points distinguishable on the side of the globe itself, all being level there and without angles, whereas in the cube there are eight points distinguished from all the others. If there were not this means of distinguishing the figures, a blind man could not learn the rudiments of geometry by touch. Nevertheless, we see that those born blind are capable of learning geometry, and have even always some rudiments of natural geometry, and that most often geometry is learned by our sight alone, without employing touch, as a paralytic, or other person to whom touch has been almost interdicted, might and even must do.

And it must be that these two geometries, that of the blind man and that of the paralytic, meet and coincide, and even reduce to the same ideas, although there are no common images. This again shows how necessary it is to distinguish *images* from *exact ideas,* which consist in definitions. It would certainly be very interesting and even instructive to examine well the ideas of one born blind to hear his descriptions of shapes. For he might come to this and he might even understand the doctrine of optics in so far as it depends upon distinct and mathematical ideas, although he would not be able to reach a conception of what chiaroscuro is, that is to say, the images of light and of colors. . . . It would also be very important to examine the ideas that a deaf and dumb man might have of non-figured things. . . . Men are very negligent in not getting an exact knowledge of the modes of thought of such persons. . . .

§ 11. [*Perception puts the difference between animals and inferior beings.*] I am inclined to believe that there is also among plants some perception and desire, because of the great analogy there is between plants and animals; and if there is a vegetable soul, as is the common opinion, it must have perception. However, I do not cease to ascribe to mechanism all that takes place in the body of plants and animals, except their first formation. Thus I agree that the movement of the plant called sensitive comes from mechanism, and I do not approve of having recourse to the soul when the detail of the phenomena of plants and animals is to be explained.

§ 14. [*Lower animals have perceptions.*] As much could be said of plants. But as to man, his perceptions are accompanied by the power of reflection which passes to the act when there is occasion. But when he is reduced to a state in which he is like one in a lethargy and almost without feeling, reflection and consciousness cease and universal truths are not thought of. Nevertheless, the innate and acquired faculties and dispositions, and even the impressions which are received in this state of confusion, do not cease for that reason, and are not effaced, although they are forgotten; they will even have their turn to contribute some day toward some noticeable effect; for nothing is useless in nature; all confusion must resolve itself; animals even, having passed through a condition of stupidity, ought to return some day to more exalted perceptions; and since simple substances last forever, it will not do to judge of eternity by some years. . . .

CHAPTER XI.

Of the faculty of discerning ideas.

§ 10. [*Brutes abstract not.*] . . . I am of the same opinion. They know apparently whiteness and notice it in chalk as in snow; but this is not yet abstraction, for that requires a consideration of what is common, separated from what is particular, and consequently there enters therein the knowledge of universal truths, which is not given to brutes. It is well observed also that the brutes that speak do not make use of words to express general ideas, and that men deprived of the use of speech and of words do not fail to invent other general signs. I am delighted that you notice the advantages of human nature.

§ 11. The brutes pass from one imagination to another by the connection which they have felt here before; for example, when the master takes a stick the dog is apprehensive of being struck. And on many occasions children, as likewise other men, have no other procedure in their passages from thought to thought. This might be called *consecution* and *reasoning* in a very broad sense. But I prefer to conform to the received usage in confining these words to man and in restricting them to the knowledge of some *reason* for the connection of perceptions which sensations alone could not give; their effect being but to cause us naturally to expect at other times the same connection which has been noticed before, although perhaps the reasons are no longer the same; a fact which often deceives those who govern them selves merely by the senses. . . .

CHAPTER XII.
Of complex ideas.

In order to render the resemblance [between the understanding and a dark room] greater it would be necessary to suppose that there was in the dark room to receive the images a cloth, which was not smooth, but diversified by folds representing innate knowledge; that, furthermore, this cloth or canvas being stretched had a sort of elasticity or power of acting, and even an action or reaction accommodated as much to past folds as to newly arrived impressions of the images. And this action would consist in certain vibrations or oscillations, such as are seen in a stretched cord when it is touched, of such a kind that it gives forth a sort of musical sound. For not only do we receive images or traces in the brain but we also form them anew when we consider *complex ideas*. Thus the cloth, which represents our brain, must be active and elastic. This comparison would explain tolerably well what takes place in the brain; but as to the soul, which is a simple substance or *monad,* it represents without extension these same varieties of extended masses and has perception of them.

§ 3. [*Complex ideas are either modes, substances, or relations.*] This division of the objects of our thoughts into substances, modes, and relations is satisfactory to me. I believe that qualities are but modifications of substances, and that the understanding adds thereto the relations. This is of more consequence than is thought.

§ 5. [*Simple and mixed modes.*] Perhaps a *dozen* or *score* are but relations and are constituted by connection with the understanding. Units are separate, and the understanding puts them together however dispersed they may be. Nevertheless, although relations are from the understanding they are not without foundation and reality. For, in the first place, understanding is the origin of things; and even the reality of all things, except simple substances, consists ultimately only of the perceptions of the phenomena of simple substances. It is often the same thing with regard to mixed modes; that is to say, that they must be referred back to relations. . . .

CHAPTER XIII.

Of simple modes, and first of those of space.

. . . § 17. [*Whether space is substance or accident, not known.*] I have reason to fear that I shall be accused of vanity in wishing to determine what you, sir, acknowledge not to know. But there is room for believing that you know more on this point than you say or believe you do. Some have believed that God is the locus of things. Lessius and Guericke, if I am not mistaken, were of this opinion; but then place contains something more than we attribute to space which we strip of all action; and in this way it is no more a substance than time, and if it has parts it could not be God. It is a relation, an order, not only among existing things, but also among possible things as they may exist. But its truth and reality is founded in God, like all the eternal truths.

It is best then to say that space is an order, but that God is its source.

§ 19. [*Substance and accident of little use in philosophy.*] . . . I acknowledge that I am of another opinion, and that I believe that the consideration of substance is a point of philosophy of the greatest importance and of the greatest fruitfulness.

CHAPTER XIV.
Of duration and its simple modes.

. . . § 16. [*It is not motion but the constant train of ideas in our minds while awake that furnishes us with the idea of duration.*] A train of perceptions awakens in us the idea of duration, but it does not make it. Our perceptions never have a train sufficiently constant and regular to correspond to that of time, which is a uniform and simple *continuum,* like a straight line. The change of perceptions gives us occasion to think of time, and it is measured by uniform changes; but if there should be nothing uniform in nature, time would not cease to be determined, just as place would not cease to be determined also if there should be no fixed or immovable body.

. . . § 24. The void which can be conceived in time, indicates, like that in space, that time and space apply as well to possible as to existing things.

§ 26. Time and space are of the nature of eternal truths which concern equally the possible and the existing.

§ 27. [*Eternity.*] But in order to derive the notion of *eternity* it is necessary to conceive more, viz., that the same reason subsists always for going farther. It is this consideration of the reasons which completes the notion of the infinite or of the indefinite in possible progress. Thus the senses alone cannot suffice to make us form these notions. And at bottom it may be said that the *idea of the absolute* is anterior in the nature of things to *that of the limits* which are added. But we do not notice the first save in beginning with what is limited and which strikes our senses. . . .

CHAPTER XVII.

Of infinity.

§ 1. [*Infinity, in its original intention, attributed to space, duration and number.*] Properly speaking, it is true that an infinity of things exists, i.e., there are always more than one can assign. But there does not exist any infinite number or line or other infinite quantity, if we take them for genuine wholes, as it is easy to prove. The scholastics who admitted a syncategorematic but not a categorematic infinite, as their language puts it, must have meant the same. The true infinite, strictly speaking, is only in the *Absolute*, which is anterior to all composition and is not formed by the addition of parts.

§ 3. [*Hence we come by the idea of infinity.*] . . . Take a straight line and prolong it in such a way that it is double the first. Now it is clear that the second, being perfectly similar to the first, can be doubled in the same way in order to give a third, which is also similar to the preceding; and the same *ratio* always holding it will never be possible to stop; thus the line can be prolonged *ad infinitum;* in such a way that the consideration of the infinite comes from that of similarity or of the same *ratio,* and its origin is the same as that of universal and necessary truths. This shows how what

gives completion to the conception of this idea is found
in us and could not come from the experiences of the
senses; just as necessary truths could not be proved by
induction nor by the senses. The idea of the *absolute* is in
us internally, like that of being. These absolutes are
nothing but the attributes of God and it can be said that
they are no less the source of ideas than God is himself
the principle of beings. The idea of the absolute in relation to space, is no other than that of the immensity of
God, and so of the others. But we deceive ourselves in
wishing to imagine an absolute space, which would be an
infinite whole, composed of parts. There is no such thing.
It is a notion which involves a contradiction, and these
infinite wholes, and their opposites, the infinitesimals,
are only admissible in the calculations of geometers, just
like the imaginary roots of algebra.

. . . § 16. [*We have no positive idea of infinity nor
of infinite duration.*] I believe that we have a positive
idea of both, and this idea will be true provided it is not
conceived as an infinite whole but as an absolute or
attribute without limits, which is the case as regards the
eternity in the necessity of the existence of God, without
depending on parts and without forming the notion by an
addition of times. From this is also seen, as I have already said, that the origin of the notion of the infinite
comes from the same source as that of necessary truths.

. . .

CHAPTER XIX.
Of the modes of thinking.

§ 1. [*Sensation, remembrance, contemplation, &c.*] It
is well to clear up these notions, and I shall try to aid

in it. I will say then that it is *sensation* when we perceive
an external object; that *remembrance* is its repetition
without the object returning; but when we know that we
have had it, it is *memory. Contemplation* is commonly
employed in a sense different from yours, namely, for a
condition where we free ourselves from business in order
to apply ourselves to some meditation. But since there is
no word that I know of which fits your notion, sir, the
one you employ may be applied to it. We give *attention*
to the objects which we distinguish and prefer to others.
When attention continues in the mind, whether the external object continues or not, and even whether it is
present or not, this is *consideration;* which tending to
knowledge without reference to action, will be *contemplation.* Attention, the aim of which is *to learn* (that is
to say, to acquire knowledge in order to preserve it), is
study. To consider in order to form some plan, is to
meditate; but revery appears to be nothing but the pursuing of certain thoughts through the pleasure taken in
them without having other end; this is why revery may
lead to insanity: one forgets self, forgets the *dic cur hic,*
hovers on dreams and chimeras, builds castles in Spain.
We can distinguish *dreams* from sensations only because they are not tied to the latter; they are, as it
were, a world apart. *Sleep* is a cessation of sensations,
and so *trance* is a very profound sleep from which one
can be aroused with difficulty, and comes from a transient internal cause, thus distinguishing it from the profound sleep which comes from a narcotic or from some
lasting injury to the functions, as in lethargy. Trances
are sometimes accompanied by *visions;* but there are some
without trance; and *vision,* it seems, is nothing but a
dream which passes for a sensation, as if it taught us
the truth of the objects. And when these visions are
divine, there is in fact truth; which may be known, for

example, when they contain particularized prophecies which the event justifies.

§ 4. [*Hence it is probable that thinking is the action, not the essence of the soul.*] Undoubtedly thought is an action and could not be the essence; but it is an essential action, and all substances have such. I have shown above, that we have always an infinity of minute perceptions without our being conscious of them. We are never without *perceptions* but it is necessary that we be often without *apperceptions,* namely, when there are no distinct perceptions. It is for want of having considered this important point, that a philosophy, loose and as little noble as solid, has prevailed among so many men of good minds, and that we have hitherto almost ignored whatever is most beautiful in souls. This has also caused men to find so much plausibility in the error which teaches that souls are of a perishable nature.

CHAPTER XX.
Of modes of pleasure and pain.

§ 1. [*Pleasure and pain, simple ideas.*] I believe that there are no perceptions which are entirely indifferent to us, but it is enough that their effect be not noticeable in order that they may be called so, for *pleasure* and *pain* appear to consist in an aid or in a noticeable impediment. I assert that this definition is not nominal and that one cannot be given.

§ 2. [*Good is what pleases.*] I am also of this opinion. The good is divided into the praiseworthy, agreeable, and useful; but at bottom I believe that it must be either itself agreeable or contributing to something else which can give us an agreeable feeling; that is to say, the good is agreeable or useful and the praiseworthy itself consists in a pleasure of the mind.

§ § 4, 5. [*Love. Hatred.*] I gave very nearly this same definition of *love* when I explained the principles of justice in the preface to my *Codex Juris Gentium Diplomaticus,* namely, that to *love* is to be led to take pleasure in the perfection, well-being or happiness of the beloved object. And for this reason we do not consider or demand any other pleasure for self than just that which is found in the well-being or pleasure of the one loved; but in this sense we do not properly love what is incapable of pleasure or of happiness, and we enjoy things of this nature without, for that reason, loving them, unless by a prosopopœia, and as if we imagine that they themselves enjoy their perfection. It is not, then, properly love when we say that we love a beautiful picture because of the pleasure we take in thinking of its perfections. But it is permissible to extend the meaning of the terms, and usage varies here. Philosophers and theologians even distinguish two kinds of love, namely, the *love* which they call *love of complacency,* which is nothing else than the desire or feeling we have for the one who gives us pleasure without our interesting ourselves as to whether he receives pleasure; and the *love of benevolence,* which is the feeling we have for him who, by his pleasure or happiness, gives the same to us. The first causes us to have in view our pleasure and the second that of others, but as making or rather constituting ours, for if it should not react upon us in some sort we could not interest ourselves in it, since it is impossible, whatever may be said, to be indifferent to one's own good. And this is how *disinterested* or non-mercenary *love* must be understood, in order to conceive well its nobleness and yet not to fall into the chimerical.

§ 6. [*Desire.*] This consideration of *uneasiness* is a

capital point, in which this author has particularly shown his penetrating and profound spirit. This is why I have given it some attention, and after having considered the matter well, it appears to me that the French word *inquiétude* (*restlessness*), if it does not sufficiently express the meaning of the author, fits nevertheless, in my opinion, the nature of the thing; and the English word uneasiness, if it stands for a displeasure, fretfulness (*chagrin*), discomfort, and in a word some effective pain, would be inappropriate. For I should prefer to say that in desire in itself there is rather a disposition and preparation for pain than pain itself. It is true that this perception sometimes does not differ from that which is in pain except in degree, but this is because the degree is the essence of pain, for it is a noticeable perception. This is also seen by the difference which there is between appetite and hunger; for when the irritation of the stomach becomes too strong it discomforts; so that it is necessary also to apply here our doctrine of perceptions too minute to be apperceived; for if what takes place in us when we have an appetite and desire were sufficiently magnified it would cause pain. This is why the infinitely wise author of our being has acted for our good, when he ordained that we should be often in ignorance and in confused perceptions. This is in order to act more promptly by instinct and not to be discomforted by the too distinct sensations of many objects, which do not altogether come back to us, and which nature has not been able to do without in order to obtain its ends. How many insects do we not swallow without our being conscious of it? how many persons do we see who having too fine a sense of smell are thereby discomforted? And how many disgusting objects should we see if our vision were sufficiently piercing? It is also by this skill that nature has given us the incitements of desire, like the rudiments or elements of pain or, so to speak, semi-pains, or (if you wish to speak so as to express yourself more forcibly) minute inapperceptible pains, to the end that we may *enjoy the advantage of evil* without being incommoded thereby. For otherwise if this perception were too distinct we would always be miserable in waiting for the good, whereas this continual victory over these semi-pains which are felt in following one's desire and satisfying in some sort this appetite or this longing, gives us many semi-pleasures, the continuation and accumulation of which (as in the continuation of the impulse of a heavy body which descends and acquires force) becomes in the end an entire and real pleasure. And at bottom without these semi-pains there would be no pleasure, and there would be no means of perceiving that something, by being an obstacle which prevents us from putting ourselves at our ease, assists us and aids us. It is also in this that the affinity of pain and of pleasure is recognized, which Socrates noticed, in the *Phaedo* of Plato, when his feet itched. This consideration of the minute aids or small deliverances and imperceptible disengagements of the arrested tendency from which noticeable pleasure finally results, serves also to give some more distinct knowledge of the confused idea which we have and ought to have *of pleasure and of pain;* just as the sensation of heat or of light results from many minute motions which express those of objects, as I have said above (see ch. 9), and do not differ therefrom save in appearance and because we are not conscious of this analysis; whereas many to-day believe that our ideas of sensible qualities differ *toto genere* from motions and from what takes place in the objects, and are something primitive and inexplicable, and even arbitrary, as if God made the soul feel what seems good to it in place of what takes place in the body; an opinion very far removed from the

true analysis of our ideas. But to return to *uneasiness,*
that is to say, to the minute imperceptible solicitations
which keep us always in suspense; these are confused
determinations such that we often do not know what
we lack, whereas in *inclinations and passions,* we at least
know what we need, although the confused perceptions
enter also into their manner of acting, and the same
passions also cause this uneasiness or longing. These impulses are like so many small springs which try to un-
bend, and which cause our machine to act. And I have
already remarked thereon, that it is through this that
we are never indifferent, when we appear to be most so,
for example, to turning to the right rather than to the
left at the end of a path. For the side which we take
comes from these insensible determinations, mingled with
the actions of objects and of the interior of the body,
which cause us to find ourselves more at ease in one than
in the other way of moving ourselves. The pendulum of
a clock is called in German *Unruhe,* that is to say,
uneasiness. It can be said that it is the same in our body,
which can never be perfectly at its ease; because if it
should be so, a new impression of objects, a slight change
in the organs, in the vessels, and in the viscera would
change at once the balance and would cause them to
make some slight effort in order to regain the best state
which they can be in; this produces a continual strife,
which causes, so to speak, the *uneasiness* of our clock;
so that this term is satisfactory to me.

§ 7. [*Joy.*] There are no words in languages, sufficiently appropriate to distinguish kindred notions. Perhaps the Latin *gaudium* approaches nearer this definition
of joy than *laetitia,* which is also translated by the word
joy; but then it seems to me to signify a state in which
pleasure predominates in us, for during the profoundest
sorrow and amidst the most piercing griefs one can take

some pleasure, as in drinking or in listening to music, but the pain predominates; and likewise amid the sharpest pains, the mind can be in joy, as happened to the martyrs.

§ 8. [*Sorrow.*] Not only the actual presence, but also the fear of an evil to come can make one sad, so that I believe the definitions of joy and of sorrow, which I have just given, agree best with usage. As to *uneasiness,* there is in pain, and consequently in sorrow, something more; and there is uneasiness even in joy, for it makes men wide awake, active, full of hope for going farther. *Joy* has been able to cause death by excess of emotion, and then there was in it even more than uneasiness.

§ § 9, 10. [*Hope and Fear.*] If uneasiness signifies a pain, I acknowledge that it always accompanies fear; but taking it for this insensible incitement which urges us on, it can also be applied to hope. The Stoics took the passions for thoughts (*opinions*); thus hope, for them, was the thought of a future good, and fear, the thought of a future evil. But I prefer to say that the passions are neither satisfactions nor displeasures, nor thoughts, but tendencies or rather modifications of the tendencies, which come from thought or from feeling, and which are accompanied by pleasure or displeasure.

§ 11. [*Despair.*] Despair taken for the passion will be a sort of strong tendency which finds itself wholly arrested, causing a violent struggle and much displeasure. But when the despair is accompanied by repose and indolence, it will be a thought rather than a passion.

§ 12. [*Anger.*] Anger seems to be something more simple and more general, since brutes, to whom no injury has been done, are susceptible of it. There is in anger a violent effort which strives to get free from the evil. The desire of vengeance may remain when one is cool and when one experiences hatred rather than anger.

§ 13. [*Envy.*] According to this [Locke's] notion,

envy would be always a praiseworthy passion and always founded upon justice, at least in my opinion. But I do not know but that envy is often entertained toward recognized merit, which one would not hesitate to misuse if one were master. Envy is even entertained of people who have a good which one would not care to have one's self. One would be content to see them deprived of it without thinking to profit by their spoils, and even without being able to hope it. For some goods are like pictures painted *in fresco,* which can be destroyed, but which cannot be taken away.

§ 17. [*Shame.*] If men took more pains to observe the overt movements which accompany the passions, it would be difficult to conceal them. As to shame, it is worthy of consideration that modest persons, when they are simply witnesses of an improper action, sometimes feel movements resembling those of shame.

CHAPTER XXI.
Of power and of liberty.

§ 1. [*The idea of power, how got.*] If *power* corresponds to the Latin *potentia,* it is opposed to *act,* and the passage from power to act is *change.* This is what Aristotle understands by the word *motion,* when he says that it is the act or perhaps *the actuation* of what is in power. We can say then that *power* in general is the possibility of change. Now change or the act of this possibility, being action in one subject and passion in another, there will be also two powers, one passive the other active. The *active* could be called *faculty* and perhaps the *passive* could be called *capacity* or *receptivity.* It is true that active power is sometimes taken in a more perfect sense, when in addition to the simple faculty there is a *tendency;* and it is thus that I employ it in my *dynamical* considerations. The word *force* might be appropriated to it in particular; and *force* would be either *entelechy* or *effort;* for *entelechy* (although Aristotle employs it so generally that it comprises also all action and all effort) appears to me more appropriate to *primitive acting forces,* and that of *effort* to *derivative forces.* There is even also a species of *passive power* more particular and more endowed with reality; it is this which is in matter when there is not only mobility, which is the capacity or receptivity for motion, but also *resistance,* which embraces *impenetrability* and *inertia.* Entelechies, that is to say, primitive or substantial tendencies, when they are accompanied by perception, are souls.

. . .

§ 4. [*The clearest idea of active power had from mind.*] . . . I am thoroughly in accord with you, that the clearest idea of active power comes to us from mind. It is also only in things which have an analogy with mind, that is to say, in entelechies, for matter properly only indicates passive power.

. . .

§ 8. [*Liberty.*] The term *liberty* is very ambiguous. There is liberty of right and of fact. According to that of *right* a slave is not free, a subject is not entirely free, but a poor man is as free as a rich man. Liberty of *fact* consists either in the power *to will* as one ought, or in the power to do what one wills. It is the *liberty of doing* of which you speak, and it has its degrees and varieties. Generally he who has most means is most free to do what he wills: but, *in particular, liberty* is understood of the use of things which are customarily in our power and especially of the free use of our body. Thus the prison or sicknesses which prevent us from giving to our body and to our limbs the motion which we wish and which we are ordinarily able to give, lessens our liberty. It is thus that a prisoner is not free, and that a paralytic has not the free use of his limbs. *Liberty to will* is also taken in two different senses. One is when it is opposed to the imperfection or to the slavery of the spirit, which is a coaction or constraint, but internal like that which comes from the passions. The other sense appears when liberty is opposed to necessity. In the first sense the Stoics said that the wise man only is free; and in fact the spirit is not free when it is occupied with a great passion, for one cannot then will as he ought to, that is to say, with the deliberation which is requisite. It is thus that God alone is perfectly free, and that created spirits are so only in so far as they are superior to the passions. And this liberty concerns properly our understanding. But the liberty of the spirit, opposed to necessity, concerns the naked will, and in so far as it is distinguished from the understanding. This it is which is called *free-will,* and it consists in this, that one wills that the strongest reasons or impressions which the understanding presents to the will do not prevent the act of the will from being contingent, and do not give it an absolute, or, so to say, metaphysical, necessity. And it is in this sense that I am accustomed to say that the understanding can determine the will, in accordance with the prevalence of perceptions and reasons, in such a way that even when it is certain and infallible, inclines without necessitating.

. . .

§ 13. [*Necessity, what.*] It seems to me that, properly speaking, although volitions are contingent, *necessity* ought not to be opposed to volition but to *contin-*

gency, . . . and that necessity ought not to be confounded with determination, for there is not less of connection or of determination in thoughts than in motions (to be determined being quite different from being pushed or forced with constraint). And if we do not always notice the reason which determines us, or rather by which we determine ourselves, it is because we are as little capable of being conscious of the whole extent of our mind and of its thoughts, most often imperceptible and confused, as we are of disentangling all the mechanisms set by nature into play in the body. Thus, if by necessity is understood the certain determination of man, which a perfect knowledge of all the circumstances of what takes place within and without the man could enable a perfect mind to foresee, it is certain that thoughts being just as determined as the motions which they represent, every free act would be necessary. But the necessary must be distinguished from the contingent though determined; and not only contingent truths are not necessary, but even their connections are not always of an absolute necessity; for it must be acknowledged that there is a difference in the manner of determination between the consequences which exist in necessary matter and those which exist in contingent matter. Geometrical and metaphysical consequences necessitate, but physical and moral incline without necessitating; the physical even having something moral and voluntary in relation to God, since the laws of motion have no other necessity than that of [the principle of] the best. Now God chooses freely although he is determined to choose the best; and as bodies themselves do not choose (God having chosen for them), usage has settled that they be called *necessary agents;* to which I am not opposed, provided the necessary and the determined be not confounded, and that it be not imagined that free beings act in an undeter-

mined manner; an error which has prevailed in certain
minds and which destroys the most important truths,
even this fundamental axiom, *that nothing occurs without reason,* without which neither the existence of God
nor other great truths could be well demonstrated. As to
constraint, it is well to distinguish two species of it. The
one *physical,* as when a man is taken to prison in spite
of himself, or is thrown over a precipice; the other
moral, as, for example, the constraint of a greater evil,
and this action although in some manner forced, is nevertheless voluntary. One can also be forced by the consideration of a greater good, as when a man is tempted
by having proposed to him a too great advantage, although this is not customarily called constraint.

. . .

§ 21. [*Liberty belongs to the agent, or man.*] When
we reason about the liberty of the will, or about the
free will, we do not ask if the man can do what he wills,
but if there is enough independence in his will itself.
We do not ask if he has his limbs free or has elbow-
room, but if he has his mind free, and in what this
consists. In this respect one intelligence could be more
free than another, and the supreme intelligence will
enjoy perfect liberty of which his creatures are not
capable.

. . .

§ § 41, 42. [*All desire happiness. Happiness, what.*]
I do not know whether the greatest pleasure is possible.
I believe rather that it can grow *ad infinitum;* for we
do not know how far our knowledge and our organs can
be extended in all that eternity which awaits us. I believe
then that *happiness* is a lasting pleasure; which could
not be so without there being a continual progress to

new pleasures. Therefore, of two persons, one of whom
will go by far more quickly and through greater pleasures than the other, each will be happy in himself and
in a unique way, although their happiness will be very
unequal. Happiness is then, so to speak, a road through
pleasures; and pleasure is merely a step and an advancement towards happiness, the shortest which can be made
according to the present impressions, but not always the
best. The right road may be missed in the desire to follow
the shortest, as the stone which goes straight may encounter obstacles too soon, which prevent it from advancing quite to the center of the earth. This shows that it is the
reason and the will which transport us toward happiness,
but that feeling and desire merely lead us to pleasure.
Now, although pleasure cannot receive a nominal definition, any more than light or color, it can, however, receive, like them, a causal definition; and I believe that
at bottom *pleasure* is a feeling of perfection and *pain*
a feeling of imperfection, provided it is noticeable enough
to cause us to be conscious of it. . . .

§ 47. [*The power to suspend the prosecution of any
desire makes way for consideration, and in this freedom
of will consists.*] The execution of our desire is suspended or arrested when this desire is not strong enough
to move us, and to overcome the trouble and inconvenience of satisfying it. . . . But when desire is strong
enough in itself to move us, if nothing prevents, it can
be arrested by contrary inclinations:—whether they consist in a simple propensity which is like the element or
the beginning of desire, or whether they extend to desire
itself. Nevertheless as these inclinations, these propensities, and these contrary desires must be found already in
the soul, it does not have them in its power, and consequently, it cannot resist in a free and voluntary way in
which the reason can share, if it had not also another

means which is that of turning the mind elsewhere. But how can we decide to do this when there is need? For there is the point, especially when we are possessed by a strong passion. There is need, therefore, that the mind be prepared beforehand, and find itself already about to go from thought to thought, in order not to stop too long in a slippery and dangerous place.

For this, it is well to accustom one's self generally not to think except in passing of certain things, in order the better to preserve the freedom of the mind. But the best way is to accustom one's self to proceed methodically, and to attach one's self to a train of thoughts the connection of which reason and not chance (that is to say, insensible and casual impressions) establishes. And in order to do this, it is well to accustom one's self to collect one's self from time to time, and to raise one's self above the present tumult of impressions, to go forth, so to say, from the place where one is, to say to one's self *"dic cur hic? respice finem,* or where are we? let us come to the point."* Men would often have need of some one, established with an official title (as Philip, the father of Alexander the Great, had), to interrupt them and to recall them to their duty. But, for lack of such an officer, it is well for us to be accustomed to perform for ourselves this office. Now being once in a condition to arrest the effect of our desires and of our passions, that is to say, to suspend action, we can find the means of combating them, be it by the contrary desires or inclinations, be it by diversion, that is to say, by occupations of another nature. It is by these methods and these artifices that we become, as it were, masters of ourselves, and that we can make ourselves think and do at the time what we should wish to will and what reason commands. Nevertheless, it is always by determined ways, and never without ground or by the imaginary principle of a perfect indifference or equilibrium, in which some would make the essence of liberty to consist; as if one could determine himself groundlessly and even against all ground, and go directly counter to the *prevalence* of the impressions and the propensities. . . .

. . .

§ 51. [*The necessity of pursuing true happiness the foundation of liberty.*] True happiness ought always to be the object of our desires, but there is ground for doubting whether it is. For often we hardly think of it, and I have remarked here more than once that the less desire is guided by reason the more it tends to present pleasure and not to happiness, that is to say, to lasting pleasure, although it tends to make it last.

. . .

CHAPTER XXIII.

Of our complex ideas of substances.

§ 1. [*Ideas of substances, how made.*] On the contrary, it is rather the *concretum* as odorous, as warm, as glittering, which comes into our minds, than the *abstractions* or qualities (for it is they which are in the substantial object and not the ideas) as, namely, heat, light, etc., which are much more difficult to comprehend. It may even be doubted whether these accidents are real existences, as in fact they are very often only relations. It is known also that it is the abstractions which occasion most difficulty when it is desired to examine them minutely, as those who are acquainted with the subtleties of the scholastics, whose most intricate speculations fall at one blow if we will banish abstract entities and resolve not to speak ordinarily except by concretes, and not to admit any other terms in the demonstrations of the sciences, but those which represent substantial subjects. Thus it is *nodum quaerere in scirpo*, if I dare say it, and to invert things, if we take the qualities or other abstract terms for what is easiest and the concrete ones for something very difficult.

§ 2. [*Our idea of substance in general.*] . . . In distinguishing two things in substance, attributes or predicates and the common subject of these predicates, it is not strange that nothing in particular can be conceived in this subject. It must necessarily be so, since we have already separated from it all the attributes in which some detail could be conceived. Therefore to demand something more in this pure *subject in general* than what is necessary in order to conceive that it is the same thing (e.g., which understands and wills, which imagines and reasons), this is to demand the impossible and to run counter to one's own supposition, made in abstracting and in conceiving separately the subject and its qualities or accidents. The same pretended difficulty could be applied to the notion of *being* and to all that is most clear and most primitive; for we could ask philosophers what they conceive in conceiving *pure being in general*; for all detail, being thereby excluded, there would be as little to say as when it is asked what *pure substance in general* is. I think, therefore, that the philosophers do not deserve to be ridiculed, as is done here in comparing them to the Indian philosopher, who when asked what the earth rested on, replied that it was a large elephant, and when asked what the elephant rested on, said that it was a great tortoise, and, finally, when pressed to tell what the tortoise rested on, was reduced to saying that it was *something, I know not what.* However, the consideration of substance, very inconsiderable as it seems to be, is not so void and sterile as is thought. Certain consequences come from it which are most important to philosophy, and which are capable of giving it a new aspect. [Cf. ch. 13, § 19.]

§§ 4, 5. [*No clear idea of substance in general.*] For my part, I believe that this opinion of our ignorance comes from our demanding a kind of knowledge which the object does not permit of. The true mark of a clear and distinct notion of an object is the means we have of knowing many truths of it by *a priori* proofs, as I have pointed out in an essay on truths and ideas inserted in the *Acta* of Leipsig of the year 1684.*

. . .

§ 15. [*Ideas of spiritual substances, as clear as of bodily substances.*] . . . It is well said, and it is very true, that the existence of the mind is *more certain* than that of sensible objects.

. . .

CHAPTER XXV.
Of relation.

§ 1. [*Relation, what.*] Relations and orders are like *entities of reason*, although they have their foundation in things; for it may be said that their reality, like that of eternal truths and possibilties, comes from the supreme reason.

. . .

CHAPTER XXVII.
Of identity and diversity.

§ 1. [*Wherein identity consists.*] There must always be, in addition to the difference of time and of place, an

* See III. 2 above ("Reflections on Knowledge, Truth and Ideas").

internal *principle* of *distinction*; and although there are
many things of the same species, it is nevertheless true
that none of them are ever perfectly alike: thus although
time and place (that is, the relation to the external) serve
us in distinguishing things which we do not well distinguish through themselves, things are none the less distinguishable in themselves. The characteristic of *identity*
and of *diversity* does not consist, therefore, in time and
in place. . . .

. . .

§ 3. [*Principium individuationis.*] *The principle of individuation* corresponds in individuals to the principle of
distinction of which I have just spoken. If two individuals were perfectly alike and equal, and (in a word)
indistinguishable in themselves, there would be no principle of individuation; and I even venture to say that
there would be no individual distinction, or different
individuals, on this condition. . . .

. . .

§ 9. [*Personal identity.*] I am also of the opinion that
consciousness, or the feeling of the *ego*, proves a moral
or personal identity. And it is in this that I distinguish
the *unceasingness* of the soul of a brute from the *immortality* of the soul of man: both retain *physical and real
identity;* but as for man, it is according to the rules of
divine providence that the soul preserve in addition moral
identity, apparent to ourselves, in order to constitute the
same person, capable consequently of feeling punishments and rewards. It appears that you, sir, hold that
this apparent identity might be preserved, even if there
should be no real identity. I should think that this might
perhaps be possible by the absolute power of God; but
according to the order of things the identity apparent to

the person himself, who himself feels the same, supposes the real identity at each *following stage,* accompanied by reflection or by the feeling of the ego: an intimate and immediate perception not naturally able to deceive. If man could be only a machine and have in addition consciousness, it would be necessary to be of your opinion, sir; but I hold that this case is not possible, at least naturally. I do not mean to say either that *personal identity* and even the *ego* do not remain in us, and that I am not that *ego* which was in the cradle, under the pretext that I no longer remember anything which I then did. It is sufficient in order to find moral identity by itself that there be a *common bond of consciousness* from a neighboring state, or even one a little removed, to another, even if some leap or forgotten interval should be mingled with it. Thus, if an illness had caused an interruption of the continuity of the connection of consciousness, so that I should not know how I had come into the present state, although I might remember more distant things, the testimony of others might fill the gap of my remembrance. I might even be punished on this testimony, if I had done some evil of deliberate purpose in an interval which I had forgotten a little while afterwards through this illness. And if I came to forget all past things, so that I should be obliged to let myself be taught anew, even to my name and to reading and writing, I could always learn from others my past life in my preceding state, as I have preserved my rights without its being necessary to divide myself into two persons, and to make myself my own heir. All this suffices for maintaining moral identity, which makes the same person. It is true that if others conspired to deceive me (as I might even be deceived by myself, by some vision, dream or illness, believing that what I dreamed had happened to me), the appearance would be false; but there are cases in which we may be morally certain of the truth upon the report of others; and in relation to God, whose bond of union with us makes the principal point of morality, error cannot enter. As regards the *ego,* it will be well to distinguish it from the *appearance of the ego* and from consciousness. The *ego* forms the real and physical identity, and the *appearance of the ego,* accompanied by truth, joins to it personal identity. Thus not wishing to say that personal identity does not extend farther than memory, I would say still less that the *ego* or physical identity depends on it. Real and personal identity is proved, as certainly as is possible in matter of fact, by present and immediate reflection; it is proved sufficiently for common use by our remembrance of the interval, or by the corroborating testimony of others. But if God changed real identity extraordinarily, personal identity would remain, provided that man should preserve the appearances of identity, the internal (that is, of consciousness) as well as the external, like those which consist in what is evident to others. Thus consciousness is not the only means of establishing personal identity, and the report of others or even other marks may take its place. But there is difficulty if a contradiction is found among these different evidences. Consciousness may be silent as in forgetfulness; but if it said very distinctly things which were contrary to the other evidences, we should be embarrassed in the decision and so appear to be suspended between two possibilities: that of the error of our memory and that of some deception in the external appearances.

. . .

§ 14. An immaterial being or mind *cannot be despoiled* of all perception of its past existence. There remain in it impressions of everything which has formerly happened to it, and it has even presentiments of everything which will happen to it; but these feelings are most often too slight to be distinguishable and for us to be conscious of them, although they may be developed some day. This continuation and connection of *perceptions* forms the same individual really; but *apperceptions* (that is, when we are conscious of past feelings) prove, farther, a moral identity and make the real identity appear. The pre-existence of souls does not appear to us through our perceptions, but if it were true, it might some day become known. . . . The late Henry More, theologian of the Anglican Church, was convinced of pre-existence, and wrote to defend it. The late M. Van Helmont, the younger, believed, with certain rabbis, in the passing of the soul of Adam into the Messiah as into the new Adam. And I do not know whether he did not believe that he himself had been one of the ancients, very able man as he was otherwise. Now, if this passing of souls was true, at least in the possible way which I have explained above (but which does not appear probable), that is, that souls, retaining subtile bodies, should pass suddenly into other gross bodies, the same individual would subsist always, in Nestor, in Socrates, and in some modern, and he might even make known his identity to that one who should sufficiently penetrate into his nature, by reason of the impressions or characters which would there remain of all that Nestor or Socrates has done, and which any sufficiently penetrating genius might read there. However, if the modern man had no internal or external means of knowing what he has been, it would be, so far as ethics is concerned, as if he had not been at all. But the probability is that nothing is neglected in the world, even in relation to morals, because God is its monarch, and his government is perfect.—Thus if souls passed into a new body, gross or sensitive, they would always retain the expression of all of which they have had perception in the old, and it would even be necessary that the new body should feel it all, so that the individual continuity will always have its real marks. . . .

. . .

§ 18. [*Object of reward and punishment.*] I confess that if God caused consciousness to be transferred to other souls, it would be necessary to treat them, according to ethical ideas, as if they were the same; but this would be to disturb the order of things groundlessly, and to make a divorce between the apperceptible and truth, which is preserved by insensible perceptions. This would not be rational, because perceptions, at present insensible, may be developed some day; for there is nothing useless, and eternity presents a large field for changes.

. . .

§ 29. [*Continued existence makes identity.*] . . . I have pointed out to you the source of true physical identity; I have shown you that morals do not contradict it, any more than memory; that they cannot always mark out physical identity to the person himself in question, nor to those who are in communication with him; but that nevertheless they never contradict physical identity, and never are divorced from it; that there are always created minds that know or may know what is the truth respecting it; but that there is reason for thinking that what is indifferent as regards persons themselves can be so only for a time.

CHAPTER XXVIII.

Of other relations.

. . . § 5 [*Moral good and evil.*] . . . I should prefer, for myself, to take as the measure of moral good and of virtue the invariable rule of reason that God has charged himself to maintain. Also we may be assured that by his means every moral good becomes physical, or as the ancients said, all that is praiseworthy is useful; whereas, in order to express the idea of the author, it would be necessary to say that moral good or evil is a *good* or *evil* of imposition or *instituted*, which he who has the power tries to bring about or to prevent by pains or recompenses. Good is that which by the general institution of God is conformed to nature or to reason.

. . .

CHAPTER XXIX.

Of clear and obscure, distinct and confused ideas.

§ 2. In a short essay on ideas, true or false or obscure, distinct or confused, inserted in the *Acta* of Leipsig in the year 1684,* I have given a definition of *clear ideas* which is common to simple ideas and to composite ones, and which accounts for what is said thereon here. . . .

. . .

§ 13. [*Complex ideas may be distinct in one part and confused in another.*] . . . This example [a chiliagon] shows that *idea* is here confounded with *image*. If someone proposes to me a regular polygon, sight and imagination could not make me understand the thousand sides which are in it; I have only a *confused* idea both of the figure and of its number, until I *distinguish* the number by counting. But having found it, I know very well the nature and the properties of the proposed polygon, in so far as they are those of a chiliagon, and consequently, I

* See "Reflections on Knowledge, Truth and Ideas," in III. 2 above.

have the idea of it; but I could not have the image of a
chiliagon, and it would be necessary to have senses and
imagination more delicate and better exercised in order
to thereby distinguish it from a polygon which should
have one side less. But knowledge of figures does not
depend upon the imagination, any more than that of
numbers, although it is of use thereto; and a mathematician may know exactly the nature of an enneagon or of
a decagon because he has the means of making and examining them, although he cannot distinguish them by
sight. It is true then that a workman or an engineer, who
should not perhaps know the nature of the figures sufficiently, might have this advantage over a great geome-
trician, that he could distinguish them by merely seeing
them without measuring them; as there are porters who
will tell the weight of what they are to carry without
the mistake of a pound, in which they will surpass the
most skillful statistician in the world. This empirical
knowledge, acquired by long practice, may have great
advantages for acting promptly, as an engineer very
often needs to do by reason of the danger to which he
exposes himself by hesitating. However this *clear image*,
or this feeling which we may have of a regular decagon
or of a weight of ninety-nine pounds, consists only in a
confused idea, since it is of no use in discovering the
nature and the properties of this weight or of the regular
decagon, which requires a *distinct idea*. And this example
serves to show better the difference between ideas, or
rather that between idea and image.

§ 15. [*Instance in eternity.*] This example does not
seem to me to fit your purpose any better; but it is very
appropriate to mine, which is to disabuse you of your
notions on this point. For there reigns here the same confusion between image and idea. We have a complete and
proper idea of eternity, since we have a definition of it,

although we have no image of it; but the idea of infinites is not formed by the composition of parts, and the errors which are committed in reasoning concerning the infinite do not come from the lack of imagery.

. . .

Book III. Words

CHAPTER I.
Of words or language in general.

. . . § 2. [*Language is primarily a social instrument.*] I believe in fact that without the desire to have ourselves understood we should never have formed any mode of language, but once formed, language serves man in reasoning by himself both through the means words give him to remember abstract thoughts and through the utility obtained by availing himself in reasoning of characters and silent thoughts; for it would require too much time to explain everything and to constantly substitute definitions for terms.

§ 3. [*On general terms.*] *General* terms serve not only for the perfection of languages but are necessary for their essential constitution. For if by *particular things* we mean individuals, it would be impossible to speak, given only *proper names* and no *appellatives*, that is, if there were only words for individuals, since at every moment there is something new turning up with individuals, accidents, and especially actions, which are the things most frequently designated. But if by particular things we mean the lowest species (*infima species*), beside the fact that it is very often difficult to determine such, it is apparent that they are really universals based on similitude. Hence, since in speaking of genera and species it is a question of more or less similitude, it is natural to notice any sort of similitudes or agreements and consequently to employ general terms of all degrees. Indeed, the most general terms, being less burdened though more comprehensive as compared to the individuals to which they apply, were very often the easiest to form and are the most useful. Thus you see that children and those who know only a little of the language they wish to speak or the subject about which they speak, use general terms like thing, plant, animal, instead of using the appropriate terms which they lack. And it is certain that all *proper* or individual *names* were originally *appellative* or general.

. . .

CHAPTER III.
Of general terms

§§ 1–5. [*Utility of general terms.*] . . . We can say then that the names of individuals were names of species given *par excellence* to some individual or other, like the name "Head" given to the most important person in a city. Thus we give the names of genera to species, that is, we will be satisfied with a more general or vaguer term to designate more particular species when we are not concerned with their differences. For example, we are content with the general name of wormwood, though there are so many species of it that a botanist (Jean Bauhin) has written a book just about them.

§ 6. [*Ideas become general by abstraction.*] I do not deny this use of abstractions, but it applies rather to ascending from species to genera than from individuals to species. For (however paradoxical it may seem) it is impossible for us to know individuals directly and to find a means of *determining* exactly the individuality of any thing except only to keep it itself; for all the circumstances may reappear; the smallest differences are imperceptible to us; space and time far from determining themselves need to be determined by the things they contain. Most important of all is the fact that *individuality* involves the infinite, and only he who understands the latter can have first-hand knowledge of the principle of individuation of this or that thing; this arises from the influence (conceived rightly) of all things in the universe on one another. It is true that it would not be so if the atoms of Democritus existed; but then it would also be true that there would be no *difference* between two *different* individuals of the same shape and size.

• • •

§ 9. [*Classes (genera and species) are names of abstract ideas.*] The art of ordering things into genera and species is of no little importance and is very useful for both judgment and memory. You know how important that is in Botany, not to speak of animals and other substances and without speaking also of moral and intelligible beings, as some call them. Order largely depends on it, and several good authors write so that their entire discourse may be reduced to divisions or subdivisions, in accordance with a method comparable to that of genera and species, and this helps not only in retaining things but also in finding them. And those persons who have arranged all sorts of notions under certain titles or categories have done something very useful.

• • •

§§ 11–18. [*Universals do not belong to real existence but to the understanding, and the essence of each species is only an abstract idea or nominal essence.*] I do not see this consequence clearly. For generality consists in the resemblance of singular things among themselves, and this resemblance is a reality. . . . Why not then seek therein also the essence of classes?

. . .

As to your statement that the qualities of gold are its nominal essence, I should prefer to say, in accord with accepted usage, that the essence of gold is what constitutes it and gives it those sensible qualities which cause us to recognize it and make up its nominal *definition*, whereas we should have a *real and causal definition* if we could explain this contexture or internal constitution. However, the nominal definition also becomes real, not through itself (for it does not make known *a priori* the possibility or generation of the body) but through experience, because we experience a body in which qualities are found together; without this fact we might doubt whether so much weight is compatible with so much malleability, just as we may doubt today whether it is possible to make glass malleable without heat. I do not have your opinion, sir, that there is some difference here between the ideas of substance and the ideas of predicates, as if the definitions of predicates (that is, of modes and objects of simple ideas) were always both real and nominal, and that those of substances were only nominal. I do admit that it is more difficult to get real definitions of bodies which are substantial beings, because their contexture is less perceptible. But it is not the same with all substances; for we have a knowledge of true substances or unities (like God and the soul) as intimate as the knowledge we have of the majority of modes. Moreover, there are predicates as little known to us as the contexture of bodies; for yellow and bitter, for example, are the objects of simple ideas or phantasms, and nevertheless we have only a confused knowledge of them, even in Mathematics where the same mode may have a nominal as well as a real definition. Few people have properly explained in what the difference in these two definitions consists, on the basis of which we ought to discern also essence and property. To my mind the difference consists in this: the real definition makes us see the possibility of what is defined, but the nominal one does not; the definition of two *parallel straight lines* which says they are in the same plane and never meet even though they are prolonged to infinity, is only a nominal one, for we may doubt at first whether that is possible. But when we understand that we can draw a line in a plane parallel to a given line provided that we take care to keep the stylus which describes the parallel constantly at the same distance from the given line, then we see at the same time that the thing is possible and why the lines have this property of never meeting which makes the definition nominal but is not the mark of parallelism except when the two lines are straight lines; whereas if at least one of them was a curve, they could be such that they could never meet and yet they would not be parallel for that reason.

. . .

CHAPTER VI.

Of the names of substances.

§ 1. [*On whether nothing is essential to individuals.*] . . . I think there is something essential to individuals, and more than you realize. It is essential to substances to act, to created substances to be acted on, to minds to think, to bodies to have extension and motion. That is, there are kinds or species to which an individual cannot cease to belong (at least naturally) once it does belong, no matter what revolutions may occur in nature. But I admit there are kinds or species accidental to individuals who may cease to belong to that kind. Thus we may cease to be healthy, handsome, learned, and even visible and palpable, but we do not cease to have life and organs and perception. I have said enough heretofore about why it seems to men that life and thought sometimes cease, although life and thought do not cease to endure and to have effects.

§ 8. [*That names conceal individual differences.*] Nothing could be more true, and I could add much information myself on that score. Books have also been written *de infido experimentorum chymicorum successu*. But the mistake consists in taking these bodies to be *similar* or uniform when they are more mixed than we realize; for we are not surprised to observe differences in *dissimilar* bodies, and physicians know only too well how different the temperaments and natures of human bodies are. In short, we shall never discover the ultimate logical species, as I have already remarked above, and never are two real or complete individuals of the same species perfectly alike.

§ 11. [*On spirits.*] There is, however, another difference still, in my system, between God and created minds, namely, it is necessary on my view that all created minds have bodies just as our soul has one.

§ 12. [*On the chain of being.*] I had intended to say elsewhere something not unlike what you have just expounded, sir, but I am very glad to be anticipated when things are said better than I should have hoped to have done. Some philosophers of ability have raised the question *utrum detur vacuum formarum*, that is, whether there are possible species that do not yet exist and which nature may have forgotten. I have reasons for believing that not all possible species are compossible in the universe, large as it is, and that is true not only for things existing contemporaneously but for the whole series of things. That is, I believe that there are necessarily species which could never have existed and will never exist since they are incompatible with that series of creatures which God has selected. But I believe that all the things that could be admitted into the perfect harmony of the universe are there. That there may be intermediate creatures between those far apart is something in conformity with this very harmony, although it is not always in the same globe or system, and what is between two species is sometimes so in relation to certain circumstances and not in relation to others. Birds which are so different from man in other respects approach him in speech; but if monkeys could speak like parrots they would go further ahead. The *law of continuity* implies that nature does not leave a void in the order it follows; but not every form or species belongs to every order. As for spirits or genii, as I hold that all created intelligences have organized bodies whose perfection corresponds to that of the intelligence or mind which is in that body by virtue of the pre-established harmony, I hold that in order to gain any conception of the perfections of spirits above us, it will help very much to imagine perfections also in the organs of bodies surpassing ours. That is where the liveliest and richest imagination and, to avail myself of an untranslatable Italian expression, *l'invenzione la più vaga* will come in handy in order to rise above ourselves. And what I have said to justify my system of harmony which exalts divine perfections beyond anything anybody dreamed, will be helpful also in obtaining ideas of creatures incomparably greater than any hitherto conceived.

§ 17. [*On whether monsters are new species.*] When it comes to determining whether monsters are of a certain species, we are very often reduced to conjectures. This shows that we are then not limited to what is internal;

since we should want to guess whether an internal nature
(such as reason in man) common to the individuals of
such a species still fits these individuals (as their birth
makes presumable), lacking as they are in so many of
the *external marks* ordinarily found in that species. But
our uncertainty has no effect on the nature of things, and
if there were such a common nature, it will be found or
not found in the monster whether we knew it or not. And
if the internal nature of no species is found in it, the
monster is well capable of being its own species. But if
there were no such internal nature in the species under
discussion, and if the matter were not decided by birth
either, then the external marks alone would determine the
species, and monsters would not belong to that species
from which they are removed, unless we take its species
with some latitude in a way that is somewhat vague; in
that case our pains in wishing to guess its species would
be in vain. This is perhaps what you mean in all your
objections to species taken as real internal essences. You
ought then to prove, sir, that no common internal specific
mark is present when a common external one is wholly
absent. But the contrary is found in the human species
where sometimes children having some monstrosity arrive
at an age when they exhibit reason. Why can something
like that not happen in other species? It is true that for
want of knowledge of them, we cannot make use of this
in order to define them but external marks take the place
of this knowledge though we recognize that they do not
suffice for an exact definition and that even nominal definitions in these cases are only conjectural; and I have
already mentioned above how provisional they are sometimes. . . .

§ 22. [*On whether we know the internal essence of
man.*] I think we have in the case of man a definition that
is real and nominal at the same time. For nothing can be

more internal to man than reason and it ordinarily makes itself well known. That is why a beard and tail [allegedly seen by travelers in an African tribe] will not be considered alongside of reason. A man of the forest though hairy will be recognized, and it is not the magot hair [of the Barbary ape] which excludes him. Imbeciles lack the use of reason, but as we know from experience that reason is often tied up and cannot appear, for this happens to men who have shown and will show reason, we probably make the same judgment regarding imbeciles upon other indications, i.e., their bodily figure. It is only by means of such indications that we presume that infants are men and that they will display reason, and we are rarely mistaken. But if there were reasonable animals with an external form a little different from ours, we would be embarrassed. That shows that our definitions when based on external marks of the body are imperfect and provisional. If anyone called himself an angel and did things far beyond us, he might be believed. If somebody else came from the moon by means of some extraordinary machine like that of Gonzales and related to us credible things about his native country, he would pass for a lunar creature; nevertheless, we might grant him citizenship and all its rights with the title of man, though he were a complete stranger to our globe; but if he asked for baptism and wished to be accepted as a proselyte of our law, I believe you would see great disputes arise among the theologians. And if commerce with these planetary men, sufficiently resembling us (according to Mr. Huyghens), were opened up, the question would deserve an ecumenical council in order to decide whether we should extend our concern for the propagation of the faith beyond our globe. Several would no doubt maintain that the rational animals of that country not being of the race of Adam have no share in the redemption of

Jesus Christ; but others would say perhaps that we do
not know enough about where Adam has always been or
what has happened to all his posterity, there having been
theologians who believed that the moon was the place of
Paradise. Perhaps, by a plurality it would be decided
safest to baptize these doubtful men on condition that
they were susceptible of it; but I doubt that they would
ever wish them to be made priests in the Roman Catholic
Church, because their consecration would always be
doubtful and we should expose people to the danger of
material idolatry, according to the hypothesis of that
Church. Fortunately, the nature of things exempts us
from all such embarrassments; nevertheless these fictions
have their use in speculation if our purpose is to become
better acquainted with our ideas.

· · ·

. . . § 27. [*Whether there are fixed limits to species.*]
I have already agreed to this [that you cannot assign fixed
limits to species], for when we are dealing with fictions
and possibilities, the transitions from species to species
may be imperceptible, and it may be sometimes about as
impossible to discriminate them as to decide how much
hair a man must have left on his head before he is bald.
This indetermination would still hold even if we should
know perfectly the internal nature of the creatures in
question. But I do not see how that prevents things from
having real essences independently of the understanding,
or prevents us from knowing them; it is true that the
names and limits of species will sometimes be like the
names of measures and weights where we must choose in
order to fix the limits. However, there is usually nothing
like that to fear, species too much alike are rarely found
together.

· · ·

§ 32. [*On whether generic ideas are only signs.*] . . .
If you take as real essences such substantial models as
a body and nothing more, an animal and nothing more
specific, a horse without individual qualities, you are
right in treating them as chimeras. And nobody has
claimed, I think, not even the greatest *Realists* of the
past that there were as many substances limited to the
generic as there are genera. But it does not follow that
if they are not that many, then they are simply *signs*. For
I have called your attention several times to the fact that
they are *possibilities* in *resemblances*. Similarly, from the
fact that colors are not always substances or extracted
dyes, it does not follow that they are imaginary. Besides
you cannot imagine nature too *liberal*; she far exceeds
anything we can discover and all advantageous compatible possibilities are found playing their rôle in the
great theatre of her performances. There used to be two
axioms among philosophers: that of the *Realists* seemed
to make nature prodigious, and that of the *Nominalists*
seemed to declare her as stingy. These axioms are both
good, provided they are understood, for nature is like a
good housekeeper who is economical when necessary in
order to be generous when and where she desires. She is
grand in effects, and sparing in the causes she employs.

. . .

BOOK IV. OF KNOWLEDGE.

CHAPTER I.

Of knowledge in general.

§§ 1 and 2. [1. *Our knowledge conversant about our
ideas.* 2. *Knowledge is the perception of the agreement or*

disagreement of two ideas.] Knowledge is employed still more generally, in such a way that it is found also in ideas or terms, before we come to propositions or truths. And it may be said that he who shall have seen attentively more pictures of plants and of animals, more figures of machines, more descriptions or representations of houses or of fortresses, who shall have read more ingenious romances, heard more curious narratives, he, I say, will have *more knowledge* than another, even if there should not be a word of truth in all which has been portrayed or related to him; for the practice which he has in representing to himself mentally many express and actual conceptions or ideas, renders him more fit to conceive what is proposed to him; and it is certain that he will be better instructed and more capable than another, who has neither seen nor read nor heard anything, provided that in these stories and representations he does not take for true that which is not true, and that these impressions do not hinder him otherwise from distinguishing the real from the imaginary, or the existing from the possible. . . . But taking *knowledge* in a narrower meaning, that is, for knowledge of truth, as you do here, sir, I say that it is very true that truth is always founded in the agreement or disagreement of ideas, but it is not true generally that our knowledge of truth is a perception of this agreement or disagreement. For when we know truth only empirically, from having experienced it, without knowing the connection of things and the reason which there is in what we have experienced, we have no perception of this agreement or disagreement, unless it be meant that we feel it confusedly without being conscious of it. But your examples, it seems, show that you always require a knowledge in which one is conscious of connection or of opposition, and this is what cannot be conceded to you. . . .

§§ 3–7. [*3. This agreement fourfold. 4. First, Of identity or diversity. 5. Secondly, Relative. 6. Thirdly, Of
co-existence. 7. Fourthly, Of real existence.*] I believe
that it may be said that connection is nothing else than
accordance or *relation*, taken generally. And I have remarked on this point that every relation is either of *comparison* or of *concurrence*. That of *comparison* gives
diversity and identity, either complete or partial; that
which makes the same or the diverse, the like or unlike.
Concurrence contains what you call co-existence, that is,
connection of existence. But when it is said that a thing
exists or that it has real existence, this existence itself
is the predicate; that is, it has a notion joined with the
idea in question, and there is connection between these
two notions. One may conceive also the *existence* of the
object of an idea, as the concurrence of this object with
the Ego. So I believe that it may be said that there is only
comparison or concurrence; but that comparison, which
marks identity or diversity, and the concurrence of the
thing with the Ego, are relations which deserve to be
distinguished among others. More exact and more profound researches might perhaps be made; but I content
myself here with making remarks.

· · ·

CHAPTER II.

Of the degrees of our knowledge.

§ 1. [*Intuitive.*] *Primitive* truths, which are known by
intuition, are of two kinds, like the *derivative*. They are
either truths of *reason*, or truths of *fact*. Truths of reason
are necessary, and those of fact are contingent. Primitive
truths of *reason* are those which I call by the general
name of *identical*, because it seems that they do nothing

but repeat the same thing without giving us any information. They are affirmative or negative. . . .

As respects *primitive truths of fact*, they are the immediate internal experiences of an *immediateness of feeling*. And here it is that the first truth of the Cartesians or of St. Augustine: *I think, hence I am*, that is, *I am a thing which thinks*, holds good. But it should be known that just as the identicals are general or particular, and that the one class is as clear as the other (since it is just as clear to say that *A is A*, as to say that *a thing is what it is*), so it is also with first truths of fact. For not only is it clear to me immediately that *I think*; but it is just as clear to me that *I have different thoughts*; that sometimes *I think of A*, and that sometimes *I think of B*, etc. Thus the Cartesian principle is good, but it is not the only one of its kind. You see by this that all *primitive truths* of reason or of fact have this in common, that they cannot be proved by anything more certain.

. . .

§ 14. [*Sensitive knowledge of particular existence.*] . . . But let us come to this controversy which the sceptics carry on with the dogmatists over the existence of things *outside of us*. We have already touched upon it, but it is necessary to return to it here. I have formerly discussed it thoroughly, both verbally and in writing, with the late Abbé Foucher, Canon of Dijon, a learned and subtle man.——Now I made him admit that the truth of sensible things consisted only in the *connection* of phenomena, which must have its reason, and that it is this which distinguishes them from dreams; but that the truth of our existence and of the cause of phenomena is of another kind, because it establishes substances; and that the sceptics spoiled whatever they say that is good, by carrying it too far, and by wishing even to extend their doubts to immediate experiences and to geometrical truths (a thing which M. Foucher, however, did not do), and to the other truths of reason, which he did a little too much. But to return to you, sir; you are right in saying that there is ordinarily a difference between feelings and imaginations; but the sceptics will say that more or less does not change the kind. Besides, although feelings are wont to be more vivid than imaginations, it is a fact nevertheless that there are cases where an imaginative person is impressed by his imaginations as much as or even more than another is by the truth of things; so that I believe that the true *criterion* as regards the objects of the senses is the *connection* of phenomena, that is, the connection of that which takes place in different places and times, and in the experience of different men, who are themselves, each to the others, very important phenomena on this score. And the connection of phenomena, which guarantees *truths of fact* in respect to sensible things outside of us, is verified by means of *truths of reason*; as the phenomena of optics are explained by geometry. However, it must be confessed that all this certainty is not of the highest degree, as you have well recognized. For it is not impossible, speaking metaphysically, that there may be a dream as continuous and lasting as the life of man; but it is a thing as contrary to reason as would be the fiction of a book which should be formed at haphazard by throwing the type together pell-mell. For the rest, it is also true that, provided the phenomena be connected, it does not matter whether they are called dreams or not, since experience shows that we are not deceived in the measures taken concerning phenomena when they are understood according to the truths of reason.

. . .

CHAPTER III.

Of the extent of human knowledge.

. . .

§ 6. [*"Whether any mere material being thinks or no."*] . . . In the first place, I declare to you, sir, that when one has only confused ideas of *thought* and of *matter,* as one ordinarily has, it is not to be wondered at if one does not see the means of solving such questions. It is as I have remarked before, that a person who has not ideas of the angles of a triangle except in the way in which one has them generally, will never think of finding out that they are always equal to two right angles. We must consider that *matter,* taken as a *complete being* (that is, *secondary matter* as opposed to *primary,* which is something simply passive and consequently incomplete), is only a mass, or that which results therefrom, and that every *real mass* supposes *simple substances* or *real unities;* and when we farther consider what belongs to the nature of these real unities, that is, *perception* and its consequences, we are transported, so to speak, into another world, that is to say, into the *intelligible world of substances,* whereas before we have been only among the *phenomena of the senses.* And this knowledge of the interior of matter sufficiently shows us of what it is naturally capable, and that every time that God shall give it organs fitted to express reasoning, the immaterial substance which reasons will not fail to be also given to it, by virtue of that harmony which is again a natural consequence of substances. Matter cannot subsist without immaterial substances, that is, without unities; after which it ought no longer to be asked whether God is at liberty to give them to it or not. And if these substances did not have in themselves the correspondence or harmony, of which I have just spoken, God would not act according to the natural order. To speak quite simply of *giving* or of *according* powers, is to return to the *naked faculties* of the schòolmen, and to imagine minute subsisting entities, which may come and go like the pigeons of a pigeon-house. It is making substances of them without thinking of it. The *primitive powers* constitute substances themselves; and the *derivative* powers, or, if you like, the faculties, are only *modes of being,* which must be derived from substances, and are not derived from matter, as a machine merely, that is, in so far as we consider it abstractly only as the *incomplete being* of primary matter, or the simply passive. Here I think that you will agree with me, sir, that it is not in the power of a mere mechanism to cause perception, sensation, reason, to arise. They must therefore spring from some other substantial thing. To wish God to act differently and give to things accidents which are not *modes of being,* or modifications derived from substances, is to resort to miracles and to what the schoolmen called the *obediential power,* by a sort of supernatural exaltation, as when certain theologians claim that the fire of hell burns disembodied souls; in which case it might be even doubted if it were the fire which acted, and if God did not himself produce the effect, by acting in place of the fire. . . .

The difficulty which remains is only in respect to those who wish to *imagine* what is only *intelligible,* as if they wanted to see sounds, or hear colors. . . .

CHAPTER IV.

Of the reality of human knowledge.

§§ 1–5. [*Knowledge placed in ideas may be all bare vision. Answer.*] Our certainty would be slight or rather none, if it had no other foundation for simple ideas than that which comes from the senses. Have you forgotten, sir, how I showed that ideas are originally in our mind and that even our thoughts come to us from our own depths, without its being possible for other creatures to have an immediate influence upon the soul. Moreover the ground of our certainty in regard to universal and eternal truths lies in the ideas themselves, independently of the senses; as also pure and intelligible ideas do not depend upon the senses, for example, that of being, of unity, of identity, etc. But the ideas of sensible qualities, as of color, of flavor, etc. (which in reality are only appearances), come to us from the senses, that is, from our confused perceptions. And the ground of the truth of contingent and particular things is in the succession, whereby the phenomena of the senses are connected just as the intelligible truths require. This is the difference which should be made between them; whereas that which you make here between simple and complex ideas, and complex ideas belonging to substances and to accidents, does not seem to me well founded, since all intelligible ideas have their archetypes in the eternal possibility of things.

. . .

CHAPTER V.
Of truth in general.

§§ 1 and 2. [1. *What truth is.* 2. *A right joining or separating of signs; i. e., ideas or words.*] . . . But what I find least to my taste in your definition of truth, is that truth is there sought in words. Thus the same meaning, being expressed in Latin, German, English, French, will not be the same truth, and it will be necessary to say with Hobbes, that truth depends on the good pleasure of men; which is speaking in a very strange way. Truth is even attributed to God, who you will admit (I think) has no need of signs. Finally, I have been already more than once surprised at the humor of your friends, who take pleasure in making essences and species, *nominal* truths.

We shall then have, also, *literal truths,* which may be distinguished into the truths of paper or of parchment, of the black of ordinary ink, or of printer's ink, if truths must be distinguished by signs. It is better, therefore, to place truths in the relation between the *objects* of ideas, which causes one to be included or not to be included in the other. This does not depend on languages and is common to us with God and the angels; and when God manifests a truth to us we acquire that which is in his understanding, for although there is an infinite difference between his ideas and ours as respects perfection and extent, it is always true that they agree in the same relation. It is therefore in this *relation* that truth must be placed, and we may distinguish between *truths,* which are independent of our good pleasure, and *expressions,* which we invent as seems good to us.

. . .

§ 11. [*Moral and metaphysical truth.*] *Moral* truth is called *veracity* by some, and *metaphysical truth* is taken commonly by metaphysicians for an attribute of being, but it is a very useless attribute and one almost void of meaning. Let us content ourselves with seeking truth in the correspondence of propositions which are in the mind with the things in question. It is true that I have also attributed truth to ideas in saying that ideas are true or false; but in that case I attribute it actually to the propositions which affirm the possibility of the object of the idea. And in this same sense it may be said farther that a *being is true,* that is to say, the proposition which affirms its actual, or at least, possible existence is true.

. . .

CHAPTER VII.
Of maxims.

§ 1. [*They are self-evident.*] This investigation is very useful and even important. But you must not imagine, sir, that it has been entirely neglected. You will find in a hundred places that the scholastic philosophers have said that these propositions are evident *ex terminis,* as soon as their terms are understood; so that they were persuaded that the force of conviction was founded on the apprehension of the terms, that is, in the connection of the ideas. But the geometricians have done much more: for they have undertaken very often to demonstrate them. . . . As regards *maxims,* they are sometimes taken for established propositions, whether they are evident or not. This might be well for beginners, whom scrupulousness arrests; but when the establishing of science is in question, it is another matter. They are also often taken thus in ethics and even by the logicians in their *Topics,* in which there is an abundance of them, but a part of this contains some which are sufficiently vague and obscure. For the rest, I said publicly and privately a long while ago that it would be important to demonstrate all the secondary axioms of which we ordinarily make use, by reducing them to *primitive,* or immediate and undemonstrable, *axioms,* which are those which I called recently and elsewhere, *identical* ones.

. . .

§ 7. It may always be said that this propositon, *I exist,* is most evident, being a proposition which cannot be proved by any other, or an *immediate truth.* And to say, *I think therefore I am,* is not properly to prove existence by thought, since to think and to be thinking are the same thing; and to say, *I am thinking* is already to say, *I am.* Nevertheless you may exclude this proposition from the number of axioms with some justice, for it is a proposition of fact, founded upon an immediate experience, and it is not a necessary proposition, whose necessity is seen in the immediate agreement of ideas. On the contrary, there is no one but God who sees how these two terms *I* and *existence* are connected, that is, why I exist. But if the axiom is taken more generally for an immediate or *non-provable* truth, it may be said that the proposition *I am* is an axiom, and in any case we may be assured that it is a *primitive truth* or *unum ex primis cognitis inter terminos complexos,* that is, that it is one of the first known statements, which is understood in the natural order of our knowledge; for it is possible that a man may never have thought of forming expressly this proposition, which is yet innate in him.

§§ 8, 9. I had further added that in the natural order to say that a thing is what it is, is prior to saying that it is not another; for here it is not a question of the history of our discoveries, which is different in different men, but of the connection and natural order of truths, which is always the same. But your remark, namely, that what the child sees is only fact, deserves still more reflection; for the experiences of the senses do not give absolutely certain truths (as you yourself observed, sir, not long ago), nor such as are free from all danger of illusion. For if it is permitted to make metaphysically possible fictions, sugar might be changed imperceptibly into a rod to punish a child if it has been naughty, just as water is changed into wine with us on Christmas Eve, if it has been well rectified [*morigené*]. But the pain (you will say) which the rod inflicts will never be the pleasure which the sugar gives. I reply that the child will think of making an express proposition concerning it as little as of remarking the axiom that it cannot be said truly that *what is, at the same time is not,* although it may very well perceive the difference between pleasure and pain, as well as the difference between perceiving and not perceiving.

§ 10. . . . Thus you must not here oppose the axiom and the example as different truths in this respect, but regard the axiom as incorporated in the example and rendering the example true. It is quite another thing when the evidence is not remarked in the example itself and when the affirmation of the example is a consequence and not merely a *subsumption* of the universal proposition, as may happen also in respect to axioms.

. . .

CHAPTER IX.

Of our knowledge of our own existence.

. . . §§ 2 and 3. [2. *A threefold knowledge of exist-ence. 3. Our knowledge of our own existence is intui-tive.*] I am fully in accord with all this. And I add that the immediate apperception of our existence and of our thoughts furnishes us the first truths *a posteriori,* or of fact, that is, the *first experiences;* as identical proposi-tions contain the first truths *a priori,* or of reason, that is, the *first lights.* Both are incapable of being proved, and may be called *immediate;* the former, because there is immediation between the understanding and its object, the latter, because there is immediation between the subject and predicate.

CHAPTER X.

Of our knowledge of the existence of God.

§ 1. . . . I do not wish to repeat what has been discussed between us concerning innate ideas and truths, among which I reckon the idea of God and the truth of his existence.

§§ 2–6. [2. *Man knows that he himself is. 3. He knows also that nothing cannot produce a being, therefore something is eternal. 4. That eternal being must be most powerful. 5. And most knowing. 6. And therefore God.*] I assure you, sir, with perfect sincerity, that I am extremely sorry to be obliged to say anything against this demonstration: but I do it in order to give you an opportunity to fill up the gap in it. It is principally in the passage where you conclude (§ 3) that something has existed from all eternity. I find ambiguity in it. If it means that *there has never been a time when nothing existed,* I agree to this; and it follows truly from the preceding propositions by a wholly mathematical sequence. For if there never had been anything, there would always have been nothing, nothing not being able to produce being; hence we ourselves would not be, which is contrary to the first truth of experience. But what follows shows at once that in saying that something has existed from all eternity, you mean an eternal thing. Nevertheless it does not follow, in virtue of what you have advanced up to this time, that if there has always been something, it has always been a certain thing, that is, that there is an eternal being. For some opponents will say that I myself have been produced by other things

and these things again by others. Farther, if some admit
eternal beings (as the Epicureans their atoms) they will
not believe themselves thereby obliged to grant an eternal
being which is alone the source of all others. For even
if they should admit that that which gives existence
gives also the other qualities and powers of a thing,
they will deny that a single thing gives existence to the
others, and they will even say that for each thing several
others must concur. Thus we will not arrive in this way
alone at one source of all powers. However, it is very
reasonable to judge that there is one, and even that the
universe is governed with wisdom. But if one believes
matter susceptible of thought, one may be disposed to
believe that it is not impossible that it may produce it.
At least it will be difficult to bring forward a proof of
it which should not show at the same time that matter
is altogether incapable of it; and supposing that our
thought comes from a thinking being, can it be taken for
granted without prejudice to the demonstration, that this
must be God?

§ 7. [*Our idea of a most perfect being, not the sole
proof of a God.*] Although I hold to innate ideas, and
particularly to that of God, I do not believe that the
demonstrations of the Cartesians drawn from the idea of
God, are perfect. . . . . This [ontological argument] is
not a paralogism, but it is an imperfect demonstration
which supposes something which has still to be proved
in order to render it mathematically evident. This is, that
it is tacitly supposed that this idea of the all-great or
all-perfect being is possible, and implies no contradiction. . . . . The other argument of M. Descartes which
undertakes to prove the existence of God because his idea
is in our soul and it must have come from the original,
is still less conclusive. For, in the first place, this argument has this defect, in common with the preceding, that

it supposes that there is in us such an idea, that is, that God is possible. . . . . And, secondly, this same argument does not sufficiently prove that the idea of God, if we have it, must come from the original. But I do not wish to delay here at present. You will say to me, sir, that recognizing in us the innate idea of God, I ought not to say that we may question whether there is one. But I permit this doubt only in relation to a strict demonstration, founded upon the idea alone. For we are sufficiently assured otherwise of the idea and of the existence of God. And you will remember that I have shown how ideas are in us, not always in such a way that we are conscious of them, but always so that we may draw them from our own depths and render them perceptible. And this is also what I believe of the idea of God, whose possibility and existence I hold to be demonstrated in more than one way. And the *Pre-established Harmony* itself furnishes a new and incontestable means of doing so. I believe besides that almost all the means which have been employed to prove the existence of God are good, and might serve, if they were perfected; and I am not at all of the opinion that the one which is drawn from the order of things is to be neglected.

§§ 9, 10. [9. *Two sorts of beings, cogitative and incogitative.* 10. *Incogitative being cannot produce a cogitative.*] I think the present reasoning the strongest in the world, and not only exact but also profound and worthy of its author. I am entirely of his opinion that no combination and modification of parts of matter, however small they may be, can produce perception; any more than the gross parts could give it (as is clearly evident), and as everything in the small parts is proportional to what may take place in the large ones. It is another important remark upon matter, which the author here makes, that it must not be taken for a thing single in number, or (as I am accustomed to say) for a true and perfect *monad* or *unity*, since it is but a *mass* of an infinite number of beings. Here this excellent author needed but one more step to reach my system. For in fact I give perception to all these infinite beings, each one of which is as an animal, endowed with a soul (or with some analogous active principle, which forms its true unity), together with what is necessary to this being in order to be passive and endowed with an organic body. Now these beings have received their nature, active and passive (that is, what they possess of immaterial and material), from a general and supreme cause, because otherwise, as the author well remarks, being independent each of the others, they could never produce that *order*, that *harmony*, that *beauty*, which we observe in nature. But this argument, which appears to be only of moral certainty, is brought to a necessity altogether metaphysical by the *new kind of harmony* which I have introduced, which is the *pre-established harmony*. For each one of these souls expressing in its manner that which takes place outside it and not being able to have any influence on other particular beings, or rather, being obliged to draw this expression from the depths of its own nature, each one must necessarily have received this nature (or this internal reason of the expressions of what is outside) from a universal cause on which all these beings depend, and which causes one to be perfectly in accord and correspondent with another; a thing which is not possible without an infinite knowledge and power, and by an artifice great as regards especially the spontaneous agreement of the mechanism with the actions of the rational soul. In regard to this, the illustrious author who made objections against it in his wonderful Dictionary, doubted whether it did not surpass all possible wisdom; saying that the wisdom of God did not appear to him too

great for such an effect, and he at least recognized that
never had the feeble conceptions which we are able to
have of the divine perfection, been so set in relief.

. . .

CHAPTER XI.

Of our knowledge of the existence of other things.

§§ 1–10. [*It is to be had only by sensation, etc.*] I
have already remarked in our preceding conversations
that the truth of sensible things is proved by their *connection,* which depends on the intellectual truths founded
in reason, and on the constant observations in sensible
things themselves, even when the reasons do not appear.
And as these reasons and observations give us the means
of judging of the future in relation to our interests, and
as success answers to our rational judgment, we could
not ask nor even have a greater certainty concerning
these objects. We can account also even for dreams and
for their slight connection with other phenomena. Nevertheless, I believe that the appellation of knowledge and
of certainty might be extended beyond actual sensations,
since clearness and manifestness extend beyond, which
I consider as a kind of certainty: and it would undoubtedly be folly to seriously doubt whether there are men
in the world when we do not see any. *To doubt seriously*
is to doubt in relation to practice, and *certainty* might
be taken for a knowledge of truth, of which one cannot
doubt in relation to practice without madness; and sometimes it is taken still more generally and applied to cases
where we cannot doubt without deserving to be greatly
blamed. But *evidence* would be a luminous certainty, that
is to say, where we do not doubt on account of the connection which we see between ideas. According to this

definition of certainty, we are certain that Constantinople is in the world, that Constantine and Alexander the Great and Julius Cæsar have lived. It is true that some peasant of Ardennes might with reason doubt of these, for want of information; but a man of letters and of the world could not do so without great derangement of mind.

§ 11. [*Past existence known by memory.*] It has already been remarked that our memory sometimes deceives us. And we believe it or not according as it is more or less vivid, and more or less connected with the things which we know. And even when we are assured of the principal fact we may often question the circumstances. . . .

§§ 13, 14. [13. *Particular propositions concerning existence are knowable.* 14. *And general propositions concerning abstract ideas.*] Your division appears to amount to mine, of *propositions of fact* and *propositions of reason.* Propositions of fact also may become general in a way, but it is by induction or observation; such that it is only a multitude of similar facts, as when it is observed that all quicksilver is evaporated by the force of fire; and this is not a perfect generalization because we do not see its necessity. General propositions of reason are necessary, although the reason also furnishes some which are not absolutely general and are only probable, as, for example, when we presume that an idea is possible until the contrary is discovered by a more exact research. There are, finally, *mixed propositions,* drawn from premises, some of which come from facts and observations, and others are necessary propositions: and such are a number of geographical and astronomical conclusions concerning the globe of the earth and the course of the stars, which spring from the combination of the observations of travelers and astronomers with the theorems of geometry and arithmetic. But as, according to the usage of logicians, *the conclusion follows the weakest of the premises* and cannot have more certainty than they, these mixed propositions have only the certainty and universality which belong to the observations. As regards *eternal truths,* it must be observed that at bottom they are all conditional and say in effect: such a thing posited, such another thing is. For example, in saying, *every figure which has three sides will also have three angles,* I do nothing but suppose that if there is a figure with three sides, *this same figure* will have three angles. . . .

The scholastics have disputed hotly *de constantia subjecti,* as they called it, that is, how the proposition made about a subject can have a real truth, if this subject does not exist. The fact is that the truth is only conditional, and says, that in case the subject ever exists, it will be found such. But it will be asked further, in what is this connection founded, since there is in it some reality which does not deceive? The reply will be that it is in the connection of ideas. But in answer it will be asked, where would these ideas be if no mind existed, and what then would become of the real foundation of this certainty of the eternal truths? This leads us finally to the ultimate ground of truths, namely, to that *Supreme and Universal Mind,* which cannot fail to exist, whose understanding, to speak truly, is the region of eternal truths, as St. Augustine has recognized and expressed in a sufficiently vivid way. And in order that it be not thought that it is unnecessary to recur to this, we must consider that these necessary truths contain the determining reason and the regulative principle of existences themselves, and, in a word, the laws of the universe. Thus these necessary truths, being anterior to the existence of contingent beings, it must be that they are founded in the existence of a necessary substance. Here it is that I find the original of the ideas and truths which are graven in our souls, not in the form of propositions, but as the sources whose opportune use will give rise presently to assertions.

CHAPTER XII.

Of the improvement of our knowledge.

. . . §§ 4–6. [*Dangerous to build upon precarious principles. But to compare clear complete ideas under steady names.*] I am surprised, sir, that you turn against maxims, that is, against evident principles, that which can and must be said against the principles assumed *gratis*. When one demands *praecognita* in the sciences, or anterior knowledges, which serve to ground science, he demands *known principles* and not arbitrary positions, the truth of which is not known; and even Aristotle understands that the inferior and subaltern sciences borrow their principles from other higher sciences where they have been demonstrated, except the first of the sciences, which we call metaphysics, which, according to him, asks nothing from the others, and furnishes them the principles of which they have need; and when he says δεῖ πιστεύειν τὸν μανθάνοντα, the apprentice must believe his master, his thought is that he must do it only while waiting, while he is not yet instructed in the higher sciences, so that it is only provisionally. Thus one is very far from receiving *gratuitous principles*. To this must be added, that even principles whose certainty is not complete may have their use if we build upon them only by demonstration; for although all the conclusions in this case are only conditional and are valid solely on the supposition that this principle is true, nevertheless, this connection itself and these conditional enunciations would at least be demonstrated; so that it were much to be desired that we had many books written in this way, where there would be no danger of error, the reader or disciple being warned of the condition. And practice will not be regulated by these conclusions except as the supposition shall be found verified otherwise. This method also serves very often itself to verify suppositions or hypotheses, when many conclusions arise from them, the truth of which is known otherwise, and sometimes this gives a perfect proof sufficient to demonstrate the truth of the hypothesis. . . .

. . . § 13. [*The true use of hypotheses.*] The art of discovering the causes of phenomena, or true hypotheses, is like the art of deciphering, where an ingenious conjecture often shortens the road very much. Lord Bacon began to put the art of experimenting into precepts, and Sir Robert Boyle had a great talent for practising it. But if the art of employing experiments and of drawing consequences therefrom is not joined to it, we shall never with the utmost cost attain to what a man of great penetration might discover at first sight. Descartes, who was assuredly such, has made a similar remark, in one of his letters, in regard to the method of the Chancellor of England; and Spinoza (whom I do not hesitate to quote when he says something good), in one of his letters to the late Mr. Oldenburg, Secretary of the Royal Society of England, printed among the posthumous works of this subtle Jew, makes a like reflection concerning a work by Mr. Boyle, who, to speak the truth, stops a little too long to draw from a great number of fine experiments no other conclusion than this which he might take for a principle, namely, that everything takes place in nature mechanically; a principle which can be rendered certain by reason alone, and never by experiments however numerous they may be.

. . .

7. ON NECESSITY AND CONTINGENCY.
(Letter to Coste, 1707)

I thank you very much for communicating to me the last additions and corrections of Locke, and I am pleased also to learn what you tell me of his last dispute with Limborch. The liberty of indifference, about which the dispute turns, and my opinion of which you, sir, ask, consists in a certain subtlety which few people trouble themselves to understand, and of which many people nevertheless reason. This carries us back to the consideration of necessity and of contingency.

A truth is *necessary* when the opposite implies contradiction, and when it is not necessary it is called *contingent*. That God exists, that all right angles are equal, etc., are necessary truths; but that I myself exist, and that there are bodies in nature which show an angle actually right, are contingent truths. For the whole universe might be otherwise; time, space, and matter being absolutely indifferent to motion and forms. And God has chosen among an infinite number of possibles what he judged most fit. But since he has chosen, it must be affirmed that everything is comprised in his choice and that nothing could be changed, since he has once for all foreseen and regulated all, he who could not regulate things piecemeal and by fits and starts. Therefore the sins and evils which he has judged proper to permit for greater goods, are comprised in his choice. This is the necessity, which can now be ascribed to things in the future, which is called *hypothetical or consequential* necessity (that is to say, founded upon the consequence of the hypothesis of the choice made), which does not destroy the contingency of things, and does not produce that absolute necessity which contingency does not allow. And nearly all theologians and philosophers (for we must except the Socinians) acknowledge the hypothetical necessity, which I have just explained, and which cannot be combated without overthrowing the attributes of God and even the nature of things.

Nevertheless, although all the facts of the universe are now certain in relation to God, or (what amounts to the same thing) are determined in themselves and even linked among themselves, it does not follow that their connection is always truly necessary; that is to say, that the truth, which pronounces that one fact follows another, is necessary. And this must be applied particularly to *voluntary actions.* When a choice is proposed, for example to go out or not to go out, it is a question whether, with all the circumstances, internal and external, motives, perceptions, dispositions, impressions, passions, inclinations taken together, I am still in a contingent state, or whether I am necessitated to make the decision, for example, to go out; that is to say, whether this proposition true and determined in fact, *In all these circumstances taken together I shall choose to go out,* is contingent or necessary. To this I reply that it is contingent, because neither I nor any other mind more enlightened than I, could demonstrate that the opposite of this truth implies contradiction. And supposing that by *liberty of indifference* is understood a liberty opposed to necessity (as I have just explained it), I acknowledge this liberty for I am really of opinion that our liberty, as well as that of God and of the blessed spirits, is exempt not only from co-action, but, furthermore, from absolute necessity, although it cannot be exempt from determination and from certainty.

But I find that there is need of great precaution here in order not to fall into a chimera which shocks the principles of good sense, and which would be what I call an *absolute indifference* or *an indifference of equilibrium*; which some conceive in liberty, and which I believe chimerical. It must be observed then that that connection, of which I just spoke, is not necessary, speaking absolutely, but that it is none the less certainly true, and that in general every time that in all the circumstances taken together the balance of deliberation is heavier on the one side than on the other, it is certain and infallible that that side will carry the day. God or the perfect sage would always choose the best that is known, and if one thing were no better than another, they would choose neither. In other intelligent subjects, passions often take the place of reason; and it can always be said in regard to the will in general that the *choice follows the greatest inclination,* under which I include everything, passions as well as reasons, true or apparent.

Nevertheless I see that there are people who imagine that we are determined sometimes to favor the side which is the less weighted; that God chooses sometimes the lesser good, everything considered; and that man chooses sometimes without object and against all his reasons, dispositions, and passions; finally, that one chooses sometimes without any reason which determines the choice. But this I hold to be false and absurd, since it is one of the greatest principles of good sense that nothing ever occurs without cause or determining reason. Thus, when God chooses, it is by reason of the best; when man chooses, it will be the side which shall have struck him most. If, moreover, he chooses that which he sees to be less useful and less agreeable, it will have become perhaps to him the most agreeable through caprice, through a spirit of contradiction, and through similar reasons of a depraved taste, which would none the less be determining reasons, even if they should not be conclusive reasons. And never can any example to the contrary be found.

Thus, although we have a liberty of indifference which saves us from necessity, we never have an indifference of equilibrium which exempts us from determining reasons; there is always something which inclines us and makes us choose, but without being able to necessitate us. And just as God is always infallibly led to the best although he is not led necessarily (other than by a moral necessity), so we are always infallibly led to that which strikes us most, but not necessarily. The contrary not implying any contradiction, it was not necessary or essential that God should create, nor that he should create this world in particular, although his wisdom and goodness should have led him to it.

It is this that M. Bayle, very subtle as he has been, has not sufficiently considered when he thought that a case similar to the ass of Buridan was possible, and that a man placed in circumstances of perfect equilibrium could none the less choose. For it must be said that the case of a perfect equilibrium is chimerical and never occurs, the universe not being able to be parted or cut into parts equal and alike. The universe is not like an ellipse or other such oval, which the straight line drawn through its centre can cut in two congruent parts. The universe has no center and its parts are infinitely varied; thus it will never happen that all will be perfectly equal and will strike equally from one side and from the other; and, although we are not always capable of perceiving all the little impressions which contribute to determine

us, there is always something which determines us between two contradictories, without the case ever being
perfectly equal on the one side and on the other.

Nevertheless, although our choice *ex datis* on all the
internal and external circumstances taken together, is
always determined, and although for the present it does
not depend upon us to change the will, it is none the
less true that we have great power over our future wills
by choosing certain objects of our attention and by
accustoming ourselves to certain ways of thinking; and
by this means we can accustom ourselves the better to
resist impressions and the better to make our reason act;
in short, we can contribute toward making ourselves will
what we ought to.

For the rest, I have elsewhere shown, that, regarding
matters in a certain metaphysical sense, we are always in
a state of perfect spontaneity, and that what is attributed to the impressions of external things comes only
from confused perceptions in us which correspond to
them, and which cannot but be given us at the start in
virtue of the pre-established harmony which establishes
the connection of each substance with all others.

If it were true, sir, that our Sevennese were prophets,
that event would not be contrary to my hypothesis of the
Pre-established Harmony and would even be in thorough
agreement with it. I have always said that the present
is big with the future and that there is a perfect connection between things however distant they may be one
from another, so that one of sufficient penetration might
read the one in the other. I should not even oppose one
who should maintain that there are globes in the universe
where prophecies are more common than on our own, as
there will perhaps be a world in which dogs will have
sufficiently good noses to scent their game at a thousand
leagues; perhaps also there are globes in which genii

have more freedom than here below to mix in the actions
of rational animals. But when the question is to reason
on what is actually practised here, our presumptive judgment must be founded on the habits of our globe, where
prophetic views of this sort are very rare. We cannot
swear that there are none, but we could wager that these
in question are not such. One of the reasons which would
most lead me to judge favorably of them would be the
judgment of M. Fatio, but it would be necessary to know
his opinion without taking it from the newspaper. If
you had with all due attention associated yourself with
a gentleman with an income of £2000 sterling who
prophesies in Greek, in Latin, and in French, although
he only knows English well, there would be no point in
refuting him. So I beg you, sir, to enlighten me more on
a matter so interesting and important. I am, etc.

8. REFUTATION OF SPINOZA
[c. 1708]

The author [Wachter] passes on (ch. 4) to Spinoza,
whom he compares with the cabalists. Spinoza (Eth.,
pt. 2, prop. 10, schol.) says: "Every one must admit that
nothing is or can be conceived without God. For it is
acknowledged by everyone that God is the sole cause
of all things, of their essence as well as of their existence; that is, God is the cause of things, not only in respect to their being made (*secundum fieri*), but also in
respect to their being (*secundum esse*)." This, from
Spinoza, the author [Wachter] appears to approve. And
it is true that we must speak of created things only as
permitted by the nature of God. But I do not think that
Spinoza has succeeded in this. Essences can in a certain
way be conceived of without God, but existences involve
God. And the very reality of essences by which they
exert an influence upon existences is from God. The

essences of things are co-eternal with God. And the very essence of God embraces all other essences to such a degree that God cannot be perfectly conceived without them. But existence cannot be conceived of without God, who is the final reason of things.

This axiom, "To the essence of a thing belongs that without which it can neither be nor be conceived," is to be applied in necessary things or in species, but not in individuals or contingent things. For individuals cannot be distinctly conceived. Hence they have no necessary connection with God, but are produced freely. God has been inclined toward these by a determining reason, but he has not been necessitated.

Spinoza (de Emend. Intel., p. 374) places among fictions the dictum, "Something can be produced from nothing." But, in truth, modes which are produced, are produced from nothing. Since there is no matter of modes, assuredly neither the mode, nor a part of it, has pre-existed, but only another mode which has disappeared and to which this present one has succeeded.

The cabalists seem to say that matter, on account of the vileness of its essence, can neither be created nor can it exist; hence, that there is absolutely no matter, or that spirit and matter, as Henry More maintains in his cabalistic theses, are one and the same thing. Spinoza, likewise, denies that God could have created any corporeal and material mass to be the subject of this world, "because," he says, "those who differ do not know by what divine power it could have been created." There is some truth in these words, but I think it is not sufficiently understood. Matter does, in reality, exist, but it is not a substance, since it is an aggregate or resultant of substances: I speak of matter as far as it is secondary or an extended mass which is not at all a homogeneous body. But that which we conceive of as homogeneous and call primary matter is something incomplete, since it is merely potential. Substance, on the contrary, is something full and active.

Spinoza believed that matter, as commonly understood, did not exist. Hence he often warns us that matter is badly defined by Descartes as extension (Ep. 73), and extension is poorly explained as a very low thing which must be divisible in space, "since (de Emend. Intel., p. 385) matter ought to be explained as an attribute expressing an eternal and infinite essence." I reply that extension, or if you prefer, primary matter, is nothing but a certain indefinite repetition of things as far as they are similar to each other or indiscernible. But just as number supposes numbered things, so extension supposes things which are repeated, and which have, in addition to common characteristics, others peculiar to themselves. These accidents, peculiar to each other, render the limits of size and shape, before only possible, actual. Merely passive matter is something very low, that is, wanting in all force, but such a thing consists only in the incomplete or in abstraction.

Spinoza (Eth., pt. 1, prop. 13, corol. and prop. 15, schol.) says: "No substance, not even corporeal substance, is divisible." This statement is not surprising according to his system, since he admits but one substance; but it is equally true in mine, although I admit innumerable substances, for, in my system, all are indivisible or *monads*.

He says (Eth., pt. 3, prop. 2, schol.) that "the mind and the body are the same thing, only expressed in two ways," and (Eth., pt. 2, prop. 7, schol.) that "thinking substance and extended substance are one and the same, known now under the attribute of thought, now under that of extension." He says in the same scholium, "This, certain Hebrews seem to have seen as through a cloud, who indeed maintain that God, the intellect of God, and the things known by it, are one and the same." This is not my opinion. Mind and body are not the same any more than are the principle of action and that of passion. Corporeal substance has a soul and an organic body, that is, a mass made up of other substances. It is true that the same substance thinks and has an extended mass joined to it, but it does not consist of this mass, since all this can be taken away from it, without altering the substance; moreover, every substance perceives, but not every substance thinks. Thought indeed belongs to the monads, especially all perception, but extension belongs to compounds. It can no more be said that God and the things known by God are one and the same thing than that the mind and the things perceived by the mind are the same. The author [Wachter] believes that Spinoza posited a common nature in which the attributes thought and extension reside, and that this nature is spiritual; but there is no extension belonging to spirits unless the word be taken in a broader sense for a certain ethereal animal such as angels were thought to be by the ancients. The author [Wachter] adds that mind and body are the modes of these attributes. But how, I ask, can the mind be the mode of thought, when it is the principle of thought? Thus the mind should rather be the attribute and thought the modification of this attribute. It is astonishing also that Spinoza, as was seen above (de Emend. Intel., p. 385), seems to deny that extension is divisible into and composed of parts; which has no meaning, unless, perchance, like space, it is not a divisible thing. But space and time are orders of things and not things.

The author [Wachter] rightly says, that God found in himself the origins of all things, as I remember Julius Scaliger once said that "things are not produced by the

passive power of matter but by the active power of God."
And I assert this of forms or of activities or entelechies.

What Spinoza (Eth., pt. 1, prop. 34) says, that "God
is, by the same necessity, the cause of himself and the
cause of all things," and (Polit. Tract., p. 270, c. 2, no.
2) that "the power of things is the power of God," I do
not admit. God exists necessarily, but he produces things
freely, and the power of things is produced by God but
is different from the divine power, and things themselves
operate, although they have received their power to act.

Spinoza (Ep. 21) says: "That everything is in God
and moves in God, I assert with Paul and perhaps with
all other philosophers, although in a different manner.
I would even dare to say that this was the opinion of
all the ancient Hebrews, so far as it can be conjectured
from certain traditions, although these are in many
ways corrupted." I think that everything is in God, not
as the part in the whole, nor as an accident in a subject,
but as place, yet a place spiritual and enduring and not
one measured or divided, is in that which is placed,
namely, just as God is immense or everywhere; the world
is present to him. And it is thus that all things are in
him; for he is where they are and where they are not,
and he remains when they pass away and he has already
been there when they come into existence.

The author [Wachter] says that it is the concordant
opinion of the cabalists that God produced certain things
mediately and others immediately. Whence he next speaks
of a certain created first principle which God made to
proceed immediately from himself, and by the mediation
of which all other things have been produced in series
and in order, and this they are wont to salute by various
names: Adam Cadmon, Messiah, the Christ, λόγος, the
word, the first-born, the first man, the celestial man,
the guide, the shepherd, the mediator, etc. Elsewhere he

gives a reason for this assertion. The fact itself is recognized by Spinoza, so that nothing is wanting except the name. "It follows," he says (Eth., pt. 1, prop. 28, schol.), "in the second place, that God cannot properly be called the remote cause of individual things, except to distinguish these from those which God produces immediately or rather which follow from his absolute nature." Moreover what those things are which are said to follow from the absolute nature of God, he explained (prop. 21) thus: "All things which follow from the absolute nature of any attribute of God must exist always and be infinite or are eternal and infinite through the same attribute."— These propositions of Spinoza, which the author cites, are wholly without foundation. God produces no infinite creature, nor could it be shown or pointed out by any argument in what respect such a creature would differ from God.

The theory of Spinoza, namely, that from each attribute there springs a particular infinite thing, from extension a certain something infinite in extension, from thought a certain infinite understanding, arises from his varied imagination of certain heterogeneous divine attributes, like thought and extension, and perhaps innumerable others: For in reality extension is not an attribute of itself since it is only the repetition of perceptions. An infinitely extended thing is only imaginary: an infinite thinking being is God himself. The things which are necessary and which proceed from the infinite nature of God, are the eternal truths. A particular creature is produced by another, and this again by another. Thus, therefore, by no conception could we reach God even if we should suppose a progress *ad infinitum,* and, notwithstanding, the last no less than the one which precedes is dependent upon God.

Tatian says, in his *Oration to the Greeks,* that there

is a spirit dwelling in the stars, the angels, the plants, the waters and men, and that this spirit, although one and the same, contains differences in itself. But this doctrine I do not approve. It is the error of the world-soul universally diffused, and which, like the air in pneumatic organs, makes different sounds in different organs. Thus when a pipe is broken, the soul will desert it and will return into the world-soul. But we must know that there are as many incorporeal substances, or if you will, souls, as there are natural, organic mechanisms.

But what Spinoza (Eth., pt. 2, prop. 13, schol.) says: "All things, although in different degrees, are animated," rests upon another strange doctrine, "for," he says, "of everything there is necessarily in God an idea, of which God is the cause, in the same way as there is an idea of the human body." But there is plainly no reason for saying that the soul is an idea. Ideas are something purely abstract, like numbers and figures, and cannot act. Ideas are abstract and numerical: the idea of each animal is a possibility, and it is an illusion to call souls immortal because ideas are eternal, as if the soul of a globe should be called eternal because the idea of a spherical body is eternal. The soul is not an idea, but the source of innumerable ideas, for it has, besides the present idea, something active, or the production of new ideas. But according to Spinoza, at any moment the soul will be different because the body being changed the idea of the body is different. Hence it is not strange if he considers creatures as transitory modifications.—The soul, therefore, is something vital or something containing active force.

Spinoza (Eth., pt. 1, prop. 16) says: "From the necessity of the divine nature must follow an infinite number of things in infinite modes, that is to say, all things which can fall under infinite intellect." This is a most false

opinion, and this error is the same as that which Descartes insinuated, viz., that matter successively assumes
all forms. Spinoza begins where Descartes ended, *in
Naturalism*. He is wrong also in saying (Ep. 58) that
"the world is the effect of the divine nature," although
he almost adds that it was not made by chance. There
is a mean between what is necessary and what is fortuitous, namely, what is free. The world is a voluntary
effect of God, but on account of inclining or prevailing
reasons. And even if the world should be supposed perpetual nevertheless it would not be necessary. God could
either not have created it or have created it otherwise,
but he was not to do it. Spinoza thinks (Ep. 49) that
"God produces the world by that necessity by which he
knows himself." But it must be replied that things are
possible in many ways, whereas it was altogether impossible that God should not know himself.—Spinoza says
(Eth., pt. 1, prop. 17, schol.): "I know that there are
many who believe that they can prove that sovereign
intelligence and free will belong to the nature of God;
for they say they know nothing more perfect to attribute
to God than that which is the highest perfection in us.
. . . . Therefore, they prefer to assert that God is indifferent to all things, and that he creates nothing except
what he has decided, by some absolute will, to create.
But I think I have shown (Prop. 16) sufficiently clearly
that all things follow from the sovereign power of God
by the same necessity; in the same way as it follows
from the nature of a triangle that its three angles are
equal to two right angles."—From the first words it is
evident that Spinoza does not attribute to God intellect
and will. He is right in denying that God is indifferent
and that he decrees anything by absolute will: he decrees
by a will which is based on reasons. That things proceed
from God as the properties of a triangle proceed from

its nature is proved by no argument, besides there is no analogy between essences and existing things.

In the scholium of Proposition 17, Spinoza says that "the intellect and the will of God agree with ours only in name, because ours are posterior and God's are prior to things"; but it does not follow from this, that they agree only in name. Elsewhere, nevertheless, he says that "thought is an attribute of God, and that particular modes of thought must be referred to it (Eth., pt. 2, prop. 1)." But the author [Wachter] thinks that he is speaking there of the eternal word of God, because he says (Eth., pt. 5) "that our mind is a part of the infinite intellect."

"The human mind," says Spinoza (Eth., pt. 5, prop. 23, proof), "cannot be entirely destroyed with the body, but there remains something of it which is eternal. But this has no relation to time, for we attribute duration to the mind only during the duration of the body." In the scholium following, he adds, "This idea which expresses the essence of the body under the form of eternity [*sub specie æternitatis*] is a certain mode of thought which belongs to the essence of the mind and which is necessarily eternal, etc." This is illusory. This idea is like the figure of the sphere, the eternity of which does not prejudge its existence, since it is but the possibility of an ideal sphere. Thus it is saying nothing to say that "our mind is eternal in so far as it expresses the body under the form of eternity," and it would be likewise eternal because it understands eternal truths as to the triangle. "Our soul has no duration nor does time relate to anything beyond the actual existence of the body." Thus Spinoza, *l. c.*, who thinks that the mind perishes with the body because he believes that only a single body remains always, although this can be transformed.

The author [Wachter] adds: "I do not see that Spi-

noza has anywhere said positively that minds migrate
from one body into another, and into different dwellings
and various regions of eternity. Nevertheless it might
be inferred from his thought." But he errs. The same
soul, to Spinoza, cannot be the idea of another body, as
the figure of a sphere is not the figure of a cylinder.
The soul, to Spinoza, is so fugitive that it does not exist
even in the present moment, and the body too only exists
in idea. Spinoza says (Eth., pt. 5, prop. 2) that "memory
and imagination disappear with the body." But I for my
part think that some imagination and some memory always remain, and that, without them, there would be no
soul. It must not be believed that the mind exists without
feeling or without a soul. A reason without imagination
and memory is a conclusion without premises. Aristotle,
also, thought that νους, mind, or the active intellect remains, and not the soul. But the soul itself acts and the
mind is passive.

Spinoza (de Emend. Intel., p. 384) says, "The ancients never, to my knowledge, conceived, as we do here,
a soul acting according to certain laws and like a spiritual *automa*" (he meant to say *automaton*). The author
[Wachter] interprets this passage of the soul alone and
not of the mind, and says that the soul acts according to
the laws of motion and according to external causes.
Both are mistaken. I say that the soul acts spontaneously
and yet like a spiritual automaton; and that this is true
also of the mind. The soul is not less exempt than the
mind from impulses from external things, and the soul
no more than the mind acts determinately; as in bodies
everything is done by motions according to the laws of
force, so in the soul everything is done through effort
or desire, according to the laws of God. The two realms
are in harmony. It is true, nevertheless, that there are
certain things in the soul which cannot be explained in

an adequate manner except by external things, and so far the soul is subject to the external; but this is not a physical influx, but so to speak a moral one, in so far, namely, as God, in creating the mind, had more regard to other things than to it itself. For in the creation and preservation of each thing he has regard to all other things.

Spinoza is wrong in calling [Eth., pt. 3, 9, schol.] the will the effort of each thing to persist in its being; for the will tends toward more particular ends and a more perfect mode of existence. He is wrong also in saying [pt. 3, prop. 7] that the effort is identical with the essence, whereas the essence is always the same and efforts vary. I do not admit that affirmation is the effort of the mind to persist in its being, that is, to preserve its ideas. We have this effort even when we affirm nothing. Moreover, with Spinoza, the mind is an idea, it does not have ideas. He is also wrong in thinking that affirmation or negation is volition, since, moreover, volition involves, in addition, the reason of the Good.

Spinoza (Ep. 2, at Oldenb.) says that "the will differs from this or that volition, just as whiteness from this or that white color: consequently, will is not the cause of volition, as humanity is not the cause of Peter and of Paul. Particular volitions have therefore need of another cause. The will is only an entity of reason." So Spinoza. But we take the will for the power of choosing, the exercise of which is the volition. Therefore it is indeed by the will that we will; but it is true that there is need of other special causes to determine the will, namely, in order that it produce a certain volition. It must be modified in a certain manner. The will does not therefore stand to volitions as the species or the abstract of the species to individuals. Mistakes are not free nor acts of will, although often we concur in our errors by free actions.

Further, Spinoza says (Tract. Polit., c. 2, no. 6), "Men conceive themselves in nature as an empire within an empire (Malcuth in Malcuth, adds the author). For they think that the human mind is not the product of natural causes, but that it is immediately created by God so independent of other things that it has absolute power of determining itself and of using rightly its reason. But experience proves to us over-abundantly that it is no more in our power to have a sound mind than to have a sound body." So Spinoza. In my opinion, each substance is an empire within an empire; but harmonizing exactly with all the rest it receives no influence from any being except it be from God, but, nevertheless, through God, its author, it depends upon all the others. It comes immediately from God and yet it is created in conformity to the other things. For the rest, not all things are equally in our power. For we are inclined more to this or to that. Malcuth, or the realm of God, does not suppress either divine or human liberty, but only the indifference of equilibrium, as they say who think there are no reasons for those actions which they do not understand.

Spinoza thinks that the mind is greatly strengthened if it knows that what happens happens necessarily: but by this compulsion he does not render the heart of the sufferer content nor cause him to feel his malady the less. He is, on the contrary, happy if he understands that good results from evil and that those things which happen are the best for us if we are wise.

From what precedes it is seen that what Spinoza says on the intellectual love of God (Eth., pt. 4, prop. 28) is only trappings for the people, since there is nothing loveable in a God who produces without choice and by necessity, without discrimination of good and evil. The true love of God is founded not in necessity but in goodness. Spinoza (de Emend. Intel., p. 388) says that "there is no science, but that we have only experience of particular things, that is, of things such that their existence has no connection with their essence, and which, consequently, are not eternal truths."—This contradicts what he said elsewhere, viz.: that all things are necessary, that all things proceed necessarily from the divine essence. Likewise he combats (Eth., pt. 2, prop. 10, schol.) those who claim that the nature of God belongs to the essence of created things, and yet he had established before [Eth., pt. 1, prop. 15] that things do not exist and cannot be conceived without God, and that they necessarily arise from him. He maintains (Eth., pt. 1, prop. 21), for this reason, that finite and temporal things cannot be produced immediately by an infinite cause, but that (Prop. 28) they are produced by other causes, individual and finite. But how will they finally then spring from God? For they cannot come from him mediately in this case, since we could never reach in this way things which are not similarly produced by another finite thing. It cannot, therefore, be said that God acts by mediating secondary causes, unless he produces secondary causes. Therefore, it is rather to be said that God produces substances and not their actions, in which he only concurs.

9. REMARKS ON THE OPINION OF MALEBRANCHE THAT *WE SEE ALL THINGS IN GOD*, WITH REFERENCE TO LOCKE'S EXAMINATION OF IT
[c. 1708]

There is, in the posthumous works of Locke published at London in 1706, 8vo., an examination of the opinion of Malebranche that we see all things in God. Locke acknowledged at the start that there are many nice thoughts and judicious reflections in the book on *The*

Search after Truth, and that this made him hope to find therein something satisfactory on the nature of our ideas. But he has remarked at the beginning (§ 2) that this father [Malebranche] makes use of what Locke calls the *argumentum ad ignorantiam,* in pretending to prove his opinion, because there is no other means of explaining the thing: but according to Mr. Locke, this argument loses its force when the feebleness of our understanding is considered. I am nevertheless of opinion that this argument is good if one can completely enumerate the means and exclude all but one. Even in Analysis, M. Frenicle employed this method of exclusion, as he called it. Nevertheless, Locke is right in saying that it is of no use to say that this hypothesis is better than others, if it is found not to explain what one would like to understand, and even to involve things which cannot be reconciled.

After having considered what is said in the first chapter of the second part of book third, where Malebranche claims that what the soul can perceive must be in immediate contact with it, Mr. Locke asks (§§ 3, 4) what it is to be in *immediate contact,* this not appearing to him intelligible except in bodies. Perhaps it might be replied that one thing acts immediately on the other. And as Malebranche, admitting that our bodies are united to our souls, adds that it is not in such a way that the soul perceives it, he is asked (§ 5) to explain that sort of union or at least in what it differs from that which he does not admit? Father Malebranche will perhaps say that he does not know the union of the soul with the body except by faith, and that the nature of body consisting in extension alone, nothing can be deduced therefrom toward explaining the soul's action on the body. He grants an inexplicable union, but he demands one which shall serve to explain the commerce of the soul and body.

He claims also to explain why material beings could not be united with the soul as is demanded; this is because these beings being extended and the soul not being so, there is no similarity [*proportion*] between them. But thereupon Locke asks very *à propos* (§ 7) if there is any more similarity between God and the soul. It seems indeed that the Reverend Father Malebranche ought to have urged not the little similarity, but the little connection, which appears between the soul and the body, while between God and his creatures there is a connection such that they could not exist without him.

When the Father says (§ 6) that there is no purely intelligible substance except God, I declare that I do not sufficiently understand him. There is something in the soul that we do not distinctly understand; and there are many things in God that we do not at all understand.

Mr. Locke (§ 8) makes a remark on the end of the Father's chapter which is tantamount to my views; for in order to show that the Father has not excluded all the means of explaining the matter, he adds: "If I should say that it is possible that God has made our souls such, and has so united them to bodies that, at certain motions of the body, the soul should have such and such perceptions but in a manner inconceivable to us, I should have said something as apparent and as instructive as that which he says." Mr. Locke in saying this seems to have had in mind my system of Pre-established Harmony, or something similar.

Mr. Locke objects (§ 20) that the sun is useless if we see it in God. As this argument applies also against my system, which claims that we see the sun in us, I answer that the sun is not made solely for us and that God wishes to show us the truth as to what is outside us. He objects (§ 22) that he does not conceive how we could see something confusedly in God, where there is no confusion. One might answer that we see things confusedly when we see too many of them at a time.

Father Malebranche having said that God is the place of spirits as space is the place of bodies, Mr. Locke says (§ 25) that he does not understand a word of this. But he understands at least what space, place and body are. He understands also that the Father draws an analogy between *space, place, body* and *God, place, spirit*. Thus a good part of what he here says is intelligible. It may merely be objected that this analogy is not proven, although some relations are easily perceived which might give occasion for the comparison. I often observe that certain persons seek by this affectation of ignorance to elude what is said to them as if they understood nothing; they do this not to reproach themselves, but either to reproach those speaking, as if their jargon was unintelligible, or to exalt themselves above the matter and those who tell it, as if it was not worthy of their attention. Nevertheless Mr. Locke is right in saying that the opinion of Father Malebranche is unintelligible in connection with his other opinions, since with him space and body are the same thing. The truth has escaped him here and he has conceived something common and immutable, to which bodies have an essential relation and which indeed produces their relation to one another. This order gives occasion for making a fiction and for conceiving space as an immutable substance; but what there is real in this notion relates to simple substances (under which spirits are included), and is found in God, who unites them.

The Father saying that ideas are representative beings, Mr. Locke asks (§ 26) if these beings are substances, modes or relations? I believe that it may be said that they are nothing but relations resulting from the attitudes of God.

When Mr. Locke declares (§ 31) that he does not understand how the variety of ideas is compatible with the simplicity of God, it appears to me that he ought not raise an objection on this score against Father Malebranche, for there is no system which can make such a thing comprehensible. We cannot comprehend the incommensurable and a thousand other things, the truth of which we nevertheless know, and which we are right in employing to explain others which are dependent on them. There is something approximating this in all simple substances where there is a variety of affections in the unity of substance.

The Father maintains that the idea of the *infinite* is prior to that of the finite. Mr. Locke objects (§ 34) that a child has the idea of a number or of a square sooner than that of the infinite. He is right, taking the ideas for images; but in taking them as the foundations of notions, he will find that in the *continuum* the notion of an extended, taken absolutely, is prior to the notion of an extended where the modification is added. This must be further applied to what is said in §§ 42 and 46.

The argument of the Father which Mr. Locke examines (§ 40), that God alone, being the goal of minds, is also their sole object, is not to be despised. It is true that it needs something in order to be called a demonstration. There is a more conclusive reason which shows that God is the sole immediate external object of minds, and that is that there is naught but he which can act on them.

It is objected (§ 41) that the Apostle begins with the knowledge of creatures in order to lead us to God and that the Father does the contrary. I believe that these methods harmonize. The one proceeds *a priori,* the other *a posteriori;* and the latter is the more common. It is true that the best way to know things is through their causes; but this is not the easiest. It requires too much attention and men ordinarily give their attention to things of sense.

In replying to § 34, I have noticed the difference there is between image and idea. It seems that this difference is combated (§ 38) by finding difficulty in the difference which there is between prehension (*sentiment*) and idea. But I think that the Father understands by prehension (*sentiment*) a perception of the imagination, whereas there may be ideas of things which are not sensible nor imaginable. I affirm that we have as clear an idea of the color of the violet as of its figure (as is objected here) but not as distinct nor as intelligible.

Mr. Locke asks if an indivisible and unextended substance can have at the same time modifications different from and even relating to inconsistent objects. I reply, Yes. That which is inconsistent in the same object is not inconsistent in the representation of different objects, conceived at the same time. It is not therefore necessary that there be different parts in the soul, as it is not necessary that there be different parts in a point although different angles come together there.

It is asked with reason (§ 43) how we know creatures, if we do not see immediately aught but God? Because the objects, the representation of which God causes us to have, have something which resembles the idea we have of substance, and it is this which makes us judge that there are other substances.

It is assumed (§ 46) that God has the idea of an angle which is the nearest to the right angle, but that he does not show it to anyone, however one may desire to have it. I reply that such an angle is a fiction, like the fraction nearest to unity, or the number nearest to zero, or the least of all numbers. The nature of continuity does not permit any such thing.

The Father had said, that we know our soul by an

inner feeling of consciousness, and that for this reason the knowledge of our soul is more imperfect than that of things, which we know in God. Mr. Locke thereon remarks very à *propos* (§ 47), that the idea of our soul being in God as well as that of other things, we should see it also in God. The truth is that we see all things in ourselves and in our souls, and that the knowledge which we have of the soul is very true and just provided that we attend to it; that it is by the knowledge which we have of the soul that we know being, substance, God himself, and that it is by reflection on our thoughts that we know extension and bodies. And it is true, nevertheless, that God gives us all there is that is positive in this, and all perfection therein involved, by an immediate and continual emanation, by virtue of the dependence on him which all creatures have; and it is thus that a good meaning may be given to the phrase that God is the object of our souls and that we see all things in him.

Perhaps the design of the Father in the saying, which is examined (§ 53) that we see the essences of things in the perfections of God and that it is the universal reason which enlightens us, tends to show that the attributes of God are the bases of the simple notions which we have of things—being, power, knowledge, diffusion, duration, taken absolutely, being in him and not being in creatures save in a limited way.

10. ON THE ACTIVE FORCE OF BODY, ON THE SOUL AND ON THE SOUL OF BRUTES.
(Letter to Wagner, 1710)

1. I willingly reply to the inquiries you make as to the nature of the soul, for I see from the doubt which you present that my view is not sufficiently clear to you,

and that this is due to some prejudice drawn from my essay, inserted in the *Acta Eruditorum,* wherein I treated, in opposition to the illustrious Sturm, of the active force of body. You say that I have there sufficiently vindicated active force for matter, and while I attribute resistance to matter, I have also attributed reaction to the same, and consequently action; that since therefore there is everywhere in matter an active principle, this principle seems to suffice for the actions of brutes, nor is there need in them of an incorruptible soul.

2. I reply, in the first place, that the active principle is not attributed by me to bare or primary matter, which is merely passive, and consists only in *antitypia* and extension; but to body or to clothed or secondary matter, which in addition contains a primitive *entelechy,* or active principle. I reply, secondly, that the resistance of bare matter is not action, but mere passivity, inasmuch as it has antitypia or impenetrability, by which indeed it resists whatever would penetrate it, but does not react, unless there be added an elastic force, which must be derived from motion, and therefore the active force of matter must be superadded. I reply, thirdly, that this active principle, this first entelechy, is, in fact, a vital principle, endowed also with the faculty of perception, and incorruptible, for reasons recently stated by me. And this is the very thing which in brutes I hold to be their soul. While, therefore, I admit active principles superadded everywhere in matter, I also posit, everywhere disseminated through it, vital or percipient principles, and thus monads, and so to speak, metaphysical atoms wanting parts and incapable of being produced or destroyed naturally.

3. You next ask my definition of *soul.* I reply that soul may be employed in a broad and in a strict sense. Broadly speaking, soul will be the same as life or vital principle,

that is, the principle of internal action existing in the
simple thing or monad, to which external action corresponds. And this correspondence of internal and external, or representation of the external in the internal,
of the composite in the simple, of multiplicity in unity,
constitutes in reality perception. But in this sense, soul
is attributed not only to animals, but also to all other
percipient beings. In the strict sense, soul is employed
as a noble species of life, or sentient life, where there is
not only the faculty of perceiving, but in addition that
of feeling, inasmuch, indeed, as attention and memory
are joined to perception. Just as, in turn, mind is a
nobler species of soul, that is, mind is rational soul,
where reason, or ratiocination from universality of truths,
is added to feeling. As therefore mind is rational soul,
so soul is sentient life, and life is perceptive principle.
I have shown, moreover, by examples and arguments,
that not all perception is feeling, but that there is also
insensible perception. For example, I could not perceive
green unless I perceived blue and yellow, from which
it results. At the same time, I do not feel blue and yellow, unless perchance a microscope is employed.

4. You will remember, moreover, that according to my
opinion, not only are all lives, all souls, all minds, all
primitive entelechies, everlasting, but also that to each
primitive entelechy or each vital principle there is perpetually united a certain natural mechanism, which
comes to us under the name of organic body: which
mechanism, moreover, even although it preserves its form
in general, remains in flux, and is, like the ship of
Theseus, perpetually repaired. Nor, therefore, can we
be certain that the smallest particle of matter received
by us at birth, remains in our body, even although the
same mechanism is by degrees completely transformed,
augmented, diminished, involved or evolved. Hence, not

only is the soul everlasting, but also some animal always remains, although no particular animal ought to be called everlasting, since the animal species does not remain; just as the caterpillar and the butterfly are not the same animal, although the same soul is in both. Every natural mechanism, therefore, has this quality, that it is never completely destructible, since, however thick a covering may be dissolved, there always remains a little mechanism not yet destroyed, like the costume of Harlequin, in the comedy, to whom, after the removal of many tunics, there always remained a fresh one. And we ought to be the less astonished at this for this reason, that nature is everywhere organic and ordered by a most wise author for certain ends, and that nothing in nature ought to be criticized as unpolished, although it may sometimes appear to our senses as but a rude mass. Thus, therefore, we escape all the difficulties which arise from the nature of a soul absolutely separated from all matter; so that, in truth, a soul or an animal before birth or after death differs from a soul or an animal living the present life only by conditions of things and degrees of perfections, but not by entire genus of being. And likewise I think that genii are minds endowed with bodies very penetrating and suitable for action, which perhaps they are able to change at will; whence they do not deserve to be called even animals. Thus all things in nature are analogous, and the subtile may be understood from the coarse, since both are constituted in the same way. God alone is substance really separated from matter, since he is *actus purus,* endowed with no passive power, which, wherever it is, constitutes matter. And, indeed, all created substances have antitypia, by which it happens naturally that one is outside another, and so penetration is excluded.

5. But although my principles are very general and

hold not less in man than in brutes, yet man stands out marvellously above brutes and approaches the genii, because from the use of reason he is capable of society with God, and thus of reward and of punishment in the divine government. And, therefore, he preserves not only life and soul like the brutes, but also self-consciousness and memory of a former state, and, in a word, personality. He is immortal, not only physically, but also morally; whence, in the strict sense, immortality is attributed only to the human soul. For if a man did not know that in the other life rewards or punishments would be awarded him for this life, there would really be no punishment, no reward; and as regards morals, it would be just as if I were extinguished and another, happier or unhappier, should succeed me. And thus I hold that souls, latent doubtless in seminal animalcules from the beginning of things, are not rational until, by conception, they are destined for human life; but when they are once made rational and rendered capable of consciousness and of society with God, I think that they never lay aside the character of citizens in the Republic of God; and since it is most justly and beautifully governed, it is a consequence that by the very laws of nature, on account of the parallelism of the kingdom of grace and of nature, souls by the force of their own actions are rendered more fit for rewards and punishments. And in this sense it may be said that virtue brings its own reward and sin its own punishment, since by a certain natural consequence, before the last state of the soul, according as it departs atoned for or unatoned for, there arises a certain natural divergence, preordained by God in nature and with divine promises and threats, and consistent with grace and justice; the intervention also being added of genii, good or bad according as we have associated with either, whose operations are certainly

natural although their nature is sublimer than ours. We
see, indeed, that a man awaking from a profound sleep, or
even recovering from apoplexy, is wont to recover the
memory of his former state. The same must be said of
death, which can render our perceptions turbid and confused but cannot entirely blot them from memory, the
use of which returning, rewards and punishments take
place. Thus the Saviour compared death to sleep. Moreover the preservation of personality and moral immortality cannot be attributed to brutes incapable of the
divine society and law.

6. No one, therefore, need fear dangerous consequences from this doctrine, since rather a true natural
theology, not only not at variance with revealed truth
but even wonderfully favorable to it, may be demonstrated by most beautiful reasoning from my principles.
Those indeed who deny souls to brutes and all perception
and organism to other parts of matter, do not sufficiently recognize the Divine Majesty, and introduce
something unworthy of God, unpolished, that is, a void
of perfections or forms, which you may call a metaphysical void, which is no less to be rejected than a
material or physical void. But those who grant true souls
and perception to brutes, and yet affirm that their souls
can perish naturally, take away thus from us the demonstration which shows that our minds cannot perish naturally, and fall into the dogma of the Socinians, who
think that souls are preserved only miraculously or by
grace, but believe that by nature they ought to perish;
which is to rob natural theology of its most important
part. Besides, the contrary can be completely demonstrated, since a substance wanting parts cannot naturally
be destroyed.

11. THE THEODICY:

ABRIDGEMENT OF THE ARGUMENT
REDUCED TO SYLLOGISTIC FORM.
[1710]

Some intelligent persons have desired that this supplement be made [to the Theodicy], and I have the more readily yielded to their wishes as in this way I have an opportunity again to remove certain difficulties and to make some observations which were not sufficiently emphasized in the work itself.

I. *Objection*. Whoever does not choose the best is lacking in power, or in knowledge, or in goodness.

God did not choose the best in creating this world.

Therefore, God has been lacking in power, or in knowledge, or in goodness.

Answer. I deny the minor, that is, the second premise of this syllogism; and our opponent proves it by this

Prosyllogism. Whoever makes things in which there is evil, which could have been made without any evil, or the making of which could have been omitted, does not choose the best.

God has made a world in which there is evil; a world, I say, which could have been made without any evil, or the making of which could have been omitted altogether.

Therefore, God has not chosen the best.

Answer. I grant the minor of this prosyllogism; for it must be confessed that there is evil in this world which God has made, and that it was possible to make a world without evil, or even not to create a world at all, for its creation has depended on the free will of God; but I deny the major, that is, the first of the two premises of the prosyllogism, and I might content myself with simply demanding its proof; but in order to make the matter clearer, I have wished to justify this denial by showing that the best plan is not always that which seeks to avoid evil, since it may happen that *the evil is accompanied by a greater good*. For example, a general of an army will prefer a great victory with a slight wound to a condition without wound and without victory. We have proved this more fully in the large work by making it clear, by instances taken from mathematics and elsewhere, that an imperfection in the part may be required for a greater perfection in the whole. In this I have followed the opinion of St. Augustine, who has said a hundred times, that God has permitted evil in order to bring about good, that is, a greater good; and that of Thomas Aquinas (in libr. II. sent. dist. 32, qu. I, art. 1), that the permitting of evil tends to the good of the universe. I have shown that the ancients called Adam's fall *felix culpa*, a happy sin, because it had been retrieved with immense advantage by the incarnation of the Son of God, who has given to the universe something nobler than anything that ever would have been among creatures except for it. For the sake of a clearer understanding, I have added, following many good authors, that it was in accordance with order and the general good that God allowed to certain creatures the opportunity of exercising their liberty, even when he foresaw that they would turn to evil, but which he could so well rectify; because it was not fitting that, in order to hinder sin, God should always act in an extraordinary manner. To overthrow this objection, therefore, it is sufficient to show that a world with evil might be better than a world without evil; but I have gone even farther, in the work, and have even proved that this universe must be in reality better than every other possible universe.

II. *Objection.* If there is more evil than good in intelligent creatures, then there is more evil than good in the whole work of God.

Now, there is more evil than good in intelligent creatures.

Therefore, there is more evil than good in the whole work of God.

Answer. I deny the major and the minor of this conditional syllogism. As to the major, I do not admit it at all, because this pretended deduction from a part to the whole, from intelligent creatures to all creatures, supposes tacitly and without proof that creatures destitute of reason cannot enter into comparison nor into account with those which possess it. But why may it not be that the surplus of good in the non-intelligent creatures which fill the world, compensates for, and even incomparably surpasses, the surplus of evil in the rational creatures? It is true that the value of the latter is greater; but, in compensation, the others are beyond comparison the more numerous, and it may be that the proportion of number and quantity surpasses that of value and of quality.

As to the minor, that is no more to be admitted; that is, it is not at all to be admitted that there is more evil than good in the intelligent creatures. There is no need even of granting that there is more evil than good in the human race, because it is possible, and in fact very probable, that the glory and the perfection of the blessed are incomparably greater than the misery and the imperfection of the damned, and that here the excellence of the total good in the smaller number exceeds the total evil in the greater number. The blessed approach the Divinity, by means of a Divine Mediator, as near as may suit these creatures, and make such progress in good as is impossible for the damned to make in evil, approach as nearly as they may to the nature of demons. God is infinite, and the devil is limited; the good may and does go to infinity, while evil has its bounds. It is therefore possible, and is credible, that in the comparison of the blessed and the damned, the contrary of that which I have said might happen in the comparison of intelligent and non-intelligent creatures, takes place; namely, it is possible that in the comparison of the happy and the unhappy, the proportion of degree exceeds that of number, and that in the comparison of intelligent and non-intelligent creatures, the proportion of number is greater than that of value. I have the right to suppose that a thing is possible so long as its impossibility is not proved; and indeed that which I have here advanced is more than a supposition.

But in the second place, if I should admit that there is more evil than good in the human race, I have still good grounds for not admitting that there is more evil than good in all intelligent creatures. For there is an inconceivable number of genii, and perhaps of other rational creatures. And an opponent could not prove that in all the City of God, composed as well of genii as of rational animals without number and of an infinity of kinds, evil exceeds good. And although in order to answer an objection, there is no need of proving that a thing is, when its mere possibility suffices; yet, in this work, I have not omitted to show that it is a consequence of the supreme perfection of the Sovereign of the universe, that the kingdom of God is the most perfect of all possible states or governments, and that consequently the little evil there is, is required for the consummation of the immense good which is found there.

III. *Objection*. If it is always impossible not to sin, it is always unjust to punish.

Now, it is always impossible not to sin; or, in other words, every sin is necessary.

Therefore, it is always unjust to punish.

The minor of this is proved thus:

1. *Prosyllogism.* All that is predetermined is necessary.

Every event is predetermined.

Therefore, every event (and consequently sin also) is necessary.

Again this second minor is proved thus:

2. *Prosyllogism.* That which is future, that which is foreseen, that which is involved in the causes, is predetermined.

Every event is such.

Therefore, every event is predetermined.

Answer. I admit in a certain sense the conclusion of the second prosyllogism, which is the minor of the first; but I shall deny the major of the first prosyllogism, namely, that every thing predetermined is necessary; understanding by the *necessity* of sinning, for example, or by the impossibility of not sinning, or of not performing any action, the necessity with which we are here concerned, that is, that which is essential and absolute, and which destroys the morality of an action and the justice of punishments. For if anyone understood another necessity or impossibility, namely, a necessity which should be only moral, or which was only hypothetical (as will be explained shortly); it is clear that I should deny the major of the objection itself. I might content myself with this answer and demand the proof of the proposition denied; but I have again desired to explain my procedure in this work, in order to better elucidate the matter and to throw more light on the whole subject, by explaining the necessity which ought to be rejected and the determination which must take place. That *necessity* which is contrary to morality and which ought to be rejected, and which would render punishment unjust,

is an insurmountable necessity which would make all
opposition useless, even if we should wish with all our
heart to avoid the necessary action, and should make all
possible efforts to that end. Now, it is manifest that this
is not applicable to voluntary actions, because we would
not perform them if we did not choose to. Also their prevision and predetermination are not absolute, but presuppose the will: if it is certain that we shall perform
them, it is not less certain that we shall choose to perform them. These voluntary actions and their consequences will not take place no matter what we **do or**
whether we wish them or not; but, *through* that which
we shall do and through that which we shall wish to **do,**
which leads to them. And this is involved in prevision
and in predetermination, and even constitutes their
ground. And the necessity of such an event is called
conditional or hypothetical, or the necessity of consequence, because it supposes the will, and the other
requisites; whereas the necessity which destroys morality
and renders punishment unjust and reward useless,
exists in things which will be whatever we may do or
whatever we may wish to do, and, in a word, is in that
which is essential; and this is what is called an absolute
necessity. Thus it is to no purpose, as regards what is
absolutely necessary, to make prohibitions or commands,
to propose penalties or prizes, to praise or to blame; it
will be none the less. On the other hand, in voluntary
actions and in that which depends upon them, precepts
armed with power to punish and to recompense are very
often of use and are included in the order of causes
which make an action exist. And it is for this reason
that not only cares and labors but also prayers are useful; God having had these prayers in view before he
regulated things and having had that consideration for
them which was proper. This is why the precept which

says *ora et labora* (pray and work), holds altogether good; and not only those who (under the vain pretext of the necessity of events) pretend that the care which business demands may be neglected, but also those who reason against prayer, fall into what the ancients even then called the *lazy sophism*. Thus the predetermination of events by causes is just what contributes to morality instead of destroying it, and causes incline the will, without compelling it. This is why the *determination* in question is not a necessitation—it is certain (to him who knows all) that the effect will follow this inclination; but this effect does not follow by a necessary consequence, that is, one the contrary of which implies contradiction. It is also by an internal inclination such as this that the will is determined, without there being any necessity. Suppose that one has the greatest passion in the world (a great thirst, for example), you will admit to me that the soul can find some reason for resisting it, if it were only that of showing its power. Thus, although one may never be in a perfect indifference of equilibrium and there may be always a preponderance of inclination for the side taken, it, nevertheless, never renders the resolution taken absolutely necessary.

IV. *Objection*. Whoever can prevent the sin of another and does not do so, but rather contributes to it although he is well informed of it, is accessory to it.

God can prevent the sin of intelligent creatures; but he does not do so, and rather contributes to it by his concurrence and by the opportunities which he brings about, although he has a perfect knowledge of it.

Hence, etc.

Answer. I deny the major of this syllogism. For it is possible that one could prevent sin, but ought not, because he could not do it without himself committing a sin, or (when God is in question) without performing an unreasonable action. Examples have been given and the application to God himself has been made. It is possible also that we contribute to evil and that sometimes we even open the road to it, in doing things which we are obliged to do; and, when we do our duty or (in speaking of God) when, after thorough consideration, we do that which reason demands, we are not responsible for the results, even when we foresee them. We do not desire these evils; but we are willing to permit them for the sake of a greater good which we cannot reasonably help preferring to other considerations. And this is a *consequent* will, which results from *antecedent* wills by which we will the good. I know that some persons, in speaking of the antecedent and consequent will of God, have understood by the *antecedent* that which wills that all men should be saved; and by the *consequent,* that which wills, in consequence of persistent sin, that some should be damned. But these are merely illustrations of a more general idea, and it may be said for the same reason that God, by his antecedent will, wills that men should not sin; and by his consequent or final and decreeing will (that which is always followed by its effect), he wills to permit them to sin, this permission being the result of superior reasons. And we have the right to say in general that the antecedent will of God tends to the production of good and the prevention of evil, each taken in itself and as if alone (*particulariter et secundum quid,* Thom. I, qu. 19, art. 6), according to the measure of the degree of each good and of each evil; but that the divine consequent or final or total will tends toward the production of as many goods as may be put together, the combination of which becomes in this way determined, and includes also the permission of some evils and the exclusion of some goods, as the best possible plan for the universe demands. Arminius, in his *Anti-perkinsus,* has very well explained that the will of God may be called consequent, not only in relation to the action of the creature considered beforehand in the divine understanding, but also in relation to other anterior divine acts of will. But this consideration of the passage cited from Thomas Aquinas, and that from Scotus (I. dist. 46, qu. XI), is enough to show that they make this distinction as I have done here. Nevertheless, if anyone objects to this use of terms let him substitute *deliberating* will, in place of antecedent, and *final* or decreeing will, in place of consequent. For I do not wish to dispute over words.

V. *Objection*. Whoever produces all that is real in a thing, is its cause.

God produces all that is real in sin.

Hence, God is the cause of sin.

Answer. I might content myself with denying the major or the minor, since the term *real* admits of interpretations which would render these propositions false. But in order to explain more clearly, I will make a distinction. *Real* signifies either that which is positive only, or, it includes also privative beings: in the first case, I deny the major and admit the minor; in the second case, I do the contrary. I might have limited myself to this, but I have chosen to proceed still farther and give the reason for this distinction. I have been very glad therefore to draw attention to the fact that every reality purely positive or absolute is a perfection; and that imperfection comes from limitation, that is, from the privative: for to limit is to refuse progress, or the greatest possible progress. Now God is the cause of all perfections and consequently of all realities considered as purely positive. But limitations or privations result from the original imperfection of creatures, which limits their receptivity. And it is with them as with a loaded vessel, which the river causes to move more or less slowly according to the weight which it carries: thus its speed depends upon the river, but the retardation which limits this speed comes from the load. Thus in the *Theodicy,* we have shown how the creature, in causing sin, is a defective cause; how errors and evil inclinations are born of privation; and how privation is accidentally efficient; and I have justified the opinion of St. Augustine (lib. I. ad Simpl. qu. 2) who explains, for example, how God makes the soul obdurate, not by giving it something evil, but because the effect of his good impression is limited by the soul's resistance and by the circumstances which contribute to this resistance, so that he does not give it all the good which would overcome its evil. *Nec* (inquit) *ab illo erogatur aliquid quo homo fit deterior, sed tantum quo fit melior non erogatur.* But if God had wished to do more, he would have had to make either other natures for creatures or other miracles to change their natures, things which the best plan could not admit. It is as if the current of the river must be more rapid than its fall admitted or that the boats should be loaded more lightly, if it were necessary to make them move more quickly. And the original limitation or imperfection of creatures requires that even the best plan of the universe could not receive more good, and could not be exempt from certain evils, which, however, are to result in a greater good. There are certain disorders in the parts which marvellously enhance the beauty of the whole; just as certain dissonances, when properly used, render harmony more beautiful. But this depends on what has already been said in answer to the first objection.

VI. *Objection.* Whoever punishes those who have done as well as it was in their power to do, is unjust.

God does so.

Hence, etc.

Answer. I deny the minor of this argument. And I believe that God always gives sufficient aid and grace to those who have a good will, that is, to those who do not reject this grace by new sin. Thus I do not admit the damnation of infants who have died without baptism or outside of the church; nor the damnation of adults who have acted according to the light which God has given them. And I believe that if *any one has followed the light which has been given him,* he will undoubtedly receive greater light when he has need of it, as the late M. Hulseman, a profound and celebrated theologian at Leipsig, has somewhere remarked; and if such a man has failed to receive it during his lifetime he will at least receive it when at the point of death.

VII. *Objection.* Whoever gives only to some, and not to all, the means which produces in them effectively a good will and salutary final faith, has not sufficient goodness.

God does this.

Hence, etc.

Answer. I deny the major of this. It is true that God could overcome the greatest resistance of the human heart; and does it, too, sometimes, either by internal grace, or by external circumstances which have a great effect on souls; but he does not always do this. Whence comes this distinction? it may be asked, and why does his goodness seem limited? It is because, as I have already said in answering the first objection, it would not have been in order always to act in an extraordinary manner, and to reverse the connection of things. The reasons of this connection, by means of which one is placed in more favorable circumstances than another, are hidden in the depths of the wisdom of God: they depend upon the universal harmony. The best plan of the universe, which God could not fail to choose, made it so. We judge from the event itself; since God has made it, it was not possible to do better. Far from being true that this conduct is contrary to goodness, it is supreme goodness which led him to it. This objection with its solution might have been drawn from what was said in regard to the first objection; but it seemed useful to touch upon it separately.

VIII. *Objection.* Whoever cannot fail to choose the best, is not free.

God cannot fail to choose the best.

Hence, God is not free.

Answer. I deny the major of this argument; it is rather true liberty, and the most perfect, to be able to use one's free will for the best, and to always exercise this power, without ever being turned aside either by external force or by internal passions, the first of which causes slavery of the body, the second, slavery of the soul. There is nothing less servile, and nothing more in accordance with the highest degree of freedom, than to be always led toward the good, and always by one's own inclination, without any constraint and without any displeasure. And to object therefore that God had need of external things, is only a sophism. He created them freely; but having proposed to himself an end, which is to exercise his goodness, wisdom has determined him to choose the means best fitted to attain this end. To call this a *need,* is to take that term in an unusual sense which frees it from all imperfection, just as when we speak of the wrath of God.

Seneca has somewhere said that God commanded but once but that he obeys always, because he obeys laws which he willed to prescribe to himself: *semel jussit, semper paret.* But he might better have said that God always commands and that he is always obeyed; for in willing, he always follows the inclination of his own

nature, and all other things always follow his will. And
as this will is always the same, it cannot be said that
he obeys only that will which he formerly had. Nevertheless, although his will is always infallible and always
tends toward the best, the evil, or the lesser good, which
he rejects, does not cease to be possible in itself; otherwise the necessity of the good would be geometrical (so
to speak), or metaphysical, and altogether absolute; the
contingency of things would be destroyed, and there
would be no choice. But this sort of necessity, which does
not destroy the possibility of the contrary, has this name
only by analogy; it becomes effective, not by the pure
essence of things, but by that which is outside of them,
above them, namely, by the will of God. This necessity
is called moral, because, to the sage, *necessity* and *what
ought to be* are equivalent things; and when it always has
its effect, as it really has in the perfect sage, that is,
in God, it may be said that it is a happy necessity. The
nearer creatures approach to it, the nearer they approach
to perfect happiness. Also this kind of necessity is not
that which we try to avoid and which destroys morality,
rewards and praise. For that which it brings, does not
happen whatever we may do or will, but because we will
it so. And a will to which it is natural to choose well,
merits praise so much the more; also it carries its reward
with it, which is sovereign happiness. And as this constitution of the divine nature gives entire satisfaction to
him who possesses it, it is also the best and the most
desirable for the creatures who are all dependent on God.
If the will of God did not have for a rule the principle of
the best, it would either tend toward evil, which would
be the worst; or it would be in some way indifferent to
good and to evil, and would be guided by chance: but a
will which would allow itself always to act by chance,
would not be worth more for the government of the uni-

verse than the fortuitous concourse of atoms, without there being any divinity therein. And even if God should abandon himself to chance only in some cases and in a certain way (as he would do, if he did not always work entirely for the best and if he were capable of preferring a lesser good to a greater, that is, an evil to a good, since that which prevents a greater good is an evil), he would be imperfect, as well as the object of his choice; he would not merit entire confidence; he would act without reason in such a case, and the government of the universe would be like certain games, equally divided between reason and chance. All this proves that this objection which is made against the choice of the best, perverts the notions of the free and of the necessary, and represents to us the best even as evil: which is either malicious or ridiculous.

12. THE PRINCIPLES OF NATURE AND OF GRACE, BASED ON REASON
[1714]

1. *Substance* is a being capable of action. It is simple or compound. *Simple substance* is that which has no parts. *Compound* substance is the collection of simple substances or *monads*. *Monas* is a Greek word which signifies unity, or that which is one.

Compounds, or bodies, are multitudes; and simple substances, lives, souls, spirits are unities. And there must be simple substances everywhere, because without simple substances there would be no compounds; and consequently all nature is full of life.

2. Monads, having no parts, cannot be formed or decomposed. They cannot begin or end naturally; and consequently last as long as the universe, which will be

changed but will not be destroyed. They cannot have shapes; otherwise they would have parts. And consequently a monad, in itself and at a given moment, could not be distinguished from another except by its internal qualities and actions, which can be nothing else than its *perceptions* (that is, representations of the compound, or of what is external, in the simple), and its *appetitions* (that is, its tendencies to pass from one perception to another), which are the principles of change. For the simplicity of substance does not prevent multiplicity of modifications, which must be found together in this same simple substance, and must consist in the variety of relations to things which are external. Just as in a *centre* or point, entirely simple as it is, there is an infinity of angles formed by the lines which meet at the point.

3. All nature is a *plenum*. There are everywhere simple substances, separated in effect from one another by activities of their own which continually change their relations; and each important simple substance, or monad, which forms the centre of a composite substance (as, for example, of an animal) and the principle of its unity, is surrounded by a *mass* composed of an infinity of other monads, which constitute the body proper of this central monad; and in accordance with the affections of its body the monad represents, as in a *centre*, the things which are outside of itself. And this *body* is *organic,* though it forms a sort of automaton or natural machine, which is a machine not only in its entirety, but also in its smallest perceptible parts. And as, because the world is a *plenum*, everything is connected and each body acts upon every other body, more or less, according to the distance, and by reaction is itself affected thereby, it follows that each monad is a living mirror, or endowed with internal activity, representative according to its point of view of the universe, and as regulated as the universe

itself. And the perceptions in the monad spring one from the other, by the law; of desires [*appétits*] or of the *final causes of good and evil*, which consist in observable, regulated or unregulated, perceptions; just as the changes of bodies and external phenomena spring one from another, by the laws of *efficient causes*, that is, of motions. Thus there is a perfect *harmony* between the perceptions of the monad and the motions of bodies, pre-established at the beginning between the system of efficient causes and that of final causes. And in this consists the accord and physical union of the soul and the body, although neither one can change the laws of the other.

4. Each monad, with a particular body, makes a living substance. Thus there is not only life everywhere, accompanied with members or organs, but there is also an infinity of degrees among monads, some dominating more or less over others. But when the monad has organs so adjusted that by their means prominence and distinctness appear in the impressions which they receive, and consequently in the perceptions which represent these (as, for example, when by means of the shape of the humors of the eyes, the rays of light are concentrated and act with more force), this may lead to *feeling* [*sentiment*], that is, to a perception accompanied by *memory*, namely, by a certain reverberation lasting a long time, so as to make itself heard upon occasion. And such a living being is called an *animal*, as its monad is called a soul. And when this soul is elevated to *reason*, it is something more sublime and is reckoned among spirits, as will soon be explained. It is true that animals are sometimes in the condition of simple living beings, and their souls in the condition of simple monads, namely, when their perceptions are not sufficiently distinct to be remembered, as happens in a deep dreamless sleep, or in a swoon. But perceptions which have become entirely

confused must be re-developed in animals, for reasons which I shall shortly (§ 12) enumerate. Thus it is well to make distinction between the *perception*, which is the inner state of the monad representing external things, and *apperception*, which is *consciousness* or the reflective knowledge of this inner state; the latter not being given to all souls, nor at all times to the same soul. And it is for want of this distinction that the Cartesians have failed, taking no account of the perceptions of which we are not conscious as people take no account of imperceptible bodies. It is this also which made the same Cartesians believe that only spirits are monads, that there is no soul of brutes, and still less other *principles of life*. And as they shocked too much the common opinion of men by refusing feeling to brutes, they have, on the other hand, accommodated themselves too much to the prejudices of the multitude, by confounding a *long swoon*, caused by a great confusion of perceptions, with *death strictly speaking*, where all perception would cease. This has confirmed the ill-founded belief in the destruction of some souls, and the bad opinion of some so-called strong minds, who have contended against the immortality of our soul.

5. There is a connection in the perceptions of animals which bears some resemblance to reason; but it is only founded in the memory of *facts* or effects, and not at all in the knowledge of *causes*. Thus a dog shuns the stick with which it has been beaten, because memory represents to it the pain which the stick had caused it. And men, in so far as they are empirics, that is to say, in three-fourths of their actions, act simply as the brutes do. For example, we expect that there will be daylight to-morrow because we have always had the experience; only an astronomer foresees it by reason, and even this prediction will finally fail when the cause of day, which is not eternal, shall

cease. But *true reasoning* depends upon necessary or eternal truths, such as those of logic, of numbers, of geometry, which establish an indubitable connection of ideas and unfailing inferences. The animals in whom these inferences are not noticed, are called *brutes*; but those which know these necessary truths are properly those which are called *rational animals*, and their souls are called *spirits*. These souls are capable of performing acts of reflection, and of considering that which is called the *ego, substance, monad, soul, spirit,* in a word, immaterial things and truths. And it is this which renders us capable of the sciences and of demonstrative knowledge.

6. Modern researches have taught us, and reason approves of it, that living beings whose organs are known to us, that is to say, plants and animals, do not come from putrefaction or from chaos, as the ancients believed, but from *pre-formed* seeds, and consequently by the transformation of pre-existing living beings. There are animalcules in the seeds of larger animals, which by means of conception assume a new dress, which they make their own, and by means of which they can nourish themselves and increase their size, in order to pass to a larger theatre and to accomplish the propagation of the large animal. It is true that the souls of spermatic human animals are not rational, and do not become so until conception destines [*determine*] these animals to human nature. And as in general animals are not born entirely in conception or *generation*, neither do they perish entirely in what we call *death*; for it is reasonable that what does not begin naturally, should not end either in the order of nature. Therefore, quitting their mask or their rags, they merely return to a more minute theatre, where they can, nevertheless, be just as sensitive and just as well ordered as in the larger. And what we have just

said of the large animals, takes place also in the generation and death of spermatic animals themselves, that is to say, they are growths of other smaller spermatic animals, in comparison with which they may pass for large; for everything extends *ad infinitum* in nature. Thus not only souls, but also animals, are ingenerable and imperishable: they are only developed, enveloped, reclothed, unclothed, transformed: souls never quit their entire body and do not pass from one body into another which is entirely new to them. There is therefore no *metempsychosis*, but there is *metamorphosis*; animals change, take and leave only parts: the same thing which happens little by little and by small invisible particles, but continually, in nutrition; and suddenly, visibly, but rarely, in conception or in death, which cause a gain or loss all at one time.

7. Thus far we have spoken as simple *physicists:* now we must advance to *metaphysics,* making use of the *great principle,* little employed in general, which teaches that *nothing happens without a sufficient reason*; that is to say, that nothing happens without its being possible for him who should sufficiently understand things, to give a reason sufficient to determine why it is so and not otherwise. This principle laid down, the first question which should rightly be asked, will be, *Why is there something rather than nothing?* For nothing is simpler and easier than something. Further, suppose that things must exist, we must be able to give a reason *why they must exist so* and not otherwise.

8. Now this sufficient reason for the existence of the universe cannot be found *in the series of contingent things,* that is, of bodies and of their representations in souls; for matter being indifferent in itself to motion and to rest, and to this or another motion, we cannot find the reason of motion in it, and still less of a certain motion.

And although the present motion which is in matter, comes from the preceding motion, and that from still another preceding, yet in this way we make no progress, go as far as we may; for the same question always remains. Thus it must be that the sufficient reason, which has no need of another reason, be outside this series of contingent things and be found in a substance which is its cause, or which is a necessary being, carrying the reason of its existence within itself; otherwise we should still not have a sufficient reason in which we could rest. And this final reason of things is called *God*.

9. This primitive simple substance must contain in itself eminently the perfections contained in the derivative substances which are its effects; thus it will have perfect power, knowledge and will: that is, it will have supreme omnipotence, omniscience and goodness. And as *justice*, taken very generally, is only goodness conformed to wisdom, there must too be supreme justice in God. The reason which has caused things to exist by him, makes them still dependent upon him in existing and in working: and they continually receive from him that which gives them any perfection; but the imperfection which remains in them, comes from the essential and original limitation of the creature.

10. It follows from the supreme perfection of God, that in creating the universe he has chosen the best possible plan, in which there is the greatest variety together with the greatest order; the best arranged ground, place, time; the most results produced in the most simple ways; the most of power, knowledge, happiness and goodness in the creatures that the universe could permit. For since all the possibles in the understanding of God laid claim to existence in proportion to their perfections, the result of all these claims must be the most perfect actual world that is possible. And without this it would not be possible

to give a reason why things have turned out so rather than otherwise.

11. The supreme wisdom of God led him to choose the *laws of motion* best adjusted and most suited to abstract or metaphysical reasons. There is preserved the same quantity of total and absolute force, or of action; the same quantity of respective force or of reaction; lastly the same quantity of directive force. Farther, action is always equal to reaction, and the whole effect is always equivalent to its full cause. And it is not surprising that we could not by the mere consideration of the *efficient causes* or of matter, account for those laws of motion which have been discovered in our time, and a part of which have been discovered by myself. For I have found that it was necessary to have recourse to *final causes*, and that these laws do not depend upon the *principle of necessity*, like logical, arithmetical and geometrical truths, but upon the *principle of fitness*, that is, upon the choice of wisdom. And this is one of the most effective and evident proofs of the existence of God, to those who can examine these matters thoroughly.

12. It follows, farther, from the perfection of the supreme author, that not only is the order of the entire universe the most perfect possible, but also that each living mirror representing the universe in accordance with its point of view, that is to say, that each *monad,* each substantial centre, must have its perceptions and its desires as well regulated as is compatible with all the rest. Whence it follows, still farther, that *souls,* that is, the most dominating monads, or rather, animals themselves, cannot fail to awaken from the state of stupor in which death or some other accident may put them.

13. For all is regulated in things, once for all, with as much order and harmony as is possible, supreme wisdom and goodness not being able to act except with perfect

harmony. The present is big with the future, the future might be read in the past, the distant is expressed in the near. One could become acquainted with the beauty of the universe in each soul, if one could unfold all its folds, which only develop perceptibly in time. But as each distinct perception of the soul includes innumerable confused perceptions, which embrace the whole universe, the soul itself knows the things of which it has perception only so far as it has distinct and clear perceptions of them; and it has perfection in proportion to its distinct perceptions. Each soul knows the infinite, knows all, but confusedly; as in walking on the seashore and hearing the great noise which it makes, I hear the particular sounds of each wave, of which the total sound is composed, but without distinguishing them. Our confused perceptions are the result of the impressions which the whole universe makes upon us. It is the same with each monad. God alone has a distinct knowledge of all, for he is the source of all. It has been well said that he is as centre everywhere, but his circumference is nowhere, since everything is immediately present to him without any distance from this centre.

14. As regards the rational soul, or *spirit*, there is something in it more than in the monads, or even in simple souls. It is not only a mirror of the universe of creatures, but also an image of the Divinity. The *spirit* has not only a perception of the works of God, but it is even capable of producing something which resembles them, although in miniature. For, to say nothing of the marvels of dreams, in which we invent without trouble (but also involuntarily) things which, when awake, we should have to think a long time in order to hit upon, our soul is architectonic also in its voluntary actions, and, discovering the sciences according to which God has regulated things (*pondere, mensura, numero, etc.*), it imitates, in

its department and in its little world, where it is permitted to exercise itself, what God does in the large world.

15. This is why all spirits, whether of men or of genii, entering by virtue of reason and of eternal truths into a sort of society with God, are members of the City of God, that is to say, of the most perfect state, formed and governed by the greatest and best of monarchs; where there is no crime without punishment, no good actions without proportionate recompense; and, finally, as much virtue and happiness as is possible; and this is not by a derangement of nature, as if what God prepares for souls disturbed the laws of bodies, but by the very order of natural things, in virtue of the harmony pre-established for all time between the *realms of nature and of grace*, between God as Architect and God as Monarch; so that *nature* itself leads to grace, and *grace*, in making use of nature, perfects it.

16. Thus although reason cannot teach us the details, reserved to Revelation, of the great future, we can be assured by this same reason that things are made in a manner surpassing our desires. God also being the most perfect and most happy, and consequently, the most lovable of substances, and *truly pure love* consisting in the state which finds pleasure in the perfections and happiness of the loved object, this love ought to give us the greatest pleasure of which we are capable, when God is its object.

17. And it is easy to love him as we ought, if we know him as I have just described. For although God is not visible to our external senses, he does not cease to be very lovable and to give very great pleasure. We see how much pleasure honors give men, although they do not at all consist in the qualities of the external senses. Martyrs and fanatics (although the emotion of the latter

·is ill-regulated) show what pleasure of the spirit can accomplish; and, what is more, even sensuous pleasures are really confusedly known intellectual pleasures. Music charms us, although its beauty only consists in the harmonies of numbers and in the reckoning of the beats or vibrations of sounding bodies, which meet at certain intervals, reckonings of which we are not conscious and which the soul nevertheless does make. The pleasures which sight finds in proportions are of the same nature; and those caused by the other senses amount to almost the same thing, although we may not be able to explain it so distinctly.

18. It may even be said that from the present time on, the *love of God* makes us enjoy a foretaste of future felicity. And although it is distinterested, it itself constitutes our greatest good and interest even if we should not seek these therein and should consider only the pleasure which it gives, without regard to the utility it produces; for it gives us perfect confidence in the goodness of our author and master, producing a true tranquillity of mind; not as with the Stoics who force themselves to patience, but by a present contentment, assuring to us also a future happiness. And besides the present pleasure, nothing can be more useful for the future; for the love of God fulfills also our hopes, and leads us in the road of supreme happiness, because by virtue of the perfect order established in the universe, everything is done in the best possible way, as much for the general good as for the greatest individual good of those who are convinced of this and are content with the divine government; this conviction cannot be wanting to those who know how to love the source of all good. It is true that supreme felicity, by whatever *beatific vision* or knowledge of God it be accompanied, can never be full; because, since God is infinite, he cannot be wholly known.

Therefore our happiness will never, and ought not, consist in full joy, where there would be nothing farther to desire, rendering our mind stupid; but in a perpetual progress to new pleasures and to new perfections.

13. THE MONADOLOGY
[1714]

1. The *monad* of which we shall here speak is merely a simple substance, which enters into composites; *simple,* that is to say, without parts.[1]

2. And there must be simple substances, since there are composites; for the composite is only a collection or *aggregatum* of simple substances.

3. Now where there are no parts, neither extension, nor figure, nor divisibility is possible. And these monads are the true atoms of nature, and, in a word, the elements of all things.

4. Their dissolution also is not at all to be feared, and there is no conceivable way in which a simple substance can perish naturally.[2]

5. For the same reason there is no conceivable way in which a simple substance can begin naturally, since it cannot be formed by composition.

6. Thus it may be said that the monads can only begin or end all at once, that is to say, they can only begin by creation and end by annihilation; whereas that which is composite begins or ends by parts.

7. There is also no way of explaining how a monad can be altered or changed in its inner being by any other creature, for nothing can be transposed within it, nor can

[1] *Théodicée,* § 10. [All footnote references to this earlier work, *Theodicy* (1710), are Leibniz's.]
[2] § 89.

there be conceived in it any internal movement which can be excited, directed, augmented or diminished within it, as can be done in composites, where there is change among the parts. The monads have no windows through which anything can enter or depart. The accidents cannot detach themselves nor go about outside of substances, as did formerly the sensible species of the Schoolmen. Thus neither substance nor accident can enter a monad from outside.

8. Nevertheless, the monads must have some qualities, otherwise they would not even be entities. And if simple substances did not differ at all in their qualities there would be no way of perceiving any change in things, since what is in the compound can only come from the simple ingredients, and the monads, if they had no qualities, would be indistinguishable from one another, seeing also they do not differ in quantity. Consequently, a plenum being supposed, each place would always receive, in any motion, only the equivalent of what it had had before, and one state of things would be indistinguishable from another.

9. It is necessary, indeed, that each monad be different from every other. For there are never in nature two beings which are exactly alike and in which it is not possible to find an internal difference, or one founded upon an intrinsic quality (*dénomination*).

10. I take it also for granted that every created being, and consequently the created monad also, is subject to change, and even that this change is continuous in each.

11. It follows from what has just been said, that the natural changes of the monads proceed from an *internal principle*, since an external cause could not influence their inner being.[3]

[3] §§ 396 and 400.

12. But, besides the principle of change, there must be an individuating *detail of changes*, which forms, so to speak, the specification and variety of the simple substances.

13. This detail must involve a multitude in the unity or in that which is simple. For since every natural change takes place by degrees, something changes and something remains; and consequently, there must be in the simple substance a plurality of affections and of relations, although it has no parts.

14. The passing state, which involves and represents a multitude in unity or in the simple substance, is nothing else than what is called *perception*, which must be distinguished from apperception or consciousness, as will appear in what follows. Here it is that the Cartesians especially failed, having taken no account of the perceptions of which we are not conscious. It is this also which made them believe that spirits only are monads and that there are no souls of brutes or of other entelechies. They, with most people, have failed to distinguish between a prolonged state of unconsciousness (*étourdissement*) and death strictly speaking, and have therefore agreed with the old scholastic prejudice of entirely separate souls, and have even confirmed ill-balanced minds in the belief in the mortality of the soul.

15. The action of the internal principle which causes the change or the passage from one perception to another, may be called *appetition*; it is true that desire cannot always completely attain to the whole perception to which it tends, but it always attains something of it and reaches new perceptions.

16. We experience in ourselves a multiplicity in a simple substance, when we find that the most trifling thought of which we are conscious involves a variety in the object. Thus all those who admit that the soul is a

simple substance ought to admit this multiplicity in the monad, and M. Bayle ought not to have found any difficulty in it, as he has done in his Dictionary, article *Rorarius*.

17. It must be confessed, moreover, that *perception* and that which depends on it *are inexplicable by mechanical causes*, that is, by figures and motions. And, supposing that there were a machine so constructed as to think, feel and have perception, we could conceive of it as enlarged and yet preserving the same proportions, so that we might enter it as into a mill. And this granted, we should only find on visiting it, pieces which push one against another, but never anything by which to explain a perception. This must be sought for, therefore, in the simple substance and not in the composite or in the machine. Furthermore, nothing but this (namely, perceptions and their changes) can be found in the simple substance. It is also in this alone that all the *internal activities* of simple substances can consist.[4]

18. The name of *entelechies* might be given to all simple substances or created monads, for they have within themselves a certain perfection (ἔχουσι τὸ ἐντελές); there is a certain sufficiency (αὐτάρκεια) which makes them the sources of their internal activities, and so to speak, incorporeal automata.[5]

19. If we choose to give the name *soul* to everything that has *perceptions* and *desires* in the general sense which I have just explained, all simple substances or created monads may be called souls, but as feeling is something more than a simple perception, I am willing that the general name of monads or entelechies shall suffice for those simple substances which have only perception, and that those substances only shall be called

[4] Preface, p. 37 (Gerhardt edition).
[5] § 87.

souls whose perception is more distinct and is accompanied by memory.

20. For we experience in ourselves a state in which we remember nothing and have no distinguishable perception, as when we fall into a swoon or when we are overpowered by a profound and dreamless sleep. In this state the soul does not differ sensibly from a simple monad; but as this state is not continuous and as the soul comes out of it, the soul is something more than a mere monad.[6]

21. And it does not at all follow that in such a state the simple substance is without any perception. This is indeed impossible, for the reasons mentioned above; for it cannot perish, nor can it subsist without some affection, which is nothing else than its perception; but when there is a great number of minute perceptions, in which nothing is distinct, we are stunned; as when we turn continually in the same direction many times in succession, whence arises a dizziness which may make us swoon, and which does not let us distinguish anything. And death may produce for a time this condition in animals.

22. And as every present state of a simple substance is naturally the consequence of its preceding state, so its present is big with its future.[7]

23. Therefore, since on being awakened from a stupor, we are *aware* of our perceptions, we must have had them immediately before, although we were unconscious of them; for one perception can come in a natural way only from another perception, as a motion can come in a natural way only from a motion.[8]

24. From this we see that if there were nothing distinct, nothing, so to speak, in relief and of a higher flavor in our perceptions, we should always be in a dazed state. This is the condition of simply bare monads.

---

[6] § 64.   [7] § 360.   [8] §§ 401 to 403.

25. We also see that nature has given to animals heightened perceptions, by the pains she has taken to furnish them with organs which collect many rays of light or many undulations of air, in order to render these more efficacious by uniting them. There is something of the same kind in odor, in taste, in touch and perhaps in a multitude of other senses which are unknown to us. And I shall presently explain how that which takes place in the soul represents that which occurs in the organs.

26. Memory furnishes souls with a sort of *consecutiveness* [association of ideas] which imitates reason, but which ought to be distinguished from it. We observe that animals, having the perception of something which strikes them and of which they have had a similar perception before, expect, through the representation in their memory, that which was associated with it in the preceding perception, and experience feelings similar to those which they had had at that time. For instance, if we show dogs a stick, they remember the pain it has caused them and whine and run.[9]

27. And the strong imagination which impresses and moves them, arises either from the magnitude or the multitude of preceding perceptions. For often a strong impression produces all at once the effect of a long-continued *habit*, or of many oft-repeated moderate perceptions.

28. Men act like the brutes, in so far as the association of their perceptions results from the principle of memory alone, resembling the empirical physicians who practice without theory; and we are simple empirics in three-fourths of our actions. For example, when we expect that there will be daylight to-morrow, we are acting as empirics, because that has up to this time always taken place. It is only the astronomer who judges of this by reason.

[9] Prelim., § 65.

29. But the knowledge of necessary and eternal truths is what distinguishes us from mere animals and furnishes us with *reason* and the sciences, raising us to a knowledge of ourselves and of God. This is what we call the rational soul or *spirit* in us.

30. It is also by the knowledge of necessary truths, and by their abstractions, that we rise to *acts of reflection,* which make us think of that which calls itself *"I",* and to observe that this or that is within *us:* and it is thus that, in thinking of ourselves, we think of being, of substance, simple or composite, of the immaterial and of God himself, conceiving that what is limited in us is in him without limits. And these reflective acts furnish the principal objects of our reasonings.[10]

31. Our reasonings are founded on *two great principles, that of contradiction,* in virtue of which we judge that to be *false* which involves contradiction, and that *true,* which is opposed or contradictory to the false.[11]

32. And *that of sufficient reason,* in virtue of which we hold that no fact can be real or existent, no statement true, unless there be a sufficient reason why it is so and not otherwise, although most often these reasons cannot be known to us.[12]

33. There are also two kinds of *truths,* those of *reasoning* and those of *fact.* Truths of reasoning are necessary and their opposite is impossible, and those of *fact* are contingent and their opposite is possible. When a truth is necessary its reason can be found by analysis, resolving it into more simple ideas and truths until we reach those which are primitive.[13]

34. It is thus that mathematicians by analysis reduce speculative *theorems* and practical *canons* to *definitions, axioms* and *postulates.*

[10] Pref., p. 27.   [11] §§ 44, 169.   [12] §§ 44, 196.
[13] §§ 170, 174, 189, 280–282, 367; Abridgment, Objection 3.

35. And there are finally simple ideas, definitions of which cannot be given; there are also axioms and postulates, in a word, *primary principles,* which cannot be proved, and indeed need no proof; and these are *identical propositions,* whose opposite involves an express contradiction.

36. But there must also be a *sufficient reason* for *contingent truths,* or those *of fact,*—that is, for the sequence of things diffused through the universe of created objects —where the resolution into particular reasons might run into a detail without limits, on account of the immense variety of the things in nature and the division of bodies *ad infinitum.* There is an infinity of figures and of movements, present and past, which enter into the efficient cause of my present writing, and there is an infinity of slight inclinations and dispositions, past and present, of my soul, which enter into the final cause.[14]

37. And as all this *detail* only involves other contingents, anterior or more detailed, each one of which needs a like analysis for its explanation, we make no advance: and the sufficient or final reason must be outside of the sequence or *series* of this detail of contingencies, however infinite it may be.

38. And thus it is that the final reason of things must be found in a necessary substance, in which the detail of changes exists only eminently, as in their source; and this is what we call God.[15]

39. Now this substance, being a sufficient reason of all this detail, which also is linked together throughout, *there is but one God, and this God is sufficient.*

40. We may also conclude that this supreme substance, which is unique, universal and necessary, having nothing outside of itself which is independent of it, and being

[14] §§ 36, 37, 44, 45, 49, 52, 121, 122, 337, 340, 344.
[15] § 7.

a pure consequence of possible being, must be incapable of limitations and must contain as much of reality as is possible.

41. Whence it follows that God is absolutely perfect, *perfection* being only the magnitude of positive reality taken in its strictest meaning, setting aside the limits or bounds in things which have them. And where there are no limits, that is, in God, perfection is absolutely infinite.[16]

42. It follows also that the creatures have their perfections from the influence of God, but that their imperfections arise from their own nature, incapable of existing without limits. For it is by this that they are distinguished from God.[17]

43. It is also true that in God is the source not only of existences but also of essences, so far as they are real, or of that which is real in the possible. This is because the understanding of God is the region of eternal truths, or of the ideas on which they depend, and because, without him, there would be nothing real in the possibilities, and not only nothing existing but also nothing possible.[18]

44. For, if there is a reality in essences or possibilities or indeed in the eternal truths, this reality must be founded in something existing and actual, and consequently in the existence of the necessary being, in whom essence involves existence, or with whom it is sufficient to be possible in order to be actual.[19]

45. Hence God alone (or the necessary being) has this prerogative, that he must exist if he is possible. And since nothing can hinder the possibility of that

[16] § 22; Preface, p. 27.

[17] §§ 20, 27–31, 153, 167, 377 seqq. [In the first copy, revised by Leibniz, the following is added: "This *original imperfection* of creatures is noticeable in the *natural inertia* of bodies. §§ 30, 380; Abridgment, Objection 5."]

[18] § 20.   [19] §§ 184, 189, 335.

which possesses no limitations, no negation, and, consequently, no contradiction, this alone is sufficient to establish the existence of God *a priori*. We have also proved it by the reality of the eternal truths. But we have a little while ago [§§ 36–39] proved it also *a posteriori*, since contingent beings exist, which can only have their final or sufficient reason in a necessary being who has the reason of his existence in himself.

46. Yet we must not imagine, as some do, that the eternal truths, being dependent upon God, are arbitrary and depend upon his will, as Descartes seems to have held, and afterwards M. Poiret. This is true only of contingent truths, the principle of which is *fitness* or the choice of the *best,* whereas necessary truths depend solely on his understanding and are its internal object.[20]

47. Thus God alone is the primitive unity or the original simple substance; of which all created or derived monads are the products, and are generated, so to speak, by continual fulgurations of the Divinity, from moment to moment, limited by the receptivity of the creature, to whom limitation is essential.[21]

48. In God is *Power,* which is the source of all; then *Knowledge,* which contains the detail of ideas; and finally *Will,* which effects changes or products according to the principle of the best. These correspond to what in created monads form the subject or basis, the perceptive faculty, and the appetitive faculty. But in God these attributes are absolutely infinite or perfect; and in the created monads or in the *entelechies* (or *perfectihabiis,* as Harmolaus Barbarus translated the word), they are only imitations proportioned to the perfection of the monads.[22]

49. The creature is said to *act* externally in so far as

[20] §§ 180, 184, 185, 335, 351, 380.
[21] §§ 382–391, 398, 395.   [22] §§ 7, 149, 150, 87.

it has perfection, and to be *acted on* by another in so far as it is imperfect. Thus *action* is attributed to the monad in so far as it has distinct perceptions, and *passivity* in so far as it has confused perceptions.[23]

50. And one creature is more perfect than another, in this that there is found in it that which serves to account *a priori* for what takes place in the other, and it is in this way that it is said to act upon the other.

51. But in simple substances the influence of one monad upon another is purely *ideal* and it can have its effect only through the intervention of God, inasmuch as in the ideas of God a monad may demand with reason that God in regulating the others from the commencement of things, have regard to it. For since a created monad can have no physical influence upon the inner being of another, it is only in this way that one can be dependent upon another.[24]

52. And hence it is that the actions and passive reactions of creatures are mutual. For God, in comparing two simple substances, finds in each one reasons which compel him to adjust the other to it, and consequently that which in certain respects is active, is according to another point of view, passive; *active* in so far as that what is known distinctly in it, serves to account for that which takes place in another; and *passive* in so far as the reason for what takes place in it, is found in that which is distinctly known in another.[25]

53. Now, as there is an infinity of possible universes in the ideas of God, and as only one of them can exist, there must be a sufficient reason for the choice of God, which determines him to select one rather than another.[26]

[23] §§ 32, 66, 386.
[24] §§ 9, 54, 65, 66, 201; Abridgment, Objection 3.
[25] § 66.
[26] §§ 8, 10, 44, 173, 196 seqq., 225, 414–416.

54. And this reason can only be found in the *fitness,* or in the degrees of perfection, which these worlds contain, each possible world having a right to claim existence according to the measure of perfection which it possesses.[27]

55. And this is the cause of the existence of the Best; namely, that his wisdom makes it known to God, his goodness makes him choose it, and his power makes him produce it.[28]

56. Now this *connection,* or this adaptation, of all created things to each and of each to all, brings it about that each simple substance has relations which express all the others, and that, consequently, it is a perpetual living mirror of the universe.[29]

57. And as the same city looked at from different sides appears entirely different, and is as if multiplied *perspectively;* so also it happens that, as a result of the infinite multitude of simple substances, there are as it were so many different universes, which are nevertheless only the perspectives of a single one, according to the different *points of view* of each monad.[30]

58. And this is the way to obtain as great a variety as possible, but with the greatest possible order; that is, it is the way to obtain as much perfection as possible.[31]

59. Moreover, this hypothesis (which I dare to call demonstrated) is the only one which brings into relief the grandeur of God. M. Bayle recognized this, when in his Dictionary (Art. *Rorarius*) he raised objections to it; in which indeed he was disposed to think that I

[27] §§ 74, 167, 350, 201, 130, 352, 345 seqq., 354. [In the first copy revised by Leibniz the following is found added here: "Thus there is nothing absolutely arbitrary."]

[28] §§ 8, 78, 80, 84, 119, 204, 206, 208; Abridgment, Objections 1 and 8.

[29] §§ 130, 360.   [30] § 147.

[31] §§ 120, 124, 241 seqq., 214, 243, 275.

attributed too much to God and more than is possible.
But he can state no reason why this universal harmony,
which brings it about that each substance expresses exactly all the others through the relations which it has
to them, is impossible.

60. Besides, we can see, in what I have just said, the
a priori reasons why things could not be otherwise than
they are. Because God, in regulating all, has had regard
to each part, and particularly to each monad, whose
nature being representative, nothing can limit it to representing only a part of things; although it may be true
that this representation is but confused as regards the
detail of the whole universe, and can be distinct only
in the case of a small part of things, that is to say, in
the case of those which are nearest or greatest in relation
to each of the monads; otherwise each monad would be
a divinity. It is not as regards the object but only as
regards the modification of the knowledge of the object,
that monads are limited. They all tend confusedly toward
the infinite, toward the whole; but they are limited and
differentiated by the degrees of their distinct perceptions.

61. And composite substances are analogous in this
respect with simple substances. For since the world is a
plenum, rendering all matter connected, and since in a
plenum every motion has some effect on distant bodies in
proportion to their distance, so that each body is affected
not only by those in contact with it, and feels in some
way all that happens to them, but also by their means
is affected by those which are in contact with the former,
with which it itself is in immediate contact, it follows
that this intercommunication extends to any distance
whatever. And consequently, each body feels all that happens in the universe, so that he who sees all, might read
in each that which happens everywhere, and even that
which has been or shall be, discovering in the present

that which is removed in time as well as in space; σύμπνοια πάντα, said Hippocrates. But a soul can read in itself only that which is distinctly represented in it. It cannot develop its laws all at once, for they reach into the infinite.

62. Thus, although each created monad represents the entire universe, it represents more distinctly the body which is particularly attached to it, and of which it forms the entelechy; and as this body expresses the whole universe through the connection of all matter in a plenum, the soul also represents the whole universe in representing this body, which belongs to it in a particular way.[32]

63. The body belonging to a monad, which is its entelechy or soul, constitutes together with the entelechy what may be called a *living being,* and together with the soul what may be called an *animal.* Now this body of a living being or of an animal is always organic, for since every monad is in its way a mirror of the universe, and since the universe is regulated in a perfect order, there must also be an order in the representative, that is, in the perceptions of the soul, and hence in the body, through which the universe is represented in the soul.[33]

64. Thus each organic body of a living being is a kind of divine machine or natural automaton, which infinitely surpasses all artificial automata. Because a machine which is made by man's art is not a machine in each one of its parts; for example, the teeth of a brass wheel have parts or fragments which to us are no longer artificial and have nothing in themselves to show the special use to which the wheel was intended in the machine. But nature's machines, that is, living bodies, are machines even in their smallest parts *ad infinitum.* Herein lies the difference between nature and art, that is, between the divine art and ours.[34]

[32] § 400.　　　[33] § 403.　　　[34] §§ 134, 146, 194, 403.

65. And the author of nature has been able to employ this divine and infinitely marvellous artifice, because each portion of matter is not only divisible *ad infinitum,* as the ancients recognized, but also each part is actually endlessly subdivided into parts, of which each has some motion of its own: otherwise it would be impossible for each portion of matter to express the whole universe.[35]

66. Whence we see that there is a world of creatures, of living beings, of animals, of entelechies, of souls, in the smallest particle of matter.

67. Each portion of matter may be conceived of as a garden full of plants, and as a pond full of fishes. But each branch of the plant, each member of the animal, each drop of its humors is also such a garden or such a pond.

68. And although the earth and air which lies between the plants of the garden, or the water between the fish of the pond, is neither plant nor fish, they yet contain more of them, but for the most part so tiny as to be imperceptible to us.

69. Therefore there is nothing fallow, nothing sterile, nothing dead in the universe, no chaos, no confusion except in appearance; somewhat as a pond would appear from a distance, in which we might see the confused movement and swarming, so to speak, of the fishes in the pond, without discerning the fish themselves.[36]

70. We see thus that each living body has a ruling entelechy, which in the animal is the soul; but the members of this living body are full of other living beings, plants, animals, each of which has also its entelechy or governing soul.

71. But it must not be imagined, as has been done by some people who have misunderstood my thought, that each soul has a mass or portion of matter belonging to it

[35] Prelim., § 70; Théod., § 195.   [36] Preface, pp. 40, 41.

or attached to it forever, and that consequently it possesses other inferior living beings, destined to its service forever. For all bodies are, like rivers, in a perpetual flux, and parts are entering into them and departing from them continually.

72. Thus the soul changes its body only gradually and by degrees, so that it is never deprived of all its organs at once. There is often a metamorphosis in animals, but never metempsychosis nor transmigration of souls. There are also no entirely *separate* souls, nor *genii* without bodies. God alone is wholly without body.[37]

73. For which reason also, it happens that there is, strictly speaking, neither absolute birth nor complete death, consisting in the separation of the soul from the body. What we call *birth* is development or growth, as what we call *death* is envelopment and diminution.

74. Philosophers have been greatly puzzled over the origin of forms, entelechies, or souls; but to-day, when we know by exact investigations upon plants, insects and animals, that the organic bodies of nature are never products of chaos or putrefaction, but always come from seeds, in which there was undoubtedly some *pre-formation*, it has been thought that not only the organic body was already there before conception, but also a soul in this body, and, in a word, the animal itself; and that by means of conception this animal has merely been prepared for a great transformation, in order to become an animal of another kind. Something similar is seen outside of birth, as when worms become flies, and caterpillars become butterflies.[38]

75. The *animals,* some of which are raised by conception to the grade of larger animals, may be called *spermatic;* but those among them, which remain in their class,

[37] Théod., § 90, 124.
[38] §§ 86, 89, 90, 187, 188, 403, 397; Preface, p. 40, seq.

that is, the most part, are born, multiply, and are destroyed like the large animals, and it is only a small number of chosen ones which pass to a larger theatre.

76. But this is only half the truth. I have, therefore, held that if the animal never commences by natural means, neither does it end by natural means; and that not only will there be no birth, but also no utter destruction or death, strictly speaking. And these reasonings, made *a posteriori* and drawn from experience, harmonize perfectly with my principles deduced *a priori,* as above [cf. 3, 4, 5].[39]

77. Thus it may be said that not only the soul (mirror of an indestructible universe) is indestructible, but also the animal itself, although its mechanism often perishes in part and takes on or puts off organic coatings.

78. These principles have given me the means of explaining naturally the union or rather the conformity of the soul and the organic body. The soul follows its own peculiar laws and the body also follows its own laws, and they agree in virtue of the *pre-established harmony* between all substances, since they are all representations of one and the same universe.[40]

79. Souls act according to the laws of final causes, by appetitions, ends and means. Bodies act in accordance with the laws of efficient causes or of motion. And the two realms, that of efficient causes and that of final causes, are in harmony with each other.

80. Descartes recognized that souls cannot impart any force to bodies, because there is always the same quantity of force in matter. Nevertheless he believed that the soul could change the direction of bodies. But this was because, in his day, the law of nature which affirms also the conservation of the same total direction in matter,

[39] § 90.
[40] Preface, p. 36; Théod., §§ 340, 352, 353, 358.

was not known. If he had known this, he would have lighted upon my system of pre-established harmony.[41]

81. According to this system, bodies act as if (what is impossible) there were no souls, and that souls act as if there were no bodies, and that both act as if each influenced the other.

82. As to *spirits* or rational souls, although I find that the same thing which I have stated (namely, that animals and souls begin only with the world and end only with the world) holds good at bottom with regard to all living beings and animals, yet there is this peculiarity in rational animals, that their spermatic animalcules, as long as they remain such, have only ordinary or sensitive souls; but as soon as those which are, so to speak, elected, attain by actual conception to human nature, their sensitive souls are elevated to the rank of reason and to the prerogative of spirits.[42]

83. Among other differences which exist between ordinary souls and minds (*esprits*), some of which I have already mentioned, there is also, this, that souls in general are the living mirrors or images of the universe of creatures, but minds or spirits are in addition images of the Divinity itself, or of the author of nature, able to know the system of the universe and to imitate something of it by architectonic samples, each mind being like a little divinity in its own department.[43]

84. Hence it is that spirits are capable of entering into a sort of society with God, and that he is, in relation to them, not only what an inventor is to his machine (as God is in relation to the other creatures), but also what a prince is to his subjects, and even a father to his children.

[41] Pref., p. 44; Théod., §§ 22, 59, 60, 53, 66, 345, 346 seqq., 354, 355.

[42] §§ 91, 397.   [43] § 147.

85. Whence it is easy to conclude that the assembly of all spirits (*esprits*) must compose the City of God, that is, the most perfect state which is possible, under the most perfect of monarchs.[44]

86. This City of God, this truly universal monarchy, is a moral world within the natural world, and the highest and most divine of the works of God; it is in this that the glory of God truly consists, for he would have none if his greatness and goodness were not known and admired by spirits. It is, too, in relation to this divine city that he properly has goodness; whereas his wisdom and his power are everywhere manifest.

87. As we have above established a perfect harmony between two natural kingdoms, the one of efficient, the other of final causes, we should also notice here another harmony between the physical kingdom of nature and the moral kingdom of grace; that is, between God considered as the architect of the mechanism of the universe and God considered as monarch of the divine city of spirits.[45]

88. This harmony makes things progress toward grace by natural means. This globe, for example, must be destroyed and repaired by natural means, at such times as the government of spirits may demand it, for the punishment of some and the reward of others.[46]

89. It may be said, farther, that God as architect satisfies in every respect God as legislator, and that therefore sins, by the order of nature and perforce even of the mechanical structure of things, must carry their punishment with them; and that in the same way, good actions will obtain their rewards by mechanical ways through their relations to bodies, although this cannot

[44] § 146; Abridgment, Objection 2.
[45] §§ 62, 72, 118, 248, 112, 130, 247.
[46] §§ 18 seqq., 110, 244, 245, 340.

and ought not always happen immediately.

90. Finally, under this perfect government, there will be no good action unrewarded, no bad action unpunished; and everything must result in the well-being of the good, that is, of those who are not disaffected in this great State, who, after having done their duty, trust in providence, and who love and imitate, as is meet, the author of all good, finding pleasure in the contemplation of his perfections, according to the nature of truly *pure love,* which takes pleasure in the happiness of the beloved. This is what causes wise and virtuous persons to work for all which seems in harmony with the divine will, presumptive or antecedent, and nevertheless to content themselves with that which God in reality brings to pass by his secret, consequent and decisive will, recognizing that if we could sufficiently understand the order of the universe, we should find that it surpasses all the wishes of the wisest, and that it is impossible to render it better than it is, not only for all in general, but also for ourselves in particular, if we are attached, as we should be, to the author of all, not only as to the architect and efficient cause of our being, but also as to our master and final cause, who ought to be the whole aim of our will, and who, alone, can make our happiness.[47]

14. ON THE DOCTRINE OF MALEBRANCHE.

(A Letter to M. Remond de Montmort, containing Remarks on the Book of Father Tertre against Father Malebranche. 1715.)

Sir, I have just received your package, and I thank you for the interesting articles which you have sent me.

[47] §§ 134 fin., 278; Preface, pp. 27, 28.

I say nothing on the continuation of Homer; but as, after the sacred books, he is the most ancient of all the authors whose works remain to us, I wish that some one would undertake to clear up the historical and geographical difficulties which remote antiquity has produced in these works, and principally in the Odyssey, relating to ancient geography; for, however fabulous the travels of Ulysses may be, it is nevertheless certain that Homer carried him into countries then spoken of but which it is difficult now to recognize.

I pass to the philosophical articles which relate to the Reverend Father Malebranche (whose loss I greatly regret), and which tend to elucidate the natural theology of the Chinese. The *Refutation* of the system of this Father, divided into three small volumes, is without doubt from a man of ability, for it is clear and ingenious. I even approve of a part of it, but part of it is too extreme. Too much divergence is here shown from the views of Descartes and of Father Malebranche, even when they are plainly good sense. It should be time to give up these enmities, which the Cartesians have perhaps drawn upon themselves by showing too much contempt for the ancients and for the Schoolmen, in whom there is nevertheless solidity meriting our attention. Thus justice ought to be shown on both sides, and we are to profit by the discoveries of both, as it is right to reject that which each advances without foundation.

1. It is right to refute the Cartesians when they say that the soul is nothing but thought; as also when they say that matter is nothing but extension. For the soul is a subject or *concretum* which thinks, and matter is an extended subject or subject endowed with extension. This is why I hold that space must not be confounded with matter, although I agree that naturally there is no void space; the scholastics are right in distinguishing the

concretes and the *abstracts,* when it is a matter of exactness.

2. I concede to the Cartesians that the soul actually always thinks, but I do not grant that it is conscious of all these thoughts. For our great perceptions and our great appetites of which we are conscious, are composed of innumerable little perceptions and little inclinations of which we cannot be conscious. And it is in the insensible perceptions that the reason is found for what occurs in us; as the reason for what takes place in sensible bodies consists in insensible movements.

3. There is good reason also for refuting Reverend Father Malebranche especially when he maintains that the soul is purely passive. I think I have demonstrated that every substance is active, and especially the soul. This is also the idea which the ancients and the moderns have had of it; and the *entelechy* of Aristotle, which has been bruited so much, is nothing but force or activity; that is, a state from which action naturally flows if nothing hinders it. But *matter, primary* and pure, taken without the souls or lives which are united to it, is purely passive; properly speaking also it is not a substance, but something incomplete. And *secondary matter,* as for example, body, is not a substance, but for another reason; which is, that it is a collection of several substances, like a pond full of fish, or a flock of sheep; and consequently it is what is called *unum per accidens,* in a word, a phenomenon. A true substance, such as an animal, is composed of an immaterial soul, and an organized body; and it is the compound of these two which is called *unum per se.*

4. As to the *efficiency of second causes,* it is again right to maintain it against the opinion of this Father. I have demonstrated that each simple substance, or monad (such as souls), follows its own laws in produc-

ing its actions, without being capable of being troubled therein by the influence of another created simple substance; and that thus bodies do not change the ethicological laws of souls, any more than souls change the physico-mechanical laws of bodies. This is why second causes really act, but without any influence of one created simple substance upon another; and souls harmonize with bodies and among themselves, in virtue of the pre-established harmony, and not at all by a mutual physical influence; except in the case of the metaphysical union of the soul and its body which makes them compose *unum per se,* an animal, a living being. It has been right, therefore, to refute the opinion of those who deny the action of second causes; but it must be done without renewing false influences, such as the *species* of the scholastics.

5. Father Malebranche made use of this argument: That extension not being a mode of being of matter, must be its substance. The author of the *Refutation* (Vol. I, p. 91) distinguishes among the positive modes of being; and he claims that extension is one of the modes of being of the second sort, which he thinks can be conceived by themselves. But these are not positive modes of being; they all consist in the variety of limitations, and none of them can be conceived save by the being of which they are the modes and ways. And as to extension it may be said that it is not a mode of being of matter, and nevertheless is not a substance either. What is it, then? you will ask, sir. I reply that it is an attribute of substances, and there is a clear difference between attributes and modes of being.

6. It appears to me, also, that the author of the *Refutation* does not combat well the opinion of the Cartesians on the infinite, which they with reason consider as prior to the finite, and of which the finite is but a limitation.

He says (p. 303 of Vol. I), that if the mind had a clear
and direct view of the infinite, Father Malebranche
would not have had need of so much reasoning to make
us think of it. But by the same argument he would reject
the very simple and very natural knowledge we have of
the Divinity. These kinds of objections amount to nothing, for there is need of labor and application in order
to give to men the attention necessary for the simplest
notions, and this end will only be reached by recalling
them to themselves from their dissipation. It is also for
this reason that the theologians who have composed
works on eternity, have had to need many discussions,
comparisons, and examples to make it well understood;
although there is nothing more simple than the notion
of eternity. But it is because, in such matters, all depends
on attention. The author adds (Vol. I, p. 307), that in
the pretended knowledge of the infinite, the mind sees
merely that lengths may be put end to end and repeated
as many times as is wished. Very good; but this author
should consider that to know this repetition can always
be made, is already to know the infinite.

7. The same author examines in his second volume the
natural theology of Father Malebranche; but his performance appears to me overdone, although he declares
that he merely presents the doubts of others. The Father
saying that God is being in general, this is taken for a
vague and notional being, as is the genus in logic; and
little more is needed to accuse Malebranche of atheism.
But I think that the Father did not understand a vague
and indeterminate being, but absolute being, which
differs from particular limited beings as absolute and
boundless space differs from a circle or square.

8. There is more likelihood of combating the opinion of
Malebranche on ideas. For there is no necessity (apparently) for taking them for something external to us. It

is sufficient to regard ideas as notions, that is to say, as modifications of our soul. It is thus that the Schoolmen, Descartes, and Arnauld regard them. But as God is the source of possibilities and consequently of ideas, the Father may be excused and even praised for having changed the terms and given to ideas a more exalted signification, in distinguishing them from notions and in taking them for perfections in God which we participate in by our knowledge. This mystical language of the Father was not then necessary; but I find it useful, for it better brings before the mind our dependence on God. It even seems that Plato, speaking of ideas, and St. Augustine, speaking of truth, had kindred thoughts, which I find very remarkable; and this is the part of Malebranche's system which I should like to have retained, with the phrases and formulas which depend on it, as I am very glad that the most solid part of the theology of the mystics is preserved. And far from saying with the author of the *Refutation* (Vol. II, p. 304), that the system of St. Augustine is *a little infected with the language and opinions of the Platonists,* I would say that it is thereby enriched and set in relief.

9. I say almost as much of the opinion of Father Malebranche when he affirms that *we see all things in God.* I say that it is an expression which may be excused and even praised, provided it be rightly taken; for it is easier to fall into mistakes in this than in the preceding article on ideas. It is, therefore, well to observe that not only in Malebranche's system but also in mine, God alone is the immediate external object of souls, exercising upon them a real influence. And although the current school seems to admit other influences, by means of certain species, which it believes that objects transmit to the soul, it does not fail to recognize that all our perfections are a continual gift of God, and a limited participation

in his infinite perfection. This suffices to show that what there is true and good in our knowledge is still an emanation from the light of God, and that it is in this sense that it may be said, that *we see all things in God*.

10. The third volume refutes the system of revealed theology of Father Malebranche, in reference especially to grace and predestination. But as I have not sufficiently studied the particular theological opinions of the author, and as I think I have sufficiently elucidated the matter in my essay *La Théodicée,* I excuse myself from entering upon it at present.

It would now remain to speak to you, sir, of the natural theology of the *Lettres Chinois,* according to what the Jesuit Father Longobardi and Father Antoine de St. Marie, of the Minorite order, report to us thereon, in the treatises which you have sent me, in order to have my opinion of them; as well as of the mode which Reverend Father Malebranche has employed to give to a cultivated Chinaman some insight into our theology. But this requires a separate letter; this which I have just written being already sufficiently long. Referring for the rest to my preceding letter, I am zealously, sir, your very humble and very obedient servant,

LEIBNIZ.

IV. ETHICS, LAW, AND CIVILIZATION

1. ON THE NOTIONS OF RIGHT AND JUSTICE *
[1693]

. . . I do not know whether, even after so many eminent writers have discussed them, the notions of *right* and of *justice* have been sufficiently cleared up. *Right* is a certain moral power, and *obligation* a moral necessity. Moreover, I understand by *moral* that which in good men is equivalent to natural: for, as a celebrated Roman jurisconsult says, things which are contrary to good morals must be regarded as things which cannot be done. A good *man* moreover is one who loves all men as much as reason allows. *Justice,* therefore, which virtue is the mistress of the affection the Greeks call love of mankind (φιλανθρωπία), will be defined, most properly, unless I am mistaken, as *the charity of the wise man* (*caritatem sapientis*), that is, charity according to the dictates of wisdom. Therefore, what Carneades is reported to have said, namely, that justice is the highest folly, because it commands us, neglecting our own interests, to care for the interests of others, comes from ignorance of the definition. *Charity* is universal benevolence, and *benevolence* is the habit of loving. Moreover to *love* is to take delight in the happiness of another, or, what amounts to the same thing, it is to regard another's happiness as one's own. Whence the difficult knot, which is also of great moment in theology, is untied, how there can be a

* From the Preface to Leibniz's *Codex Juris Gentium Diplomaticus.*

disinterested love, which is free from hope and from fear, and from regard for personal advantage; it is evident that the joy of those whose joy enters into our own delights us, for those things which delight are sought for their own sake. And just as the contemplation of beautiful objects is itself agreeable, and a painting by Raphael affects him who understands it, even if it brings no riches, in such a way that it is kept before his eyes and regarded with delight, as a symbol of love; so when the beautiful object is at the same time also capable of happiness, his affection passes over into true love. But the *divine love* surpasses other loves because God can be loved with the greatest result, since nothing is at once happier than God, and nothing more beautiful and more worthy of happiness can be known than he. And since he also possesses the highest power and wisdom, his happiness does not only enter into ours (if we are wise, that is love him) but it also constitutes it. Since, moreover, wisdom ought to direct charity, there will be need of defining it also. I think, however, that the notions of men are best satisfied if we say that *wisdom* is nothing else than the very science of happiness. Thus we are brought back again to the notion of *happiness,* to explain which this is not the place.

From this source flows *natural right,* of which there are *three grades; strict right* in commutative justice, *equity* (or charity in the narrow sense of the word) in distributive justice, finally *piety* (or probity) in universal justice: whence spring the rules, to injure no one, to concede to each his own, to live honorably (or rather piously), as well as the most general and commonly recognized precepts of right, just as I formerly outlined it in my youthful essay, *De Methodo Juris.**

* *Methodus nova discendae docendaeque Jurisprudentiae* (1667).

The law of bare or *strict right* is, *No one is to be injured,* unless within the state a cause for action be given, and outside the state the right of war; whence comes the justice which philosophers call *commutative* and the right which Grotius calls legal claim (*facultas*). The higher grade I call *equity,* or, if you prefer, charity (namely, in the narrower sense), which I extend beyond the rigor of bare right to those obligations also to the performance of which we may not be forced; such as gratitude, almsgiving, to which we have, according to Grotius, not a *legal* but a *moral right.*

And just as it belonged to the lowest grade to injure no one, so to the middle grade it belongs, *To do good to all;* but so far only as is fitting to each or so far as each deserves, so that it is not possible to favor all equally. Thus this is the sphere of *distributive* justice, and the law of right here is that which commands us to give to each his due (*suum cuique tribui*). And to this the political laws in the commonwealth extend which secure the happiness of the subjects, and along with this bring it about that those who had only a moral right acquire a legal right, that is, that they are able to demand that others perform what is fair. And while in the lowest grade of right the differences among men were not regarded, except those which arise from the particular affair itself, but all men are held as equals, now, however, in this higher grade, merits are weighed; whence privileges, rewards, punishments have their place. This difference in the grade of right Xenophon has excellently sketched, with the boy Cyrus as example, who, chosen as judge between two boys, the stronger of whom had exchanged coats with the other by force, because he had found the coat of the other more fitting to his figure, and his own coat to the figure of the other, had pronounced in favor of the robber: but it was pointed out

by his teacher that the question here was not whom the
coat might fit, but to whom it belonged, and that Cyrus's
form of giving judgment could only then be employed
rightly, when he himself had coats to distribute. For
equity itself commends to us strict right in affairs, that
is, equality among men, except when a weighty reason
of greater good commands us to recede from it. Moreover, what is called respect of persons has its place not
in exchanging goods with others, but in distributing our
own or public goods.

The highest degree of right I have called by the name
of probity or rather *piety*. For what has been hitherto
said can be so understood as to be confined to the relations of mortal life. And, moreover, bare or strict right
springs from the need of preserving peace; equity or
charity extends to something more: viz., while each one
benefits the other as much as he can, he increases his
own happiness in that of the other; and, in a word, strict
right avoids misery, the highest right tends to happiness, but happiness such as belongs to mortality. But
that we ought to subordinate life itself and whatever
makes this life desirable, to the great good of others; that,
moreover, the greatest griefs ought to be endured for the
sake of others; this is more beautifully taught by philosophers than solidly demonstrated. For the honor and
glory and joyous feeling in the virtue of one's own soul,
to which, under the name of honor, they appeal, are goods
of thought or of the mind, and, moreover, have great
superiority, but not with all men and for all bitterness
of evils, since all men are not equally affected by the
imagination; especially those whom neither a liberal education nor a free-born mode of living or the discipline of
life or of sect has accustomed to the estimation of honor
and to the appreciation of the goods of the soul. But in
order to establish by a general demonstration that all

that is worthy is useful, and all that is base is injurious, the immortality of the soul, and the director of the universe, God, must be assumed. Thus it is that we know that we all live in the most perfect state under a monarch who on account of his wisdom cannot be deceived and on account of his power cannot be eluded; and he too is so lovable that to serve such a master is happiness. Therefore, he who loses his soul for this master, as Christ teaches, wins it. By his power and providence it comes to pass that all *right* passes over into fact, that no one is injured except by himself, that nothing done rightly is without its reward, no sin without punishment. Since, as Christ has divinely taught, all our hairs are numbered, and even a cup of water is not given in vain to one thirsting, so nothing is neglected in the Commonwealth of the Universe. It is on this account that *justice* is called *universal* and includes all other virtues; for that also which otherwise does not concern the interest of another, e.g., that we do not misuse our body or our property, this is also forbidden outside of human laws, by natural right, i.e., by the eternal laws of the divine monarchy, since we are indebted to God for our existence and for what we have. For as it is to the interest of the State so it is much more to that of the Universe that no one make a bad use of his own. Here, therefore, that highest law of right receives its force, which commands us *to live honorably* (i.e., piously). And in this sense it is rightly put by learned men among the things to be demanded, that the natural law and the law of nations be taught according to the doctrines of Christianity, that is (from the example of Christ), the sublime things, the divine things of the wise. Thus we think we have explained most fitly the three precepts of right, or three degrees of justice, and to have pointed out the sources of natural law. . . .

2. ETHICAL DEFINITIONS
(From a Letter to Nicaise, 1697)

As to charity or disinterested love, on which I see embarrassing disputes have arisen, I think that one could not extricate one's self better than by giving a true definition of love. I believe that in the preface to the work [*Codex Juris Gentium Diplomaticus*] which is known to you, sir, I have formerly so done in noting the source of justice. For JUSTICE is fundamentally nothing else than charity conformed to wisdom. CHARITY is universal benevolence. BENEVOLENCE is a disposition or inclination to love and it has the same relation to love that habit has to act. And LOVE is this act or active state of the soul which makes us find our pleasure in the happiness or satisfaction of others. This definition, as I have since noted, is capable of solving the enigma of disinterested love, and of distinguishing it from the bonds of interest or debauchery. I remember that in a conversation, which I had several years ago with the Count ———— and other friends, in which human love alone was spoken of, this difficulty was considered, and my solution was found satisfactory. When one loves a person sincerely one does not seek one's own advantage or a pleasure severed from that of the beloved person, but one seeks one's pleasure in the contentment and in the felicity of this person. And if this felicity did not please in itself, but merely because of an advantage resulting therefrom to us, this would no longer be pure and sincere love. It must be then that pleasure is immediately found in this felicity, and that grief is found in the unhappiness of the beloved person. For whatever produces pleasure immediately through itself is also desired for itself, as constituting (at least in part) the end of our wishes, and as something which enters into our own felicity and gives us satisfaction.

This serves to reconcile two truths which appear incompatible; for we do all for our own good, and it is impossible for us to have other feelings whatever we may say. Nevertheless we do not yet love altogether purely, when we seek the good of the beloved object not for itself and because it itself pleases us, but because of an advantage which we foresee from it. But it is apparent from the notion of love which we have just given that we seek at the same time our good for ourselves and the good of the beloved object for it itself, when the good of this object is immediately, finally (*ultimato*) and through itself our end, our pleasure and our good; as happens in regard to all the things wished for because they are pleasing in themselves, and are consequently good of themselves, even if one should have no regard to consequences; these are ends and not means.

Now divine love is infinitely above the loves of creatures, for other objects worthy of being loved constitute in fact part of our contentment or our happiness, in so far as their perfection touches us, while on the other hand the felicity of God does not compose a part of our happiness, but the whole. He is its source and not its accessory, and since the pleasures of lovable earthly objects can injure by their consequences, only the pleasure taken in the enjoyment of the divine perfections is surely and absolutely good, without danger or excess being possible.

These considerations show in what the true disinterestedness of pure love consists, which cannot be severed from our own contentment and felicity, as M. de la Trappe has well remarked, because our true felicity embraces essentially the knowledge of the felicity of God

and of the divine perfections, that is to say, the love of
God. And consequently it is impossible to prefer one to
the other by a thought founded in distinct notions. And
to wish to sever one's self from one's self and from one's
own good is to play with words; or if you wish to go to
the effects, it is to fall into an extravagant quietism, it
is to desire a stupid, or rather affected and simulated
inaction in which under pretext of resignation and of
the annihilation of the soul swallowed up in God, one
may go to libertinism in practice, or at least to a hidden
speculative atheism, such as that of Averroes and of
others more ancient, who taught that our soul finally lost
itself in the universal spirit, and that this is perfect union
with God.

(From another Letter to Nicaise, 1698)

The error concerning pure love appears to be a misunderstanding, which as I have already said to you, sir,
comes perhaps from not paying sufficient attention to
forming definitions of terms.

To LOVE truly and disinterestedly is nothing else than
to be led to find pleasure in the perfections or in the
felicity of the object, and consequently to experience
grief in what may be contrary to these perfections. This
love has properly for its object subjects susceptible of
felicity; but some resemblance of this is found as regards
objects which have perfections without being aware of
it, as for example, a beautiful picture. He who finds
pleasure in contemplating it and would find pain in seeing it ruined even if it should belong to another, would
love it, so to speak, with a distinterested love. This could
not be said of another who should merely have in view
gain in selling it or the winning of applause by showing
it, without further caring whether or not it were ruined
when it should no longer belong to him. This shows that

pleasure and action cannot be taken away from love without destroying it, and that M. des Preaux in the beautiful verses which you sent me, was right both in recommending the importance of the divine love and in opposing a love which is chimerical and without effect. I have explained my definition in the preface of my *Codex Juris Gentium Diplomaticus* (published before these new disputes arose), because I had need of it in order to give the definition of JUSTICE, which in my opinion is nothing but charity regulated according to wisdom. Now CHARITY being a universal benevolence, and BENEVOLENCE being a habit of loving, it was necessary to define what it is to love. And since to LOVE is to have a feeling which makes us find pleasure in what conduces to the happiness of the beloved object, and since WISDOM (which makes the rule of justice) is nothing but the science of happiness, I showed by this analysis that happiness is the basis of justice, and that those who would give the true elements of jurisprudence, which I do not find laid down as they should be, ought to begin by establishing the science of happiness, which does not yet appear well determined, although books on Ethics are full of discourses on blessedness or the sovereign good.

As PLEASURE, which is nothing but the feeling of rare perfection, is one of the principal points of HAPPINESS, which in turn consists in a lasting condition of possession of what is necessary in order to taste pleasure, it were to be desired that the science of pleasures which the late M. Lautin meditated had been completed.

(The following Ethical Definitions, translated from the Latin,* are undated.)
Justice is the charity of the wise.
Charity is general benevolence.

* Erdmann edition (1840), p. 670.

Benevolence is the habit of love.

To love anyone is to delight in his happiness.

Wisdom is the science of happiness.

Happiness is durable joy.

Joy is a state of pleasure.

Pleasure or delight is a sense of perfection, that is, a sense of something which helps or which sustains some power.

He is perfected whose power is augmented or helped.

Demonstrate this Hypothesis elsewhere:

The world is governed by the wisest and most powerful of monarchs, whom we call God.

Propositions.

The end or aim of God is his own joy or love of himself.

God created creatures, and especially those endowed with mind, for his own glory or from love of himself.

God created all things in accordance with the greatest harmony or beauty possible.

God loves all.

God bestows on all as much as is possible.

Neither hatred, nor wrath, nor sadness, nor envy, belong to God.

God loves to be loved or loves those loving him.

God loves souls in proportion to the perfection which he has given to each of them.

The perfection of the universe, or harmony of things, does not allow all minds to be equally perfect.

The question why God has given to one mind more perfection than to another, is among senseless questions, as if you should ask whether the foot is too large or the shoe pinching the foot is too small. And this is a mystery, ignorance of which has obscured the whole doctrine of the predestination and justice of God.

He who does not obey God is not the friend of God.

He who obeys God from fear is not yet the friend of God.

He who loves God above all things is at length the friend of God.

He who does not seek the common good does not obey God.

He who does not seek the glory of God does not obey God.

He who at the same time seeks the glory of God and the common good obeys God.

He who does not in his acts recognize God does not sufficiently love God.

He who is displeased by some things in the acts of God does not think God perfect.

He who thinks God does some things from absolute good pleasure, having no reason, or from irrational or indifferent liberty, does not think God perfect.

He who thinks God acts in the best possible way acknowledges that God is perfect.

Whoever does not delight in the contemplation of the divine perfection does not love God.

All creatures serve the felicity or glory of God in the degree of their perfection.

Whoever against his will serves the felicity of God does not love God.

Whoever places his own felicity in relation with the divine felicity, loves himself and loves finally God.

He who loves God endeavors to learn his will.

He who loves God obeys God's will.

He who loves God loves all.

Every wise man endeavors to do good to all.

Every wise man does good to many.

Every wise man is a friend of God.

The wiser one is the happier he is.

Every wise man is just.

Every just man is happy.

3. ON DESTINY OR MUTUAL DEPENDENCE

That everything comes to pass through an established destiny or mutual dependence is as certain as three times three are nine. For this mutual dependence consists in the fact that everything is linked to everything else, like a chain, and in the fact that everything will unfailingly happen in a predestined way, as unfailingly as that something has to happen when it does.

The ancient poets, like Homer and others, have spoken of the golden chain which Jupiter dangled from heaven, and which cannot be broken arbitrarily by man whose place is fixed in the chain. And this chain consists in the succession of causes and effects.

That is to say, every cause has its determinate effect which is reducible to the former, if a single cause operates; when there are many causes, their co-operation produces a certain inevitable effect or resultant according to the measure of the forces involved, and this is true when not only two but 10 or 1000, or even an infinite number of things act together as actually happens in the world.

Mathematics or the art of measuring can beautifully explain such things, since everything in nature is equally circumscribed by number, measure, and weight or force. For example, when a ball meets another ball in the open air, and we know their magnitudes and direction and speed before meeting, we can then predict and calculate how they will rebound and what kind of course they will take after the collision. For there are elegant laws of collision, and they hold for as many balls as you please, and for as many other objects with shapes other than that of a ball.

Thus we see that everything in the whole wide world proceeds mathematically, that is, infallibly, so that if one had enough insight into the inner parts of things and also enough memory and understanding to take in all the circumstances and calculate them, he would be a prophet; he would see the future in the present as in a mirror.

Just as we find that flora and fauna already have their own structures in the seed, which can be somewhat modified by external events, so we may say that the whole future world lies in the present and is completely foreshadowed in it, for nothing entirely outside the present exists which can affect it.

However, it is impossible for a limited understanding to foresee future things with all their circumstances, because the world consists of infinite things working together, so that nothing too small or remote can be dismissed which does not convey some effect in proportion to its magnitude. And often, such small things cause very important changes. I used to say a fly can change the whole state, in case it should buzz around a great king's nose while he is weighing important counsels of state; for he may be at a point in his understanding when arguments on both sides seem equally strong, and that side will win which impresses his mind most; the difference in the outcome can be caused by the fly which prevents or distracts him from considering the justice of the other side with the result that he yields to his inclination at the moment.

Those who understand something of artillery fire, know how small changes can cause a ball to take quite a different course. So it was by a small chance that Turenne (for example) was hit by a bullet, but if that had not happened the whole war would have then taken another turn, and things today would have come out differently. So also, we know that a spark of fire, should it fall into a powder-magazine, can destroy a whole population.

And even this effect of small things causes those who do not consider things correctly to imagine some things happen accidentally and are not determined by destiny, for this distinction arises not in the facts but in our understanding, just as one who does not comprehend the large number of small things belonging to every particular effect and does not recognize any cause he does not see, will then imagine that aces turn up in dice simply by chance.

This infallibility of destiny can help us attain a composure of mind, . . . precisely because we discover in numbers, figures, forces, and all measurable things of which we have an adequate conception, that they are not only just and perfect but also quite harmonious and beautiful, in short, that they cannot be improved nor can anything conceivably better be hoped for.

Indeed we cannot see such a harmony so long as we do not enjoy the right point of view, just as a picture in perspective is best appreciated only from certain standpoints and cannot be seen properly from another angle.

It is only with the eyes of the understanding that we can place ourselves in a point of view which the eyes of the body do not and cannot occupy. For example, if we consider the course of the stars from where we stand on our earth's sphere, we obtain a wonderfully complicated structure which astronomers, just in the last few thousand years, have been able to reduce to a few certain laws, and these laws are so difficult and confusing that King Alfonso of Castille, having let tables be drawn up of celestial motions to fill up the lack of accurate knowledge, is supposed to have said that if he had been God's counsellor, the world would have been laid out better.

However, after it had been finally discovered that we must place our eye at the sun if we want to view the celestial motions correctly, and that as a result everything comes out wonderfully beautiful, then we see that the supposed disorder and complication were the fault of our understanding and not of nature.

A similar order should be judged to hold for everything which we come across. And if we cannot always find the right viewpoint with our understanding, yet we should be content to know that there is the fact that we might take pleasure in all things if we understood them properly, and thus already find in that fact some satisfaction. It is exactly as we take pleasure in the doings of a friend or prince when we have completely good faith in him, that is, when we are assured of his understanding and good will, regardless of whether we always quite see why he behaves as he does, and even when he often externally appears not to be doing the right thing.

And it is precisely this satisfaction with the universal supreme order, no matter what happens, when we do our duty, that const tutes the right basis of true religion. And the resultant composure in our understanding also serves to give us pleasure. And just as nothing is more agreeable to man's senses than musical harmony, so there is nothing more agreeable than the wonderful harmony of nature, of which music is only a foretaste and small sample. For that reason I take my stand on the thoughts of high-minded people, whose position requires them to seek a great part of their pleasure in the investigation of natural wonders and majestic, beautiful truths, which are hidden in solid, worthwhile sciences. Beautiful dis-

coveries are not commendable simply for the profit of
those who advance them, but they also promote the building up of enterprise and serve human well-being, including even the preservation of health. In any case, these
discoveries throw such light on the whole masterful
work of nature and offer such pleasure stemming therefrom, that he who misses these things is to be compared
with a man who must always grope in the dark; on the
other hand, he who is enlightened by these researches can
elevate himself to a height from which everything appears as it would to one looking down from the stars.
If also the masterpieces of nature were not of any concern to people, the knowledge of truth would be subse-
quently regarded by them as not so good as ignorance.
For ignorant and superstitious people are satisfied with
any sort of false imagining. Hence, when nature is not
being appraised by people with understanding and virtue, it is better to deal with others who are acquainted
with the truth. It would be immeasurably absurd in itself
and contrary to all order if it should be deemed that
want of understanding could provide any judgment in
this matter. And because everything in nature has its
cause and is ordered in every respect, it is impossible
not to consider understanding and conduct based on
understanding (that is, virtue) better than the contrary.
Since nature brings everything into order, he who stands
closest to that order already can most easily arrive at
an orderly contemplation or orderly conception, that is,
at a felt satisfaction, precisely because there can be no
higher satisfaction than to consider and see how good
everything is and that nothing possibly better is to be
wished.

It might be said, on the other hand, that evil is not
evil in itself but only in the one who does evil, and
though punishment does indeed befit him, on the whole,

however, nature knows how to bring it about that the evil supposed to be present in evil persons leads to a very much better state of things than if she had not permitted the evil to occur at all. Indeed, we prefer that no appearance of evil remain and that things become so improved that as a result we might know not only in general that everything is good and well, but might also understand it concretely, in fact, actually feel it. For the greater and livelier our contentment and pleasure in such an understanding and feeling, the more do all hardships become mitigated and even annihilated. Only we must for that reason remember that such mitigation is not always feasible, and that it is even better so. Just as it had to take time before men finally discovered that the right point of view of celestial motions is in the sun, so we must observe that our soul, when it is well directed, will finally and gradually attain more nearly the concept and feeling of such beauty in nature, as soon and as much as is feasible.

Furthermore, because everything works for the best, it follows that those persons must sooner and better attain the satisfaction of this contemplation who through their understanding have better opened up for themselves the road to it. To the extent that their conduct is guided rationally and systematically by their best idea towards the good, that is, by their virtue, so also by working especially for the happiness of others do they find their own happiness. In this investigation of truth and of the majestic wonder of the highest, progressive working of everything in nature, seeing as correct knowledge also depends on it, men are helped to reach that high point on which virtue, satisfaction, and true happiness hang.

We finally come to the two great laws which reason teaches us concerning the hang of destiny itself and the incomparable order it includes: first, that we should regard as good and proper everything that has already happened or is happening, as though we might be seeing them from the right viewpoint; secondly, that in all future things or events that are yet to happen, we should seek to do the good and proper thing as much as is in our power and according to our best conception, and thus come nearer to the right point of view as much as it is possible for us to do. Of these two rules, the former gives us every possible satisfaction in the present, and the latter paves the way to a future, far greater happiness and joy.

4. NEW PROPOSALS

Since we live in an age which tries to go deeply into things, those who love the general good must make an effort to take advantage of this inclination which may not last long among men; especially if by mishap or lack of method they are not helped much, they will be prone to relapse some day into indifference and finally into ignorance. However, the fact remains that Mathematics, the masterpiece of human reasoning, has never made so much progress, and if Medicine does not yet advance commensurately with the fine progress of the physical sciences, it is perhaps only for lack of a sound order of researches which sovereigns might institute in order to make a little more available the advantages mankind has already gained over nature. Civil History and everything called "belles lettres" are widely published. And although what we can obtain from the Greek and Latin writers is not yet completely exhausted, and there are some beautiful passages yet to be collected, we can nonetheless be confident that the aim or principle is clear.

For some time now work is being done on the History of the Middle Ages; by pulling out chests of archives and wiping the dust off old papers, scholars are helping to throw light on the origins, changes, and embroilments of sovereigns by means of a quantity of chronicles, documents, and memoirs. It will soon be necessary to go and make inquiries among the Chinese and Arabs in order to complete the history of mankind to the extent that we can obtain it from the extant works or monuments, whether they be in writing or on stones or metals, or even in the memory of men, for we must not neglect tradition, and I maintain that of everything not written the spoken languages themselves are the best and the most significant remains of the past on which we can draw for light on the origins of peoples, and often, on the origins of things. I know that several philosophers and mathematicians poke fun at these factual researches, but we see, on the other hand, that men of the world usually like nothing so much as the study of History and dislike or leave to professionals anything smacking of scientific reasoning. I believe that both sides go to extremes in these judgments. History would be of great utility were it only to support men in their desire for glory which is the motive behind most of their fine deeds; surely the respect sovereigns themselves have for the judgment of posterity often produces a good effect. I wish History would sometimes include a little of the style of the Novel, especially when there are motives involved which are carefully hidden, but history always tells us enough about them to make us gain from the events narrated. In all it has provided excellent lessons at the hands of the greatest men who have experienced good and bad successes, and nothing is more convenient than to learn at somebody else's expense. The History of Antiquity is an absolute necessity for the proof of the truth of religion,

and apart from the excellence of the doctrine, it is from
its wholly divine origin that our religion is distinguished
from all others which do not approach it in any fashion.
Therein lies perhaps the best use of the most refined and
profound criticism, offering sincere testimony to those
great truths by ancient authors carefully examined, and
if Mohammedans, pagans, and even free-thinkers do not
surrender to reason, we may say that it is chiefly due
to their not knowing ancient history, those knowing nothing at all of it remain children (as that Egyptian in his
talk with Solon properly judged the Greeks to be). But
if I attach much importance to these admirable historical studies which lead us in a fashion into the secret
of providence, I do not underestimate the way of the
sciences for becoming acquainted with the magnificence
of Divine Wisdom whose traces are found in the ideas
God has put into our soul and into the structure of
bodies he has supplied for our use. In a word I value
any sort of discoveries in whatever subject-matter there
is, and I see that usually it is for lack of knowing the
relations and consequences of things that people turn
their backs on the works and concerns of others, a sure
indication of pettiness of mind. Serious persons usually
err in failing to appreciate how much insight and uncertain opinions we must use in the course of practical
matters and in practical sciences like politics and medicine. In these occupations we are like gamblers who must
make up their minds and place a bet even when there
is no certainty of the outcome. There is a science which
governs us in these very uncertainties for the sake of
discovering in what direction the greatest appearances
point. But it is an astonishing fact that this science is
almost unknown and that logicians have not yet examined
the degrees of probability or likelihood in conjectures or
proofs even though the estimation of probability is as

sure as numbers. This estimation can and should serve us not in order to arrive at a certitude, which is impossible, but in order to act with the utmost possible reasonableness on the facts or information given us. After doing so we shall have nothing to regret, and at least we shall succeed most often, provided that we imitate wise gamblers and good business men who divide their money in several small risks, rather than commit themselves to fortune in one stroke and thus expose themselves to sudden bankruptcy. There is then a science about the most uncertain matters which informs us demonstratively of the degrees of appearance and uncertainty. The skill of experienced persons often consists of knowing by routine habit what choice they should make; however, as they most often continue to judge superficially, philosophers and mathematicians could be of great help to them if they would henceforth examine these practical matters, and would not rest in their abstract speculations alone, making the mistake of wanting to dig into places where it is necessary only to sound the bottom. On the other hand, we see that worldly men often take too many chances, boldly choosing the side most in accord with their taste or prejudices, whether they make up their minds to act or remain in a state of indecision. For the ordinary statesman takes only to easy and superficial thoughts such as a wit often finds at the tip of his tongue; and when it comes to thinking seriously, they give up. Whence, the exact and profound sciences which they regard as a painful business are not to their liking; but they are punished for this laziness in their own jurisdiction and in the management of their affairs, for while they debauch in verbal intercourse and superficial views, they neglect what is often the dryest part of their occupation, namely, finances and militia, which are both nearly all mathematical, as are commerce, manufactures, navigation, artillery, and other matters he may have to judge.

Jurisprudence itself is a science having very much to do with reasoning, and among the ancients I find nothing which approaches the style of geometers as much as that of the pandects. As to theology it is very plain how indispensable to it are Metaphysics, on the one hand, and history and languages, on the other. Of all the things in this world after tranquillity of mind, nothing is more important than health whose preservation or restoration requires profound studies in physics and mechanics. How often do we become wretched through ignorance alone or through overlooking some easy reasoning or observation already made which would not escape us if we would apply ourselves as we should, and if men would make use of their advantages? That is why I maintain that we must neglect nothing and that all men should be particularly concerned with the search for truth. And as there are certain mechanical tools which no head of a family fails to possess (though there are other special instruments left to each artisan for his particular job), so we all ought to try to acquire the general science capable of enlightening us everywhere. And as we are all curious to know at least the prices and often the uses of the manufactured products or tools which we cannot make ourselves, so that we can at least purchase and use them when needed, in the same way we ought to know the true value and utility, and to some extent the history, of the sciences and arts with which we do not meddle, in order to recognize how in the republic of letters everything conspires to the perfection of the mind and to the advantage of mankind. This may be compared to a city in which all the trades being well managed and on a sound basis contribute to making the city more prosperous.

I believe two things would be necessary for men to take advantage of their opportunities and to do everything they could to contribute to their own happiness, at least in the matter of knowledge, for I do not touch here on what pertains to the rectifying of their will. These two things are, *first* an exact INVENTORY of all the knowledge acquired but dispersed and badly arranged (at least of that knowledge which appears to be most important at the beginning), and *secondly,* the GENERAL SCIENCE which should give us not only the means to use knowledge already acquired but also the Method of judging and discovering, in order to go further and supply what we want. This inventory I speak of would be very different from systems and dictionaries, and would be composed only of Lists or enumerations, Tables, or Progressions which would serve to keep always before us, during some reflection or deliberation of any sort, the catalogue of facts and circumstances and the most important assumptions and maxims which ought to serve as the basis of reasoning. But I admit that such an enterprise cannot be the work of a single man nor even of a few persons. Nevertheless, I believe that while waiting for something better, it would be possible through the effort of a few able and industrious people to arrive easily at something approaching it. This would be worth incomparably more than our present confusion in which it seems our very riches make us poor, somewhat like what would happen in a big store which lacked the order necessary to find anything one needed, for it is tantamount to having nothing as to having it without being able to use it. But as the general science also helps to make up an orderly inventory, for it is to the particular sciences what the science of accounting is to a merchant or financier, it is with the general science that we shall still have to begin.

5. ESSAY ON A NEW PLAN OF A
CERTAIN SCIENCE
(About which the opinions of the most Intelligent
are asked)

Of all our losses, loss of time and of opportunities is the most incalculably invaluable. However, we scarcely take notice of them except when there is no time left and regrets are superfluous. We may say that solid and useful knowledge is the greatest treasure of mankind, and if it ever belonged to a century to make it grow and profit from it, that century is our own. Yet I do not see ourselves doing what we should in order to enjoy as we should either this grace from heaven or the glorious inclination of the greatest Princes to encourage the growth of the Sciences and Arts.

All our felicity consists chiefly in two principal points: the first is the satisfaction of the mind (which we know to be the effect of true piety and good morality), and the second is the health of the body which is undoubtedly the most precious of terrestrial goods. But both points are equally neglected and it is not surprising that the consideration of our future life (a condition which we can know only through faith) makes so little an impression on minds, since the examples set by those who have gotten themselves into present and visible misery through their derangements and through the neglect of their health may convert any of those who take the same road.

That reveals that often the most enlightened have only superficial thoughts about everything which does not flatter the senses at first, or their vanity or avarice, not for lack of penetration but for lack of attentiveness, and it seems that they never think seriously of anything but the most trivial things.

I believe that one of the biggest reasons for this negligence is the despair of improving matters and the very bad opinion entertained of human nature, for many persons are prejudiced by a secret incredulity disposing them to imagine that man is carried away by the general torrent of nature with the rest of the animals, that all we try to do is pure vanity, and that from all this nonsense it is better to choose the most pleasant piece.

There are some who imagine that reason serves only to afflict us, and that far from seeking truth, we must flee from it deliberately, because the truth will only help to increase our misery by showing us too well our insignificance.

As to the Sciences and Arts, several are persuaded that only the most material have any importance, as mechanics and mathematics, and that the others are only beautiful illusions appropriate to providing a comfortable living for those who cultivate them and to keep peoples in dutiful subjection. They expect nothing from medicine except when they are sick, they make fun of the law while they are not faced with a suit, and they set their mind against Theology until they have to think of death.

But this inconsistency in our judgments which we ourselves abandon at the first approach of danger, is evidence enough that they rest only on superficiality and laziness. It is not the most informed who are the quickest to pronounce judgment, and those who reflect find more reason to admire the excellence of human nature than to despise it. For after all, in this understanding which raises us above the universe in order to contemplate it, and causes us to know necessary and eternal truths which the universe itself is obliged to follow, do we not have a sample of the divine nature since nothing is more real nor more divine than the truth and the understanding which answers to it. Those who are versed in the profound studies of Geometry and Numbers where truth reveals itself quite nakedly, admire at each moment the order of things, and when they contemplate some progression in the rank of magnitudes where there appears to be irregularity, they always find after an exact discussion that everything is admirably well arranged and that this apparent disorder brings out by contrast the greatest beauty. There is every appearance that nature everywhere wears this order, that this wonderful understanding she has given to our soul cannot end up in nothing, and that the wisdom, justice and goodness of the author of things would be evident not only in the government of men but in their formation, were we only as able to envisage the universal harmony as we are able to examine the particular concinnity of the mechanism of our body.

But if there were as much uncertainty on one side as on the other, would it not be fitting to make at least a trial of our power before despairing of success? Do we not see every day new discoveries not only in the arts but also in philosophy and in medicine? Why should it not be possible to come to some considerable relief from our troubles? I shall be told that so many centuries had worked fruitlessly. But considering the matter more closely, we see that the majority of those who have dealt with the sciences have simply copied from one another or amused themselves. It is almost a disgrace to mankind that so few have truly worked to make discoveries; we owe nearly everything we know (apart from accidental experiences) to a handful of persons, the others only having begun to make progress. That is why with all the learned men we have to day I believe, if a great Monarch would make some powerful effort, or if a considerable number of individuals of ability freed from other concerns would take to the task required, that we

could make great progress in a short time, and enjoy
the fruit of our labors ourselves. In the manner which
we take to it at present, that enjoyment will be reserved
for posterity.

6. AN ODD THOUGHT CONCERNING A
NEW SORT OF EXHIBITION

(or rather, an Academy of Sciences; Paris, Sept. 1675)

[The following unfamiliar fragment of Leibniz's *
illustrates an aspect of his thought often inadequately
emphasized in textbooks of the history of philosophy.
Along with his recognized interest in pure logic, mathematics, and *a priori* metaphysics and theology, he was,
as this text shows, as zealous as any Baconian for the
promotion not only of empirical investigations but also
of their mechanical applications, and for the diffusion of
knowledge of these and enthusiasm for them among the
general public. The project here outlined was not, indeed, unrelated to current tendencies of the period. More
or less "scientific" museums were in the seventeenth century coming into fashion, and in a number of European
cities those maintained either by princely houses or by
private naturalists or other *savants* were among the
show-places visited by educated travellers. Such were
the museum of the Settalas, father and son, in Milan;
that of Berend Ten Broeke (Bernardus Paludanus,
1550–1633) at Enkhuizen in Holland; Kircher's famous
museum, visited by Evelyn in 1644, and bequeathed in
1680 to the Jesuit College in Rome; and the Tradescants'
"Ark" in London, "considered to be the most extensive

* Reprinted in part from JOURNAL OF THE HISTORY OF IDEAS,
April, 1940, Vol. I, No. 2, pages 232–240, with Professor A. O.
Lovejoy's collaboration.

collection in Europe at the time," which, purchased by
Elias Ashmole in 1659, became the nucleus of the Ash-
molean Museum. Many of these were chiefly or solely
collections of "natural" rarities (*rariora naturalia*),
rather than of recent inventions and discoveries, but
examples of the latter, in some cases, found place in the
collections. Leibniz's project, therefore, was not without
precedent; but it is distinguished by its special emphasis
on the comprehensive exhibition of recent progress in
science and the practical arts in all countries, and by the
popular appeal at which he aimed. And the text shows,
in the originator of the Calculus and the author of the
Monadology, the talents of a great showman; like the
director of a latter-day World's Fair, he shrewdly insists
upon the indispensability of amusements and spectacles
(including seventeenth-century equivalents of moving
pictures), and even gambling rooms, in order both to
lure the multitude to the scientific and technological
exhibits and to increase the revenues of the enterprise.
He hoped, it will be noted, that the exposition would be
so successful that it would become permanent, and would
develop into a self-supporting "academy" for the encouragement and prosecution of further investigations
and inventions. The Paris *Académie des Sciences* (1666)
and the Royal Society (1662) had already been established, but not as outgrowths of popular exhibitions. The
Berlin *Akademie der Wissenschaften* was founded nearly
thirty years later, upon a quite different plan drawn up
by Leibniz; but his "odd idea" of 1675 appears to have
been the germ of his own conception of such an institution.]

The Exhibition which took place at Paris on the river
Seine, of a Machine for walking on water, gave birth
in me to the following thought. However odd the idea

may appear, it could not fail to be of importance, were it carried out.

Suppose that some persons of means with an interest in curiosities, especially in machines, should agree to have public expositions made of such things. To this end, it would be necessary for them to raise a fund in order to meet necessary expenses. . . .[1] It would be all the better if one could dispense with the great noblemen, even with persons powerful at court; and it would be well to have private individuals able to defray the necessary expenses. For a powerful nobleman would monopolize the business when he found it successful. If things went well, one could always have protectors at court.

Beside the persons capable of defraying the expenses, we should also need persons who could constantly invent new things. But as too many would give rise to disorders, I believe that it would be better to have no more than two or three directors who would employ all others and determine the conditions for certain exhibitions, limiting them to a certain period or to as long a period as the principals desire, or until a certain sum of money supplied by them had been repaid. The persons to be employed should be painters, sculptors, carpenters, watchmakers, and other such folk. We may add gradually mathematicians, engineers, architects, boat-builders, entainers, musicians, poets, book-binders, typographers, engravers, and others.

The exhibitions would include Magic Lanterns (we might begin with these), flights, artificial meteors, all sorts of optical wonders; a representation of the heavens and stars and of comets; a globe like that of Gottorp at Jena; fire-works, water fountains, strangely shaped

[1] Leibniz here names several prominent members of Louis XIV's court who might be induced to advance the money.

boats; Mandragoras and other rare plants. Unusual and rare animals. A Royal Circle. Figures of animals. Royal Machine with races between artificial horses. Prize for Archery. Exhibitions of battle scenes. Fortifications built of wood. On an elevated stage, representations of charity, cruelty,—etc.—all in imitation of the maker of the art—things that I have seen. An instructor in fortification would explain the use of all war games. Infantry drill of Martinet. Cavalry exercise. Naval combats in miniature on a canal. Extraordinary Concerts. Rare instruments of Music. Speaking trumpets. Counterfeit gems and jewelry.

The Show could always be combined with some story or comedy. Theatre of nature and of art. Swimming. Extraordinary rope-dancer. Perilous leap. Show how a child can raise a heavy weight with a thread. Anatomical theater followed by garden of medicinal herbs, laboratory. . . . For besides public exhibitions there will be private ones such as small adding machines,[2] in others Pictures, Medals, Library. New experiments on water, air, vacuum: for the large exhibitions, one would make use of Mons. Guericke's machine of 24 horses, etc., for the small ones, a strong globe.[3] Many things from Mons.

---

[2] Leibniz himself had invented a multiplying machine about 1671. Cf. *A Source Book in Mathematics,* edited by D. E. Smith (1929), pp. 173–181. Pascal had constructed the first adding machine (1642), but Leibniz says he did not know of it in 1671 (*ibid.,* p. 174).

[3] Otto von Guericke (1602–86) was Mayor of Magdeburg, (1646), famous for his public demonstration of two teams of horses which could not pull apart the hemispheres of a small hollow globe voided of air. "Otto von Guericke's globe" refers either to this hollow globe voided of air by the air-pump he invented (imitated by Robert Boyle), or to a sulphur-globe with which he was the first to make static electricity by friction and to make the earliest observations of the conduction of such electricity.

Dalencé's establishment, *item,* the magnet. Mons. Denis [4]
or Mons. ———— would explain them. One would even
distribute certain rarities,[5] *e.g.,* those pixtriques, etc.
Operations of transfusion and infusion would be made.[6]
Item, for holiday spectators, who would be told the
weather for the next day, whether it will rain or not,
by means of the little man in the cabinet of Father
Kircher.[7] We will bring the man from England who eats
fire, etc., if he is still alive. Through a Telescope we
could show the moon at night along with other heavenly
bodies. We could send for the water drinker.[8] We could
test machines which would throw things exactly at a given
point. Exhibits of the muscles, nerves, bones: *item,* ma-

[4] Denis Papin: amanuensis of Huygens in experiments on air-
pump; author of *Experiences du vuide,* 1674. Denis Papin "had
the idea of obtaining power on the air-pump principle, and had
tried, or at least suggested, the use of either gunpowder or
condensed steam for the purpose; but Hooke, we are told, regarded the whole scheme as impractical." (A. Wolf, *History of
Science, Technology, and Philosophy in the Eighteenth Century,*
Chapter XXIV, Technology, VII The Steam Engine, pp. 611–
612.) Papin had, along with Guericke and Boyle, also experi-
mented on the intensity of sound in various densities of the
media (*ibid.,* 175).

[5] Here Leibniz wrote in the margin: "preferably different
rooms like palace shops in the same house where private parties
having rented the rooms, would show the rarities."

[6] Leibniz appended a note to the effect that the Director's
office could serve as a clearing-house for all exhibitions; by
charging a fee that would go to the Academy, the latter would
be self-supporting.

[7] A weather-forecaster invented by Athanasius Kircher (1601–
80), German mathematician and Jesuit; his *Polygraphia, seu
artificium linguarum quo cum omnibus mundi populis poterit
quis respondere* (1663), interested Leibniz in connection with
his own attempts to invent a universal language.

[8] Leibniz explains the trick in a note, by indicating the use of
concealed tubes in the mouth and alimentary tract of the water-
drinker.

chine representing the human body. Insects of Mons. Swammerdam, Goedartis . . . , Myrmeleon. Shop of *Mepitus Galinée* and *des Billets*. Arts of Mons. Thevenot. Amusing and colloquial disputes. Exhibit of *camera obscura*. Paintings which can be seen only with a . . . , from one angle presenting one picture, from another, quite a different one, like that of a certain Mons. a l'isle, v.d.— farms as at Versailles on the edge of a Canal. Public diversions (such as) pictures on oiled paper and burning lamps or lanterns. There could be figures who could walk, with a little illumination inside them, so as to show whatever might be printed on the paper. For magic lanterns, there would be not only simple objects painted on something transparent, but also detachable moving pictures of very unusual and grotesque objects, which it would be possible to make.[9]

Ballets of horses. Races round a ring and Turkish head. Artificial machines, such as I have seen in Germany. Power of a mirror to kindle a fire. Gilgevis de Callinus. Chess game . . . showing men on a stage, as in Haychaffle. Pageant in the German style. Other sorts of elaborate games could be taught and performed.

Play an entire comedy with the amusing games of all sorts of countries. People would imitate these games at

[9] Here Leibniz wrote in the margin: "I had almost forgotten that we might establish an Academy of games or more generally, Academy of pleasures. But I prefer the first name because it is more fashionable. There would be games of cards and of dice."—(Leibniz adds details of games to be played, admission tickets, etc.) "It would be, at the same time, a respectable [gaming] rooms as at Blyeme's." . . . "There would be several houses or Academies of this nature through the city. These houses or rooms would be built in such a way that the director of the house could hear and see everything said and done without any one perceiving him, by means of mirrors and openings, something that would be very important for the state and a species of political confessional." . . . (rest torn).

home. There might be in the building provision for a game of tennis, and for other games, inventing perhaps new sorts of useful games.

There might be established some training Academies and Colleges for youth: perhaps join them to the College of the Four Nations [in Paris]. Comedies of the styles, debates of each country, a Hindu comedy, a Turkish, a Persian, etc. Comedies of the trades, one for each trade, which would show their skills, peculiarities, jokes, masterpieces, special and ridiculous styles. In other comedies, Italian and French clowns who would perform their buffooneries. Flying dragons of fire, etc., could be made of oiled paper, illuminated. Wind-mills, thin boards that can go against the wind, the chariot of sails from Holland or rather from China. Instruments that play by themselves. Shells, etc. Hauz's machine of an artificial cavalry and infantry in battle. The experiment of breaking a glass by shouting. *Petter* should come. Inventions of Monsieur Weigel. Show the equality of the oscillations of pendula.

People at the Academy should be forbidden from swearing and blasphemy, for under that pretext, Academies of the sort we are describing have been put under suspicion. . . . The pretext would be met, were it to become fashionable to admire fine players or performers. And those who broke the rules should give something, not to the cards but to the house, for in this matter it would be to the advantage of those who play to observe the law. But if a troupe of players were in a rare case unrestrained, and disobeyed this law, admission to any house should be denied by simply excluding them. . . .

[Rules of playing and gambling follow, ending with the statement:] Gambling would be the finest occasion in the world for initiating a thing as agreeable and useful to the public as the present plan. For we must offer the public some bait, take advantage of its weakness and deceive it in order to cure it. Is there anything so just as making use of extravagance in order to establish order?

Games of "chasse passe" (pass the hunter). Map games. These things might be made part of comedies played by a performer. At the end the opera will be added to all this, along with many other things; pantomime in comedies in the Italian and German style would be of interest. When the curtain is down it would not be bad to know what to do in the interim. Something might be shown in the dark, and magic lanterns would be appropriate for that. The actions of these transparent marionettes might be accompanied by a few words or songs. Performances might be given of Roman antiquities or of great men. In a word, all sorts of shows.

The use of this enterprise to the public as well as to the individual, would be greater than might be imagined. As to the public, it would open people's eyes, stimulate inventions, present beautiful sights, instruct people with an endless number of useful or ingenious novelties. All those who produce a new invention or ingenious design might come and find a medium for getting their inventions known, and obtain some profit from that. It would be a general clearing house for all inventions, and would become a museum of everything that could be imagined. A Menagerie. Simple machines. Observatory. Anatomical theater. Museums of rarities. All people with curious minds would write to it. This would be the way to spread these things abroad. There would be added Academies, colleges, tennis courts and other games, concerts, galleries of paintings. Conferences and lectures.

The profit for the private individual would apparently be great. Optical curiosities would hardly cost much and would constitute a large part of these inventions. All respectable people (*tous les honnêtes gens*) would want to see these curiosities in order to be able to talk about them; and even ladies of fashion would want to be taken there, and more than once. There would always be an inducement to improve things further, and it would be a good thing if those who undertook it were assured of the project in other large cities [10] such as Rome, Venice, Vienna, Amsterdam, Hamburg, by persons enjoying privileges from kings and republics. It could even serve to establish everywhere an Assembly of Academies of Sciences, which would be self-supporting, and would not cease producing fine things.[11] Perhaps some curious Princes and distinguished persons would contribute some of their wealth for the public satisfaction and the growth of the sciences. In short, everybody would be aroused and, so to speak, awakened; and the enterprise might have consequences as fine and as important as could be imagined, which would some day perhaps be admired by posterity. . . . [At the end Leibniz added the following:] At the close a purchasing office would be added. A register of catalogs and other useful

[10] "Having a fund, there would be a perpetual income from interest and from other sources, such as the information of companies for new manufactures."—Leibniz's marginal note.

[11] How manifold Leibniz conceived the aims of such academies to be, can be seen by an extract from one of his letters to Prince Eugene, besieger of the Turks. In this letter, the activities of academies of science extend to historical works and investigations of charts and manuscripts, a library for the newest publications in literature, a museum of coins and antiquities, a theater of nature and art, a chemical laboratory, an observatory, a shop for models and machines, a botanical garden, a museum of minerals and rocks, schools for anatomy and surgery, an annual physico-medical History of the Seasons and Statistics of the Interior, research-expeditions in the fields of art, nature and literature, salaries and encouragement of persons devoted to these tasks of research and discovery, prizes and gratuities to inventors.

things. Bring together the Marionettes du Marmis and the Pygmies. Shadows might be added to these, either on stage or at the ends near the spectators, where there are lights, and little wooden figures, so agitated that they will throw their shadow against the paper in very startling and magnified proportions. But in order to prevent this shadow world from appearing all on one plane, resort to perspectives might bring about diminishing sizes of shadows. They will approach the center from the edge and that will make it appear as if they are coming forward from the rear. They will increase in size because of their distance from the light, a thing easily managed. There will be no end of wonderful metamorphoses, perilous leaps, flights. Circle of the Magi who transform whoever appear into demons of hell. Then of a sudden, all would be darkened. The same trick could be produced by subduing all lights except that one alone which is near the movable little wooden figures. This remaining light with the aid of a Magic Lantern would throw against the wall admirably beautiful and moving figures which obey the same laws of perspective. All of this would be accompanied by song from below the stage. The little figures would be moved from below or by their weight, so that whatever is used to move them is invisible. Song and music would accompany everything.

7. ON AN ACADEMY OF ARTS AND SCIENCES

(Letter to Peter the Great, 1716)

Very august, very powerful, very indomitable Czar,
Very gracious Sir:

Since your Royal Majesty has kindly given me to believe at Torgau that my projects were not displeasing to him, I hastened to have a terrestrial magnetic sphere built, such as has never been seen, and which permits navigators to steer more safely on the ocean. And if in every bit of ten years new observations are made with the magnetic needle, and if as a result of them new magnetic spheres are built for the use of navigators, we should then have something which might take the place of longitudes, or of what the Dutch call East and West; and these observations should be renewed until the time when we have a durable result.

But as the magnetic needle undergoes not only a declination *in a horizontal plane* but also *in a vertical plane,* and as it is of the highest necessity to make the observation of both carefully, I have also built for that purpose a special instrument of inclination, and it would be desirable to observe the inclination as well as the declination at different intervals and in diverse places of the great empire of Russia, for that would render navigation an immense service.

I await the orders Your Majesty promised to give me, and I refer moreover to the written propositions, very humbly submitted to him at Torgau, constantly with the thought that despite the difficult times of war, thanks to a favorable disposition Your Majesty will not lose any time (the most precious of all the things God has made), and that without too much expense, Your Highness may soon be able to contribute generously to the progress and extension of the arts and sciences.

I wanted to add an extract of Chinese or Cathayan (*Cataisiennes*) letters which clearly prove the good intentions which exist there concerning the sciences and how much Your Majesty would help to unite Europe and China.

. . . G.W. de Leibniz

P.S. Very gracious Sir: Probably, Baron Urbich may have mentioned, and Your Majesty will deign to remem-

ber, that I have entered into negotiations with the Prince
Elector of Hanover, and then that the Prince of Kurakin
has established and concluded treaties on the negotiations. Although I count many years of service in administration and law, and though I have been consulted for
a long time by great princes, I nevertheless consider the
arts and sciences as more elevated, and capable of increasing the glory of God and the welfare of mankind,
for it is especially in the sciences and the knowledge of
nature and art that we see the wonders of God, his
power, wisdom and goodness; and furthermore, the arts
and sciences are the true treasure of mankind; they
show the superiority of art over nature and distinguish
civilized people from barbarians.

That is why, since my youth, I have given myself to
the sciences that I loved; I was fortunate, despite numerous occupations abroad, to arrive at important discoveries, which have been praised in the writings of distinguished and impartial persons. I needed only a great
prince who might want to interest himself sufficiently in
the thing; I hope to have found one in Your Majesty
who wishes and can take the best measures on this subject in his great empire. Your Czarist Majesty, by means
of projects worthy of a hero, and by putting them into
execution will be able to procure the well-being and
prosperity not only of our contemporaries but also of
future generations, and chiefly to make himself useful to
the Russians and other Slavic peoples, as Fohi was to
the Chinese, Hermes to the Egyptians, Zoroaster to the
North of Asia, Arminius to the Germans in the south,
Odin to the Germans in the north, and Almanzor to the
Saracens.

It seems that God has decided that science should
make a tour of the world and penetrate as far as Scythia,
that he has designated Your Majesty to be his instrument

for that purpose, while Your Majesty is in a position to draw from Europe on one side and from China on the other what there is of the best, and to perfect the institutions of both these countries by means of wise reforms. For considering that everything that has to do with education is still to be done for the greatest part of his empire, and that one starts, so to speak, with a blank sheet, one will be able thus to avoid so many errors which have imperceptibly slipped in; we know that a palace, built entirely anew, rises much better than one which, after several centuries of existence, has to be repaired and is subject to numerous alterations.

What constitutes this new and vast edifice, are libraries, museums, theaters of rarities, workshops of models, objects of art, chemical laboratories, and astronomical observatories; objects which it is not necessary to have all at once, but little by little, while there is room for submitting a few projects tending to obtain the most urgent things without enormous expense.

The important thing is to procure from different places men capable of responding to the plans one proposes, men who would be installed in Your Majesty's empire in order to instruct young people faithfully, since victuals are cheap in Russia and there will be little expense to pay for those who will be installed in the country.

I should regard myself very proud, very pleased and highly rewarded to be able to render Your Majesty any service in a work so worthy and pleasing to God; for I am not one of those impassioned patriots of one country alone, but I work for the well-being of the whole of mankind, for I consider heaven as my country and cultivated men as my compatriots, and I prefer to render a good many services to the Russians than a few to the Germans or other Europeans, even though I might enjoy among the latter leisure, fame and fortune; but not being able any longer to be of so great a use, it is to my liking and inclination to concern myself with the general welfare.

It is to this end that I have for a long time now been in touch with Europe and even China, that for many years I have been a member of the Royal Societies of France and England, and that, in addition, I have been president of the Royal Society of Prussia, which will make every effort to reply to the noble plans of Your Majesty, witness the request addressed to His Highness, Duke Rudolph of Brunswick-Luneburg. This Society which the King founded according to my plans, has been established on such a basis that it scarcely costs the King anything to maintain; this can not only happen but be realized with greater profit in the great empire of his Czarist Majesty, and become glorious by his renown.

. . . 5. We could also to the same end establish a sound commerce between Moscow and China, in order to transplant in Moscow and in Europe the sciences and arts known in China, but unknown among us. We could thus increase the importance of our manufactures and the *commodities* of life, and Moscow would extract not a little profit from it. I know from my correspondence with the Catholic missionaries in China that they are the ones who introduce our commodities and our sciences, but that the Chinese are not generous in exchange, and that they seek to keep society busy with other things. It will follow that when the Chinese will have learnt from us what they wish to know they will then close their doors.

6. The new and marvelous discovery I have made, namely, the secret of deciphering the old characters of the famous Fohi, one of the first kings and philosophers of China, who lived more than 3000 years ago, will especially be agreeable to the Chinese and procure an entry for us. I succeeded by myself in discovering a new mode

of counting,* and I have found that this new method
sheds a great deal of light on all of mathematics, and
that, thanks to it, we may discover things we have had
difficulty with. By putting together all the matter it is
likely that this old Fohi had the key of this method, as
we can see in the characters themselves, and, from what
Father Kircher in his *China illustrata* and Father Couplet
and others have published. It can be seen from the large
figure of 64 characters, called the Li-King among the
Chinese, which Father Bonnet has sent by including a
Chinese copy which is in harmony with the discovery that
I communicated to him.

7. . . . One further research to light up the history,
geography, origin and migrations of peoples . . . would
be to make samples of the variety of languages spoken
in that immense monarchy either on the border by means
of interpreters living not only in Moscow but also in
frontier cities, in Archangel, Tobolski in Siberia, Kezar,
Astruban, Nepschin, Azof.—But it would be in the interest of Christendom and of human civilization that
there be made complete dictionaries and grammars of
the languages opposite one another, not in dialects but
radicalites, and we should translate into these languages
a few useful and spiritual books and even the Bible.

* The binary system, in which 2 is the base. Leibniz deciphered
the Chinese trigrams with the use of this system of numbers.

TABLE OF SOURCES OF SELECTIONS
IN THIS VOLUME
Based on the Following Editions of Leibniz:

B.-C.   A. Buchenau and Ernst Cassirer, *G. W. Leibniz Philosophische Werke* (4 vols.): *Hauptschriften zur Grundlegung der Philosophie* (2 vols., Leipzig, 1924).

COUT.   Louis Couturat, *Opuscules et fragments inédits de Leibniz* (Paris, 1903). Latin and French.

D.   George Martin Duncan, *The Philosophical Works of Leibniz*, Second (Revised) Edition (New Haven, 1908). Has been revised again in the selections used in this volume.

E.   J. Erdmann, *Leibnitii Opera Philosophica quae extant Latina, Gallica, Germanica Omnia*, Berlin, 1840.

F.   Foucher de Careil, *Oeuvres de Leibniz* (7 vols., Paris, 1859–1875); Tome IV: *Histoire et politique* (1862); Tome VII: *Leibniz et les académies. Leibniz et Pierre le Grand* (1875).

GERH.   C. I. Gerhardt, *Die philosophischen Schriften von Gottfried Wilhelm Leibniz* (7 vols., Berlin, 1875–1890).

GERL.   Ernst Gerland, *Leibnizens nachgelassene Schriften physikalischen, mechanischen, und technischen Inhalts* (Leipzig, 1906). No. 134.

LANG.   Alfred G. Langley, *New Essays Concerning Human Understanding*. Macmillan Co., 1896. Second edition, 1916.

LAT.   Robert Latta, *Leibniz: The Monadology and Other Philosophical Writings*. London, Oxford University Press, 1898. Revised in the selections used in this volume.

601

M.-C.   George R. Montgomery, *Leibniz: Discourse on Metaphysics, Correspondence with Arnauld, and Monadology*, translation revised by Albert R. Chandler. Open Court Publishing Co., 1924.

The next two books were used in the Introduction:

Preussischen Akademie der Wissenschaften, *Leibniz: Sämtliche Schriften und Briefe* (Darmstadt, 1923–1931), Reihe 1–4.

Bertrand Russell, *A Critical Exposition of the Philosophy of Leibniz, with an Appendix of Leading Passages*. Cambridge University Press, 1900,[1] 1937.[2]

Asterisks indicate selections not hitherto translated into English. Duncan's, Langley's, and Latta's translations require further revision.

I

1. Extract from "Juris et aequi elementa." B.-C., vol. II, pp. 504–506, from G. Mollat, *Rechtsphilosophisches aus Leibnizens ungedruckten Schriften* (Leipzig, 1885), pp. 20 ff.

*2. "De la méthode d'universalité." COUT., pp. 97 f. and p. 144.

*3. "Dialogus, August, 1677," GERH., vol. VII, pp. 190–194.

"Dialog über die Verknüpfung zwischen Dingen und Worten," B.-C., vol. I, pp. 16–21.

*4. "Préface à la Science Générale," COUT., pp. 153–157.

*5. "Zur allgemeinen Characteristik," B.-C., vol. I, pp. 30–38. Untitled, according to GERH., vol. VII, pp. 184–189.

*5a. *"Principia calculi rationalis,"* COUT., pp. 229–231.

*5b. Untitled fragment. COUT., p. 326.

II

IV